The Nature of New Testament Theology

The Nature of New Testament Theology

Essays in Honour of Robert Morgan

Edited by
Christopher Rowland and
Christopher Tuckett

Blackwell
Publishing

BLACKWELL PUBLISHING
350 Main Street, Malden, MA 02148-5020, USA
9600 Garsington Road, Oxford OX4 2DQ, UK
550 Swanston Street, Carlton, Victoria 3053, Australia

First published 2006 by Blackwell Publishing Ltd

1 2006

Library of Congress Cataloging-in-Publication Data

The nature of New Testament theology / edited by Christopher Rowland and Christopher Tuckett.
    p. cm.
    Includes bibliographical references and index.
    ISBN-13: 978-1-4051-1175-1 (hardcover : alk. paper)
    ISBN-10: 1-4051-1175-5 (hardcover : alk. paper)
    ISBN-13: 978-1-4051-1174-4 (pbk. : alk. paper)
    ISBN-10: 1-4051-1174-7 (pbk. : alk. paper)   1. Bible. N.T.—Theology.
I. Rowland, Christopher, 1947–   II. Tuckett, C. M. (Christopher Mark)

    BS2397.N38 2006
    230′.0415—dc22

                    2005017018

A catalogue record for this title is available from the British Library.

Set in 10.5 on 12.5 pt Garamond
by SNP Best-set Typesetter Ltd, Hong Kong
Printed and bound in Singapore
by Fabulous Printers Pte Ltd

The publisher's policy is to use permanent paper from mills that operate a sustainable forestry policy, and which has been manufactured from pulp processed using acid-free and elementary chlorine-free practices. Furthermore, the publisher ensures that the text paper and cover board used have met acceptable environmental accreditation standards.

For further information on
Blackwell Publishing, visit our website:
www.blackwellpublishing.com

Contents

Contributors

John Ashton taught New Testament Studies in Oxford until his retirement in 1996.

John Barton is Oriel and Laing Professor of the Interpretation of Holy Scripture in the University of Oxford.

Zoë Bennett is Director of Postgraduate Studies in Pastoral Theology, Anglia Ruskin University and the Cambridge Theological Federation.

Adela Yarbro Collins is the Buckingham Professor of New Testament Criticism at the Yale University Divinity School.

Philip Esler is the Chief Executive of the UK Arts and Humanities Research Council (during a period of leave from the University of St Andrews, where he is Professor of Biblical Criticism).

Morna Hooker is Lady Margaret's Professor Emerita in the University of Cambridge, and a Fellow of Robinson College.

Luke Timothy Johnson is the Robert W. Woodruff Professor of New Testament and Christian Origins at the Candler School of Theology, Emory University, Georgia.

Leander E. Keck is Winkley Professor of Biblical Theology Emeritus at Yale University.

Ulrich Luz is Professor Emeritus of New Testament at the University of Bern, Switzerland.

Margaret Y. MacDonald is Professor of Religious Studies at St Francis Xavier University, Canada.

John Muddiman is G.B. Caird Fellow in New Testament at Mansfield College, Oxford.

Heikki Räisänen is Professor of New Testament Studies in the University of Helsinki and Academy Professor at the Academy of Finland.

Christopher Rowland is Dean Ireland's Professor of Exegesis of Holy Scripture at the University of Oxford and a Fellow of Queen's College, Oxford.

Gerd Theissen is Professor of New Testament Theology in the University of Heidelberg.

Christopher Tuckett is Professor of New Testament Studies in the University of Oxford.

Francis Watson holds the Kirby Laing Chair in New Testament Exegesis at the University of Aberdeen.

Rowan Williams is Archbishop of Canterbury.

Michael Wolter is Professor of New Testament Studies in the University of Bonn, Germany.

Frances Young is Professor Emeritus of Theology in the University of Birmingham.

Abbreviations

AB	Anchor Bible
ANRW	*Aufstieg und Niedergang der römischen Welt*
BTB	*Biblical Theology Bulletin*
BZ	*Biblische Zeitschrift*
CBQ	*Catholic Biblical Quarterly*
EKK	Evangelisch-katholisch Kommentar
ET	English Translation
EvTh	*Evangelische Theologie*
ExpT	*Expository Times*
HBT	*Horizons in Biblical Theology*
JAAR	*Journal of the American Academy of Religion*
JBL	*Journal of Biblical Literature*
JR	*Journal of Religion*
JRS	*Journal of Roman Studies*
JSNT	*Journal for the Study of the New Testament*
JSNTSup	Journal for the Study of the New Testament Supplement Series
JSOTSup	Journal for the Study of the Old Testament Supplement Series
KuD	*Kerygma und Dogma*
NovT	*Novum Testamentum*
NTOA	Novum Testamentum et orbis antiquus
NTS	*New Testament Studies*
SJT	*Scottish Journal of Theology*
StNT	Studien zum Neuen Testament
TEH	Theologische Existenz heute
UTB	Uni-Taschenbücher
WUNT	Wissenschafliche Untersuchungen zum Neuen Testament
ZNW	*Zeitschrift für die neutestamentliche Wissenschaft*
ZTK	*Zeitschrift für Theologie und die Kirche*

Preface

We are delighted to offer this collection of essays to Bob Morgan, a remarkable friend, scholar and mentor. It is on a subject which is close to Bob's heart and which he has written about over many years with insight and a formidable knowledge of the subject matter. It would be fair to say that he introduced us both to the meaning of this particular branch of the exegetical discipline and we have continued to benefit from his writing and even more from engagement with him personally over the years.

Bob's has been an unusual contribution to theological life. He has been at the very heart of a network of colleagues who have come to rely on his judgement and knowledge and have found his wisdom has propelled them into areas which they scarcely would have explored without Bob's inspiration. The personal contact as much as the writings themselves have been instrumental in modelling a way of engaging with the biblical texts. Bob has taken to heart the words of his beloved Paul when he asks the Corinthians to imitate him. What Bob has done for generations of students in Lancaster and Oxford, and in the church courses which he has taught down the years, is to offer a model of the theological task informed and inspired by Scripture. There are many who would like to have been part of this volume who join with those of us who have contributed to it in expressing gratitude for Bob's work over the years.

For Bob, New Testament theology has never been an end in itself. Pastoral ministry in Sandford-on-Thames, just outside Oxford, has for nearly the last 20 years been a central part of Bob's life. The dialectic between church and academy has been a more and more explicit part of his writing and has always been a central ingredient in his interpretative work. In this the inspiration of Ernst Käsemann is everywhere apparent. Bob's work perhaps lacks the controversial side of Käsemann's exegetical essays, but the commitment to the life and concerns of the contemporary church is the motor of his intellectual life, without which we would not understand his work.

The present collection is an attempt to offer an up-to-date guide to discussion and study of 'The theology of the New Testament', a discipline which is not without its critics and the articulation of which is a very much contested area. Distinguished colleagues from different parts of the world have come together to explore the different facets of this task. Their distinction and the readiness with which they agreed to write for this volume is itself testimony to the esteem in which Bob is held. It is offered to him as a tribute of affection and esteem and in the hope that it will be a catalyst for him continuing to spur us on to new endeavours in the area of study which he has made his own and to which he has contributed so much.

Within New Testament studies generally, the study of what some call 'The theology of the New Testament' has a potentially central, if contested, position in the discipline, as Bob Morgan has demonstrated in a lifetime of immersion in the subject. The debate over its character, and what exactly is – or should be – constituted by a 'theology of the New Testament', can indeed go to the very heart of the nature of theology and its place in a modern academic – and secular – university. To illustrate some of the problems involved, it may be helpful to set out the questions which were posed to the authors of this volume as questions which might be borne in mind when writing their contributions:

- Is there such an entity as 'New Testament theology'?
- If so, how does it differ from study of the thought of early Christianity?
- Is New Testament theology inherently confessional?
- What is/should be included in a New Testament theology (anything in the New Testament? Or only particular elements, e.g. 'highlights' such as Paul and John)?
- Does the teaching of the historical Jesus belong within a New Testament theology?
- Is a New Testament theology a theology of texts or of historical authors?
- Is 'the' theology of the New Testament a single entity, or a collection of different theologies?
- Is the search for a unity in possible diversity desirable and/or justifiable?
- Is New Testament theology an attempt to systematize what the text meant or an attempt to illuminate faith and practice in the contemporary world?

The rise of historical scholarship since the Enlightenment illuminated the distinctiveness and the social context of the emerging Christian theological discourse found in the New Testament but also established the problematic character of the intellectual engagement with the canonical texts and their implication of that work for contemporary faith communities. It has been easy to see 'theology', and in particular 'New Testament theology', as an essentially descriptive task, in which the various aspects of a particular biblical book are systematically presented. And indeed for some, a 'New Testament theology' is and should be just that (although they may seek to avoid the term 'theology' for such an enterprise). For others, however, such a task does not go to the heart of what is (or should be) a 'New Testament theology', nor does it do justice to its vitality as an intellectual exploration, in which biblical exegesis is not an end in itself but a necessary tool of a contemporary understanding of theology and life. As such the 'theology of the New Testament' is not a deductive enterprise but an inductive, exploratory task, in which the complex dialectic of exegetical engagement and a contemporary agenda, where through a philosophical hermeneutic (as Rudolf Bultmann's *Theology of the New Testament*) or a self-aware praxis (as in liberationist hermeneutics) provides a potent means of doing theology. No doubt this kind of theology is deeply rooted in the intellectual movement set in train by the Reformation, but its distinctive contemporary contours set the historical concerns of exegesis in an altogether different intellectual engagement with the text as compared with a narrowly historical approach to the text.

This collection of essays exhibits both the descriptive and the existential (in the non-technical sense of that word) approaches to what is called 'New Testament theology'. No attempt has been made here to reconcile the different approaches, nor to impose uniformity on divergent positions adopted. It is inspired by Robert Morgan's work over the years. We trust that he will appreciate the collection and, whatever his disagreements with particular approaches, he will recognize the stimulus he has given which has enabled us to continue the dialogue to which he has been such a distinguished contributor.

Christopher Rowland
Christopher Tuckett

Foreword: Reading, Criticism, Performance

Rowan Williams

Sometimes I read a text because I want to know what the text knows. The text invites or provokes; it suggests to me a world that is not my habitual place of residence, emotionally or imaginatively, but where I could live and imagine myself quite differently. Other readers of the text may reinforce the invitation or provocation; the text has made something possible for them that could not have opened up otherwise. So I begin to read, attempting to bracket those things I take for granted so that I can follow the contour of a new landscape. Perhaps I can think of myself 'performing' a script, assuming a role, realizing a movement or action prescribed; and in that act of performance discovering capacity I had been unaware of. In the process, there will be transitions, bridging moments in the text's composition, that will be obscure to me; there will be bits that I simply don't know how to perform, how to realize. Other readers/ performers may help me, but there may not be a quick resolution. The success of my performance will not decide the worth of the text, but may rather take me back to the beginning, aware that the text's world is still real, but that I have yet to find the right way of realizing it here and now. There is no last performance, no reading that leaves nothing to do.

Sometimes I read a text because I want to know what the text doesn't know. The text speaks unconsciously of its location, its cultural world; it suggests obliquely how it works as a tool in particular contexts; it shows how prevailing images and ideas in the world of the text make some sorts of connections and bridges seem obvious, while a reader now will know that these connections rest on misunderstanding or error. Other readers of the text may not have seen the questions; they share the non-knowing of the text and they add new areas of complexity to the tracing of what isn't known. Only in making plain what the text doesn't know, and its other readers haven't seen, can I read the text for what it is and judge what it has to say to me or anyone now. There is no final reading, because of course I bring to the task what I myself don't know, and another reader, knowing something different or more than I will find other things that the text doesn't know.

This is more or less to paraphrase some of what Karl Barth says in the preface to the third edition of his Romans commentary, where he locks horns with Bultmann over the principles of theological exegesis. The former model is what Barth speaks of in terms of 'loyalty' to the text or its author; and he notes that it is not something peculiar to biblical exegesis but belongs to the very nature of literary interpretation. It is not possible to go so far in performative reading (I happily acknowledge my debt to Nicholas Lash and Frances Young for the crucial metaphor of performance in this context) and then turn around and comment upon the ideas or the style from outside (Barth 1933, pp. 18ff.). What is needed is what Barth calls reading, thinking and writing *with* (not *on*) the text and its author (pp. 17–18). It is worth noting, in passing, that Barth regularly speaks of author rather than text, in a way redolent of a residual nineteenth century assumption that the text is the transcription of the contents of an author's mind; but we shall return to this a little later. But only by this close, performative reading do we become able to see beyond the text, to see in some measure what the text sees or envisages – which, for Barth, is not first and foremost the world consciously *addressed* by the text, but the world consciously inhabited by the text. And in the case of Paul's letter to the Romans, the world inhabited is a world under God's judgement and God's grace; stand alongside Paul and your commentary will be – as Barth's unmistakably is – a sustained exercise in recreating Paul's movement of thought, pursuing, repeating, improvizing on the theme: performance of a very distinctive kind.

Barth is determined to put clear blue water between this exercise and the work of historical criticism, and his assault on Bultmann in these pages is very much to do with Bultmann's mixing of the two sorts of reading. Bultmann's exegesis is apparently committed to some sort of performance; it works for conversion, it assumes that the text invites. Yet it uses the tools of historical criticism to distinguish between what the text *uniquely* knows and what it merely reproduces from the repertoire of what its ambient cultural/religious world knows. Thus it is an exegesis which determines what is performable. And Barth's problem with this is that it, in effect, determines in advance the limits of what the text knows; how then can it actually invite into another world? The reader has already

decided the limit of what can be learned. 'I am completely unable', says
Barth, 'to understand Bultmann's demand that I should mingle fire and
water' (Barth 1933, p. 18). The effect of such a mingling is in fact to
deprive theological reading of its integrity – that theological reading
which is defined by its loyalty, its willingness to follow the *Sachdialektik*
of the text in its entirety.

This refers back to Barth's preface to the second edition of his commentary a year earlier (1921), but takes it further. The earlier preface
moves rather rapidly in its argument from a perfunctory defence of historical criticism as a means of establishing a sound working text to the
assertion that true and full historical criticism is always in search of
the fundamental dialectic of the text; it cannot be satisfied with a com-
placently baffled statement that such and such a doctrine is simply part
of Paul's inaccessible world (Barth 1933, pp. 6ff.). 'The critical historian
needs to be more critical . . . Intelligent comment means that I am driven
on till I stand with nothing before me but the enigma of the matter; till
the document seems hardly to exist as a document; till I have almost forgotten that I am not its author' (Barth 1933, p. 8). This implies that there
is a proper progression from strictly 'critical' issues to *Sachkritik* – or
rather to the extraordinary depth of 'performative' reading implied in the
goal of almost forgetting the distance between author and reader. But
the reply to Bultmann seems to point in a slightly different direction.
Bultmann's idea of historical criticism is far more than the production
of a good textual apparatus: it really is about the *matter* of the text, the
understanding of its world, the movement and logic of its thought. But
what Barth cannot accept in it is the final reservation: it cannot be 'loyal';
it will, by discriminating between the conditioned and the uncondi-
tioned, the time-bound myth and the eternal word of judgement, refuse
the sharpest interpretative challenge of all. What if the text is an indis-
tinguishable melange of human words precisely *in* whose complexity
the Word of divine invitation is uttered? No detail can be ignored, no
detail can be absolutized. The 'relativity' or ambiguity of the text as a
whole (Barth 1933, p. 19) is what speaks, what 'knows'; we cannot know
what the text knows without that sort of hermenuetical patience that
will not exercise surgical discrimination but seek to follow how the
whole of what is on the page can be performable.

So from the 1921 picture, a relatively simple one, of plunging into the
text once the preliminary critical work is done, Barth seems to be moving
to a position where the critical enterprise is allowed free play up to the
limits of the text itself. To be able to identify, in Bultmannian fashion,
all the 'words of men', the 'other spirits', that determine the actual shape
of a Pauline argument is, Barth implies, entirely compatible with his own

exegesis of performance. There is no sanctified area where historical criticism is not allowed to penetrate. The problem arises only when this process is used to sift the Word of God from human words, the Spirit of Christ from other spirits. The otherness of Christ's Spirit, God's Word, is not that of a particular 'area' of the text or the writer's mind. So being brought into the new world of the text is not a matter of finding where the boundary lies within the text between old and new, God and the human spirit. 'The whole is *litera*, that is, voices of those other spirits. The problem is whether the whole must not be understood in relation to the true subject matter which is – The Spirit of Christ' (Barth 1933, p. 17).

The point could be expressed, I think, in this way. For Bultmann (as Barth reads him, not wholly unfairly), what Paul knows about God (and what we want to know from him) is an area of his overall knowledge sharply distinct from his 'knowing' of other things – and thus from his not-knowing of other things, his sharing in the mythology of his day. For Barth, Paul's knowing of God is inseparable from all he knows and doesn't know, from the actuality of his humanity in all its conditionedness. To stand without reserve with Paul in this human vulnerability is the only way of knowing what he knows of God. To stand where he stands is to locate and share his relation to his true subject matter – his entire being in the presence of God's wrath and grace. This adumbrates the later Barth's provocative remarks about the Bible in the *Church Dogmatics*, insisting that the Bible should not be regarded as inspired because it is (or to the degree that it is) manifestly *inspiring* in human terms, any more than belief in the divinity and Lordship of Christ is connected to any judgement about his human impressiveness (e.g. Barth 1975, pp. 112–13; 1956, pp. 506–7, 509–10, 674–5). So the performative reader acknowledges that the only way of knowing what Paul knew about God (and he 'knows of God what most of us do not know' wrote Barth in 1921; Barth 1933, p. 11) is through the reader's radical displacement. It does not make historical criticism impossible; on the contrary. It resigns the field to it, in one way. It simply affirms that the necessary self-consciousness of the critic cannot co-exist in the same practice as a performance of the text.

In fact, this allows us to clarify a little the potential tangle about author and text. There is a sense in which the text 'knows' more than the author. That is, what the text in its performability makes possible is not confined by what the author, even the inspired scriptural author, is aware of in the event of composition. To be loyal to the text is not quite the same as being loyal to the author, if being loyal to the author means only that I seek to share what was in the author's mind in writing. Standing with or alongside Paul as Barth describes it can also be standing with the indeterminacy of his conscious conception of the work – standing with him precisely *as* author, that is as someone responsible for a text that will live beyond his own conception. The displaced reader enters the world of a writer who is also in one way 'displaced', not in control, enters the world in which what is significant is 'the true subject matter', which is always in excess of what is consciously known.

The significance of this for thinking through what 'New Testament theology' might mean and for clarifying the relation of historical and theological study is plain. If we want to read the New Testament from a desire to know what it *alone* knows, we have to find how to 'perform' it. This is not immediately connected with any exercise in historical reconstruction; we are not reading in order to find out what Paul or (more pointedly, perhaps) John knew about certain events, what ideas they held in common with their contemporaries, what map, chronological or geographical, they used to find their way in the world. Other sources might tell us some of that, and this particular text will find a place in a cumulative work of reconstruction, no doubt, filling out some details and being itself supplemented by others. But what is the full specificity of *this* text or set of texts, what makes this itself as a literary reality, a distinct version of the world? Put it another way: why did this particular text have to come into being (assuming that texts are written because they are needed)? Only the following through of its actual literary movement can help us here. And when the text makes claims about God, we have to take it that the knowledge of the world inhabited by the text will require from us as readers a particularly intense suspension of the ego and its current modes of knowing and constructing the world. A 'theology' of the New Testament, or indeed of Scripture in general, must be in substantial part a method and a rationale for such suspension. That is to say, it must show us where and how to read in such a way that we 'perform', stand with, the text; and it must spell out the character, the grammar, of Christian talk about God in such a way that we see why knowledge of this God cannot be a matter of knowing facts about God alongside facts about other matters, why this God is not to be located within particular boundaries in a text or an authorial mind. If we want to make a connection that Barth, as I have suggested, clearly implies, we should have to say that this is related to the Chalcedonian claim that the divinity of God in Christ is not an aspect or area of Christ's historical identity but a pervasive, transforming, ironic presence which makes this identity the integral identity it is.

One further point worth drawing out is what Barth outlines in his first discussion of Scripture in the *Dogmatics*. We have to tread carefully in handling this distinction between theological and historical. It will not do to return to a Bultmannian identification of the timeless kerygma buried in a conditioned myth and a contingent narrative. If God is not a specialized area of otherness inside the world as far as the text is concerned, neither is God a specialized area of otherness in history, a presence suspending history; God is active in communicating with us in history – in memory, narrative, actual process. If our reading/performing of the text tempts us to think that the specific location of the text in history doesn't matter, that its interpretation has nothing to do with the circumstances of its production, we not only 'dematerialise' the text (as we would in any instance of literary interpretation or realisation), we imagine the act of God in relation to the text as if it were something detached from the human act of writing, and thus from all the complex cultural and local embeddedness that shapes it. Thus, while historical criticism will not tell us what is cultural and local and what is of God, what it will and should do for us is to monitor attempts at performance/ realisation/ exegesis that are straightforwardly incompatible with what can be known about the contingent world in which the text is formed. In this sense, historical criticism has a powerful, if in a sense negative, role for theological interpretation, for good theological reasons (Barth 1975, pp. 325–30).

'The historical component in theological interpretation of the New Testament is essential if Scripture is to remain definitive of Christian belief. It helps preserve the givenness of revelation *ab extra* and makes possible some degree of consensus about valid meanings by excluding arbitrary interpretations from doctrinal contexts' (Morgan 2003, p. 34). This simple but magisterial judgement of Bob Morgan's, from an essay of 2003, represents the fruit of a long reflection on the issues touched upon in these pages. He has always defended the need for Christology to be allowed to develop without anxious dependence on historical reconstruction, and he has some suitably sceptical words in this same essay for some fashionable attempts in this direction. But he has also a vivid sense of the entire logic of Scriptural interpretation requiring a sensitivity to the necessary – if never sufficient – conditions for reading or performing Scripture in a way faithful to what it really is. This balance has long made him hard to categorize in the simplistic oppositions that can mark the world of New Testament study. He is not a programmatic sceptic nor a conservative historicist. Instead, I suggest, he is someone who has very fully grasped the difference and the tension between the kinds of reading with which I began. He has been consistently alive to the fact that the biblical texts are texts for 'performance'; they invite a transfer of allegiance and domicile, a new world. Watching these texts being performed as and where they should be, in the sacramental assembly of worshippers, is to see how our world becomes other, how it is possible to live otherwise. Seeing the performance of the texts in the closely related context of labour and witness for the Kingdom in a world of gross injustice and inhumanity likewise invites us to be judged and remade and commissioned. Both liturgy and transforming action (or should we say transforming action, liturgical and otherwise?) spell out what a Barthian 'loyalty' to the text might be. Yet to be always aware at the same time of the risks of turning the texts into abstract patterns, of idealizing them and refusing to entertain the question of what they don't know – this too is crucial to the fullness of theological labour. But it needs the most careful mapping if we are to avoid the massive category mistakes of some who try to do their theology out of their critical conclusions.

Bob Morgan has negotiated this tightrope with elegance and profundity for decades; and I hope he will not mind being displayed in these introductory remarks as a practical illustration of how Barth's discriminations can work within a serious and professional practice of critical scholarship. The professional world of biblical scholarship is not a sermon class, and there is a good deal in past practice that has to be unlearned, by so-called radicals and conservatives alike (for radicals too preach sermons, as the work of the Jesus Seminar makes all too plain). It is possible never to ask or want to ask – in the sense earlier defined – what the text knows, and yet to be a first class commentator of one kind. But for those who cannot let the text lie as if it were unperformable, those who continue to watch what happens in its performance in the community, there needs to be theologically alert guidance in helping us see what role the critical enterprise does and doesn't have in the art of performance. That is the guidance that Bob Morgan has offered; this volume speaks eloquently of the authority with which he has addressed both categories of biblical readers and the contribution he continues to make to the work of discrimination here outlined.

References

Barth, Karl, *The Epistle to the Romans*, (translated from the sixth edition by Edwyn C. Hoskyns; Oxford: Oxford University Press, 1933).
Barth, Karl, *Church Dogmatics I.2. The Doctrine of the Word of God*, (trans. G. T. Thomson and Harold Knight; Edinburgh: T. and T. Clark, 1956).
Barth, Karl, *Church Dogmatics I.1. The Doctrine of the Word of God*, second edition, (trans. G. Bromiley; Edinburgh: T. and T. Clark, 1975).
Morgan, Robert, 'Jesus Christ, the Wisdom of God (2)', in *Reading Texts, Seeking Wisdom. Scripture and Theology* (eds David Ford and Graham Stanton; London: SCM Press, 2003) pp. 22–37.

Chapter 1

History and Theology in New Testament Studies

John Ashton, Paris

At the height of the German Enlightenment many German thinkers were coming to attach increasing importance to history, and in 1787 J.P. Gabler, following the trend, sought to invest New Testament (NT) theology with respectability by giving it a properly historical dimension. He advocated a two-stage process to ensure for theology, or rather dogma, a solidly established foundation. Yet at the same time he continued to apply the term 'biblical theology' to the first, preliminary stage of historical enquiry. This was a potential source of confusion; and when William Wrede, more than a century later (1897), argued that in his own field of the New Testament the term 'New Testament theology' should be replaced by a title indicating more accurately the true nature of the scholarly enterprise, he helped to perpetuate the confusion by continuing to employ the term he deprecated until the very last page of his long essay 'On the Task and Method of so-called New Testament Theology'. So, for instance, he writes: 'I have called the separation of the New Testament writings from those related to them . . . downright mistaken in biblical theology' (Morgan 1973, p. 191 n. 62). What he means, of course, is that such a separation is mistaken in the history of early Christian religion. Somewhat surprisingly he leaves a place for theology, albeit a small one, in his proposed title, which reads, in full, 'the history of early Christian religion and theology' (p. 116). This was no doubt because, as he freely admits, there are properly theological elements at least in Paul and John. Nevertheless the addition is in one respect unfortunate because it has allowed the confusion between the two quite distinct disciplines of history and theology to persist. It is one thing to include some treatment of Paul's theology as part of a general history of the breakaway of the Christian movement from Judaism, asking, for instance, as Wrede did, how his 'Pharasaic Jewish theology became, through the experience of his conversion and what followed it, transformed into his Christian theology' (p. 107), quite another to isolate it for special treatment and use it as a sort of compendium of subsequent Christian doctrine, a tendency whose origins lie deep in the Protestant Reformation. Albert Schweitzer, writing in 1911, says of Reformation exegesis, that 'it reads its own ideas into Paul in order to receive them back clothed in apostolic authority' (Schweitzer 1912, p. 2). This is just what Wrede was complaining about in his own predecessors and contemporaries, but it is a practice that still lives on.

Wrede's seminal essay remained untranslated into English until 1973 when it was published by Robert Morgan along with a strong rebuttal of Wrede's key thesis by Adolf Schlatter and a magisterial introduction by Morgan himself. The purpose of the present chapter, written with admiration and respect in honour of Robert Morgan, is to suggest in a friendly way (for he is one of my closest friends) some of the limitations and possibilities of the project of a full-scale New Testament theology that is so close to his own heart. (By New Testament theology I mean an interpretation of the NT designed to be religiously significant to present-day readers – roughly what Morgan calls the strong sense of theology.)

In adding the term 'theology', almost as an afterthought, to his general title, Wrede was already, as I have suggested, conceding too much. For in speaking blithely of 'the theology' of this or that NT author, scholars are enabled to ignore the properly *religious* aspect of their writings and of the experiences they record. The two founders of Christianity, Jesus and Paul, were not in the first place religious *thinkers* but religious figures; and the only words Jesus is said to have written (in a spurious insertion into John's Gospel) were in sand. Nowadays, not only his miracles but also the amazing religious experiences attributed to him in the Gospels, his baptism and transfiguration, are generally dismissed as legendary. Even the Apocalypse, reporting what on the face of it are religious experiences of a truly astonishing kind, is often – when discussed at all – drained of life by being placed on the same dusty shelf as the letters of Peter and James, as if apocalypse was nothing more than yet another literary genre. Klaus Berger, one of the very few NT scholars to have taken Wrede's admonitions seriously, nevertheless entitles his big book *Theologiegeschichte des Urchristentums* (Berger 1994), perhaps because he felt uneasy with the alternative: *Religionsgeschichte*.

If, despite Wrede's powerful arguments against allowing dogmatic interests to intrude upon their academic study of the New Testament, theology has continued to play a major role in the work of the majority of biblical scholars, it is equally true that history has occupied an important place in works designated NT theologies. It is not altogether clear whether Wrede himself agreed with Gabler in thinking that after the history there was further work to be done. He was certainly not interested himself in theology in the strong sense of applying lessons learned from a study of the Bible to the life of the Christian community.

By far the most important New Testament theology in the twentieth century, as is commonly agreed, is that of Rudolf Bultmann, and for the purposes of the present chapter some consideration needs to be given of the ways in which Bultmann succeeded in muddying the waters still further. In a foreword to a collection of his own essays published in 1967, Bultmann agrees with the editor's assessment of his career: 'He rightly stresses as the dominant characteristic of my work that I have been resolutely concerned to effect a unity between exegesis and theology, but in such a way that exegesis in fact takes precedence' (Bultmann 1967, p. vii).

There can be no doubt that exegesis, rigorously conducted as an exercise in historical criticism, was an art in which Bultmann excelled; but many of his readers might well feel that in his work as a whole theology has had the upper hand. At any rate his New Testament theology is a strange mixture of history and theology of the kind that Wrede deplored. The book opens with the notorious assertion that 'the message of Jesus is a presupposition for the theology of the New Testament rather than part of that theology itself.' This of course is only true if Jesus' preaching is levered out of the Gospels in which it has come down to us and forced to stand, somewhat uncertainly (for no two scholars reconstruct it in quite the same way), on its own. Each of the Synoptic Gospels, including its record of Jesus' message, remains an important document in the history of the early church. For the historian it is equally important to attempt a reconstruction of what Bultmann calls 'the kerygma of the earliest church (*Urgemeinde*)', but this belonged to a period that preceded the first writing of the New Testament, Paul's first letter to the Thessalonians, and so it is hard to see why it is included in a theology of the *New Testament*, There is no reason why a New Testament theology rightly understood should begin with history, every reason why it should begin with the Gospels. Taken as a whole, moreover, the first part of Bultmann's book cannot be said either to be fully consonant with Wrede's proposals for a history of early Christianity, since in a major section on 'the theology of the Hellenistic church aside from Paul' Bultmann brings in a number of writings that were composed after, in some cases long after, all the authentic letters of Paul. Historically speaking this makes no sense.

The Problem of the Canon

At some point or some period between the second and the fourth centuries, the 27 writings that go to make up the little book Christians call the New Testament were accepted by the church as canonical, that is to say as authoritative records of their own faith. In spite of some disagreements and adjustments they have remained so ever since.

The problem for scholars interested in the early history of Christianity, a problem highlighted by Wrede, is that there are many other non-canonical writings, no less important for the understanding of the history of the period, that historians need to take into account. The writings of the NT itself are burdened, Wrede points out, with dogmatic predicates like 'normative' that say nothing about their character as documents: 'no NT writing was ever born with the predicate "canonical" attached' (Morgan 1973, p. 70). What is more, some of them – 1 Peter, 2 Peter, along with James and Jude – are too small to serve as sources for any significant doctrinal material. It would be stupid to suppose that all an author's thoughts could be contained in what is little more than a snippet of a letter.

These, however – and this must be stressed – are not problems for the theologian, for whom the canon remains a valid concept and its writings 'normative' in a sense that cannot be predicated of any others. Preoccupied as he was with the need to correct the dogmatic prejudices of his own contemporaries, Wrede did not even consider the possibility that some of them might wish to carry on with theology in the strong sense and use historical studies, as Gabler had suggested, simply to provide their theological reflections with a solid basis in scholarship.

Wrede at one point reinforces his argument with the disparaging comment that 'anyone who accepts without question the idea of the canon places himself under the authority of the bishops and theologians of these [the second to fourth] centuries' (Morgan 1973, p. 71). Morgan responds that this is 'by no means obviously true' (Morgan 1973, p. 5). But Wrede is right here, and he might have added to the bishops of the second and fourth centuries the whole subsequent tradition of the Christian Church, East and West. But why should this worry someone who is engaged *ex professo* in theology rather than history? The discomfort arises from trying to wear two hats at the same time. A theologian who puts history before theology in more than a merely temporal sense runs the risk of subordinating the NT witnesses to extraneous considerations that may obscure the message they continue to carry for Christian readers.

In my view the problem of the canon is a pseudo-problem, one that disappears before a clearly drawn distinction between history and theology.

The Old Testament

Morgan comments that the question of 'how [a Christian] reading of the OT is related to the NT is by no means easily answered' (Morgan 1995, p. 129). But this is perhaps because it is the wrong question. I do not know when Christian scholars began to devote to the OT the kind of specialized and undivided attention that would result in a work meriting the name of a Christian reading of the Old Testament. But this was certainly not how the first Christians looked at it.

Once again we may start by distinguishing history from theology. Historically speaking the two Testaments belong quite literally to different eras. In any *history* of early Christianity the OT's relevance is restricted to the light it can shed upon the attitudes and behaviour of the men and women, Jews and Christians, who lived centuries after it was composed.

For NT *theology* its relevance is much greater, because with the solitary exception of James (and who knows how he would have answered the question?) the OT, mostly in the Greek translation we call the Septuagint, is for the authors of the NT what gives intelligibility to their faith in the crucified Messiah: think how often the little word *dei* occurs in the Gospels in connection with the fulfilment of prophecy. As theologians themselves, the NT writers drew lessons from what was still to them the only Scripture they knew (*he graphe*) and applied these to their own faith in ways that can seem peculiar and disconcerting to an attentive reader versed in the principles of critical exegesis. Matthew, for instance, in one of his fulfilment prophecies, explains Jesus' eventual return from the flight into Egypt by quoting Hosea: 'out of Egypt I have called my son' (Hos 11:1; Matt 2:15). A Jewish reader might well feel astonished, even offended, by this seemingly trivial application of Hosea's pithy summary of the grand events of the Exodus. Equally, however, Matthew is prepared to apply to Jesus' healing miracles a line from Isaiah to which later Christian writers would attach a different and much more sombre meaning: 'he took our infirmities and bore our diseases' (Isa 53:4; Matt 8:17).

It is clear from these two examples that in many cases a historical critical reading of the OT is of no help whatever in interpreting the NT. A further point may be made, this time from Paul. In Galatians Paul attaches an enormous amount of emphasis to the word *sperma*, which occurs often in the early chapters of Genesis in reference to the seed of Abraham. He insists that 'the promises were made to Abraham and to his offspring. It does not say, "And to offsprings", referring to many; but, referring to one, "And to your offspring", which is Christ' (Gal 3:16). Yet the Hebrew word translated as *sperma never* has a singular reference: when used of a human individual it *always* refers to his descendants in their entirety. Here and often elsewhere in the NT the interpreter will benefit much more from a knowledge of the exegetical practices of the rabbis, who base their own interpretations of the sacred text (*midrashim*, re-readings) upon this and other such grammatical peculiarities, not upon a critical study of the OT itself. A few verses further on, stressing that God's covenant with Abraham (Genesis 15) was based on a promise, not a contract, Paul exhibits breath-taking chutzpah by deliberately avoiding all mention of Genesis 17, in which an alternative version of the covenant with Abraham stipulates that all his descendants should be circumcised. To have introduced this text here would have left Paul's original argument in tatters.

Morgan is no doubt right, then, to assert that 'a NTT that did not speak of the OT would be inadequate both to the NT authors' witness to the revelation of God in Jesus Christ and to most modern interpreters' understanding of this'; but wrong to conclude, as he does, 'We are forced back upon the misleading phrase *biblical theology*' (Morgan 1995, p. 129). NT theologians do not need to be OT theologians also.

The Historical Jesus

With one important exception NT theologians are content to employ historical methods and conclusions as external aids to interpretation. The exception is the historical Jesus, or (as it has been called since the publication in 1910 of an English version of Albert Schweitzer's famous book) 'the quest of the historical Jesus'.

Many discussions of the legitimacy and possibility of the quest are vitiated by a failure to observe the crucial distinction between the Jesus of history who lived and died in Palestine in the first century of the Common Era and the historical Jesus as hypothetically reconstructed by historians. The former is remembered in the pages of the Gospels, the latter is an artificial construct of modern research. One example of this confusion may suffice. Ernst Käsemann, one of the initiators of the New Quest, responding angrily to the rejection of the whole project by his teacher, Bultmann, puts the question, as he says, in a nutshell: 'does the

NT kerygma count the historical Jesus among the criteria of its own validity?' (Käsemann 1968, p. 48). This question he answers himself with a resounding Yes, as if no other answer was conceivable. But we must distinguish: 'historical Jesus' could mean simply 'Jesus of Nazareth as he figures in the pages of the Gospels'. In that case the answer is plain enough, for a No would amount to a rejection of the Gospels themselves. But it could equally well mean, especially in the context of Käsemann's article 'Jesus as an object of historical research'. If so, the answer is surely that, with the possible exception of Luke (not an ally whom Käsemann would welcome), neither the NT nor its authors show any interest in historical research.

What Schweitzer said of the nineteenth-century quest seems to me equally true of the twentieth: 'it was not only each epoch that found its reflection in Jesus; each individual created him in accordance with his own character. There is no historical task which so reveals a man's true self as the writing of a Life of Jesus' (Schweitzer 1910, p. 4). Yet the difficulty (I would say impossibility) of arriving at a picture of Jesus that would satisfy everybody qualified to assess it has left dozens of would-be biographers undeterred. Historians (and others) continue to argue with one another whether Jesus was really a homespun Cynic philosopher, a social reformer, or an eschatological preacher deeply sympathetic to the Pharasaic culture all around him. And in any case the virtual impossibility of writing a reliable biography of Jesus does not mean that nothing at all can be said with any assurance about his life and teaching.

When we turn to theology, however, the picture changes. In 1892 strong objections against favouring what he called the so-called historical Jesus over the true biblical Christ were put forward by Martin Kähler. He pointed out that faith cannot be founded on historical research, which is always in principle subject to revision. The liberal theologians, who were still interested in scraping off the dogmatic overlay that had in their view obscured the Jesus of Christian faith, ignored Kähler's arguments. For them true Christianity consisted in the acceptance of Jesus' message of God's fatherly love for mankind and the moral teaching that went along with it (summed up by Harnack as 'the higher righteousness'). This watered-down version of the Christian faith was scornfully dismissed by the dialectical theologians who came to the fore in Germany after the First World War. They replaced it by what is commonly called a kerygmatic theology, which holds that the true object of Christian faith is not the Jesus of history but the Risen Christ, Messiah and Son of God, as proclaimed by Paul (and John). For the purposes of New Testament theology, by far the most significant of the dialectical theologians is Rudolf Bultmann, who added to Kähler's arguments against the questers the more profound theological objection that reliance upon historical research amounts to an offence against the Lutheran principle of justification by faith alone.

Whatever the merits and relevance of Bultmann's high-minded Lutheranism in this matter, he is surely right to insist that the Christ of the kerygma is not a historical figure which could enjoy continuity with the Jesus of history. This is a key feature of his theology, and one that more conservative theologians not surprisingly jib at. It depends upon the perception that whereas the Jesus of history is a flesh-and-blood human being, the kerygmatic Christ is a mythical figure inaccessible to human reason. It may be possible to replace the challenging term 'mythical' with one less offensive to pious ears, but Bultmann's basic point is surely correct. He is right too to point out that the Synoptists, in combining as they do historical report and kerygmatic Christology, are not aiming to give historical legitimacy to the Christ-kerygma but the other way round: by viewing the history of Jesus in the light of the kerygma (i.e. of the proclamation of faith in the Risen Lord) they are purposely giving their Gospels legitimacy as vehicles of that proclamation (see Bultmann 1964, pp. 24–5).

From an admittedly rather cursory survey of the vast array of attempts to further research into the life of Jesus, my own impression is that none has succeeded in proving convincingly the *theological* relevance of this research. Nils Dahl, one of the few really great twentieth-century scholars, responded to Bultmann by asserting that 'though the Gospels may be proclamation and witness it would be *contrary to the intention of the evangelists* to declare inquiry into the history of the narratives as irrelevant' (Dahl 1991, p. 103, my italics). Had this been so one would expect the many detailed disagreements between the Gospels to have provoked an immediate debate about which of them was right in each instance. Quite the opposite occurred: the grander differences of theme and emphasis between the Gospels prompted Irenaeus, in the middle of the second century, to insist that all four had to be read together in order to provide a fully rounded picture of Jesus as man, prophet, priest and Son of God.

'Because of the special authority ascribed to the words of the Lord in the New Testament,' argues Dahl, 'we cannot regard the question of the genuineness or nongenuineness of a word as completely irrelevant for theology' (1991, p. 108). But does not the very fact that they have been included in the Gospels or elsewhere in the NT *as* the words of Jesus bestow a special authority on them? 'It is more blessed to give than to receive' (Acts 20:35), a saying of triply dubious authenticity, is surely no less precious or powerful for that. Suppose for a moment that we had the means of distinguishing with certainty between all the authentic and inauthentic sayings attributed to Jesus. This would no doubt involve the use of such a fine and discriminating homing device that the results of the search would look pitifully meagre, and some of them (for example the divorce saying in Mark 10:1–12) difficult to live with. And what in any case should we do with the great bulk number of sayings that had slipped through the net, including all the long discourses in the Fourth Gospel?

Though he rejects any continuity between the Jesus of history and the kerygmatic Christ, Bultmann does nevertheless allow a continuity between the kerygma, which clearly presupposes the Jesus of history (without whom there would never have been any kerygma at all) and the activity, especially the preaching activity, of Jesus. Here are two historical facts: Jesus proclaimed the kingdom of God; the first Christians proclaimed the Risen Christ. Generally reticent about what can be said with any assurance about the historical Jesus, Bultmann does admit 'somewhat cautiously' that we can say something. His list is not a long one but even so it includes some items (as do all such lists) that are contested by other scholars, such as Jesus' polemic against Jewish legalism and his eschatological message of the breaking-in of the kingdom. Then he adds an important rider. 'The greatest embarrassment to the attempt to reconstruct a portrait of Jesus is the fact that we cannot know how Jesus understood his end, his death. It is symptomatic that it is practically universally assumed that Jesus went consciously to his suffering and death and that he understood this as the organic or necessary conclusion to his activity. But how do we know this, when prophecies of the passion must be understood by critical research as *vaticinia ex eventu?*' (Bultmann 1964, p. 23). We do not even know, Bultmann concludes, whether he found any meaning in it himself: 'we may not conceal from ourselves the possibility that he suffered a collapse [*daß er zusammengebrochen ist*]' (p. 24).

All this is extremely contentious. But Bultmann is talking about possibilities here, not certainties. He is simply saying that there is no certainty to be had, and issuing a warning to prospective biographers of Jesus of the sheer precariousness of the whole enterprise. But have any of them listened? The proliferation of Lives of Jesus, from professional scholars and interested amateurs alike, continues unabated. To a disinterested observer there seems little significant difference between the original quest, the new quest, and the self-proclaimed third quest. Armed with the chisels and levers of critical exegesis, the would-be biographers industriously prise out from the pages of the Synoptic Gospels (and occasionally from the Fourth Gospel too and their own imagination) the material they need to enable them to piece together a convincing historical figure. Some of these, naturally, are more lifelike than others, but most of them are simply puppets dancing obediently to strings tugged by their creators.

One of the most impressive attempts to reflect theologically on the Synoptic Gospels is Bultmann's own *Jesus* (1926), translated into English as *Jesus and the Word* (1934). True, Bultmann does base himself here on what he considers to be the oldest layer of Jesus' sayings, but without pretending to confine himself to those whose authenticity he thinks he can prove. Moreover he deliberately eschews any attempt to offer a portrait of the personality of Jesus, pointing out that it is characteristic of all great men ('Plato or Jesus, Dante or Luther, Napoleon or Goethe') that they are more interested in their work than in their own personalities, and that in Jesus' case his work is chiefly to be found in his words. There are enough of these for Bultmann to present his own readers with a challenging interpretation of his own. A present-day theologian, modelling herself on Bultmann's example, would certainly offer a very different interpretation and a different kind of challenge. But this, surely, is the stuff of New Testament theology.

When, much later, Bultmann came to write his own monumental New Testament theology he omitted any direct treatment of the Synoptic Gospels because, as we have seen, he considered the message of Jesus to be simply a presupposition rather than a part of the theology of the NT. But it is only by making a bizarre and unacknowledged excision in what the term NT actually denotes that he can justify this omission, for the Synoptic Gospels occupy a substantial place in this little book. More importantly they also occupy a place in the kerygmatic message of early Christianity, proclaiming as they do, however paradoxically and contradictorily, the identity of the Jesus whose story they are telling with the Risen Lord whom Christians worship.

Just how, in what position and in what order NT theologians should deal with the Synoptic Gospels must be left to them to decide. But that they should be included somewhere in any New Testament theology with pretensions to completeness seems to me beyond question.

Applicatio

Any New Testament theology worth its salt must be seen to offer a meaningful interpretation of the NT to the community for which it is written. This is the aspect of theology traditionally called *applicatio*. History, including the history of the Christian religion, is interested in *meaning*, that is to say with understanding the period it is concerned with and the written documents that belong to this. Theology must go further: not just meaning but *meaning for*.

One reason why Bultmann's theology is so impressive is that he has managed to find in the Christian kerygma (Paul and John) the timeless challenges that will always confront human beings, in virtue of their sheer humanity. But precisely because they are timeless they fail to address the particular problems, moral, social, political, that continue to emerge from one generation to the next. A theology that does address these questions will have to sacrifice Bultmann's grand vision for something smaller and more fragmentary. What this would look like I cannot say.

All authoritative texts require interpretation. Luther's *Scriptura ipsius interpres* (Scripture its own interpreter) cleverly disposed of the dogmatic barnacles with which the Bible had become encrusted, but relied upon an assumption of the unity of Scripture (itself a dogmatic principle!) that proved in the long run unsustainable. So what could take its place? Recognising that the Bible itself could not be simply and simplistically identified with revelation, Bultmann substituted for Luther's *Scriptura ipsius interpres* his own principle of *Sachkritik*.

Sachkritik, Morgan tells us, 'has been variously translated into English as "content criticism, material criticism of the content", "objective criticism" (!), "theological criticism", "critical interpretation" and "critical study of the content"' (1973, p. 42). None of these translations is very perspicuous. *Sache* is a difficult word to render satisfactorily in English: it can mean subject matter, affair, concern, content, point, circumstance; it can also mean object, article, thing. *Bei der Sache bleiben* means to stick to the point. I guess that *Sache* corresponds quite closely to the Latin *res*, and that it lies behind Luther's brilliant epigram, *qui non intellegit rem non potest ex verbis sensum elicere*: you will make no sense of the words if you don't understand what they're all about: what the words are all about: the heart of the matter: *die Sache*.

As a principle of interpretation this sounds fine, but of course you first have to discover the central message, *die Sache*, and then you have to apply it. The search for the core message involves the putting into practice of another of Luther's principles. Since he was still able to conceive Scripture as a whole, for him it was the whole of Scripture that guides the understanding of each individual passage, yet at the same time the grasp of the whole can only be reached through the cumulative understanding of the individual passages in their entirety. This principle, known as the hermeneutical circle, is, I think, valid in itself, but even if one believes, as Luther did, that there is a single literal meaning ascertainable throughout Scripture, it is virtually impossible to apply it in practice. (In fact Luther used *Sachkritik* before the term had even been coined: *crux sola est nostra theologia* [our theology is the cross, and nothing but the cross].) We know now that the Old Testament was not written with the New in mind, so in his own biblical theology Bultmann could quite reasonably devote all his attention to the New Testament. In fact he is much more selective than that. Because he mixes up history and theology he can and does treat different parts of the text differently. Of the three parts of his book, only the second, dealing with Paul and John, is theological in the strong sense. Many of his brief analyses of the other NT writings are shrewd and insightful, but he makes no effort to derive theological lessons from them. In the single page devoted to the Letter of James, for instance, he contents himself with pointing out that it is irreconcilable with the theology of Paul.

In spite of these serious difficulties there is still a lot to be said for the method of *Sachkritik*. As Morgan points out: 'if the aim of theological interpretation is to achieve some correlation between the theologian's apprehension of Christianity and what he finds in the tradition, then some method for rejecting tradition is inevitable, and there is no reason why it should not be used on biblical tradition, once it is agreed that this is not in itself revelation' (1973, p. 43). The problem lies in the phrase 'the theologian's apprehension of Christianity,' not because the use of the word Christianity implies that what is being considered here is much larger than a single little book (this seems to me inevitable), but because of the risk that any single theologian's apprehension of Christianity is in the nature of the case highly subjective and open to challenge by others. Morgan is alert to the danger of what he calls 'the premature application of a method which is all too likely to do violence to a historical text in making it correspond to the interpreter's own view' (ibid.) (I am not entirely clear whether he thinks that the risk of violence to the text is inherent in the method itself or simply in its premature application.)

It seems then that another hermeneutic is required, perhaps one in which the problems affecting biblical theology can be seen in a broader context. Just such a hermeneutic is urged very powerfully by H.-G. Gadamer in his classic study, now 45 years old, *Wahrheit und Methode* (1960) (ET *Truth and Method* 1975).

Theology has at least two lessons to learn from Gadamer. First, there is his convincing dismissal of the idea that it is possible to transport oneself back into the past as on a magic carpet, and once arrived survey the work one is studying through the eyes of its author. But he retains from this idea, which goes back at least as far as Schleiermacher and is still clearly present, say, in the second edition of Barth's commentary on Romans, the clear implication that an ancient text may continue to be have meaning for later generations.

Indeed the meaning of such a text, insists Gadamer, is indefinitely extendible, because its horizon (*Horizont*) ceaselessly edges outwards as it impacts upon readers of later generations. Gadamer gives this unceasing outward movement the name of *Wirkungsgeschichte* (literally 'history of impact'), and the act or process whereby someone outside the circle of the work's original readers reaches an understanding of it he calls *Horizontverschmelzung* (fusion of horizons). A fusion is required because however much the horizon of the work may shift, the interpreter's own horizon is always different. 'The conscious act of this fusion', he says, is the task of *das wirkungsgeschichtliches Bewußtsein* (literally, the history-of-impact consciousness): 'it is, in fact, the central problem of hermeneutics. It is the problem of application that exists in all understanding' (Gadamer 1975, p. 274). (Gadamer's theory cannot be discussed in detail here; but the new model is certainly an improvement upon the magic-carpet theory it has supplanted.)

Gadamer immediately goes on to argue that the three skills required in the interpretation of an ancient text, to which German Pietism gave the names of *subtilitas intelligendi, explicandi* and *applicandi*, are really inseparable, three aspects of a single process which, he continues, may be seen to apply to the whole broad field of humanistic studies, including ethics, history (on which subject he appeals to Bultmann), literary criticism and, most significantly, law.

Here, in fact, is Gadamer's second notable contribution to the proper understanding of the true nature of biblical interpretation: his recognition of its structural resemblance to legal hermeneutics. In both cases we have to do with ancient authoritative texts that have a meaning in the present that cannot in the nature of the case have been envisaged by their authors. Judge or jurors on the one hand, theologians or preachers on the other, are confronted with the task of finding a new meaning: not, insists Gadamer, arbitrarily, but according to the right sense of the law. (One might have expected him to use a term like 'spirit of the law' here, but he avoids doing so, no doubt because the word 'spirit' is encumbered by too much philosophical baggage.)

Gadamer says of preaching (and he would surely say the same of theological interpretation of the Bible) that unlike a legal verdict, it is not 'a creative supplement to the text it is interpreting.... Scripture is the word of God, and that means that it has an absolute priority over the teaching of those who interpret it' (1975, p. 295). But he has failed at this point, I think, properly to unpack the term 'word of God'; moreover it is just as true of, say, the American Constitution as of Scripture that it has an absolute priority over the teaching of its interpreters.

For all his insights, Gadamer is far from offering solutions to all the problems confronting the NT theologian. For one thing, he is surprisingly optimistic about the likelihood that legal experts and (implicitly) theologians and preachers will agree upon the significance of the text they are interpreting. The fact is that members of the Supreme Court on the one hand, and theologians on the other, can and do disagree among themselves. And there is nothing in *Truth and Method* to advise us on how to resolve these disagreements.

Given this situation, what sort of criteria can be found for assessing the rightness or wrongness of a particular interpretation? The answer, quite clearly, is None. Each and every proposed criterion is always open to challenge.

Is there any way out of this impasse? The history of bitter disagreements between theologians of different branches of the church over the centuries, often focused on a single verse or group of verses, suggests that the answer is No. In their reading of the Gospel of John the Eastern and Western churches continue to disagree on how much weight to put on John 16:7, the source of the famous *filioque* clause in the creed that is still a bone of contention between the Roman and the Eastern churches.

And what of the continuing row between two wings of the Anglican Communion on the subject of homosexuality? Rom 1:27, and just as clearly 1 Cor 6:9, which excludes active and passive homosexuals (*malakoi* and *arsenokoitai*) from the Kingdom of God, may no doubt be disposed of by the dexterous employment of a little *Sachkritik*, an exercise which I will attempt in a moment. But this is not a solution that is likely to impress the conservative wing. Those who support homosexual rights generally appeal to the welcome Jesus extended to sinners (though he always told them to repent) and to the vulnerable and dispossessed.

Perhaps, however, there is something more to be said after all. Ed Sanders, introducing his book, *Paul, the Law, and the Jewish People* (1983), comments perceptively on the difficulty of 'distinguishing between the reasons for which he held a view and the arguments he adduces in favor of it' (p. 4). Not only is this distinction of crucial importance in itself, but it may be applied not just to Paul but to his successors, who, like him, constantly appeal to Scripture for support. In all cases if we manage to discover the reasons that lie behind the arguments actually alleged in support of a particular case, we are much closer to a proper understanding than if, scrabbling on the surface, we fail to penetrate beneath the words on the page.

What is more, in confronting disagreements, ancient or modern, between interpreters belonging to the same tradition, we should recognize that their appeals to the Bible are in themselves arguments, not reasons. Many of their reasons may proceed from motives that have nothing to do with the Bible or theology. But others (and it is important to acknowledge this) are to be found buried in an understanding of the

Bible that has come to them without their realizing it through a much more deep-rooted tradition. It may be true that in most cases when they turn to the Bible to bolster their case they already know what they want to find there. But this presupposition or prejudice, call it what you will, will often belong and stem from a *tradition* (something well spotted by Gadamer). No one has put the matter with more insight than Hugh Kenner, who speaks of 'the whispering forest of all traditional poetries, where the very words to which millions of minds respond have helped to form the minds that respond to them' (Kenner 1972, p. 521).

Consequently, turning back to Paul, we should not attach too much importance to his apparent misreadings of the OT. These texts are simply the arguments he has lying to hand: he uses them when it suits his purpose, to persuade his readers that the Crucified Messiah has super-seded the Law. And if *this* is his message, is it not permissible to include in 'the Law' clauses that he himself, without giving the matter much thought, continued to regard as valid? The example that Sanders uses to illustrate his observation is Paul's teaching, in 1 Corinthians 11, that women should pray with their heads covered. Paul's arguments are abstruse, but the *reason* for his position, Sanders concludes, is simply that he was Jewish (Sanders 1983, 4). Nobody pays any attention to 1 Corinthians 11 nowadays, but Paul's reason for condemning homosexuality, along with a list of other sins, in 1 Cor 6:9 is the same: he was Jewish. Such a startlingly original thinker in many respects, Paul was a conservative when it came to morals, carrying most of his ethical teaching around with him in two bags, one labelled Jewish, the other Stoic, and opening them only when he needed a list of virtues or vices like the one in 1 Corinthians 6. (Another very radical thinker with surprisingly conservative moral views was René Descartes, as can be seen, Gadamer [1975, p. 248] points out, from his cor-respondence with Elizabeth, Princess of Bohemia.) Jesus, on the other hand, at any rate the Jesus of the Synoptic Gospels, was a truly revolution-ary moral thinker who, unlike Paul, always reflected upon the moral aspect of a situation; and so when it comes to moral issues, provided that they remember that Jesus too was a man of his time, New Testament theolo-gians have better reasons for turning to him than to Paul.

Conclusion

This chapter has been largely dominated by the distinction between history and dogma so forcefully argued by Wrede. How do things look if we substitute exegesis (plus theology) for Wrede's dogma? It is often suggested that the two disciplines are intertwined, or that they have been placed in adjacent, insufficiently watertight compartments. The picture of the two disciplines seeping unstoppably into the wrong box is unhelpful. Exegesis is the attempt to understand the meaning of a text; accounting for its genesis, a very different matter, is the business of history. The two disciplines often work with the same material, but their formal object, as the scholastics would call it, is different. Gabler realized that theologians have to start by being historians. As such they must follow the agreed procedures for historical study. In the case of the NT this may compel them to make use of a lot of extraneous material too. This was clearly perceived by Wrede. But when they turn to the actual practice of exegesis they are dealing with texts, and their approach must now be a literary one. In the past, I suspect, acutely aware (rightly so) that sound exegesis must be historically based, Morgan may have given his theology too much of a historical slant. In his recent writing, however, he shows that he now perceives his work as a New Testament exegete and theologian to require a more literary approach. Having grasped, as an exegete, the meaning of the NT writings in context, he can then, as a theologian, apply this to the present-day circumstances of the Anglican Communion to which he is proud to belong. He has my heartfelt good wishes in this ambitious enterprise.

References

Berger, K., *Theologiegeschichte des Urchristentums: Theologie des Neuen Testaments* (Tübingen: Francke Verlag, 1994).

Bultmann, R., *Exegetica* (ed. E. Dinkler; Tübingen, 1967).

Bultmann, R., *Jesus and the Word* (New York, 1934).

Bultmann, R., 'The primitive Christian kerygma and the Historical Jesus', in *The Historical Jesus and the Kerygmatic Christ* (eds C.E. Braaten and R.A. Harrisville; Nashville, 1964), pp. 15-42.

Bultmann, Rudolf, *Theologie des Neuen Testaments* (2 vols; Tübingen: Mohr Siebeck, 1948-53). ET *Theology of the New Testament* (2 vols; New York: Scribner, 1951-55). References are to the English version.

Dahl, N.A., 'The problem of the Historical Jesus', *Jesus the Christ* (ed. D.H. Juel; Minneapolis, 1991), pp. 81-111.

Gadamer, H.-G., *Truth and Method* (London, 1975).

Kähler, M., *The so-called Historical Jesus and the Historic, Biblical Christ* (Philadelphia: Fortress, 1964).

Käsemann, E., 'Blind alleys in the "Jesus of History" controversy', *New Testament Questions of Today* (Philadelphia: Fortress, 1969), pp. 23-65.

Kenner, H., *The Pound Era* (London, 1972).

Morgan, R., *The Nature of New Testament Theology* (London: SCM/Naperville, IL: Alec R. Allenson, 1973).

Morgan, R., 'New Testament theology', *Biblical Theology: Problems and Perspectives in Honor of J. Christiaan Beker* (eds Steven J. Kraftchick, Charles D. Myers, Jr. and Ben C. Ollenburger; Nashville, 1995), pp. 104-30.

Sanders, E.P., *Paul, the Law, and the Jewish People* (Philadelphia: Fortress, 1983).

Schweitzer, A., *The Quest of the Historical Jesus: A Critical Study of its Progress From Reimarus to Wrede* (trans. W. Montgomery, with a preface by F.C. Burkitt; London: A. & C. Black, 1910).

Schweitzer, A., *Paul and His Interpreters: A Critical History* (trans. W. Montgomery; London: A. & C. Black, 1912).

Wrede, W., 'The task and methods of "New Testament theology"', in R. Morgan, *The Nature of New Testament Theology* (London: SCM/Naperville, IL: Alec R. Allenson, 1973), pp. 68-116.

Chapter 2

Biblical Theology: an Old Testament Perspective

John Barton, Oxford

A recurring theme in biblical study over the last century or so has been the sense of a disconnection between biblical studies and theology, and in particular a rift between the work of biblical critics and the religious life of the Christian churches. The work of Gerhard von Rad in Germany, and of the so-called 'Biblical Theology Movement' in North America and Britain, were attempts to move beyond what was seen as the somewhat positivistic, obscurantist and even reductionist character of traditional biblical scholarship, and to reconnect biblical study with faith. That there have been positivistic strains in the study of the Bible cannot be doubted. To anyone interested in theological issues, the work of (for example) the Albright school of biblical archaeology certainly seems to veer in a positivistic direction; and the same can be said of the minute work of dissection involved in conventional source or redaction criticism, which after all are still very much alive in our discipline, especially though not exclusively in the German-speaking world. It is an understandable reaction to such tendencies to want to stress again the theological and religious character of the Bible, and to want to put biblical scholarship at the service of the Church rather than primarily of the academic community.

Among recent attempts to heal this perceived rift one thinks at once of the work of Brevard Childs (see, for example, Childs 1979 and 1992). His programme, the 'canonical approach' to the Bible, was born of a basic sympathy with the aims of the Biblical Theology Movement but a sense (shared by many others) that that movement had failed to deliver what it promised, being based on certain false premises. His alternative proposals have had a vast effect on the state of biblical studies today. For every scholar who directly espouses the canonical approach in exactly the form Childs proposed it – and those are not few – there are 10 more who ask quite different questions of the Bible than they would have asked before Childs began his work, even if they are not aware of this themselves. At any conference now you hear the question, 'What of the final form of the text?' or 'What does this text mean in its whole scriptural context?': questions that were not asked in this form before Childs came along.

But my own starting point lies rather with the seminal work of Gabler in 1787, which argued that biblical theology – not just biblical study, but biblical *theology* – is a descriptive and historical discipline first and foremost (see Gabler 1787; on Gabler, see the important discussion in Morgan 1987).[1] As we shall see, this does not mean that it is inherently either positivistic or reductionist. But it does mean that its first concern is with what the biblical texts mean within their original context, and this may be called an anti-canonical tendency in the sense that it does not regard the question about the text's place in the finished corpus of Scripture as the first question to be asked. Gabler himself wanted to connect biblical study, so understood, with theology proper. Once you had asked what the biblical text meant in itself, you were to be free to go on and ask what theological implications it had for constructive theology. Indeed, unless you did so, it was not clear why you would be bothering with the study of the text in the first place. But this was to be quite explicitly a second step: the establishment of the text's meaning, and the question about its importance within theology, could not legitimately be collapsed into a single question. The findings of biblical scholars, indeed even of biblical theologians, were to provide raw material for theology. This is a picture deeply disliked by proponents of canonical approaches, but essential in Gabler's strategy.

An attachment to Gabler's model can only mean seeing biblical study, and particularly biblical theology, as essentially belonging to the history of ideas. Studying what the Bible has to say about matters of theology is not different in kind from studying the ideas of Plato, or of one of the Christian Fathers, or of Luther, or even of a modern theologian. In each case there is, in the same way as Gabler argued for the Bible, necessarily a two-stage procedure. First we have to establish as objectively as we can what the thinker in question actually taught or teaches. We shall fail in this if our prior conviction that this thinker must be right makes us prejudge what he or she actually says. As a second stage, we go on to ask what the teaching in question has to say to us today. The process, as I just remarked, cannot legitimately be collapsed into only one stage. But this does *not* mean that the question about the text's significance for us is somehow being downplayed or turned into a matter of secondary importance. To take a secular example, ancient philosophers strive to discover what Plato actually taught. But that does not mean they habitually block out the question of whether what he taught is important or remains true. It is simply that this is a further question, and neither of the two questions is reducible to the other. In a similar way, I would argue that it is essential in biblical study to begin by asking the question – which you can call a historical or a descriptive or even a positivistic question if you will – of what the text in fact means.

Because the text in question comes from such a remote and unfamiliar culture, this will inevitably entail a good deal of historical reconstruction: nineteenth-century scholars were correct in that. And some will be so absorbed by the detail of all this that they never personally move on to questions about the abiding significance of the text's ideas. Nevertheless that is a legitimate question, and it is no surprise if most people who study the Bible want to go on and ask it. All study of the history of ideas, after all, invites the question how far the ideas studied remain important. Very few historians of ideas are simply historians: mostly they are thinkers who want to apply the ideas they study to the contemporary world. And this is certainly no less true of biblical scholars – indeed it is in some ways more true, precisely because of the great importance these particular texts have in the Christian community. This does not imply a special hermeneutic: it simply calls for an ability to compare the results of investigation into the meaning of the Old Testament text with theological convictions found in other theological disciplines, such as historical theology and systematics.

Biblical study, on this model, is a theological discipline not because it has a special theological method, unlike that used in the study of other texts, but because the subject matter of the Bible is almost exclusively theological. This is religious literature. Presumably ancient Israel had some secular literature, and a little of it has turned up in the small range of inscriptions found in Palestine: legal documents, steles announcing victories, above all commercial documents. But hardly any of it found its way into the Old Testament, which is quite unremittingly theological in content. (This is even more true of the New Testament, which does not even hint at 'secular' writing within the early Christian community.) Historians will be interested in such history as the Old Testament contains, and literary scholars in its narrative techniques, its poems, its style. Linguists will be interested in the languages it is written in. But theologians will surely be interested in its theological ideas, and since these appear on every page, it would be odd to devote oneself to the study of the Bible without being concerned for them. Thus biblical study is a *theological* discipline almost whether or not it seeks to be: only by steadfastly ignoring what the Bible is about can one insist on pursuing a non-theological study of it.

This does not mean, however, that biblical study is possible only from within a particular confessional position, or that non-Christians cannot possibly understand it. It demands empathy – all texts do; it does not demand belief. It remains a question whether those who have no belief in the God about whom the Bible talks are ever really likely to take much interest in it. My own suspicion is that they are not, though they are missing something of important cultural value even to them by not knowing this exciting text. But being realistic I would expect Old Testament study to remain largely a pursuit of committed Christians and Jews, while warmly welcoming the interest of any other people who can be convinced of its value. At the same time, however, I would continue to stress its essentially descriptive, or (in Childs's terms) 'historical', character: the history of ideas is a kind of history, not a kind of systematic or constructive theology, even if its subject matter happens to be the biblical text.

How does Old Testament study actually work if it is seen as part of the history of ideas? It will be clear from all I have said that I see it as what people usually call a 'historical-critical' activity, concerned with the so-called 'original meaning' – I put both these expressions in scare quotes, and will explain why later. But producing a 'historical' description of the 'original meaning' of a text is a far from positivistic operation. There are questions a biblical critic is bound to raise in trying to describe the theological content of a biblical text historically which cannot be answered by using only historical-critical tools in a narrow sense of that term. As a theologian, one needs to know how the concepts and insights to be found in ancient Israelite literature relate to those of people standing in the later theological traditions that ultimately take their rise from the biblical text and its interpretation. One needs to understand how biblical concepts connect with what came out of them as well as with what came before them. Reception history or *Wirkungsgeschichte*, the history of a text's effects, are just as much history as the study of the text's antecedents, and neither can be ignored by the biblical scholar. We must, and we also can, pose our own theological questions to the Old Testament text, just as we can pose them to the works of Plato or to the Greek tragedians. If exegetes do not do this, it is unlikely that anyone else will – or if they do, they will do so in ignorance of what the biblical text really means, and will make little headway. And to do so is to be more than merely a purveyor of raw material to the systematician, even though the task is still a fully historical one and is not itself systematic theology.

The biblical scholar's task is to describe the theological ideas of the biblical texts. This task, however, is far from being a merely positivistic or antiquarian one. It inevitably contains a heavy element of interpretation. To describe phenomena discovered within the text one must often use concepts which would not have been directly comprehensible to the biblical authors themselves – because they are our concepts – and yet which for us as modern readers provide the best way into the ancient text. We are forced, in fact, to compare the religious categories of the ancient Israelites with our own. Although complete mutual understanding will never occur, we have to try to instigate a kind of dialogue between their concepts and ours. Our reconstruction of the original categories used in the text is bound in some measure to be flawed, but that ought not to lead to a kind of nihilism or extreme cultural relativism, according to which ancient and modern concepts are so radically different that dialogue is always automatically impossible.

I should like to illustrate what I mean with an example I have developed elsewhere: the idea of divine omnipotence (see Barton 1995). In this case we are dealing with a theme in Christian and Jewish theology in which the relationship between the basic biblical texts from which the theme ultimately derives, and the theological assertions of latter times, is a strangely ambiguous one. The theme undoubtedly does derive from biblical tradition; but it developed in directions which, though in some sense continuous with its roots, would not have been readily recognizable to those who first thought of the idea. Yet the later developments contributed to a sort of hermeneutical framework within which the older texts have tended to be read. Thus the biblical text started a process which led to its own partial misinterpretation. Something operated that might nowadays be called a feedback loop.

The omnipotence of God is a central tenet of both Judaism and Christianity. Christians and Jews alike read the Old Testament in the light of their conviction that God can do everything, and that he has the totality of all that exists under his control. They take it for granted that the biblical texts, which are read as according with this way of thinking, do really exemplify that belief. But, as any biblical scholar knows, the matter is actually a good deal more complicated than this. The Old Testament's own conceptuality is some distance removed from later Jewish and Christian ideas of divine omnipotence. For example, the God of whom the Old Testament speaks is entirely free to change his mind, and does so on a number of well-known occasions: in response to pleading by Abraham (Gen 18:23–33), Moses (Exod 32:31–4) and Amos (Amos 7:1–4), and in the matter of Saul, whom he 'repents' of having made king (1 Sam 15:10). In traditional theological discussion omnipotence precisely means that God cannot be prevailed on to change his mind and never has to repent, since he controls everything anyway. For the Old Testament, the power of God is seen precisely in the fact that he *can* change his mind: he is not, like some pagan deity, limited by his own past decisions, he can be flexible, he is not tied to his own rulings like Darius in Daniel 6, who cannot change his decree because of the 'laws of the Medes and Persians'. Sovereign freedom rather than philosophically defined omnipotence characterizes the God of Israel, and that is why he is so much to be respected: he can adapt to each new situation, do what is appropriate, an idea which some interpreters think is expressed in the parable of the farmer at the end of Isa 28:23-9, who adjusts his work from season to season and is not condemned to a monotonous predictability. In Old Testament terms, divine power and divine immutability are mutually exclusive, rather than going hand in hand as they have in much Christian reflection.

This tension between what the text implies when read on its own terms and what tradition has read out of it requires deep theological reflection. Even if we try to be as 'purely descriptive', as 'historical-critical', as possible in our account of the thought forms of ancient Israel, we still have to decide what concepts to employ in explaining to ourselves and others what is going on in the text. In describing ideas of the power of God we come up against the fact that the idea of omnipotence ultimately derives from the Old Testament. Without the prophets (especially perhaps Ezekiel), without the Psalms, without the Pentateuch, neither Judaism nor Christianity would have been likely to produce or discover the notion of divine omnipotence. Yet this idea developed within Jewish and Christian religious and theological culture in ways so far removed from what the biblical text itself implies, that we falsify that text if we simply project the later idea back on to it. The texts have been ultimately responsible for ideas that lead to misunderstanding if we use them to interpret those same texts. To explicate this fact requires historical-critical acumen, but also theological skills that go beyond the merely historical-critical. It demands exactly what is needed of the good historian of ideas: an ability to see both similarity and difference, and to be able both to trace development, and yet distinguish direct development from indirect, and to be aware of the part played by reception history. Such work is definitely theologically engaged, yet not on the same model as in a 'canonical' approach, because it is much more historically orientated.

In more recent times the idea of divine omnipotence has changed again. Theologians such as Karl Barth have in fact approached it more as an expression of what I have called God's sovereign freedom, than as the philosophical concept of an ability to do absolutely anything. This represents in many ways a recapturing of an essential biblical insight, and its re-expression in modern theological terms. But we can only see that it does indeed mark a return to a biblical category because we know

what the alternatives are, and because we are able to clear away interpretations lying between ourselves and the Bible sufficiently to compare
Barth's ideas with the text itself, rather than with traditions about how
the text is to be read. Establishing the true sense of the text requires an
ability to distinguish it both from the traditional reading and from one
such as Barth's: only then can we see that Barth's is probably nearer to
that sense. Barth does not provide a hermeneutical lens through which
to read the text, but a set of theological formulations which we can
compare with the text.

In all this I am not proposing a new model for the practice of biblical
criticism or biblical theology. All I am doing is to describe and analyse a
little what biblical scholars do anyway, and have done at least since the
Reformation and the Renaissance. Here there is a real difference between
my position and that being put forward by proponents of canonical and
other newer approaches, including some of the newer literary interpretations. As we saw at the beginning, much that is new in biblical study,
including the work of Childs, is predicated on the perception that biblical
studies have become detached or alienated from theology or from the
Church's life. This was also true of the Biblical Theology Movement from
the 1940s to the early 1960s. It took as its given a sense that biblical study
had become too untheological, and needed to be reconnected with
Christian faith. My own belief is that this was not in fact the case. The
idea that biblical study is getting divorced from Christian belief is not a
recurring fact but a recurring *topos*, a kind of fixed idea that can be used
to justify new programmes, but which in fact is usually false. I do not
believe that, until the very *recent* rise of departments of biblical studies
that do have a genuinely secular character (to which I shall return), there
was in fact much biblical study divorced from theology or from Church
life. Even the most 'positivistic' scholars – to take two examples, source
critics of the age of Wellhausen, or archaeologically orientated students
of the Bible such as the Albright school – were nearly always deeply
concerned with Christian faith and life. Most biblical commentaries have
always been produced by religious publishing houses; most biblical scholars have taught in confessional settings. Paradoxically, it is only in the last
few years, at the very same time as canonical approaches have made their
mark, that really secular biblical study has been getting off the ground in
the Anglo-Saxon world. In the German-speaking world it has still hardly
arrived. Biblical studies tend to remain allied to theology in very many
settings, and most people who study the biblical text still do it for religious reasons and always have done so.

So now I should like to propose a different story about the development of Old Testament studies from that commonly accepted nowadays,

a story that may make some of these issues appear in a different light. The study of the Old Testament, I should want to say, has almost always had a critical component: in that sense 'biblical criticism' is not a wholly modern development. Certainly the Bible was seen as special in what we call the ages of faith, that is, in the patristic and medieval periods, but this did not mean that people turned to it only for religious information in a narrow sense of that term. Hans Frei, in his *The Eclipse of Biblical Narrative* (Frei 1974), showed how much the Bible was regarded as a kind of encyclopaedia, not simply as a book of religious teaching. Nor does it mean that they were unaware of many of the difficulties – inconsistencies and discrepancies in the text – that became the basis for, for example, nineteenth-century work on the sources of the Pentateuch.

The important shift at the Reformation was the concern to read the text without the authoritative guidance allegedly supplied by the Church's magisterium. The novel element was the freedom to ask what the text meant in itself, rather than in an ecclesiastically determined context. This inevitably led scholars to notice that the text did not always say what we should want it to say, and therefore that it must inhabit a world somewhat different from our own: and with that insight most of what is nowadays called historical criticism is already present in essence. The turn to reason did not arrive only with the Enlightenment, nor the turn to history only in the nineteenth century; both are already implied in the major shifts of the Reformation period, though it is obvious that both were greatly developed and enhanced during those later periods. But the motivation for this kind of biblical criticism was in essence theological, not antiquarian or historicist or positivistic. The motivation was to discover what the Old Testament text said to us, in contradistinction to what the Church authorities *told* us it said to us.

What happened in the nineteenth century was that history came to be seen as the primary route towards an understanding of textual meaning. This development in biblical studies of course correlates with wider developments in the scholarly world, and we know that Old Testament scholars such as Wellhausen were deeply influenced by classical historians: Niebuhr, Ranke, Mommsen. Even so, the main quest remained the elucidation of the biblical text and the discovery of what it really meant. People came to see more clearly, in the light of the new explosion in historiography, that you need a much broader knowledge of the historical background than had previously been felt necessary if you were properly to understand a text from an ancient culture. So great was the necessary knowledge that scholars might very well devote all their time to reconstructing it, and never actually turn back to elucidating the biblical text; they might leave that task for others. But this did not mean

that the enterprise of Old Testament studies ceased to be seen as ultimately a theological one. Even Wellhausen, one of the most freethinking
scholars of the late nineteenth century, did not want to leave his theological chair: he became convinced that he needed to do so, because others
perceived his work as undermining the faith, not because he so perceived
it himself. One might say the same of his ally, William Robertson Smith,
in Scotland. Smith lost his chair because others judged his conclusions
to be incompatible with Christianity, but he himself always maintained
that they were part of his Christian commitment. It would be entirely
untrue to say that his work was not theological in intention, and indeed
everyone saw it as theological – it was simply that, from an orthodox
perspective, it contained the wrong kind of theology.

If we turn to the twentieth century, we find a similar picture in many
ways. However 'historical-critical' their commentaries may have been and
however unfruitful for faith some perceived them as being, the great
majority of biblical scholars always saw their work on the Old Testament
as part of a theological discipline. One important shift that occurred in
the twentieth century, but well before Childs, was towards reading biblical texts in their 'final form', rather than being concerned with their
original constituent parts. That can already be seen in Gerhard von Rad.
Von Rad quotes with approval the comment of Franz Rosenzweig that
R, the symbol for the redactor in the Pentateuch, ought really to be read
as *rabbenu*, 'our master', because it is the text as it comes from the
final redactor's hand that is the authoritative text. Consequently von Rad
devotes a lot of attention to the finished form, to the edited Pentateuch,
rather than exclusively to J, E, D and P as some older scholars had done
(see von Rad 1956).

This anticipates the ideas of Childs to a considerable extent. It also
anticipates another characteristic twentieth-century 'turn', the turn to literary approaches that concentrate similarly on the text as it now confronts
us, rather than on the sources from which it may have been composed.
Yet this literary interest in the final form is rarely devoid of a theological
concern. Though some secular critics studied the Old Testament in a literary way – Roland Barthes (1988) would be an example – the majority of
literary critics of the Bible turn out to have a religious interest, too.
Sometimes this has been a conservative interest. Some scholars have found
the emphasis on reading the final form attractive because they really
believe there never were any sources anyway, and believe this because of
a conservative or even fundamentalist commitment. Others simply think,
as Childs does, that 'final form' exegesis is more productive theologically
than source- or form-critical models of Old Testament study. Not very many
have pursued literary approaches simply because they had a purely secular

interest in the Bible, though that is undoubtedly true of some, and as we shall see is now at last *beginning* to be increasingly the case.

Thus, in my own understanding of the story of Old Testament study, there never was a time when theological interests went away, so that they then needed at some point to be restored. It is not the case now that Old Testament study is predominantly a secular discipline that has lost touch with theology or with the churches. People *say* that biblical scholars are out of touch with what ordinary Christians are concerned with. Insofar as biblical scholars pursue difficult technical studies, such as textual criticism or Hebrew grammar or redaction history, of course they are not doing things that the ordinary Bible reader will be much interested in. But it is not true that they are usually unconcerned for the effect of their studies on practical biblical exegesis as that concerns the ordinary believer: on the contrary, the great majority of Old Testament scholars are still actively engaged in the life of the churches, and that is true even in places where not all students of the Bible are also candidates for ordination and ministry in one of the churches. In Oxford, for example, the greater part of theology students are not ministerial candidates but study the subject because they have a general intellectual interest in it. It is nevertheless true that the majority of them are Christians, and it is also true that very nearly all those who teach Old Testament in Oxford are also active themselves in the life of the Church, preach regularly, and are concerned for the ordinary believers with whom their work brings them into contact. Nearly all would also call themselves theologians rather than 'orientalists'. This is a common pattern in much of the world of biblical studies, and it suggests that most Old Testament scholars still see their study as a theological discipline.

What can be said, however, is that in the very recent past there has at last developed a style of Old Testament study that *is* genuinely secular, and not interested in theological issues. I would stress what a recent development this is, but there is no doubt that it is growing fast. People who study the Old Testament in this way belong to departments of *biblical* studies, rather than of theological or religious studies. In Britain the main example is the Department of Biblical Studies at Sheffield, but there are many such departments in the USA. Here biblical studies are – for the first time in their history, I would argue – detached from theological concerns. The text is read primarily as ancient literature, and the scholars involved are not interested at all in possible theological implications. Indeed, they tend to argue that the trouble with traditional biblical study is exactly that it has been too theological. David Clines and Philip Davies in Sheffield both try to show that Old Testament scholarship, where it has claimed a kind of intellectual objectivity, has in fact been controlled mostly by theological concerns, and that these have distorted it. If they are right, then they help me to make my own case that Old Testament study has usually been theological. Clines, in his book *Interested Parties* (Clines 1995), argues, for example, that commentators on the prophets have nearly always assumed that the prophets were right in their condemnations of contemporary Israel or Judah, and have very seldom questioned the truth of what the prophets allege. They have assumed this because of a prior commitment to the authority and inspiration of the prophetic books. This commitment proceeds from religious rather than historical or cultural concerns. Clines succeeds in showing, I think, that there have indeed been very few Old Testament scholars in the past who have not approached the biblical text with a certain reverence. To him this shows just how partisan biblical scholarship has been. In the same way Philip Davies in his *In Search of 'Ancient Israel'* (Davies 1992) argues that scholars have approached the Old Testament narratives with a settled conviction that they must tell an essentially true story, the story of 'Israel', and have been far too ready to give the text the benefit of the doubt when it might strike a really impartial observer as legendary or fictitious.

So the case these scholars make is that, so far from Old Testament study having been insufficiently theological, and needing to be brought back into connection with the Church, it has nearly always been all too theological anyway, serving a mainly ecclesiastical interest even when its practitioners have claimed to be acting as impartial historians. For them, Old Testament studies has been all too much a theological discipline, and ought to become less so if it is to survive as an intellectually respectable and honest pursuit.

This way of thinking about the history of Old Testament studies stresses how theological they have nearly always been, and how little in reality they have been detached from the life of the churches. Of course it is always possible to find a scholar who was interested, let us say, in only the use of the preposition *min* in biblical Hebrew, and to ask scornfully what possible significance that could have for theology. But, for one thing, that is to ignore the fact that small-scale academic issues can have larger-scale consequences, and that we need scholars who can do the microscopic work even though of course they cannot for ever be spelling out wider implications. For another, it is to forget that even such scholars usually work in a context in which the religious importance of the Bible is more or less taken for granted. It is the very authority of the Bible that makes people concerned for issues at such a microscopic level, in a way they seldom are in the case of other texts.

Old Testament study has always, until very recently, been a largely theological discipline. I do not say that essentially in either praise or

blame, but as a statement of fact. But my own opinion is that, though it
need not remain a theological discipline to continue to be worthwhile
and have its own integrity, it probably has more of a future if it does. For
it will continue to be the case that the majority of people who take an
interest in the Old Testament will be those for whom it is religiously significant. In other words, I do not regret the establishment of secular
departments of biblical studies; and I believe that scholars such as Clines
and Davies are right to point out to us how past commentators have
smuggled in their religious convictions to their academic work in illicit
ways. But I still think that the most important aspect of the Old Testament
is the theological content of most of its texts, and that it is therefore
natural for this to continue to be the focus of interest in the future as it
has been in the past.

But I do not believe that in this we can dispense with the historical-
critical approach to our texts, and therefore I do not personally find the
programme for the future implied in the canonical approach, or even in
works such as von Rad's *Theology*, the most hopeful for the future of Old
Testament study as a theological discipline. In both there is an attempt to
make the Old Testament deliver a directly theological message, that is, to
tell us what we should now believe; whereas historical method implies
rather a two-stage process, in which we first ask what the text means in
itself, and only then go on to ask what significance it has for us. In my
judgement modern canonical readings too often collapse this into a single
process, and thereby threaten the objectivity of our reading of what is
actually there in the text. But a concern for this objectivity should certainly not be what I have called positivistic. It requires deep theological
understanding, a knowledge of the history of the text's reception, and an
ability to engage in a lively dialogue between present and past: all features
that are essential in general in the study of the history of ideas.

Thus I share the concern of scholars such as Childs with the theological content of the Old Testament, but I approach this from a rather different angle, since I believe that such a concern has in any case nearly
always been part of the study of these texts, even during phases which
are referred to as 'historical-critical'. To use Krister Stendahl's now famous
distinction, biblical scholars have nearly always been interested in both
what the text *meant* and what the text *means* (see Stendahl 1962). I am
not happy with that way of putting this distinction, however, since it
identifies what I would see as the text's actual meaning, that is, the
meaning it has against its own background, as somehow a past meaning;
and that already sells the pass, inviting us to see what it now 'means' as
something newer and more relevant. Implicit in my way of presenting
the matter is that texts actually do have meanings, which do not change

over time. But they also have significance, and biblical scholarship certainly cannot afford to ignore this dimension (for the distinction compare Hirsch 1967). My own belief is that they have very rarely done so, and so my plea is the very unexciting one: please go on doing what you are doing anyway, rather than looking for new programmes that will change the face of our discipline. The so-called historical critics got it largely right: it is we who misinterpret them as mere positivists. Traditional biblical criticism is already a rich, many-layered, dense discipline, which has contributed and continues to contribute a great deal to the Church's life and thought.

Note

1. It is a great pleasure to dedicate this essay to Robert Morgan, who has been such a close colleague for many years.

References

Barthes, R., 'Wrestling with the angel: textual analysis of Genesis 32:23–33', in R. Barthes, *The Semiotic Challenge* (New York, 1988), pp. 246–60.
Barton, J., 'Alttestamentliche Theologie nach Albertz?', *Religionsgeschichte oder Theologie des Alten Testaments* (Jahrbuch für biblische Theologie 10, 1995), pp. 25–34.
Childs, B.S., *Introduction to the Old Testament as Scripture* (Philadelphia and London, 1979).
Childs, B.S., *Biblical Theology of the Old and New Testament: Theological Reflections on the Christian Bible* (London, 1992).Clines, D.J.A., *Interested Parties: The Ideology of Writers and Readers of the Hebrew Bible* (JSOTSup 205; Sheffield, 1995).
Davies, P.R., *In Search of 'Ancient Israel'* (Sheffield, 1992).
Frei, H.W., *The Eclipse of Biblical Narrative: A Study in Eighteenth- and Nineteenth-Century Hermeneutics* (New Haven: Yale University Press, 1974).
Gabler, J.P., *Oratio de iusto discrimine theologiae biblicae et dogmaticae regundisque recte utriusque finibus* (Altdorf, 1787); reprinted in his *Kleine theologische Schriften* II (Ulm, 1831), pp. 179–98.
Hirsch, Jr, E.D., *Validity in Interpretation* (New Haven and London, 1967).
Morgan, R., 'Gabler's bicentenary', *ExpT* 98 (1987), 164–8.
Rad, G. von, *Theologie des Alten Testaments* (2 vols; Munich 1957 and 1962); ET *Old Testament Theology* (2 vols; Edinburgh and London, 1962 and 1965).
Rad, G. von, *Das erste Buch Mose* Genesis (Göttingen, 1956); ET *Genesis* (London, 1961, revised edition 1963).
Stendahl, K., 'Biblical theology, contemporary', *Interpreter's Dictionary of the Bible* (1962).

Chapter 3

Apocalypticism and New Testament Theology

Adela Yarbro Collins, Yale

In his article on biblical theology, Krister Stendahl (1962) argued that the distinction between what the Bible meant and what it means only came sharply into focus with the work of the history-of-religion school. This distinction began to have a significant effect on biblical theology in the 1920s. Before that, conservatives and liberals alike were convinced that the Bible contained revelation of eternal truths that could be extracted from the cultural and historical forms in which they were expressed. The conservatives emphasized the passages that fitted with their own theological and ethical values and then harmonized the others with those so that they could claim that the whole of Scripture was revelatory. The liberals arrived at their notion of pure revelation by more drastic, reductionist measures. By source and other kinds of criticism, they arrived at the 'original' teaching of a prophet or of Jesus, which often fitted well with their own values. Karl Barth's commentary on Romans, however, as well as Rudolf Bultmann's *Theology of the New Testament* and Oscar Cullmann's *Christ and Time* all reflected, in different ways, consciousness of the historical and cultural distance between the biblical texts and the modern situation. In his own programmatic essay, Stendahl advocated that a distinction be made between descriptive study of the actual theologies that are expressed in the Bible and attempts to construct a normative and systematic theology that could be called biblical.

Stendahl's proposal may be seen as one of the results of a long process of change in the interpretation of the Bible and in hermeneutics, the study of the principles and rules of interpretation, that has been described and analysed by Hans Frei (1974). In the West before the rise of historical criticism in the eighteenth century, Christian reading of the Bible was realistic, that is, both literal and historical. Precritical realistic reading assumed that the Bible described historical occurrences and that all of these could be combined into one great narrative that included the past of the biblical writers and the present of the interpreters. Figural reading helped to unify all the stories into one comprehensive narrative. Earlier biblical stories were seen as figures or types of later ones. Beginning already in the seventeenth century, however, readers of the Bible, both radicals and conservatives, began to make a distinction between biblical narrative and historical reality. The question then arose whether the biblical narratives can be confirmed by the study of historical reality. Thus the realistic narrative reading of the Bible began to break down. Literal or verbal meaning was separated from historical meaning. Figurative or typological reading became problematic. It was problematic logically because it came to be assumed that any statement has only one meaning. Historically, it became incredible that sayings and events of one period of time could predict those of a later time. Literal and figural readings, which were once united, came apart. Their successors, historical criticism and biblical theology, had different values and methods and became more and more difficult to combine. The interpreters that Frei studied focused on Genesis 1–3 and the Synoptic Gospels. Much of the discussion, however, is relevant for the theme of apocalypticism, since apocalyptic ideas and expectations are often expressed in narrative form.

A Selective History of Relevant Scholarship

Many see the beginning of the discipline of biblical theology in a lecture of Johann Philipp Gabler (1787). He 'was the first to state clearly that dogmatic theology must depend on the results of exegesis, which to him meant historical-critical analysis of the texts' (Frei 1974, p. 163). Like most interpreters of the late eighteenth century, he gave the subject matter of the texts priority over their actual wording (1974, p. 254). He attributed a historical origin to biblical theology, but a didactic origin to dogmatic theology. Dogmatic theology, in his view, teaches what each theologian philosophizes rationally about divine things. He argued that one must distinguish between the opinions that pertain only to a particular time and place of the past and those that pertain to the unchanging doctrine of salvation. Gabler did not mention the topic of apocalypticism or eschatology in his lecture. This lack may be explained, in part, by the lecture's quite general and abstract character. Another important factor is that apocalypticism was yet to be 'rediscovered' (Koch 1970).

As historical criticism advanced, the unity of the New Testament was questioned, as well as the unity of the Bible as a whole. Hegel interpreted history as a process in which the Spirit was progressively unfolding itself. Ferdinand Christian Baur used this idea as his hermeneutical principle in his New Testament theology (1864). He raised the question whether Jesus' understanding of the kingdom of God was similar to what he called the material ideas that Jews of that time had about the messianic kingdom. His answer was an emphatic no. Jesus spiritualized the concept of the messianic reign to such a degree that nothing was left of those material ideas. On the contrary, the kingdom of God in the teaching of Jesus was a community based on ethical-religious conditions, whose ultimate aim lay in the transcendent world (p. 70).

Baur interpreted the parousia and the End in Paul's teaching as the triumph of the principle of life over the principle of death and the overcoming of evil. All creation returns to God and becomes an eternal unity (pp. 202–5). Whereas Paul departed from Judaism to the greatest extent among the writers of the New Testament, the author of the book of Revelation, whom he took to be John the son of Zebedee, is the closest to it (p. 211). The thoroughly figurative language of the work is not unique in the New Testament, just more elaborate. He opposed the particularism of the Apocalypse to the universalism of Paul, inferring from chapter seven, for example, that Gentiles are saved only insofar as they join the community of the 12 tribes of Israel (p. 212). In his discussion of the Christology of the book, he remarked that the author speaks from below. Everything metaphysical is outside his worldview (pp. 214–19). Baur's treatment of the work concludes with the comment that the imagistic character of the Apocalypse makes it impossible very often to express its ideas in a particular dogmatic concept (p. 230).

Bernhard Weiss' New Testament theology is an example of the conservative approach in the second half of the nineteenth century (1868/ 1880). His treatment of the delay of the parousia is apologetic and harmonizing. In the section on the return of the Messiah and the judgement, he acknowledged that many passages imply that at least 'some of His hearers will yet see the coming completion of the kingdom of God' (1. 148). He also noted passages that seem to imply a long delay, but declared that it was 'mere critical arbitrariness to regard all such statements simply as a later expression of disappointed expectations' (1. 149). Rather, Jesus warned his hearers not to be deceived by false Messiahs etc. and that the end would come suddenly and unexpectedly.

In the same context, Weiss made a valiant attempt to salvage the pre-critical understanding of the unity of biblical narrative and history. He argued that:

> Although the consummation of all things is not brought about in the natural way of historical development, it is nevertheless a condition of its commencement, that the time has become ripe for it (1. 149).

Just as the Messiah could not appear until the time was fulfilled (Mark 1:15), so:

> according to the divinely appointed course of the historical development, certain events must have taken place before He returns; and from these, as its foretokens, men can then discern the nearness of the divinely appointed moment of the consummation. Upon this fundamental thought of apocalyptic prophecy rests also the prophecy of Jesus regarding His return (1. 149–50).

Weiss inferred that, since the judgement is linked to the consummation of all things, the End cannot come until the world has made itself ripe for judgement by 'making full the measure of its guilt' (1. 150). He argued that, in the first century, only the Jewish people had filled up the measure of their sins by rejecting the Messiah. Thus, the destruction of Jerusalem was the beginning of the final judgement. In Weiss' theology, the destruction of Jerusalem in the first century serves as a figure or type of the final judgement.

Since Weiss took the position that Paul had written 2 Thessalonians, he was able to harmonize Paul's teaching on the parousia with the synoptic apocalyptic discourse, which he accepted as 'Jesus' words of prophecy'. Both texts, in his view, express the expectation that the parousia will also be the day of judgement on which the Antichrist will be annihilated (1. 313–15).

With regard to the book of Revelation, he concluded that the thousand-year reign is the fulfillment of the promises of the Old Testament, but for the true Israel, rather than literal Israel. Here again, typology serves to unite the two Testaments. This hope for an earthly consummation splits the idea of the day of the Lord into two parts. The first leads to the triumph of the kingdom of God on earth. The second, to its final, heavenly consummation (2. 263).

Whereas Weiss' work is a prominent example of conservative historically oriented New Testament theology, the textbook on the topic by Heinrich Julius Holtzmann (1911) is a liberal example. An important event, however, had taken place between the publication of the third edition of Bernhard Weiss' New Testament theology and the first edition of Holtzmann's. That event was the publication of a book by Bernhard's son, Johannes Weiss (1892). Johannes was also the son-in-law of Albrecht Ritschl, and respectfully delayed the publication of this book until after

Ritschl's death. In this work the younger Weiss applied the research of the history-of-religion school to the apocalypticism of the New Testament. In the process, he pointed out the significance for the interpretation of the New Testament of the rediscovery of ancient apocalypticism in the nineteenth century. He argued that the kingdom of God, as proclaimed by Jesus, was not an ethical society to be brought about by human effort, but a radical transformation to be effected by divine power. This new perspective is one with which Holtzmann grappled in constructing his New Testament theology.

Under the influence of the history-of-religion school, Holtzmann interpreted the historical Jesus and all the writings of the New Testament in relation to contemporary forms of Judaism. By reducing the relevant apocalyptic passages through the application of various types of criticism, however, he was able to conclude that only a simple apocalypticism could be attributed to the historical Jesus, which had its characteristic expression in the metaphor of the 'thief in the night' (Luke 12:39/Matt 24:43). The purpose of such apocalypticism is not to communicate eschatological knowledge, but to admonish the audience to faithfulness and watchfulness. Those passages, in contrast, that involve a technical, organized pattern of ideas, serving the quest for eschatological knowledge, belong to a later stage. These synoptic traditions belong to the same category as 2 Thessalonians and the Johannine Apocalypse (1. 403–4). He argued that the history of the exegesis of these synoptic passages manifests the same pathological hue as that of the Pauline and Johannine texts just mentioned. With regard to the synoptic tradition, the religious need for self-deception is even more evident. It is impossible to find a logical unity in all the scattered and various synoptic eschatological materials or to avoid the painful fact of a still unfulfilled prophecy. The last remark is made in explicit criticism of Bernhard Weiss (1. 404–5). It is the attractive simplicity of the ethical genius of Jesus that underlies the various forms of Christianity and that keeps his memory alive (1. 418).

According to Holtzmann, the conviction that Jesus would return was common to all forms of early Christian teaching. This was the necessary correlate to the belief in his resurrection (1. 433). He considered the conviction that Christ would return to be illusory and evaluated it as an inadequate means of expressing the great spiritual impulse that his followers had received from Jesus. Early Christian apocalyptic fanaticism was fundamentally only the expression of the intense perception of the decisive position that their leader had been given in God's world (1. 436).

Holtzmann viewed the book of Revelation as an artistic example of the genre 'apocalypse' attested by contemporary Jewish texts. He followed contemporary exegesis in concluding that the work contained

Jewish sources and had come into being in successive stages of composition and editing. It is thus not surprising that he considered it to lack theological coherence and unity: 'Unadulterated Judaism and fully developed Christianity lie without any connection side by side' (1. 539–40). The vivid depiction of the end-time serves the work's purpose of rousing and strengthening the spirits of the communities. The result is the extravagant portrait of the future that is characteristic of nationalistic messianism (1. 542).

Karl Barth revived theological-biblical exegesis and challenged the focus on historical research favoured by the liberals and the history-of-religion school. In his comment on Rom 7:6a, 'But now we have been discharged from the law,' he redescribed Paul's eschatology in the following terms:

> The heaven which bounds this world of ours is rent asunder in the eternal 'Moment' of apprehension, in the light of resurrection, in the light of God, in order that our vision may have space to perceive, not what men think and will and do, but what God thinks and wills and does....we stand, nevertheless, already in the primal and ultimate history where all ambiguity, all polarity, every 'not only – but also', is *done away*, because God is all in all. We stand already where the temporal order, from which we cannot escape, stands over against us as one completed whole, bounded by the Day of Jesus Christ; where we know ourselves to be finally liberated from the coils of our humanity, in which as religious men, we are bound and throttled (1919/1922, p. 237).

Barth created a constructive analogy between Paul's language about Law and his own critique of contemporary religion. But his redescription of Paul's eschatology did not take sufficiently into account its temporal dimension and Paul's insistence on individual transformation in a communal context.

Rudolf Bultmann's (1948–53) theological interpretation of the New Testament dominated much of the twentieth century because he combined the highest level of scholarly research, valued by the liberals and the historians of religion, with the emphasis on the text and theology revived by Barth. Rather than adopt a biblicist position, however, Bultmann took a hermeneutical approach. He included a discussion of the message of Jesus, but only as one of the presuppositions of New Testament theology (1. 3–32). He found the dominant concept of Jesus' message to be the kingdom or reign of God. Like Holtzmann, Bultmann interpreted the notion of the kingdom of God as an eschatological concept. That reign will come in a miraculous way, brought about by God with no human assistance (1. 4). Although Bultmann placed the message of Jesus in the context of Jewish eschatological expectations, he argued that his thought was not determined by the national hope of a restoration of the idealized kingdom of David. Rather, the perspective of Jesus was more similar to the hope attested by Jewish apocalyptic literature, according to which a cosmic catastrophe will abolish all conditions of the present world. He described this type of hope as pessimistic and dualistic: the present age is evil because Satan has gained control of the world; the new age to come will be glorious (1. 4–5). Like Holtzmann, Bultmann concluded that Jesus took over the apocalyptic picture of the future 'with significant reduction of detail' (1. 6). Bultmann redescribed the message of Jesus in terms of existential philosophy. He proposed 'that "eschatological existence" bears all the marks of what Martin Heidegger call[ed] "authentic existence"' (Kelsey 1975, p. 77). The exhortation to 'Keep ready or get ready' for the reign of God that is breaking in is restated as a '*call to decision*' in the present time which is 'the *time of decision*' (Bultmann 1948–53: 1. 9).

Bultmann's discussion of the theology of Paul is organized according to anthropological concepts, not dogmatic or doctrinal topics. There is no separate treatment of Paul's eschatology. The discussion of faith includes the topic 'Faith as Eschatological Occurrence'. Bultmann took up the common expression 'salvation-occurrence', referring to Jesus' death and resurrection, and placed it rightly in its ancient context by rephrasing it as 'the eschatological occurrence'. He then redescribed the latter in existential terms: faith, as 'the newly opened way of salvation', is a '*new possibility*' for authentic existence. The possibility of faith is actualized in 'the individual's decision of faith', which is itself 'eschatological occurrence'. The 'existing of a Christian in the faith that operates in love is eschatological occurrence: a being created anew' (1. 329–30).

The book of Revelation is treated briefly under the headings of 'The Development of Doctrine' and 'Christology and Soteriology'. Bultmann concluded that it 'has to be termed a weakly Christianized Judaism' (2. 175).

In the epilogue, Bultmann affirmed that his presentation of New Testament theology stands:

on the one hand, within the tradition of the historical-critical and the history-of-religion schools and seeks, on the other hand, to avoid their mistake which consists of the tearing apart of the act of thinking from the act of living and hence of a failure to recognize the intent of theological utterances (2. 250–1).

He also affirmed that, in this work, the reconstruction of the history of early Christianity stands in the service of the interpretation of the New

Testament writings 'under the presupposition that they have something to say to the present'. Connecting theological thoughts to the act of living means, for him, 'explication of believing self-understanding' (2. 251).

Until about 1960, apocalypticism was an obscure field studied by specialists. In that year, however, Ernst Käsemann published an essay in which he argued that 'Apocalyptic was the mother of all Christian theology – since we cannot really class the preaching of Jesus as theology' (1960, p. 102). Around the same time, apocalypticism had attracted the attention of the systematic theologian Wolfhart Pannenberg, who argued that the apocalyptic concept of history was 'both the presupposition of the historical thinking of the west and the horizon which spans the whole of Christian theology in general' (Koch 1970, p. 14).

Pannenberg published an essay (1961) in which he presented and defended the following theses:

1. The self-revelation of God in the biblical witnesses is not of a direct type in the sense of a theophany, but is indirect and brought about by means of the historical acts of God.
2. Revelation is not comprehended completely in the beginning, but at the end of the revealing history.
3. In distinction from special manifestations of the deity, the historical revelation is open to anyone who has eyes to see. It has a universal character.
4. The universal revelation of the deity of God is not yet realized in the history of Israel, but first in the fate of Jesus of Nazareth, insofar as the end of all events is anticipated in his fate.
5. The Christ event does not reveal the deity of the God of Israel as an isolated event, but rather insofar as it is a part of the history of God with Israel.
6. In the formulation of the non-Jewish conceptions of revelation in the Gentile Christian Church, the universality of the eschatological self-vindication of God in the fate of Jesus comes to actual expression.
7. The word relates itself to revelation as foretelling, forthtelling, and report.

Pannenberg's position may be clarified by comparison with that of G. Ernest Wright. In his book *God Who Acts*, Wright argued that the authoritative aspect of Scripture is biblical narrative, which is to be construed as confessional recital concerning God's self-revelation in historical events (Kelsey 1975, pp. 32–3). Pannenberg's work is similar to Wright's to the extent that he also finds the authoritative aspect of Scripture in biblical narrative because it reveals God's acts and thus reveals God. He differs from Wright in two important respects. First, Pannenberg argued that revelation occurs by means of history, but not in any particular event or series of events. God can be known only in the final event which provides the vantage point from which all history may be seen as God's activity. The final event is anticipated in the resurrection of Jesus. Secondly, Pannenberg rejected the distinction, made by Wright, between 'facts' and 'evaluations' and the related notion that revelation occurs when events are interpreted 'by the eyes of faith'. For Pannenberg, biblical narrative, as word, foretells or promises God's action and forthtells the ethical obligations that revelation imposes. The one event that can be reported is the resurrection of Jesus because it is the only event that is revelatory in itself (Kelsey 1975, pp. 53–4). By 'report' Pannenberg (1961, p. 154) does not mean 'an objective and detached chronological description of' the event of the resurrection, but rather the proclamation that was set in motion by the appearances of Jesus.

Like Gabler, Pannenberg (1991, p. 7) distinguished between 'what is historically relative in the traditional teaching and what is its abiding core'. Unlike Gabler, he did not speak about unchanging and truly divine ideas. He did, however, speak about some kind of 'truth' that underlies the various historically and culturally determined formulations. Each epoch has to reformulate that truth in its own terms, but 'the truth which systematic theology tries to reformulate should recognizably be the same truth that had been intended under different forms of language and thought in the great theological systems of the past and in the teaching of the church throughout the ages' (ibid.). But if, as he admits, the forms of language and thought are 'passing', it is hard to see how the 'truth' that underlies the various thoughts and forms of language can be discerned. The rationality of his thought and his insistence on a transcendent truth is in tension with the imaginative and figurative language of apocalypticism. Pannenberg (1969, p. 52) rightly saw, however, that the eschatology of Jesus as expounded by Bultmann and the young Barth 'is timeless and deprived of its temporal meaning'.

In the mid-1960s, another theologian, Jürgen Moltmann, attempted 'to restore eschatology from its obscure peripheral position to its place in the centre of Christian dogmatics' (Koch 1970, p. 107). Moltmann argued that:

> The eschatological is not one element *of* Christianity, but it is the medium of Christian faith as such, the key in which everything in it is set, the glow that suffuses everything here in the dawn of an expected new day. For Christian faith lives from the raising of the crucified Christ, and strains after the promises of the universal future of Christ. Eschatology is the passionate suffering and passionate longing kindled by the Messiah (1964, p. 16).

He spoke about the kingdom of God being present 'as promise and hope for the future horizon of all things' (p. 223). Its presence stands in contradiction to a corrupt reality. In keeping with the political and social climate of the universities in Western Europe and the United States in the 1960s, Moltmann interpreted the kingdom of God in an activist sense:

> Not to be conformed to this world does not mean merely to be transformed in oneself, but to transform in opposition and creative expectation the face of the world in the midst of which one believes, hopes and loves (p. 330).

In 1974, the American theologian Carl E. Braaten published a book under the influence of Pannenberg, in which he affirmed that:

> To have an eschatology . . . is to believe that the essence of things lies in their future; nothing that exists is exactly as it ought to be; everything is subject to the call for radical conversion; and all are heirs of the promise of fulfillment (p. 6).

Some later developments will be discussed in the next section.

Approaches to New Testament Theology in a Pluralistic Situation

There are two main ways of construing the audience and purpose of New Testament theology. One way is to say that the activity of constructing such a theology takes place in and for the Church. David Kelsey has provided an analogous construal for theology in general. He has argued that Scripture is not a 'perfect source' for theology and that the relation between Scripture and theology is not genetic. The normativity of Scripture for theology means that theological proposals ought to be apt in a Christian way. In other words, theological proposals 'are assessed over against a *discrimen*', that is, a pair of criteria, namely, 'the presence of God among the faithful in conjunction with the uses of scripture in the church's common life' (1975, p. 193). The other way to construe New Testament theology is to say, as Bultmann did in his epilogue, that the discipline stands in the service of the interpretation of the New Testament writings 'under the presupposition that they have something to say to the present' (2. 251). This general formulation suggests that it is worthwhile to interpret the New Testament in a way that may be intelligible to unbelievers as well as to believers. The work of Paul Tillich seems to have had a similar goal, as have all projects described as 'public theology' (Tracy 1981).

Even if one decides to produce a work of New Testament theology for the Church, one needs to come to terms with the fact that the Church is diverse. Not only that, but many denominations themselves are made up of members with widely varying views about what it means to be Christian. So for both reasons, the desirability of constructing a public New Testament theology and the diversity of the Church, it is wise to affirm that apocalypticism may be related to theology in a variety of ways. This variety may be imagined as positions on a spectrum that ranges from those based on non-theistic philosophical approaches at one end to fundamentalist approaches at the other.

The work of Max Horkheimer is an example of non-theistic philosophical thought which could serve as a starting point for articulating the significance of apocalypticism today. Horkheimer, a critical theorist of the Frankfurt School, saw the critical task of philosophy 'in salvaging the truth in religion in the spirit of the Enlightenment' (Habermas 2002, pp. 95–6). In his view,

> The productive form of criticism directed to the way things are, which expressed itself in earlier periods as belief in a heavenly judge, is today the struggle for more reasonable conditions in social life (Horkheimer 1970, p. 36).

He 'once expressed the quintessence of his critical theory in the remark: "The longing that the murderer should not triumph over his innocent victim"' (Moltmann 1973, p. 223; Horkheimer 1970, p. 11). He considered 'the longing for perfect righteousness' to be characteristic of living religion. Perfect righteousness

> can never be realized in secular history; for even if a better society were to resolve the present social disorder, it could not make good past misery nor neutralize past distress in an all-embracing nature (1970, p. 69).

In Moltmann's account of Horkheimer's critical theory, 'innocent suffering puts the idea of a righteous God in question', and conversely, 'longing for the righteousness of the wholly other puts suffering in question and makes it conscious sorrow'. Consciousness of sorrow is a protest against suffering that is 'not content with any answer and keeps the question alive' (Moltmann 1973, p. 225).

Tina Pippin's (1992) feminist reading of the book of Revelation may be placed at the non-theistic, public end of the spectrum. In her book she moves from ideological and political readings to Marxist-feminist readings and makes use of studies of the fantastic in her interpretation. Her main methods are ideology-critique and narratology. Her study is one critical way of asking what this apocalyptic work has to say in the present. Eventually, postcolonial readings may also be illuminating in that regard.

Again with respect to the non-theistic end of the spectrum, let us consider how the work of Jürgen Habermas may provide a framework for interpreting apocalypticism in the context of a public theology. Habermas was one of Horkheimer's successors in the Frankfurt School. He argued against Horkheimer's late philosophical thought by stating, for instance:

> The idea that it is vain to strive for unconditional meaning without God betrays not just a metaphysical need; the remark itself is an instance of the metaphysics that not only philosophers but even theologians themselves must today get along without (2002, p. 96).

Habermas characterizes modernity or postmodernity as 'postmetaphysical' because he believes that Immanuel Kant and others have offered an 'irreversible critique of metaphysics' (2002, p. 99; Meyer 2004, p. 128). He thus rejects an absolute or theistic understanding of unconditional meaning. Instead, he adopts Charles Peirce's pragmatic understanding of language and reason and proposes a more modest 'transcendence from within,' which is grounded in the inescapable presupposition of an ideal communication community that underlies the validity claims of everyday speech. It is this more modest secular hope, which 'recovers the meaning of the unconditional without recourse to God or an Absolute,' that distinguishes postmetaphysical thought from religion (Habermas 2002, p. 108; Meyer 2004, p. 128).

Although Habermas 'denies the cognitive claims and public role of religion, [he] has, over the past few decades, come to accept a limited role for religion as a source of private consolation' (Meyer 2004, p. 129). He distinguished the philosophical 'significance of unconditionality' from:

> an unconditional meaning that offers consolation. On the premises of postmetaphysical thought, philosophy cannot provide a substitute for the consolation whereby religion invests the unavoidable suffering and un-recompensed injustice, the contingencies of need, loneliness, sickness and death, with new significance and teaches us to bear them (Habermas 2002, p. 108).

The consolation of which Habermas spoke is a particularly powerful effect of apocalyptic texts of the New Testament. The book of Revelation depicts suffering in the framework of a conflict between the creator, the

redeemer and those loyal to them, on one side, and the deceitful, slander-
ous Satan along with the murderous and exploitative powers associated
with him, on the other side. In an important step towards the Christian
idea of the martyr, Revelation portrays the one who suffers because of
loyalty to the forces of creation and redemption as a 'witness' and boldly
describes such suffering and death as 'conquering'. The Gospel of Mark
employs an apocalyptic trope in arguing in a narrative way that it was
necessary that the Son of Man suffer, die and rise from the dead. In its
teaching on discipleship, the suffering that the followers of Jesus meet
is depicted as taking up one's cross and following Jesus. Suffering or
death resulting from the violence of other human beings or from any
other cause is transfigured and made meaningful by association with the
account of Jesus' suffering, death and ultimate vindication.

At the other end of the spectrum are fundamentalist interpretations
like those of Hal Lindsey. A strength of Lindsey's interpretation of the
book of Revelation is his recognition of its deep and extensive political
character. Weaknesses are the one-dimensional interpretation of biblical
symbols and the lack of a critical attitude to the politics of American
society (Yarbro Collins 1984, 1986; Rowland 1998, pp. 543–4).

In contrast to Lindsey, William Stringfellow rejected the common practice of construing the Bible from an American perspective and aimed at
understanding the America of the early 1970s biblically (1973, p. 13).
Instead of the usual procedure of identifying the beast and other figures
of chaos and evil with the enemies of the United States, he applies those
images to America, as a death-dealing world power.

Near the same end of the spectrum, are evangelical and other conservative Christians of our time who can read or hear the apocalyptic narratives of the New Testament in a way similar to the precritical, realistic
mode described by Hans Frei. Some of these readers, like Hal Lindsey,
take the texts literally and still work at harmonizing their diverse perspectives and expectations. Others take them seriously, but not quite so literally. The important thing for them is the fulfilment of prophecies about
the return of Christ and the last judgement, to be followed by appropriate rewards and punishments.

A number of positions occupy the middle of the spectrum. Some of
these are explicitly theistic; others are not. One such position is analogous
to 'the fundamental moral intuition that guided Horkheimer throughout
his life' (Habermas 2002, p. 96). This is the approach that interprets
apocalyptic literature in terms of moral education and formation. One
could argue, as Socrates does in the *Phaido*, that the stories about the
fate of the dead, which describe a better afterlife for those who have
led good lives and terrible punishments for egregious sinners, are not

certainly true, but likely. Or, one could suspend disbelief and experience the rhetorical power of the narratives in a kind of second naiveté. The latter seems to be the approach suggested by Plato's Socrates, when with humour and irony he describes language about the afterlife as 'magical spells' that we should sing to each other every day in order to heal our souls (*Phaido* 77e, 115e; Klauck 2004, p. 20).

As Lautaro Lanzillotta has argued, 'The moral educational purpose of apocalyptic literature' is evident in 'its subjects, its characters, and its scenarios' (2003, p. 133). The main feature of the created world in these works is the opposition between characters and figures embodying good and evil or legitimate, just power and illegitimate, lawless power. The plots generally end with the vanquishing of evil or illegitimate power and the triumph of good or legitimate power. The human beings who ally themselves with the forces of good are rewarded at the End, whereas those who associate with the forces of evil are punished. In many apocalyptic texts, there is an emphasis on the rewards and glorious destiny of the righteous and the punishments and ill fate of the wicked. This theme dominates the post-New Testament apocalyptic Christian texts, such as the Apocalypse of Peter.

Often, 'the scenario of the Last Judgement . . . displays before the eyes of the righteous a complete inversion of the unjust state of things according to a system of values implicitly defended by the text'. The chaotic situation in which the wicked and the unjust prosper and oppress the weak, the defenceless and the innocent will be transformed into order when all receive appropriate retribution for their deeds. The readers or audiences of apocalyptic texts are moved to accept the normative values in the displayed value system, which provides 'the touchstone for correct behaviour' (Lanzillotta 2003, pp. 134–5).

Some apocalypses, such as Daniel and the book of Revelation, take up traditional combat myths, normally used to assimilate the human king to the divine king and to celebrate the establishment, renewal or continuation of a particular king's reign. Daniel and Revelation, however, invert the myths so that the current human king is associated with the rebellious monster, rather than with the god who conquers the beast (Yarbro Collins 1998, 176–84). A similar revolutionary perspective is evident in the implicit moral teaching of apocalyptic texts. The day of the Last Judgement describes the fall of those whose consistently unjust and exploitative behaviour has established the norm of the status quo. The scenario in which their fall is narrated 'implies the superseding of the unjust current system of values by a righteous one'. Apocalyptic texts may therefore also be called revolutionary from a moral perspective,

since their vivid depiction of judgement, reward and punishment sub-
verts what counts as acceptable behaviour in the present (Lanzillotta
2003, p. 136).

Another position in the middle of the spectrum is the liberal strategy
of deriving abstract ideas from the narrative detail of the texts. This activity is not so different from some kinds of precritical reading. Besides the
realistic historical kind of reading, precritical interpretation included a
distinction between the 'narrative level of the Bible and the deeper theological meaning or spiritual significance implicit within it' (Steinmetz
1997, p. 27). In his essay on the superiority of precritical exegesis, David
Steinmetz has argued that 'What appears to be history may be metaphor
or figure. . . . The interpreter must demythologize the text in order to grasp
the sacred mystery cloaked in the language of actual events' (p. 28).

For example, one could argue that apocalyptic texts express the idea
of the sovereignty of God over all creation, that is, over time, space and
human destiny. Such a deity is the classic dogmatic *Deus revelatus*. Or,
in cases like Mark's affirmation that Jesus' death was part of the divine
plan, one could argue that a God who makes such a plan is a hidden God,
a *Deus absconditus* (Guttenberger 2004, pp. 343–4).

R.H. Charles praised the authors of apocalyptic texts for transforming
the traditional expectation of an endless 'existence in the unblessed
abode of Sheol or Hades' into 'the hope of a blessed immortality' (1914,
pp. 9–10, 17–18). Charles also defended the value of apocalypticism
against scholars like 'Harnack in Germany and Professor Porter in Yale
University' (p. 15). He argued, against most scholars of his time, that the
move from prophecy to apocalypticism was not a decline, but an advance,
because it grasped the unity of all history – human, cosmological and
spiritual – 'a unity following naturally as a corollary of the unity of God
preached by the prophets' (p. 24); whereas the scope of prophecy was
limited with regard to space and time, 'that of apocalyptic was as wide
as the universe and as unlimited as time' (p. 32). With regard to ethics,
Charles confirmed the consensus that prophecy was 'the greatest ethical
force in the ancient world' (p. 29). But he rejected the attempt by
'advanced liberals' to differentiate prophecy and apocalypticism 'on the
ground that apocalyptic and ethics are distinct, and that ethics are the
kernel and apocalyptic the husk, which Christianity shed when it ceased
to need it' (p. 30). In the language of his time, Charles affirmed the unity
of form and content in apocalyptic texts, arguing that apocalyptic language as such is imbued with ethical import.

In his Schweich Lectures on the book of Revelation, given shortly after
the end of the First World War, Charles articulated 'the object of the seer',

which he believed was 'highly relevant then, yet never so relevant to the
conditions and needs of the world as at the present day' (1922, pp. viii,
74). He concluded that the object of the seer:

> is to proclaim the coming of God's kingdom on earth, and to assure the
> Christian Church of the final triumph of goodness, not only in the indi-
> vidual and within the borders of the Church itself, not only throughout
> the kingdoms of the world and in their relations to one another, but also
> throughout the whole universe. Thus its Gospel was from the beginning
> at once individualistic and corporate, national and international, and cosmic
> (p. 74).

Charles rightly rejected the view, common then and now, that apocalypticism is pessimistic. Recognizing 'the full horrors of the evils that are
threatening to engulf the world', the author of Revelation never despairs
of 'the ultimate victory of God's cause on earth' (p. 75). He also rightly
perceived the political character of the work:

> John the Seer insists . . . that there can be no divergence between the
> moral laws binding on the individual and those incumbent on the State, or
> any voluntary society or corporation within the State (ibid.).

Another position in the middle of the spectrum is the approach of
Walter Wink. In the period of protest and social experimentation in the
late 1960s and early 1970s, he argued that 'there is a sense in which we
can speak of apocalyptic visions as possessing an objective symbolic
content'. In other words, 'they may be the faithful reflection in symbolic
terms of the menace and promise of the hour'. Like some of Bultmann's
critics, he concluded that apocalyptic visions are deeply political, 'having
the most radical consequences for society, as even a casual reading of the
history of apocalyptic should make clear'. Far from being irrelevant or
quietistic, '[a]pocalyptic images have enormous power to elicit action'.
Retrieving and expanding Bultmann's interpretation, however, he remarked that 'Nothing is so revolutionary as a new paradigm of . . .
authentic existence in community' (1970, p. 18). In his later work (Wink
1984–92) he took up some of the issues engaged by Stringfellow.
    Another approach that may be placed on the middle of the spectrum
is the process of interpretation in which analogies are found between a
biblical text and its way of addressing its original situation and the way
the interpreter wishes to address a contemporary situation. The book
of Revelation played such a role in late twentieth-century liberation
theology. In her preface to a short commentary on the book of Revelation,
Elisabeth Schüssler Fiorenza (1981) made an analogy between the deaths

of Oscar Romero, Elisabeth Käsemann, Karen Silkwood and Steve Biko, on the one hand, and those murdered unjustly in John's time. Allan Boesak related the images of the beast and Babylon to the struggle against apartheid in South Africa. The notes in the Brazilian *Bíblia Sagrada* aimed at putting the book of Revelation into dialogue with the situation of its readers, recalling Christians to a prophetic role of involvement in liberating activity. The goal is radical transformation, the birth of a new world of justice. John's Apocalypse played a similar role in the basic ecclesial communities in Latin America (Rowland 1998, pp. 547-9). A related way of reading Revelation in the northern hemisphere is:

> as revealing the true nature of a world in which violence and destruction are prevalent. The story of the Lamb who is slain offers a critique of human history and of our delusions, of the violence we use to maintain the status quo, and of the lies with which we disguise the oppression of the victim (Kovacs and Rowland 2004, pp. 249-50).

This self-critical approach has some of the same virtues as Stringfellow's reading.

Conclusion

So where do things stand with the proposal by Krister Stendahl with which this study began? The project of attempting to understand and describe what a particular passage, book of the Bible or biblical writer 'meant' is clear enough in its aims and methods. The interpretive community of historical critics has rules and procedures that are applied in judging whether an article or book is successful in its attempt to do so. But when biblical scholars attempt to articulate the meaning that a passage, book or biblical writer has for their own time, the distinction that Stendahl called for is not made, at least not in a clear and clean manner. It seems that when biblical scholars aim at expressing 'what it means', they do not begin with a historical description of what the relevant part of Scripture 'meant'. Rather they read and construe Scripture in a different manner.

The most successful of the works of New Testament theology treated here is Bultmann's. Although there are important dimensions of the texts that he did not take up into his theological interpretation, his work was effective in large part *because* he did not distinguish between 'what it meant' and 'what it means' in his works addressed to a general audience. He began with description of the texts from a historical point of view, but moved quickly and almost imperceptibly from that approach into a deceptively simple philosophical and theological reading. His work is like a seamless garment in which the textual and the historical are woven together with the philosophical and the theological threads. Another reason for his success, from a scholarly point of view, is that his theological interpretation did not conflict unduly with the historical readings of his time. The omissions were significant – the communal and the cosmic dimensions – but his redescriptions had a recognizable structure or shape that could be seen to 'fit' the texts, even when read historically. His redescriptions were obviously not identical with the texts as historically read, but they were congruent with them.

Bultmann's synthesis is of course dated today, since existential philosophy no longer has the appeal it had in the mid-twentieth century. For the future, I would argue that Stendahl's proposal be heeded by those who aim at a historical reading of New Testament and related texts. Theological warrants should never be used to justify historical claims. Those, however, who aim at a theological interpretation need not, and probably should not, begin with the results of historical analysis of the texts. What is needed is a holistic approach that construes the text in terms of the interpreter's philosophical and theological premises or in terms of whatever conceptual framework takes the place of such premises. Theological interpretations that avoid contradicting the results of historical study, however, are likely to be more persuasive than those that do.

References

Barth, Karl, *Der Römerbrief* (Bern: Bäschlin, 1919; 2nd rev. ed. München: Kaiser, 1922). ET from the 6th ed.: *The Epistle to the Romans* (Oxford: Oxford University Press, 1933).

Baur, Ferdinand Christian, *Vorlesungen über Neutestamentliche Theologie* (ed. Ferdinand Friedrich Baur; Leipzig: Fues's Verlag [L.W. Reisland], 1864. Reprinted: Wissenschaftliche Buchgesellschaft, Darmstadt, 1973).

Braaten, Carl E., *Eschatology and Ethics: Essays on the Theology and Ethics of the Kingdom of God* (Minneapolis, MN: Augsburg, 1974).

Bultmann, Rudolf, *Theologie des Neuen Testaments* (2 vols; Tübingen: Mohr Siebeck, 1948-53). ET *Theology of the New Testament* (2 vols; New York: Scribner, 1951-55). References are to the English version.

Charles, R.H., *Religious Development between the Old and the New Testaments* (London: Williams & Norgate; New York: Henry Holt, 1914).

Charles, R.H., *Lectures on the Apocalypse.* The Schweich Lectures, 1919 (actually delivered in 1920) (London: British Academy/Oxford University Press, 1922).

Frei, H.W., *The Eclipse of Biblical Narrative: A Study in Eighteenth- and Nineteenth-Century Hermeneutics* (New Haven: Yale University Press, 1974).

Gabler, Johann Philipp, 'An oration on the proper distinction between biblical and dogmatic theology and the specific objectives of each' (1787), in Ben C. Ollenburger, Elmer A. Martens and Gerhard F. Hasel (eds), *The Flowering of Old Testament Theology: A Reader in Twentieth-Century Old Testament Theology, 1930-1990* (Winona Lake, IN: Eisenbrauns, 1992), pp. 3-19.

Guttenberger, Gudrun, *Die Gottesvorstellung im Markusevangelium* (Berlin/New York: De Gruyter, 2004).

Habermas, Jürgen, *Religion and Rationality: Essays on Reason, God and Modernity* (Oxford/Cambridge: Blackwell Publishers/Polity Press, 2002).

Holtzmann, Heinrich Julius, *Lehrbuch der Neutestamentlichen Theologie* (2 vols; 2nd rev. ed. Tübingen: Mohr Siebeck, 1911. 1st ed. 1896-1897).

Horkheimer, Max, *Kritische Theorie* (2 vols; Frankfurt am Main: Fischer, 1968). ET *Critical Theory* (New York: Seabury/Continuum, 1972). References are to the English.

Horkheimer, Max, *Die Sehnsucht nach dem ganz Anderen: Ein Interview mit Kommentar von Helmut Gumnior* (Hamburg: Furche-Verlag, 1970).

Käsemann, Ernst, 'Die Anfänge christlicher Theologie', *ZTK* 57 (1960), 218-37. ET 'The beginnings of Christian theology', in *idem, New Testament Questions of Today* (Philadelphia: Fortress, 1969), pp. 82-107. Reference is to the English version.

Kelsey, David H., *The Uses of Scripture in Recent Theology* (Philadelphia: Fortress, 1975).

Klauck, Hans-Josef, 'Himmlisches Haus und irdische Bleibe: Eschatologische Metaphorik in Antike und Christentum', *NTS* 50 (2004), 5-35.

Koch, Klaus, *Ratlos vor der Apokalyptik* (Gütersloh: Mohn, 1970). ET *The Rediscovery of Apocalyptic* (Naperville, IL: Allenson, 1972). References are to the English.

Kovacs, Judith and Rowland, Christopher, *Revelation: The Apocalypse of Jesus Christ* (Oxford: Blackwell Publishing, 2004).

Lanzillotta, Lautaro Roig, 'Does punishment reward the righteous? The justice pattern underlying the *Apocalypse of Peter*', in Jan N. Bremmer and Istvan Czachesz (eds), *The Apocalypse of Peter* (Leuven: Peeters, 2003), pp. 127-57.

Meyer, William J., Review of Jürgen Habermas (2002), in *JR* 84 (2004), 128-9.

Moltmann, Jürgen, *Theologie der Hoffnung* (München: Kaiser, 1964). ET *Theology of Hope* (New York: Harper & Row, 1967). References are to the English version.

Moltmann, Jürgen, *Der gekreuzigte Gott* (München: Kaiser, 1973). ET *The Crucified God* (New York/Minneapolis: Harper & Row/Fortress, 1974/1993). References are to the English version.

Ollenburger, Ben C., 'What Krister Stendahl "meant" - A normative critique of "Descriptive Biblical Theology"', *HBT* 8 (1986), 61-98.

Pannenberg, Wolfhart, 'Dogmatische Thesen zur Lehre von der Offenbarung', in *idem* (ed.) *Offenbarung als Geschichte*, (Göttingen: Vandenhoeck & Ruprecht, 1961), pp. 91-114. ET 'Dogmatic theses on the doctrine of Revelation', in *idem* (ed.), *Revelation as History* (New York: Macmillan; London: Collier-Macmillan, 1968), pp. 123-58. References are to the English.

Pannenberg, Wolfhart, *Theology and the Kingdom of God* (Philadelphia: Westminster, 1969).

Pannenberg, Wolfhart, *An Introduction to Systematic Theology* (Grand Rapids, MI: Eerdmans, 1991).

Pippin, Tina, *Death and Desire: The Rhetoric of Gender in the Apocalypse of John* (Louisville, KY: Westminster John Knox Press, 1992).

Rowland, Christopher C., 'The book of Revelation: introduction, commentary and reflections', in Leander E., Keck *et al.* (eds), *The New Interpreter's Bible* (vol. 12; Nashville, TN: Abingdon Press, 1998), pp. 501–743.

Schüssler Fiorenza, Elisabeth, *Invitation to the Book of Revelation: A Commentary on the Apocalypse with Complete Text from the Jerusalem Bible* (Garden City, NY: Doubleday Image Books, 1981).

Steinmetz, David C., 'The superiority of pre-critical exegesis', in Stephen E. Fowl (ed.), *The Theological Interpretation of Scripture: Classic and Contemporary Readings* (Oxford, UK/Cambridge, MA: Blackwell Publishers, 1997).

Stendahl, Krister, 'Biblical theology, contemporary', *The Interpreter's Dictionary of the Bible* 1 (1962), pp. 418–32. Reprinted in *idem, Meanings: The Bible as Document and as Guide* (Philadelphia: Fortress, 1984), pp. 11–44.

Stringfellow, William, *An Ethic for Christians and Other Aliens in a Strange Land* (Waco, TX: Word Books, 1973).

Tracy, David, *The Analogical Imagination: Christian Theology and the Culture of Pluralism* (New York: Crossroad, 1981).

Weiss, Bernhard, *Lehrbuch der biblischen Theologie des Neuen Testaments* (Berlin: Hertz, 1868; 3rd ed. 1880). ET of 3rd ed.: *Biblical Theology of the New Testament* (2 vols; Edinburgh: T. & T. Clark, 1882–1883). References are to the English.

Weiss, Johannes, *Die Predigt Jesu vom Reich Gottes* (Göttingen: Vandenhoeck & Ruprecht, 1892; 2nd ed. 1900). ET *Jesus' Proclamation of the Kingdom of God* (Philadelphia: Fortress, 1971).

Wink, Walter, 'Apocalypse in our time', *Katallagete* 3 (1970), 13–18.

Wink, Walter, *The Powers* (3 vols; Philadelphia: Fortress, 1984–92).

Yarbro Collins, Adela, 'Fundamentalist interpretation of biblical symbols', in Marla Selvidge (ed.), *Fundamentalism Today: What Makes it So Attractive?* (Elgin, IL: Brethren Press, 1984), pp. 107–14.

Yarbro Collins, Adela, 'Reading the book of Revelation in the twentieth century', *Interpretation* 40 (1986), 229–42.

Yarbro Collins, Adela, 'Pergamon in early Christian literature', in Helmut Koester (ed.), *Pergamon: Citadel of the Gods: Archaeological Record, Literary Description, and Religious Development* (Harrisburg, PA: Trinity Press International, 1998), pp. 163–84.

Chapter 4

New Testament Interpretation as Interpersonal Communion: the Case for a Socio-Theological Hermeneutics

Philip F. Esler, St Andrews

Introductory Observations

At one point in his 1973 work *The Nature of New Testament Theology* Robert Morgan makes the following observation in the course of insisting that the word 'theology' does not appear in the phrase 'New Testament theology' by accident:

> Most people's interest in the New Testament, including their historical interest in it, has been engendered by its significance for Christian faith. The discipline has been developed in the interests of traditional Christian faith and also out of hostility to it, but not with indifference to it (p. 22).

There are nearly one billion people on earth who call themselves Christians and seek to live a Christian life. For them the pages of the New Testament contain the primary information concerning God's intervention in the world through Jesus Christ and its immediate aftermath –

information that bears directly on the nature of their current existence and identity and speaks of their ultimate destiny. The New Testament is not just any old text from the Greco-Roman past. Rather, it has shaped and enriched the Christian faithful in heart, mind and spirit for the last two millennia and will continue to do so as long as Christianity lasts. Morgan is pointing out that it is this life-shaping function of the text for Christians that has motivated most research into the New Testament, whether to endorse this role or, probably less often, to subvert it, and that, accordingly, it is reasonable to employ the concept of New Testament theology in relation to work that recognizes this dimension.

Robert Morgan's own life – balancing the demands of a New Testament position in Oxford with the pastorship of an Anglican parish at Sandford-on-Thames (a few miles out of Oxford) – represents an exemplary attempt both to bring into close and positive alignment a penetrating insight into the New Testament and a very active Christian life, but also to produce some of the finest work ever on the character of 'New Testament theology' (see especially Morgan 1973, 1987, 1996, 2002, Morgan and Pye 1977, Morgan with Barton 1988).

I am in complete agreement with Morgan that there is a continuing role for (at least some) New Testament critics to be actively concerned with considering how its 27 constituent works can continue to foster Christian beliefs, experience and hope. We differ merely in the approach each of us takes to promote that end. Although I am happy to concede the reasonableness of applying the word 'theological' (or 'socio-theological') to that enterprise, I have serious misgivings concerning the ability of 'New Testament theology' from its inception in the eighteenth century onward to the present to deliver the result Morgan and I both wish to see.

My aim in this essay is to set out a different approach to the question of New Testament theology that utilizes social-scientific ideas and perspectives. Since I have recently set out my views on in this subject in a monograph (Esler 2005), I will endeavour here to offer an overview of that extended argument.

Johann Philipp Gabler and New Testament Theology

It is fair to say that the whole enterprise of New Testament theology as it is generally conceived reflects in various ways the programme of its founder Johann Philipp Gabler in 1787, even though Gabler's views themselves were not particularly influential and later writers moved in different directions. Gabler was largely responding to a widespread opinion in the late eighteenth century that Lutheran dogmatic theology had become too remote from the Bible, even to the extent of moving in philosophical and scholastic directions that Luther himself had opposed (see Boers 1979). Gabler's aim was to encourage a closer connection between biblical insights and Lutheran theology. Gabler distinguished between religion and theology as follows:

> (R)eligion is passed on by the doctrine in the Scriptures, teaching what each Christian ought to know and believe and do in order to secure happiness in this life and in the life to come. Religion then, is every-day, transparently clear knowledge; but theology is subtle, learned knowledge, surrounded by a retinue of many disciplines, and by the same token derived not only from the sacred Scripture but also from elsewhere, especially from the domain of philosophy and history.

Then he went on to distinguish between biblical and dogmatic theology:

> there is truly a biblical theology, of historical origin, conveying what the holy writers felt about divine matters; on the other hand there is a dogmatic theology of didactic origin, teaching what each theologian philosophises rationally about divine things, according to the measure of his ability or of the times, age, place, sect, school, and other similar factors (Sandys-Wunsch and Eldredge 1980, p. 137).

Gabler proposed that the Bible should be investigated using historical techniques in order to separate 'those things which in the sacred books refer most immediately to their own times and to the men of those times from those pure notions which divine providence wished to be characteristic of all times and places' (Sandys-Wunsch and Eldredge 1980, p. 138). Sustaining this view were sentiments similar to the one that Lessing had expressed 10 years earlier when he declared that the 'accidental truths of history can never become the proof of necessary truths of reason' (Lessing 1957, p. 53).[1] Lessing had famously encapsulated his opposition to the notion that the fact of the resurrection of Jesus Christ in the past could prove that he *is* the Son of God *now* in the statement 'That, then, is the ugly, broad ditch which I cannot get across, however often and however earnestly I have tried to make the leap' (Lessing 1957, p. 55).

Gabler believed that theological truths discovered in the Bible through its historical investigation could then be utilized by dogmatic theologians. As Boers notes, 'Biblical theology was intended for a specific purpose, that is, to serve dogmatic theology by providing it with an independent base. With regard to its purpose, thus, biblical theology was not independent of dogmatic theology' (Boers 1979, p. 27). In this aim Gabler was

motivated by an attempt to understand the theological task as a whole
(Boers 1979, p. 30).

Two problems with Gabler's approach (even if, as noted above, it was
not in itself particularly influential) should be noted. First, it has no role
for the historical analysis of the Bible to feed theological ideas directly
into the religion of ordinary Christians. Secondly, it assumes that theological truth is not to be found in the historical details themselves, but only
in aspects that transcended their particular contexts and were valid for
all times and all places. Robert Morgan has noted with characteristic
clarity one problem of the latter assumption:

> Sketching the bare outline of the Christian symbol-system in isolation from
> its successive social contexts can only have a regulative function. The bibli-
> cal witness may have more purchase on contemporary reality when seen
> in its own historically conditioned reality (Morgan 1986–7, p. 168).

Another way to express this is to say that Gabler's view entails the
unlikely notion that modern Christians, struggling to do God's will and
to maintain their identity in their own epoch, cannot derive useful
assistance from investigating how the first people who followed Christ
did God's will and held onto their new identity in their particular time
and place.

Space is lacking here to offer a roll-call of all New Testament theologians who, if not influenced directly by Gabler, nevertheless are marked
by these two dominant assumptions in his approach.[2] Early in the twentieth century, however, Bultmann's plea for demythologizing, which
entailed extracting kernels of universal truth from the ancient biblical
husks in which they were lodged, seems to have been a descendant of
Lessing's 'ugly, broad ditch' and meant a certain dehistoricizing of the
New Testament. In the last two decades, moreover, we have witnessed
the significant phenomenon of scholars such as Brevard Childs and
Francis Watson, each in their different ways, calling for theological interpretations of the Bible that are rather unsympathetic (although in varying
ways) to a role for the historical understanding of the texts in their original contexts (see Childs 1970, 1979, 1984, 1985, 1992, and Watson 1993,
1994, 1997, 2000).

The perspective that I find more appealing is the opposite of this. It
was expressed most vividly by Krister Stendahl in an essay published in
1962 on contemporary biblical theology. Stendahl made a strong case for
what he described as the 'descriptive task' in biblical theology, which he
traced back to the 'history-of-religions school' (*religionsgeschichtliche
Schule*) in the late nineteenth and early twentieth century. Such investiga-

tion stressed the difference between biblical and modern times and forced scholars who wanted to explore the biblical texts in this way to creep out of their 'Western and twentieth-century skin' and identify themselves 'with the feelings and thought patterns of the past' (Stendahl 1962, p. 418). I am entirely convinced by the foundation for Stendahl's view, which was the sheer value inherent in the distance of the biblical material from us:

> For the life of the church such a consistent descriptive approach is a great and promising asset which enables the church, its teaching and preaching ministry, to be exposed to the Bible in its original intention and intensity, as an ever new challenge to thought, faith, and response (Stendahl 1962, p. 431).

Toward the end of his 1962 essay Stendahl made a remark that I consider to be of profound importance in formulating an approach to the New Testament theology that takes seriously the historical distance between ourselves and its 27 constituent documents: '*A theology which retains history as a theologically charged category finds in its ecclesiology the overarching principles of interpretation and meaning.*' Such a theology, moreover, 'does not permit its ecclesiology to be transferred to the second last chapter in its systematic works, followed by that on an equally inactivated eschatology' (Stendahl 1962, p. 428, emphasis added).

A Social and Theological Model of Persons in Communion

If ecclesiology is to be central, it becomes necessary to think about how we might conceive of a relationship between us and the persons responsible for producing the New Testament writings. My answer is to propose a model of dialogue and communion between those first Christ-followers who composed the 27 documents of the New Testament and ourselves. This model is necessarily intercultural, given the great cultural distance between us and them, and critical, since there will be areas in which their ways (the acceptance of slavery, for example) are not our ways. Although the model is based initially upon the situation of communion *inter vivos*, I later proceed to propose ways of incorporating the fact that the New Testament authors and their original audiences are long dead. This model is both social and theological. Yet it is predicated upon the fundamental necessity of attempting to understand our biblical forebears in all their historical particularity. It is not a body of systematic theological truth that depends upon ignoring or eliminating the historical distinctiveness of the New Testament writings. Rather, it renders articulate the theological foundations of what we are doing when we try to grasp the original meanings of the New Testament as composed by persons who, like us, belonged (or belong?) to the Body of Christ and experienced the same Holy Spirit in spite of the gulf between us and them.

If asked why I find the model I am about to summarize attractive, I can only answer that it comes from some deep part of how I see the world that goes back to my upbringing.[3] In proceeding with this model of interpersonal communion, I am, accordingly, articulating my instincts as much as simply selecting promising theory from the options available because of its intellectual force.

One foundational idea for my approach comes from Martin Buber's 1923 work *Ich und Dich* ('I and You'). Since Buber was concerned with relationships between persons and their relationship with God, his position embraces both social and theological aspects of human experience. Buber drew a sharp distinction between our attitude to other persons and our attitude to things. In the former one human subject, 'I', confronts another 'You', whereas in the latter a person contemplates and experiences an object. When 'I' encounters 'You' a meeting occurs that goes to the heart of our shared humanity (Buber 1970, p. 55). Elsewhere he states, 'The basic word I-You establishes the world of relation' (Buber 1970, p. 56) Relations are foundational for our humanity. Only in relation to other persons do we truly become ourselves: 'Man becomes an I through a You' (Buber 1970, p. 80).

Buber strongly distinguished his position from that of Heidegger, of which he was sharply (and rightly) critical. Buber insisted that for Heidegger a human being of 'real existence', who in Heidegger's view was the goal of life, is not the person who lives with another person, but a person who can no longer live with another, a person 'who now knows a real life only in communication with himself'. Heidegger 'absolutizes the temporally conditioned situation of the radically solitary man, and wants to derive the essence of human existence from the experience of a nightmare' (Buber 1947, p. 168). Heidegger's self is '*a closed system*': 'Existence is completed in self-being; there is no way beyond this for Heidegger' (Buber 1947, p. 171). Buber's model of human existence as completed in the relation between two subject stood in stark opposition to this view.

At times in *I and You* Buber touched on the significance of language. The relation between persons he had in mind, he said at one point, 'enters language'. He developed his thoughts on dialogue more fully elsewhere. In 'Dialogue', for example, Buber (1924) described 'genuine dialogue' as occurring when 'each of the participants really has in mind the other or others in their present and particular being and turns to them with the intention of establishing a living mutual relation between himself and them' (Buber 1947, p. 19).[4]

It was fundamental to Buber's understanding of community that those who comprise it do not need to agree on everything. At the heart of the I-You relation, that is necessary for community, lies a recognition of otherness, of the fact that others are different from oneself: 'Only men who are truly capable of saying *Thou* to one another can truly say *We* to one another' (Buber 1947, p. 176). Furthermore, by '*We*' Buber meant 'a community of several independent persons, who have reached a self and self-responsibility, the community resting on the basis of this self and self-responsibility, and being made possible by them' (Buber 1947, p. 175). There are very significant expressions of similar ideas in 'Distance and Relation'. His fundamental insight is that 'Genuine conversation, and therefore every actual fulfillment of relation between men, means acceptance of otherness'. The critical factor is the disposition that the participants have toward one another, not that they should agree. The recognition of difference in human relations lies at the basis of Buber's insistence that we must retain a critical attitude in relation to the views of others.

One possible objection to Buber's understanding was that it was largely atemporal. To address this issue I call in aid the work of Franz Rosenzweig (1886–1929). In his major work, *The Star of Redemption* (1921), Rosenzweig generated a new model for the I-You relationship that eschewed the atemporality that had marked Buber's presentation and built instead on the temporal nature of speech between persons (Rosenzweig 1971).[5] Rosenzweig described the 'wholly real employment of language' as the centre-piece of the entire book (Rosenzweig 1971, p. 174). That is, he understood the meaning of persons and their reality in the world fundamentally in relation to speech and dialogue:

> For speech is truly mankind's morning gift from the Creator, and yet at the same time it is the common property of all the children of men, in which each has his particular share and, finally, it is the seal of humanity in man (Rosenzweig 1971, p. 110).

This oral dimension upon which Rosenzweig insisted is a vital ingredient in our model in view of the fact that the New Testament documents came into existence in what was largely an oral culture and would have been heard rather than read by their initial audiences.

The next step is to amplify this model in relation to the intercultural dimension. Yet there is nothing new in the notion of intercultural communication. All across the world every day people set off to spend long periods of time in cultures very different from their own. They include diplomats, health professionals, volunteers abroad, aid workers, business people, emigrants and students, to name only a few. It is likely that they will all experience 'culture shock' when they arrive at their destination – the painful appreciation that their customary ways of thinking, feeling and behaving stemming from their own culture are quite different to those of the locals, thus exposing them to feelings of awkwardness and inadequacy.[6] Fortunately there is an extensive literature on intercultural communication offering assistance to those in this predicament. A good example is the work by William B. Gudykunst and Young Yun Kim entitled *Communicating with Strangers: An Approach to Intercultural Communication* (see Gudykunst and Kim 2003). This area of enquiry is relevant because the cultural distance between us and our ancestors in faith raises issues of comprehension and awareness similar to those encountered by any person who immerses him- or herself in a foreign culture today. The good news from works like those of Gudykunst and Kim is that representatives of cultures that are very different from one another can learn to sensitize themselves to the other in such a way as to allow significant communication and even interdependence.

This stress on personal inter-relation and communion derived from social theory is matched by the recent turn among theologians from monadic to relational notions of the human person. Boethius had famously defined a person as 'an individual substance with a rational nature' (*Est autem persona rationalis naturae individua substantia*).[7] The definition of the self proposed by Descartes (1596–1650) as a 'thinking thing' (*res cogitans*) and the tendency of idealist philosophies in the modern period to define a person in terms of self-consciousness both reflect the legacy of Boethius (Pannenberg 1985, pp. 236–7). In the last century, however, there has been a strong reaction against this whole individualistic approach to the person among theologians. Wolfhart Pannenberg summarizes what has happened as follows:

> Since the end of the nineteenth century there has been a growing desire to avoid taking as the starting point of thought either the isolated subject or an abstract, supraindividual subject which exists only in the form of individual subjects but which is asserted to be the basis of all experience (Pannenberg 1985, p. 179).

This development constitutes a theological reaction against individualistic construals of the person which have not only been widespread among theologians and philosophers, but have also been dominant in many northern European and North American cultures. A clear example of the impetus toward this outlook in philosophy is evident in John MacMurray's Gifford lectures in 1953–4 entitled *The Form of the Personal*, (1891–1976), where MacMurray mounted a vigorous philosophical attack on the notion of the person as a thinking subject (usually accompanied by a pronounced mind–body dualism). He argued that mutuality was the hallmark of personal identity (see MacMurray 1957, 1961). In the last few decades John Zizioulas has been an influential theological voice urging the reassessment of the nature of the human person in relation to the person of God. In an important essay published in 1975 he outlined a strongly relational position and developed his position in a 1985 monograph entitled *Being as Communion*. It is also possible to integrate these insights into an understanding of the Trinity. An example in point is the important 1992 monograph by Catherine LaCugna, *God For Us: The Trinity and Christian Life*. Here, under the primary influence of Zizioulas, and also to a lesser extent in positive response to MacMurray, feminist and liberation theologies and Catholic and Orthodox moral theologies, LaCugna presents a powerful case for an ontology that privileges persons-in-communion, the persons in question comprising the three persons of the Trinity and human beings.

Interesting New Testament confirmation that we are on the right track with this model exists in the beginning of 1 John:

> That which was from the beginning (*ap' archês*), which we have heard, which we have seen with our eyes, which we have looked upon and touched with our hands, concerning the word of life – the life was made manifest, and we have seen it, and testify to it, and proclaim to you the eternal life which was with the Father and was made manifest to us – that which we have seen and heard we proclaim also to you, so that you may have communion (*koinônia*) with us; and our communion (*koinônia*) is with the Father and with his Son Jesus Christ (1 John 1:1–3).[8]

In this programmatic statement the author announces that he and whoever else among his contemporaries are included in the expression 'we' have had first-hand sensory experience, *from the beginning*, of the word of life made manifest and that he will proclaim it to 'you', his audience, to that they may have communion with them, a communion that is also with the Father and the Son. Thus, the foundational events of salvation in Christ are to be communicated in an oral framework of proclamation and listening that leads to communion between those sending the message and those receiving it, a communion that is also with the Father and the Son.

The Knowability of the Past and the Importance
of the Author

An attempt to engage in intercultural communion with the Christ-followers who produced the writings of the New Testament presupposes both
that the past is knowable and that it makes sense to read texts such as
these with an eye on what their authors wished to convey by them. Since
both of these presuppositions have been strongly challenged in the last
few decades, they require defending.

Most of us believe that what has happened in the past is in some sense
knowable, that there is some such thing as an 'historical fact'. Until the
1970s, most historians and cultural analysts would probably have been
happy with the definition of an historical fact as defined by British historian Richard Evans:

> A historical fact is something that happened in history and can be verified
> as such through the traces history has left behind. Whether or not a histo-
> rian has actually carried out the act of verification is irrelevant to its fac-
> tuality: it really is there entirely independently of the historian (Evans 1997,
> p. 76).

Jacques Derrida has mounted what has probably been the most influential challenge to this type of view. At a literary conference in Johns
Hopkins University in 1966 he announced the broad outlines of his
project, which has come to be known as deconstruction and which forms
an important strand in postmodernist thought.[9] Although the character
of Derrida's writing is such that summarizing his thought is not easy, even
at this early stage it is clear that he was announcing that reality was
affected by a major transformation in which it had become decentred:

> This was the moment when language invaded the universal problematic,
> the moment when, in the absence of a center or origin, everything became
> discourse.... that is to say, a system in which the central signified, the
> original or transcendental signified, is never absolutely present outside a
> system of differences. The absence of the transcendental signified extends
> the domain and the play of signification infinitely (Derrida 1981, p. 280).

What does all this rather portentous language mean? Critically important is the distinction between 'signifiers' and 'signified'. For Derrida each
time a word, a signifier, is uttered, the relationship between it and other
words changes. Language is thus an infinite play of significations. In the
quotation just given Derrida seems to be saying that there is no reality

apart from language. There is no 'transcendental signified'. This seems perilously close to asserting that everything is merely an arrangement of words and that nothing exists outside language – a position that Richard Evans does indeed attribute to him (Evans 1997, p.95, citing Derrida 1976, 1981, 1983). Although Kevin Vanhoozer has tried to defend Derrida (Vanhoozer 1998), it is extremely difficult to deny that Derrida seems to be asserting that there is no ground for meaning beyond language systems. This seems implausible in the extreme, not only in the face of realities such as the Holocaust, a difficult subject for Derrida when it emerged in 1987 that his supporter Paul de Man had written unfavourably of the Jews in a Nazi-controlled paper in Belgium during the Second World War, but even in relation to less fraught subjects, such as what I did yesterday.[10]

Hans Gadamer's work 1979 work *Truth and Method* has also been extremely influential, and yet, his notion of the 'fusion of horizons', actually represents a potential obstacle to the approach I am essaying here; I say 'potential' because Gadamer's argument is fatally flawed in this area. Gadamer favours the view (to an extent based on the thought of Martin Heidegger) that time is no longer primarily a gulf to be bridged but is actually 'the supportive ground of process in which the present is rooted' (Gadamer 1979, p. 264). Gadamer insists on the priority of the viewpoint of the person reading an historical text:

> Every age has to understand a transmitted text in its own way, for the text is part of the whole of the tradition in which the age takes an objective interest and in which it seeks to understand itself (Gadamer 1979, p. 263).

Thiselton accurately interprets Gadamer to mean by this statement that we 'cannot, as it were, leave the present to go back into the past and to view the past solely on its own terms', since the 'very meaning which the text has for us is partly shaped by our own place in a tradition which reaches the present' (Thiselton 1980, p. 306). The horizon of the past and the horizon of the present 'fuse', so that we cannot appreciate the past on its own terms. Gadamer supports this notion with a comparison from human conversation. For Gadamer the only true conversation is when we are 'seeking agreement concerning an object' (Gadamer 1979, p. 270). This is completely unsatisfactory. Gadamer's model of conversation rests on the *sentimental* notion that we are only truly speaking to one another if we are trying to reach agreement. Interpreted a little more bleakly, however, he is actually opposing the mutual co-existence of different views and is indefensibly advocating the *hegemonic* assertion of sameness over difference. In other words, 'You're only free to agree'.

As we have seen, Buber, on the other hand, recognized that true conversation will frequently involve disagreement. Knowing the other in his or her otherness, not to the extent they agree with me, is a feature of human conversation and occurs even in cross-cultural contexts.

When one reads the New Testament expressly in a Christian context, in the belief that it has vital things to tell us about the condition and aspirations of human beings in relation to themselves, the cosmos and God, it is unhelpful to regard these texts as literary documents where, possibly, authorial intention is of little concern. Even Wimsatt and Beardsley, whose 1946 essay on 'The Intentional Fallacy' seems to many to have excluded authorial intention as a useful notion in biblical interpretation, made it clear that their views were restricted to poems. At one point they said: 'In this respect poetry differs from practical messages, which are successful if and only if we correctly infer the intention' (Wimsatt 1954, p. 5). Since the New Testament works were essentially written with the intention enunciated in John 20:31 (whether they say so expressly or not), they are practical messages where authorial intention must be addressed.

Another way of putting this is to say, with Gadamer (and here we enter upon a more satisfactory aspect of his hermeneutics), that our experience of literature is similar to that of play, in that 'all those purposive relations which determine active and caring existence have not simply disappeared, but in a curious way acquire a different quality' (Gadamer 1979, p. 91). Both players and readers tend to lose themselves in the experience (Gadamer 1979, p. 92). If we read the New Testament in a Christian context, however, we are pushed into reality, not isolated from it. Again, we may use J.L. Austin's speech act theory (see Austin 1962, Searle 1969), by which the messages of the New Testament have illocutionary or perlocutionary force, whereas, as Richard Ohmann has suggested:

> [A] literary work is a discourse abstracted, or detached, from the circumstances and conditions which make illocutionary acts possible; hence it is a discourse without illocutionary force (Ohmann 1971, p. 13, emphasis original).

What, next, of the proposal made by critics such as Roland Barthes and Paul Ricoeur that the reading process is predicated on the 'death of the author'. A central part of Ricoeur's argument is the distinction he claims exists between speaking and writing (see Ricoeur 1976, pp. 25–44). The 'problem of writing', he claims, 'is identical to that of the fixation of discourse in some exterior bearer, whether it be stone, papyrus, or paper, which is other than the human voice. This inscription, substituted for the immediate vocal, physiognomic, or gestural expression, is in itself a tremendous cultural achievement. *The human fact disappears*. Now material "marks" convey the message' (Ricoeur 1976, p. 26, emphasis added). It is very difficult seriously to entertain such a view. Ricoeur is proposing that *the human dimension of a discourse is not conveyed by its contents!* A single example will reveal its implausibility. If Ricoeur was correct on this, it would follow that the 'human fact' is present in a young man saying to a young woman 'I love you', but has disappeared in a letter he sends her bearing exactly the same words!

'Whereas spoken discourse,' Ricoeur assures us, 'is addressed to someone who is determined in advance by the dialogical situation – it is addressed to you, the second person – a written text is addressed to an unknown reader and potentially to whoever knows how to read'. He describes this as 'the universalization of the audience' and says that by it 'discourse is liberated from the narrowness of the face-to-face situation' (Ricoeur 1976, p. 31). But what is wrong with the face-to-face situation? Why is this narrow? Or again, he says, 'Thanks to writing, man and only man has a world and not just a situation' (Ricoeur 1976, p. 36). Here we have the remarkable notion that writing is necessary for and indeed constitutive of the world. It is an impossible proposition that entails that all the pre-literate peoples in human history (and, one must presume, the numerous illiterate members of literate cultures) had and have only a 'situation', not a 'world'. This is the view of a Western intellectual at home in his study.[11] His theory of what happens when an author's work is published represents a form of dehumanization and depersonalization with very little to be said for it.

None of this is to deny that every act of communication is imperfect; we do not quite say what we mean and our conversation partners understand our utterances in their own distinctive ways. Wolgang Iser's account of the reading process rests upon this type of phenomenon. Iser notes that it 'is the virtuality of a text that gives rise to its dynamic nature'. This means that the text is 'infinitely richer than any of its individual realizations' (Iser 1974, p. 280). As the reader uses the various perspectives offered by the text in order to relate its patterns to one another, this process results in the awakening of responses within the reader (Iser 1974, p. 275).

On re-examination, Friedrich Schleiermacher, much maligned as insisting on an unattainable knowledge of an author's pscyhe, emerges as the propounder of an approach to hermeneutics closely cognate with what I am advocating here. To many observers, Friedrich Schleiermacher's aim of 'understanding an author better than he understood himself' is a serious flaw in his hermeneutics. But one needs to consider the context.

Schleiermacher in his personal life was always a great conversationalist and even translated the *Dialogues of Plato* (published in 1804). He was committed to the dialogical and the inter-relational. When one actually looks at his hermeneutic corpus, it becomes clear that by understanding an author he really meant the understanding that we can deduce from the communication. At one point in his notes, for example, Schleiermacher says, '*Since we have no direct knowledge of what was in the author's mind* (emphasis added), we must try to become aware of many things of which he himself may have been unconscious, except in so far as he reflects upon his own work and becomes his own reader' (Schleiermacher 1977, p. 112).[12] For Schleiermacher this was the way to understand a communication, whether in spoken or written form. He was on solid ground.

1 Corinthians 10–14 as a Test Case for Interpersonal Communion

It is worthwhile briefly to consider one part of the New Testament to see how it reflects this model with respect to communion between Christ-followers *inter vivos*. A particularly rich source for this is 1 Corinthians 10-14. We need to bear in mind that this was a context where the vast majority of the population was illiterate (see Harris 1989 and Hezser 2001). Members of the Christ-followers became socialized into the movement by hearing not reading. Paul's culture accordingly represents an environment where Martin Buber and Franz Rosenzweig's advocacy of speech and dialogue as fundamental to the relational nature of the human person is confirmed with notable strength.

A major reason prompting Paul to write to the Corinthians was the need to combat tendencies toward divisiveness or even factionalism. He wants to persuade them to become unified.[13] In 1 Corinthians 10 there is an extensive treatment of true and false communion. One key expression of communion, *koinônia*, actually appears in 1 Cor 10:16-17:

> The cup of blessing which we bless, is it not communion (*koinônia*) with the blood of Christ? The bread which we break, is it not communion (*koinônia*) with the body of Christ? Because the bread which we break is one, we, although many, are one body, for we all share in the one bread.

In 1 Cor 10:21-2 Paul underlines the seriousness of engaging in communion with the Lord and with demons. Serious sanction is threatened. In 1 Cor 11:17-34 there is another discussion over the Lord's

Supper, this time in relation to practices attending its celebration in the congregation.

In addition, Paul's community in Corinth (and elsewhere) was the site of a flourishing array of spoken phenomena. During their meetings the members gave burst to prophecy, teaching, apocalypses, psalms, glosso-lalia and its interpretation. In addition, either at the meetings (the princi-pal focus of 1 Corinthians 12 and 14), or in other contexts, the spoken word also had a role in healings, miracles, distinguishing between spirits, and in assistance and guidance. In each case the use of language was central to the life and identity of the person in Christ. All of these min-istries involved the spoken word, even if some did so more than others. We are dealing with oral phenomena. For Rosenzweig, speech, and not writing, was humanity's morning gift from the creator and both he and Buber placed the spoken word ahead of writing. In Paul's communities we witness the centrality of interpersonal communion through speech.

The Effect of Writing on Interpersonal Communion

Central to my overall approach is the insistence that the introduction of writing into the communications between the early Christ-followers did not significantly affect the character of their communion or the role of such communion in their emerging understanding of existence and identity. Given that the documents some of them left are our main means of access to them, this is a significant result.

Thus, the earliest proclaimers of the gospel were determined to keep alive the sense of personal connection even when spatial separation meant that face-to-face communication and communion were impossible. They did this through use of letters, as exemplified in Paul's epistolary practice. Paul frequently mentioned in his letters that he continually bore in remembrance and prayed for those he had left behind in communities he had founded and even for the members of congregations, such as in Rome, he had never visited (cf. Rom 1:8; 1 Cor 1:3, 16:23; 2 Cor 13:9; Phil 1:3-5; Gal 6:18; 1 Thess 1:2; 5:28). In addition, the proto-trinitarian shape of Paul's thought in Rom 15:30-1, where he exhorts the Romans to act in solidarity with him, coheres closely with the trinitarian dimension to the model of socio-theological communion set out above.

In a culture such as this where an overwhelming proportion of the population was illiterate, the despatch of letters (which comprise the greater part of the New Testament by number) that would be read out to the congregation of Christ-followers at their destination represented minimal change to their established mode of communication. The position is different, but not fundamentally so, in relation to the documents of the corpus that are narrative in form: the Gospels, Acts and the Apocalypse. In the first-century Mediterranean context, where the majority of the population was illiterate, Christ-followers must have first come across these documents (better seen as 'scripts' for performance than as 'texts') when they head them read aloud at their meetings. It is also probable that on their very first recitation the audience knew the identity of their composers.

In the first century or so, 'scripture' (*graphê*) meant the various writings of what we now call the Old Testament (cf. Rom 1:2 and 2 Tim 3:16). In those early days, the proclamation about the life, death and resurrection of Jesus circulated in oral form. As late as 120–40 CE Papias could still say he preferred these oral communications to the written message of books, such as Matthew and Mark (cited in Eusebius, *Ecclesiastical History* 3.39.4). As James Barr has noted, the 'idea of a Christian faith governed by Christian written holy scriptures was not an essential part of the foundation plan of Christianity' (Barr 1983, p. 12).

In the fuller version of my argument, I explain how the earlier discussion of the validity of history and the continuing role of authorial intention applies to the way we read the New Testament. Its 27 'scripts' came into existence as expressions of intense interpersonal communications in a largely oral culture. There is no obligation on us to let the valorization of texts, in printed form – and the subsequent rise of accompanying practices of solitary reading that have occurred only since the invention of printing in the fifteenth century – deflect us from using historical approaches to continue to access them in the same way.

Ways to Model Communion

Yet all of the New Testament authors are long dead. In what sense can we have communion with them? Perhaps the idea is not that radical. As a matter of empirical fact, many Christians have always considered that those of their number who died in Christ were in some sense still present. There are a number of ways to model such communion and as my aim is to be inclusive rather than exclusive I am content if any one of them works, even though my own theological preference is for a high theology of the communion of saints that is current in the Roman Catholic church, all of the autocephalous Orthodox churches and also in some Reformed and Protestant traditions, some Anglicans especially. There is a particularly lively debate at present as to the post-mortem status of those who have died in Christ.[14]

On the other hand, the communion of saints is one of the least explored dimensions of Christian theology, as Elizabeth Johnson has shown in her important recent book (Johnson 1998). Space prevents a treatment of the biblical traditions that lay behind such a tradition, with Hebrews 10–12 being particularly significant. Certainly in Christian writers from the late first and second centuries it is common to find a belief in both a temporary disembodied existence after death that will be concluded by resurrection (see Perham 1980).

One way to model the communion is in relation to our respect for the deceased author of these texts. Here the argument revolves round adopting an 'allocratic' mode of interpretation, that is, one in which the voice of the other (*allos*) prevails (*kratei*), rather than an autocratic one, where the reader disregards the other and produces his or her own (*autos*) meaning from the text. E.D. Hirsch ventures to assert in relation to any text that unless there is 'a powerful overriding value in disregarding an author's intention, we who interpret as a vocation should not disregard it' (Hirsch 1976, p. 90). This applies even though the authors are dead, since although the dead have no rights we are well used to the obligation on us in many contexts to honour their memory. Such an obligation is triggered by virtue of their having been progenitors of the group to which we belong and depend upon for our religious identity and beliefs.

A second way to model the communion is to see those who produced the New Testament as our ancestors in faith. Admittedly, this idea will have a more powerful resonance in some contexts, such as in traditional African and Chinese cultures, than in others. Nevertheless, even in the West the idea has been given a recent stimulus by discoveries in the area of mitochondrial DNA which shows, for example, that all human beings probably descend from a human population in Africa about 100,000 years ago and that virtually all Europeans can trace their ancestry back to one of seven women who lived between 45,000 and 10,000 years ago (see Sykes 2001). My proposal is that the moral obligation we feel in relation to the memory of our own recent dead also exists to honour the memory of our ancestors in faith who first accepted and lived in consequence of the Gospel of Christ, especially the actual persons who composed the letters and other writings which now comprise the New Testament and the actual persons to whom they were first directed, all those, in short, who formed part of the communicative process which resulted in the writings we now possess.

A third way to model the communion is through the processes of collective memory, using notions of collective memory developed by Maurice Halbwachs (see Halbwachs 1950, 1980, 1992). The key idea here is that the groups to which we belong contribute in a major way to our store of memories and thus shape our identity, our sense of who we are. By bringing into remembrance the messages (in their original meaning) of the New Testament authors we enter into this process, itself a form of communion with them. Two important passages in the New Testament which expressly refer to the memorialization of the saints, both concerning women, deserve notice: the Magnificat in Luke 1:46–55 (especially v. 48: 'For behold, henceforth all generations will call me blessed') and Jesus' remark concerning the woman who anoints him at Bethany in the Gospels of Mark and Matthew ('Amen I say to you, wherever the gospel is proclaimed in the whole world, what this woman has done will be spoken of in memory of her'; Mark 14:9; cf. Matt 26:13). While they enrich our present identity, the words of those who speak in and through the New Testament documents come to us not as binding decrees but as revelations of the possibilities of life in Christ lived in the time of the formation of the faith and shaped by the distinctive cultures in which they emerged. By remembering what they have been in the past, we can gain a fresh sense of what we can be, now or in the future.

A fourth mode of communion is by relating to the New Testament authors as 'saints' in the symbolic mode eloquently advocated by Elizabeth Johnson. We are able to understand the living and the dead in Christ along the lines of what she calls the 'companionship model':

> then saints in heaven are not situated *between* believers and Christ in a hierarchy of patronage, but are *with* their companions on earth in one community of grace. Then calling on a saint in heaven to 'pray for us' is one particular, limited, concrete expression of this solidarity in the Spirit, through the ages and across various modes of human existence (Johnson 1998, p. 132).

Yet since in our postmodern condition of spiritual agnosticism, she suggests, we have problems with the idea of communication with the dead, this invocation should be

> read as symbolic rather than literal address, calling the other by name with request for a prayer is a concrete act by which we join our lives for God.... the invocation of any saint, in Rahner's luminous words, 'is always the invocation of *all* saints, i. e., an act by which we take refuge in faith in the all-enfolding community of all the redeemed' (Johnson 1998, p. 135).

The fifth and final mode is that of communion of saints in the fullest sense, one that makes the greatest demands on our faith. The awkwardness Western culture feels in the face of death makes this a difficult subject to broach. For on the one hand we (unlike our parents) are denied exposure to the bodies of our deceased relatives by their speedy removal to mortuaries and on the other we are routinely exposed to cinematic representations of violent death, so that we have become largely inured to the phenomenon in that form. Paralleling our alienation from the naturalness and reality of death has been a growing lack of interest in what, if anything, lies beyond it.[15]

Nevertheless, there has been a belief among Christians from as early as the second century CE to the present (virtually all of them prior to the Reformation and a large number since) that those who died in Christ were still alive and that it was possible to ask them to pray to God on one's behalf. Such a belief clearly presupposes that a part of each person (a 'soul') lives on after death and this in turn depends upon a particular construal of the human person. The most theologically attractive version of this option is 'integrative dualism'. Here the person is seen as a composite of separable 'parts', but is to be identified with the whole, which usually functions as a unity. One of the parts survives death (in a highly attenuated form), but hopes for vindication depend on the resurrection of the whole person.[16] Aquinas was of this view. It is worth noting that another understanding of the human person is attracting growing interest in certain Christian circles. It is known as 'non-reductive materialism'. In this view, there is no spiritual essence or soul separable from the physical being examined by science. Christian hope lies in resurrection. Again, although the constraints of this chapter do not permit a discussion of the subject here, it is worth noting that a major problem with 'non-reductive materialism' is that if nothing survives death and vindication lies only in resurrection it is difficult to avoid the conclusion that what will be raised is not 'me' but a 'replica of me'. Accordingly, integrative dualism offers the richest theological model for communion with those who produced the New Testament writings.

Conclusion

We are left then with a different vision of New Testament theology. While I see these texts as impacting upon and enriching the experience, faith and identity of Christians today, my interest is very different from Gabler's proposal of using historical analysis to isolate from them elements which apply to all times and places. Rather, I am advocating a model of cross-cultural communication where we seek to understand these first-century persons in their distinctive cultural and historical context. Their very embeddedness in so alien a context and their generating very distinctive Christian modes of being in the world and before God are the factors that make our I-You encounters with them potentially so enriching.

In the full version of this project I conclude with an analysis of how Christians today can encounter Paul speaking in Romans in this way.[17] In Romans we have an elaborate and profound attempt to represent the identity of the Christ-movement in a manner dominated by the reconciliation of ethnic difference between Judean and Greek, where the theological truth of the oneness of God who makes righteous all without distinction provides the foundation for the common identity found in Christ. In a world still riven by ethnic conflict this message will continue to resonate for us –not *in spite of* the historical particularities within which Paul launched his message but precisely *through* them. By our intercultural communion with him as a bearer of a heavily contextualized message on bringing Judeans and Greeks together in Christ we are immeasurably enriched in relation to similar phenomena in our time and place, both in understanding and acting upon them.

Notes

1. Note that Stendahl, apparently responding to this view of Lessing, accurately interprets him to be saying 'eternal truth cannot be derived from historical data' (1962, p. 426).
2. Heikki Räisänen (1990) has recently shown some interest in Gabler.
3. I set out details in Chapter 2 of my *New Testament Theology*.
4. 'Dialogue' is here cited in the English translation by Ronald Gregor Smith in Buber 1947, pp. 1–39.
5. The original German edition (*Stern der Erlösung*, begun while Rosenzweig was a soldier in the First World War) appeared in 1921.
6. The phrase 'culture shock' was devised by anthropologist K. Oberg in the 1950s (see Oberg 1960).
7. Boethius, *De duabus naturis* PL 64: 1343C.
8. ET is from the RSV, slightly modified, especially by substituting 'communion' for 'fellowship'.
9. For the text of this lecture, see Derrida 1970 and 1981.
10. On the consequences of the Holocaust for postmodernist history, see the essays in Friedlander 1992. On the Paul de Man controversy, see Hamacher, Hertz and Keenan 1988 and 1989.
11. Cf. Ricoeur 1976, p. 37: 'For me, the world is the ensemble of references opened up by every kind of text . . . that I have read, understood, and loved'.
12. A similar point has been noted by Jeanrond 1991, p. 47.
13. See the persuasive case for this position made by Mitchell 1992.
14. As prominent examples, see the recent works by Warren Brown *et al.* 1998 and N.T. Wright 2003.
15. See the powerful expression of loss of our sense of connection with the dead in Rahner 1971, pp. 6–7.

16. See the discussion in Brown *et al.* 1998.
17. See Chapter 12 of Esler 2005. This argument is, in turn, based on the under-standing of Romans I have advanced in Esler 2003.

References

Austin, J.L., *How to Do Things with Words* (Oxford: Clarendon, 1962).
Barr, James, *Holy Scripture: Canon, Authority, Criticism* (Oxford: Oxford University Press, 1983).
Boers, Hendrikus, *What is New Testament Theology?* (Philadelphia: Fortress Press, 1979).
Brown, Warren, Murphy, Nancey and Malony, H. Newton (eds), *Whatever Happened to the Soul: Scientific and Theological Portraits of Human Nature* (Minneapolis: Fortress Press, 1988).
Buber, Martin, *I and Thou* (ET of *Ich und Dich* [1923] by Ronald Gregor Smith; Edinburgh: T. & T. Clark, 1937).
Buber, Martin, *Between Man and Man* (ET by Ronald Gregor Smith; London: Kegan Paul, 1947).
Buber, Martin, *The Knowledge of Man* (edited with an introductory essay by Maurice Friedman; ET by Maurice Friedman and Ronald Grigor Smith; London: George Allen & Unwin, 1965).
Buber, Martin, *I and Thou* (ET [with a prologue and notes] of *Ich und Dich* [1923] by Walter Kaufmann. Edinburgh: T. & T. Clark, 1970).
Childs, Brevard S., *Biblical Theology in Crisis* (Philadelphia: Westminster, 1970).
Childs, Brevard S., *Introduction to the Old Testament as Scripture* (London: SCM, 1979).
Childs, Brevard S., *New Testament as Canon: An Introduction* (London: SCM, 1984).
Childs, Brevard S., *Old Testament Theology in a Canonical Context* (London: SCM, 1985).
Childs, Brevard S., *Biblical Theology of the Old and New Testaments* (London: SCM, 1992).
Derrida, Jacques, 'Structure, sign and play in the discourse of the human sciences', in R. Macksey and E. Donato (eds), *The Languages of Criticism and the Sciences of Man* (Baltimore: Johns Hopkins University Press, 1970), pp. 247–65 (also in Derrida 1978).
Derrida, Jacques, *Of Grammatology* (Baltimore: Johns Hopkins University Press, 1976).
Derrida, Jacques, *Writing and Difference* (Chicago: University of Chicago Press, 1978).
Derrida, Jacques, *Positions* (London: Athlone, 1981).
Derrida, Jacques, *Dissemination* (Chicago: University of Chicago Press, 1983).
Esler, Philip F., *Conflict and Identity in Romans: The Social Setting of Paul's Letter* (Minneapolis: Fortress Press, 2003).

Esler, Philip F., *New Testament Theology: Communion and Community* (Minneapolis: Fortress Press, 2005).

Evans, Richard J., *In Defence of History* (London: Granta Books, 1997).

Friedländer, Saul (ed.), *Probing the Limits of Postmodernism: Nazism and the "Final Solution"* (Cambridge, MA: Harvard University Press, 1992).

Gabler, Johann Philipp, 'De justo discrimine theologiae biblicae et dogmaticae regundisque recte utriusque finibus' (1787). ET 'On the proper distinction between biblical theology and dogmatic theology and the specific objectives of each'), in Sandys-Wunsch and Eldredge 1980, 134–44.

Gadamer, Hans-Georg, *Truth and Method* (2nd ed.; ET of the second [1965] edition of *Wahrheit und Methode*; London: Sheed and Ward, 1979).

Gudykunst, William B. and Kim, Young Yun, *Communicating with Strangers: An Approach to Intercultural Communication* (4th ed.; Boston: McGraw-Hill, 2003).

Halbwachs, Maurice, *La Mémoire Collective* (Paris: Presses Universitaires de France, 1950).

Halbwachs, Maurice, *The Collective Memory* (Partial ET of the 1950 French original *La Mémoire Collective*; New York: Harper Colophon Books, 1980).

Halbwachs, Maurice, *On Collective Memory. The Heritage of Sociology* (edited, translated with an introduction by Lewis A. Coser; Chicago: University of Chicago Press, 1992). (This is a translation of large parts of *Les cadres sociaux de la mémoire* [1925] and the concluding chapter of *La topographie légendaire des évangiles en terre saint. Étude de mémoire collective* [1941].)

Hamacher, Werner, Hertz, Neil and Keenan, Thomas, *Wartime Journalism, 1939–1943, by Paul de Man* (Lincoln, Nebraska: University of Nebraska Press, 1988).

Hamacher, Werner, Hertz, Neil and Keenan, Thomas, *Responses: On Paul de Man's Wartime Journalism* (Lincoln, Nebraska: University of Nebraska Press, 1989).

Harris, William V., *Ancient Literacy* (Cambridge, MA: Harvard University Press, 1989).

Hezser, Catherine, *Jewish Literacy in Roman Palestine* (Tübingen: Mohr Siebeck, 2001).

Hirsch, E.D., *The Aims of Interpretation* (Chicago: University of Chicago Press, 1976).

Iser, Wolfgang, *The Implied Reader: Patterns of Communication in Prose Fiction from Bunyan to Beckett* (Baltimore: Johns Hopkins University Press, 1974).

Johnson, Elizabeth A., *Friends of God and Prophets: A Feminist Theological Reading of the Communion of Saints* (London: SCM Press, 1998).

Jeanrond, Werner, *Theological Hermeneutics: Development and Significance* (London: SCM Press, 1991).

LaCugna, Catherine, *God For Us: The Trinity and Christian Life* (San Francisco: HarperSanFrancisco, 1992).

Lessing, Gottholt, *Lessing's Theological Writings* (Selections in translation with an introductory essay by Henry Chadwick; Stanford, CA: Stanford University Press, 1957).

Macksey, Richard and Donato, Eugene (eds), *The Languages of Criticism and the Sciences of Man* (Baltimore: Johns Hopkins University Press, 1970).

MacMurray, John, *The Form of the Personal. Vol. 1, The Self as Agent; being the Gifford lectures delivered in the University of Glasgow in 1953* (London: Faber, 1957).

MacMurray, John, *The Form of the Personal. Vol. 2, Persons in Relation; being the Gifford Lectures delivered in the University of Glasgow in 1954* (London: Faber, 1961).

Mitchell, Margaret M., *Paul and the Rhetoric of Reconciliation: An Exegetical Investigation of the Language and Composition of 1 Corinthians* (Louisville, KY: Westminster/John Knox, 1992).

Morgan, Robert, *The Nature of New Testament Theology: The Contribution of William Wrede and Adolf Schlatter* (London: SCM Press, 1973).

Morgan, Robert, 'Gabler's bicentenary', *ExpT* 98 (1986-7), 164-8.

Morgan, Robert, 'The historical Jesus and the theology of the New Testament', in L.D. Hurst and N.T. Wright (eds), *Studies in Christology in Memory of G.B. Caird* (Oxford: Clarendon, 1987), pp. 187-206.

Morgan, Robert, 'Can the critical study of Scripture provide a doctrinal norm?', *JR* 76 (1996), 206-32.

Morgan, Robert, 'The Letters of Paul in the context of a New Testament theology', in J. Capel Anderson (ed.), *Pauline Conversations in Context: Essays in Honor of Calvin Roetzel* (Sheffield: Sheffield Academic Press, 2002), pp. 241-61.

Morgan, Robert, with Barton, John, *Biblical Interpretation* (Oxford: Oxford University Press, 1988).

Morgan, Robert and Pye, Michael, *Ernst Troeltsch: Writings on Theology and Religion* (London: Duckworth, 1977).

Oberg, K., 'Culture shock: adjustment to new cultural environments', *Practical Anthropology* 7 (1960), 177-82.

Ohmann, Richard, 'Speech acts and the definition of literature', *Philosophy and Rhetoric* 4 (1971), 1-19.

Pannenberg, Wolfhart, *Anthropology in Theological Perspective* (ET Edinburgh: T. & T. Clark, 1985).

Perham, Michael, *The Communion of Saints: An Examination of the Place of the Christian Dead in the Belief, Worship, and Calendars of the Church* (London: Alcuin Clubs/SPCK, 1980).

Rahner, Karl, 'Why and how can we venerate the saints?', *Theological Investigations: Volume VIII. Further Theology of the Spiritual Life 2* (ET London and New York: Darton, Longman and Todd/Herder and Herder, 1971), pp. 3-23.

Räisänen, Heikki, *Beyond New Testament Theology: A Story and a Programme* (London and Philadelphia: SCM Press and Trinity Press International, 1990).

Ricoeur, Paul, *Interpretation Theory: Discourse and the Surplus of Meaning* (Fort Worth: Texas Christian University Press, 1976).

Rosenzweig, Franz, *The Star of Redemption* (ET of 2nd ed.; London: Routledge & Kegan Paul, 1971). (German original *Stern der Erlösung* 1921).

Sandys-Wunsch, John and Eldredge, Laurence, 'J.P. Gabler and the distinction between biblical and dogmatic theology: translation, commentary, and discussion of his originality', *SJT* 33 (1980), 133–58.

Schleiermacher, Friedrich, *Hermeneutics: The Handwritten Manuscripts* (edited by Heinz Kimmerle and translated by James Duke and Jack Forsman; Missoula, Montana: Scholars Press, 1977).

Searle, John R., *Speech Acts* (Cambridge: Cambridge University Press, 1969).

Stendahl, Krister, 'Biblical theology, contemporary', *The Interpreter's Dictionary of the Bible* (Nashville: Abingdon Press, 1962), pp. 8–32.

Sykes, Bryan, *The Seven Daughters of Eve* (London: Bantam Press, 2001).

Thiselton, Anthony C., *The Two Horizons: New Testament, Hermeneutics and Philosophical Description with Special Reference to Heidegger, Bultmann, Gadamer, and Wittengenstein* (Grand Rapids, MI: Eerdmans, 1980).

Vanhoozer, Kevin J., *Is There a Meaning in This Text? The Bible, the Reader, and The Morality of Literary Knowledge* (Grand Rapids: Zondervan, 1998).

Watson, Francis (ed.), *The Open Text: New Directions for Biblical Studies* (London: SCM, 1993).

Watson, Francis, *Text, Church and World* (Edinburgh: T. & T. Clark, 1994).

Watson, Francis, *Text and Truth: Redefining Biblical Theology* (Edinburgh: T. & T. Clark, 1997).

Watson, Francis, *Agape, Eros, Gender: Towards a Pauline Sexual Ethic* (Cambridge: Cambridge University Press, 2000).

Wimsatt, William K., *The Verbal Icon* (Lexington: University of Kentucky Press, 1954).

Wimsatt, William K. and Beardsley, Monroe C., 'The intentional fallacy' (1946), reprinted in Wimsatt 1954, 3–18.

Wright, N.T., *The Resurrection of the Son of God* (London: SPCK, 2003).

Zizioulas, John D., 'Human capacity and human incapacity: a theological exploration of personhood', *SJT* 28 (1975), 401–48.

Zizioulas, John D., *Being as Communion: Studies in Personhood and the Church* (London: Darton Longman and Todd, 1985).

Chapter 5

The Nature of New Testament Theology

Morna Hooker, Cambridge

Introduction

What *is* New Testament theology? The answers to this question are so many and so various that they would appear to be largely dependent on the understanding of those who attempt to define it. To the New Testament scholar, however, New Testament theology is primarily an historical discipline. Our difficulties lie chiefly in knowing how to approach it and analyse it.

The editors have helped us here by allocating a particular topic to each contributor. Yet to be asked to focus on Christology can hardly be said to narrow down the field of research, for in a sense *all* New Testament theology is Christology. Our New Testament books focus on the figure of Jesus precisely because he is the new element in the situation. New Testament authors were not concerned to write a systematic 'theology', but were reacting to the life, death and resurrection of Jesus, whom they believed to be God's Messiah or Christ. The evangelists were concerned to write 'the good news about Jesus Christ' (Mark 1:1). The letter writers – above all, Paul – wrote pastoral letters to those who responded to this good news and were endeavouring to live by it. Christological statements often seem to occur in these letters only incidentally, but the fact that they are introduced at all demonstrates how relevant Christology was to Christian life. As we read the New Testament, it would seem that Christ is in the foreground, while God is in the background.

Yet it is precisely because God *is* 'in the background' that we have a New Testament at all. We must beware of being misled by the fact that its books focus so clearly on the figure of Jesus, for the basic assumption that undergirds them all is this: that in Christ, *God* has been at work, revealing his salvation. For Paul, this meant that what took place in and through Jesus was due to 'the grace of God' (Rom 5:15-16) who, 'in Christ, was reconciling the world to himself' (2 Cor 5:19).[1] John expressed the same belief, in statements attributed to Jesus himself: Jesus was sent by God (John 5:30), and the words Jesus speaks and the works he does are the words and works of God, so that once again, God can be said to be 'in him' (John 8:46-7; 10:37-8). Although Mark heads his story 'the good news about Jesus Christ', the origin of this 'good news' is God himself, and was promised by him long before, in holy scripture (Mark 1:2; cf. Rom 1:1-4). The Epistle to the Hebrews opens with the declaration that '*God*, who spoke in time past to our fathers in many different ways through the prophets, has now spoken to us by a son', while the message preached by Peter in the early chapters of Acts speaks of *God* raising Jesus from the dead and making him Lord and Messiah (Acts 2:32, 36), and of the way in which *God* has fulfilled his promises through him (Acts 3:13, 15, 18-21, 26). Above all, it was this conviction that God had raised Jesus from the dead that was crucial for Christian faith.

We see, then, that though Jesus is in the foreground throughout the New Testament, with the result that the vital question for believers came to be the one he is said to have put to his disciples, 'Who do you say that I am?' – a question that dominated the early Church's doctrinal controversies – the more fundamental question was: 'What has *God* done – in Christ?' It was the answers they gave to this question that not only enabled them to answer the question about Jesus' identity, but led to a new understanding of God as the 'Father of our Lord Jesus Christ' (2 Cor 11:31).

In the New Testament, as in the old, the nature of God is revealed by what he does. In Christ, God showed his love for humankind (Rom 5:8); in Christ's death, God revealed his glory, that is his nature (John 12:28); through Christ, men and women came to recognize that God's salvation was meant for all people (Luke 2:30-2), and that the Gentiles were included in God's covenant with Israel. New Testament theology is focused on Christ, not merely because he was at the forefront of their experience, but because it was in pondering the meaning of his life, death and resurrection that Christian believers found themselves reshaping their entire theology. Their experience of Christ affected their understanding of God and his purpose for the world, their grasp of the work of the Holy Spirit and the nature of God's people, together with their hope for the future, and forced them to rethink the way in which God's demand that his people be holy as he himself is holy might be fulfilled.

Dynamic, not Static

Summing up the implications of the opening paragraphs of his *New Testament Theology*, George Caird wrote: 'it follows that there is no such thing as New Testament theology' (1994, p. 4). It might seem an unpropitious beginning! Yet Caird was right, for as we have noted already, our New Testament authors were not attempting to write a 'theology', but were engaged in apologetic and dialogue. The real problem with talking about 'New Testament theology', however, is that it suggests something static and complete, whereas what we have in the New Testament is a number of different people all 'doing theology' in different situations. We do not have an inanimate corpse, labelled 'New Testament theology', laid out on a mortuary slab and waiting for dissection; rather we have a series of photographs of people vigorously engaged in the process of 'theologizing', trying to work out the significance of their faith. To use a biblical metaphor, we have something that was in the process of being written by the living Spirit on hearts of flesh, not a closed system that had been carved on tablets of stone, and was no longer capable of development and change (2 Cor 3:1-6).

In reading the New Testament, we find ourselves conversing with first-century Christians who were attempting to think out the meaning of the life, death and resurrection of Jesus. In the early years that meant primarily trying to understand the 'Christ event' in relation to the Holy Scriptures and to what, as Jews, they already knew about God. We find that their ideas developed as they did so, and as they realized the implications of what they were claiming for Jesus. And as new situations and problems arose, they expressed their faith in new ways. The content of their belief was inextricably bound up with the context in which they lived and worked, so that the form in which they expressed their belief necessarily changed as their circumstances changed, in order to be meaningful. But that context itself changed and shaped their belief.

We see an example of this at the simplest level in the basic response to the question 'Who is Jesus?' The earliest confession of faith seems to have been 'Jesus is the Messiah' (Mark 8:29), a message that would have been understandable in the Jewish context in which it was first proclaimed (Acts 2:36; 5:42). The evangelists all make plain that the 'good news' they are announcing concerns Jesus the Messiah (Matt 1:1, 18; Mark 1:1, 34; Luke 2:11, 26; John 1:18, 41; 20:31). Paul, preaching the Gospel in the Gentile world, could hardly expect his converts to find such a confession meaningful. Although he continually referred to Jesus as *Christos*, the Greek form of *Messiah*, the confession which made most sense in this new context was 'Jesus is Lord' (Rom 10:9; 1 Cor 12:3; Phil 2:11). Questions regarding the origin and background of this term are endlessly asked, and are given widely divergent answers: some argue that it derives from the Old Testament understanding of God as 'Lord' (cf. Rom 10:13); others that it reflects pagan belief in 'gods many and lords many' (1 Cor 8:5); others that it is a direct denial of the claims of Caesar (Phil 2:11; 3:20). We need, however, to distinguish *origin* from *context*. If we are asking who first used the title 'Lord' for Jesus, the answer seems to be 'Jewish Christians', since the phrase *marana tha* (1 Cor 16:22), meaning 'Our Lord, come!' (or 'Our Lord has come'), which Paul apparently expected his readers to understand, is Aramaic. It is clear that Paul's own use of the term was shaped by the Old Testament; he appears, for example, to have been influenced by Ps 110:1 (Rom 8:34; 1 Cor 15:25). Gentiles listening to his message, however, would have heard it against the background of their previous belief in many gods and many lords: now they were assured that there was only *one* Lord (1 Cor 8:6), who had been enthroned by the one true God (Phil 2:9-11). But at some stage it came to have a more particular resonance, because they were living in the Roman Empire, where exclusive claims came to be made in time for Caesar. Whether the cult of the emperor was already a political force in the time of Paul is not clear; what is certain is that the confession 'Jesus is Lord' took on a new significance when it was seen as fundamentally opposed to the confession of Caesar as Lord (*Martyrdom of Polycarp* 8:2).

New terms are needed to express belief as the Gospel moves into different contexts, and as new circumstances arise. The old terms, when they are used in new settings, are interpreted differently. Inevitably, then, the belief itself changes: something is gained, and something is lost. Once again, the term 'Messiah' provides a good example. It is unlikely that the Greek form of the word, 'Christos', had already replaced 'Jesus' as a name by the time that Paul took the Gospel to Gentiles, and he could easily have referred to Jesus by his name, which would have been more comprehensible to his converts. The fact that Paul continued to use the term 'Christ' in an alien context suggests that it was important to his understanding of the Gospel. And indeed, the word 'Messiah' reflects his understanding of God's purpose for the world and the role of Israel in the divine plans, for it was through his 'Messiah' ('anointed one') that God had fulfilled his promises to Israel (Rom 9:5, cf. 1:3): it was because Jesus was the Messiah that, like the kings before him, he could be the representative of his nation, and that God could recreate his people 'in Christ'. In the Gentile world, however, the full significance of the term was easily forgotten, if it was ever understood. It therefore rapidly came to be used

THE NATURE OF NEW TESTAMENT THEOLOGY

merely as another name for Jesus. Yet this change signalled far more than a forgetting of the term's full meaning; when Christians forgot the real significance of the name 'Christ', it became easier for them to cut adrift from Judaism.

If 'Messiah' lost its significance in the Gentile world, another appellation, 'the Son of God', gained new layers of meaning. In Old Testament usage, the phrase was used of Israel herself (Exod 4:22; Hos 11:1) or of Israel's king (2 Sam 7:14; Ps 2:7). The dual use is unsurprising since, as we have noted already, the king was regarded as the representative of his people. As 'son of God', however, the king was also the representative of God. It is hardly surprising, then, if we find both Paul and John speaking of God 'sending' his son (Rom 8:3; Gal 4:4; John 3:17; 1 John 4:9–10, 14; the verbs vary, but the meaning appears to be the same). Because children often resemble their parents, a son of God was naturally understood to have been obedient to his father. In the book of Wisdom, written shortly before the Christian era, the righteous man is described as 'God's son'. Whatever Jesus did as God's son must, then, have been the will of God. This understanding is reflected in the Gospels, and in particular in the passion narratives. In an extraordinary twist to the story in Mark and Matthew, Jesus' executioner watches him die and proclaims him to be 'Son of God'. Both evangelists had earlier linked the disciples' realization that Jesus is 'Son of God' with Jesus' attempts to explain that this meant suffering and death (Matt 16:16, 21; Mark 9:7, 12). For Jesus, sonship meant obedience to the will of God,[2] whom he addresses as 'Abba', meaning 'Father' (Matt 26:39, 42; Mark 14:36). All three Synoptic evangelists describe how Jesus is challenged by the high priest to say whether or not he is 'the Son of God', and how it is his response (however enigmatic) to this final question that leads to his crucifixion (Matt 26:63–5; Mark 14:61–3; Luke 22:70–1). In the Fourth Gospel, the 'hour' of Jesus' death is seen as the purpose of his ministry, and by his death he glorifies God (John 12:27). In dying, Jesus both discloses (17:1–5) and achieves (19:30) God's plan for the world, which is to give eternal life to all who trust in him (3:16).

For Paul, too, the term 'Son of God' expresses Jesus' closeness to his Father. The Gospel of God which Paul proclaims is the Gospel 'about God's Son' (Rom 1:1–3, 9). That Gospel concerns the death and resurrection of his Son (Rom 5:10). Paul speaks not only of God giving up his Son to death (Rom 8:32), but of the Son giving himself up (Gal 2:20): Father and Son are united in purpose, and the Son is obedient to the Father's will. So God 'sent his Son' (Rom 8:3; Gal 4:4); but, as in the Johannine literature, this 'sending' has redemptive purpose: the Son of God shares human weakness, and by identifying himself with men and women, enables them to share his death and resurrection, and so to be 'conformed to his image' (Rom 8:29) and to become 'sons of God', addressing God as 'Abba' (Rom 8:14-15; Gal 4:4-6). In Christ, their future is secure, for the Son of God will come again from heaven (1 Thess 1:10), but though everything will finally be subject to him, the Son himself is subject to God (1 Cor 15:24-8).

Paul's insistence that those who trust in God and in what God has done in Christ share the likeness of God's Son points us back to the Jewish origins of his thought. God had called *Israel* to be his Son; now, 'in Christ' – that is, in the Messiah – Christian believers had inherited the promises made to Abraham, and had been made 'sons of God' (Gal 3:26).[3] This 'sonship' brought them immense privileges, for they were now heirs of God's promises, but it also brought the requirement to obey God: for Paul, however, 'obedience' no longer meant obedience to the Law, but the obedience that sprang from faith, which he termed the 'obedience of faith' (Rom 1:5; 16:26). As an apostle, Paul believed himself to have been called by God to be a role model of the Christian life, since God had been pleased 'to reveal his Son in me' (Gal 2:16);[4] his task was like that of a mother giving birth to children who would be like Christ, their elder brother (Gal 4:19). Those who were truly 'like Christ' were truly human, for they were what God had intended men and women to be – like God himself.

In a pagan world, however, Paul's words would once again have been understood somewhat differently. The term 'Son of God' would have suggested a divine being of some kind, and according to the myths of the ancient world, the sons of the gods were not characterized by obedience to their parents. The notion that the Son of God had been sent would have been interpreted as indicating not so much the purpose of the sender as the descent of a 'heavenly' being into the world. Inevitably, then, new questions began to be asked – e.g. about the Son's pre-existence. As time went by, Paul's language about Jesus as Son of God was understood as spelling out his 'divinity', and the term no longer reminded Christians of their calling, but separated Christ from them. According to the later exegesis of the Church, 'the Son of God' expressed Christ's divinity, while the term 'the Son of man' referred to his humanity. Were those who read New Testament language in this way distorting its meaning, or were they drawing out the implications of its teaching in ways that were appropriate to their own culture? Unfortunately, what tended to happen was that the later interpretation came to be seen as the authoritative and only way of understanding the text, with the result that 'New Testament theology' was not only identified with the theology of a later community, but was itself regarded as though it were set in stone.

The Gospel of/about Jesus

The most fundamental shift of perspective had, of course, taken place even earlier, when the Christian faith was first born. With the death and resurrection of Jesus (to quote Bultmann's famous words), 'the proclaimer became the proclaimed' (1952, p. 33). New Testament scholars agree on very little, but on one thing there is unanimity: what Jesus proclaimed was the Kingdom of God. Yet the message of his followers was clearly centred on Jesus himself. The shift is nicely reflected in the enigmatic opening words of Mark's Gospel: 'The Gospel (Good News) of Jesus Christ'. Mark might perhaps mean the good news proclaimed *by* Jesus, but what he goes on to write is the good news *about* him.

This shift is even clearer, of course, when we turn to the Fourth Gospel. While it is true that the Synoptic tradition reflects the beliefs of the community, the focus of Jesus' teaching in the Synoptic Gospels is the Kingdom of God, not Jesus himself. Jesus speaks only rarely about himself, and when he does, he demands secrecy (Mark 8:27–30 and //s), or refers enigmatically to his approaching suffering and vindication (Mark 8:31–3 and //s). It is only during the 'trial' before the high priest that Jesus is said to have agreed that the terms 'Messiah' and 'Son of God' were appropriate ways of referring to him (Mark 14:61–2 and //s). The evangelists preferred to show their readers how they should interpret the figure of Jesus by their editorial comments and through their arrangement of the material rather than by putting claims into the mouth of Jesus. In John, however, we are dealing with tradition that has been radically modified by Christian belief. There are, to be sure, echoes of sayings and stories found in the Synoptics, but the picture of Jesus presented by John is very different. Instead of implicit Christology, we have explicit claims. Jesus speaks of himself openly as 'the Son' (John 5:20–3 etc.), and acknowledges that he is the Messiah (John 4:25–6; 11:24–5). He makes extraordinary claims for himself in the 'I am' sayings. No longer is Jesus' message about the Kingdom of God: rather, it is about Jesus himself. This is a different kind of apologetic, which spells out clearly the claims of the Christian community about Jesus by placing them in the mouth of Jesus himself. John's concern was to persuade his readers to 'believe that Jesus is the Christ the Son of God, and through believing, might have life in his name' (20:31). But though his method was very different from that of the other evangelists, their purpose was similar, for they, too, were concerned to write 'the good news about Jesus'.

The difference between the message of Jesus and the message about Jesus is not, however, as great as might at first appear, since the message of Jesus himself contained implicit claims. Although Jesus proclaimed the Kingdom of God – or rather the Rule of God – that rule was very closely bound up with his own person, so that in a very real sense it was embodied in him. His message – directed to his own people, the Jews – was a message of good news (Matt 4:23; Mark 1:14; Luke 4:18), for while he demanded repentance (Matt 4:17; Mark 1:15; Luke 5:32), he offered 'release to the captives and recovery of sight to the blind' (Luke 4:18). According to all the Gospels, the salvation he spoke of was experienced by those whom he healed. While there are obvious historical problems surrounding some of the miracle stories, there seems to be a firm tradition that Jesus did possess extraordinary powers of healing, and that what he did made as much impact as what he said. Although it is only in the Fourth Gospel that the miracles are described as 'signs' and that their significance is spelt out, it is clear that the other evangelists, too, see the healing miracles as integral to Jesus' message. All three Synoptic writers spell this out at the beginning of their accounts of Jesus' ministry: Matthew tells us that Jesus travelled through Galilee, 'proclaiming the good news of the kingdom, and curing every disease and every sickness' (Matt 4:23); Mark describes how Jesus taught in the synagogue at Capernaum, amazing everyone with the authority with which he taught and expelled unclean spirits (Mark 1:22, 27); and Luke tells how Jesus read the opening verses of Isaiah 61 in the synagogue at Nazareth, and then declared, 'Today this scripture has been fulfilled in your hearing' (Luke 4:16–21).

The evangelists interpreted the miracles, not as mere 'signs and wonders', but as embodying Jesus' message. It is not surprising if the authority with which he spoke and acted raised questions about the source of his authority (Mark 3:22 and //s; 11:28 and //s). The evangelists provide their answer to this question in their opening paragraphs, and though their methods are very different, their answer is the same: the story of Jesus is the story of how God fulfilled his promises to his people, the story of what God did in and through him. They expect us to read their narratives in the light of this knowledge, while providing reminders from time to time, in words attributed to Jesus, of why he is acting as he does: thus we are told that his exorcisms are the work of the Holy Spirit (Matt 12:28; Mark 3:23–30); that he is sent by God (Matt 15:24; Mark 9:37 and //s; 15:24; Luke 4:18; John *passim*); that he came for a purpose (Mark 10:45; Luke 19:10; John 10:10); and that what happens to him – even his suffering and death – is in accord with God's will (Mark 14:35–6 and //s; Matt 26:56: Mark 14:49; John 12:27–8).

Many of these statements are honed by opposition, and those who raise questions about Jesus' authority in the Gospels are his opponents. The reaction of those who took exception to his teaching was, in effect, to say, 'Who does he think he is?' So we see that the question about Jesus' authority moves easily into the question 'Who, then, is this?' (Mark 4:41). For his followers, it was not enough to say 'he was sent by God'; faith required labels, definitions, confessions, all of which would summarize and express what they believed about him.

The Use of Titles

Much of the discussion of New Testament Christology in the twentieth century centred on the investigation of titles. This was hardly surprising, since terms such as 'Messiah', 'Lord', and 'Son of God' tend to be used in confessions of faith. Yet it is important to remember that these 'titles' are succinct ways of expressing beliefs, shorthand summaries which, as we have seen, convey a range of ideas that differ according to the situation of those who hear them. Indeed, 'Son of God' is primarily an expression of a relationship rather than a title (Ps 2:7; Rom 1:3; John 3:16). There is little in the Synoptic tradition to suggest that Jesus referred to himself as 'Son of God' (Matt 11:25-7//Luke 10:21-2 is the remarkable exception), but there are clear indications that he thought of God as his Father (Mark 14:36 and //s), and could therefore be described by God himself as his Son (Mark 1:11 and //s; 9:7 and //s). 'Messiah' is used in the Old Testament only as an adjective (1 Sam 2:10), not as a title, and once again expresses a relationship to God. Was Jesus perhaps thought of as 'anointed' by God, or by the Spirit of God (Luke 4:18, quoting Isa 61:1), before he was confessed as 'the Messiah'?

The Gospels preserve answers to the question of Jesus' identity that were later considered inadequate: he was addressed as 'teacher' by both friends and enemies (Matt 8:19; Mark 4:38; 12:14, 19; Luke 12:13; John 11:28); he was considered by many to be a prophet (Mark 6:15//Luke 9:8; Mark 8:28 and //s; Luke 24:19; John 4:19), perhaps even *the* prophet spoken of by Moses (Deut 18:15; John 6:14; 7:40). Jesus is said to have spoken of himself in terms of a prophet (Matt 3:57//Mark 6:4; Luke 4:24; 13:33). But is that how he thought of himself? Or did he believe himself to be 'the Messiah'?

The question of the 'messianic self-consciousness of Jesus' dominated a great deal of christological investigation in the twentieth century. The answer was regarded by many scholars as being of great significance for Christian faith. Typical of their approach is this comment, dating from 1945: *'The Church cannot indefinitely continue to believe about Jesus what he did not know to be true about himself.'* (Bowman, 1945, p. 108, italics original). The conviction expressed so forcefully here was diametrically opposed to the position of those such as Rudolf Bultmann, who denied that Jesus thought of himself as Messiah, as Servant, or as Son of man, and considered this unimportant for Christian belief (Bultmann 1952, 26–32). Such titles, it was argued, can tell us only about the beliefs of the early Christians, not those of Jesus himself. Moreover, it would seem that Jesus himself was not as obsessed with his own person as he was later assumed to be. The important question which emerged from this scholarly battle proved to be a rather different one; not 'Did Jesus or did he not think of himself as "the Messiah"?' but rather 'Is there continuity, as well as discontinuity, between the beliefs, words and actions of Jesus and those of the early Church? Did he behave in such a way that his followers felt themselves compelled to speak of him as "Messiah"?'

Undoubtedly the most enigmatic of all the so-called 'messianic titles' applied to Jesus is the one which he himself is said to have used: 'the Son of man'. The Greek phrase ὁ υἱὸς τοῦ ἀνθρώπου – 'the son of the man' – is a literal translation from Aramaic, and must have puzzled Greek-speaking audiences. Unlike all other titles, it was not used by others (with the exception of Acts 7:56), but by Jesus alone. This means that there can be little doubt that Jesus used the phrase. But was he thinking of himself, as the Gospels suggest, or of a future eschatological figure, as has been argued by some twentieth-century scholars (typical of this view is Hahn 1969, pp. 15–67)? Or was the phrase an Aramaic idiom, a modest way of referring to oneself, which was misunderstood by the Greek-speaking Church (as argued by Vermes 1973, pp. 160–91)? A more traditional view understands Jesus to have been referring to himself, but questions whether the phrase should properly be described as a 'title' (Hooker 1979). Rather, as in Dan 7:13, to which many of the Son of man sayings allude, 'the Son of man' is the description of a role. The phrase hints at the role of the man 'Adam', who was created by God to rule under him over the earth (Ps 8:4–8).[5] In particular, it points to the role of Israel, God's people (Dan 7:13; Ps 80:17;[6] 2 Esdras 6:53–9). Although Jesus used the term as a self-designation, it is notable how frequently what is said about 'the Son of man' clearly involves others: the Son of man must suffer, die and be vindicated, but his disciples must be prepared to follow his example (Mark 8:31–8 and //s); the Son of man came to serve, and his disciples must also serve one another (Mark 10:43–5 and //s); when the Son of man comes in glory, his elect will share his triumph (Matt 24:30–1// Mark 13:26–7).

The answers we give to these questions about the origin and use of the phrase 'the Son of man' are important, not only because of the light they throw on Jesus' own understanding of his ministry, but also because of their relevance to the question of the relationship of Jesus' own beliefs to the development of 'New Testament theology'. Is Jesus' *own* theology part of the picture, and how much continuity do we expect between the way Jesus saw his own mission and the way the Church interpreted him? If Jesus used the phrase 'the Son of man' to refer to his own mission, why did the early Church not consider it to be an appropriate way to express their beliefs about him? If he spoke of someone else as 'the Son of man', did the Church radically distort his teaching in identifying him with this figure? If he used the phrase merely as an idiomatic way of saying 'I', is there anything in his teaching to explain why the Church created so many sayings about 'the Son of man'? These last two explanations of the phrase both require that we assume that the early Church misunderstood Jesus' own words and gave them a very different meaning. And neither of them provides us with any insight regarding Jesus' understanding of his own mission. How did he perceive his own role?

Yet the fact that the Gospels all testify to Jesus' use of the term as a way of referring to his mission suggests that there is an important element of continuity here. Jesus clearly used the phrase, and it was sufficiently distinctive and characteristic of him to be remembered. Why was it important to him? Can we find other signs of continuity, not necessarily in the 'title' itself, but in what Jesus is recorded as saying *about* 'the Son of man'? In other words, are these sayings echoed elsewhere in the New Testament? Those who regard the sayings as creations of the Church will, of course, argue that any parallels between the Son of man sayings and the theology of Paul and John merely confirm that the sayings reflect the Church's beliefs. But might those beliefs in fact be founded on what Jesus himself said about 'the Son of man'?

One of the remarkable features of New Testament Christology is the close association between Jesus and the believing community which is assumed to exist by the majority of its authors. The clearest expression of this idea is perhaps to be found in Paul, in his use of the phrase 'in Christ' to describe the believer's relationship to Christ. He spells out that relationship in different ways, describing Christians as joined to Christ – and to each other – by being members of Christ's body (1 Cor 12:12-27; Rom 12:4-5) or by being built into the temple whose foundation is Christ (1 Cor 3:11-17). Such is the close relationship of believers with Christ that they can be said to have been baptized into Christ, and so into his death (Gal 3:27; Rom 6:3), but those who share his death will also share his resurrection (Rom 6:5) – indeed, Christ already lives within them (Gal 2:20).

It would seem that, for Paul, this close relationship is founded on the fact that as *Christos*, that is *Messiah*, Jesus is a representative figure. It is by union with him that Gentiles are made 'the seed of Abraham' (Gal

3:16, 26-9), and it is through him that they share in the promises made to Israel (Rom 9:1-5). What happens to Christians takes place because they are *in* Christ - or it takes place *with* Christ or *through* Christ. It is surely for this reason that Paul rarely uses the name 'Jesus' on its own, preferring to speak of 'Christ', of 'Jesus Christ', or of 'Christ Jesus'.

In the opening paragraph of Romans, Paul tells us that Christ was born 'of the seed of David' (1:3): by birth, then, he was qualified to be 'Messiah'. Elsewhere, Paul speaks of Jesus being born of a Jew (Gal 4:4). Christ's identity with his people is important - as is his identify with the human condition in general (Rom 8:3; 2 Cor 5:21; 8:9). It is necessary for him to be Jewish, in order to represent Israel, just as it is necessary for him to be human, in order to represent humanity. But his Davidic descent is 'according to the flesh'. God, on the other hand, is Spirit, and acts in power: the reason why Christ is able to save his people is that by the resurrection of the dead, God proclaimed him Son of God in power (Rom 1:4). Remarkably, Paul speaks here of the resurrection of the dead in the plural: is he perhaps already hinting at Christ's representative role? In Romans 5, we realize that this representative role is not confined to his relationship with Israel, since now he is compared and contrasted with Adam. Paul's argument here is based on the Jewish understanding of Adam (the name means 'man') as a representative figure, whose sin brings death to all his descendants. In contrast to Adam's disobedience, which brings condemnation to all, we have Christ's obedience, which brings life to all (Rom 5:12-21). Yet Paul insists throughout that though this is effected by Christ's obedience, it is God who is at work, and it is because of his grace that the results of Adam's fall are reversed (5:15-17, 20-1).

In Christ, therefore, we have what is in effect a new creation (2 Cor 5:17; Rom 8:19-25). Christ's resurrection will be shared by believers (6:5), who will be openly revealed to be what *he* is, God's 'sons' (8:19, 29). So, in him, men and women attain to the glory which comes from those who see God face to face (8:30; 2 Cor 3:18), a glory which they lost when Adam sinned (Rom 1:23; 3:23). In terms of what Paul terms the flesh, men and women are like Adam, made from dust and returning to dust; but at the resurrection of the dead they will share the likeness of Christ, who is 'the last Adam' (1 Cor 15:20-27a; 42-9). Christ is thus the model of what men and women should be, the true 'image of God' (2 Cor 6:6), after whom Adam was fashioned (Gen 1:26). Not surprisingly, he fulfils the words of Ps 8:7 about the role of humanity in the world (1 Cor 15:27). We find, then, that when Paul attempts to spell out *how* men and women are affected by Christ's obedient death and resurrection, he uses 'Adam' language, and that the ideas, as well as the language, are reminiscent of the Son of man sayings in the Gospels.

The Fourth Evangelist, too, emphasizes the union between Christ and his followers: they are dependent on him, as are branches on a tree (John 15:1-11). The fact that John speaks of a vine tree is significant, since the vine was a symbol for Israel (Ps. 80: 8, 14, where it is linked with the 'son of man' in v.17). John does not refer to the Son of man here, but at the beginning of this section he has described how Jesus washed his disciples' feet – a dramatic representation of the saying found in Mark 10:45. Since 'servants are not greater than their master' (13:16), the disciples must do the same, but *because* they 'are not greater than their master' (15:20) they, like him, will be persecuted. 'Son of man' Christology underlies passages such as these, even where the term is not used.

In Heb 2:6-7 we have the one clear citation of Ps 8:4ff. in the New Testament. The passage refers to humans, and the author comments that, contrary to the promise in the Psalm, all things are *not* yet subject to them; but, he adds, it *has* been fulfilled in the case of Jesus, who has 'tasted death for everyone'. He is 'the pioneer of their salvation', who sanctifies those who, with him, share the same heavenly Father. Thus Heb 2:5-18 elaborates the idea of Jesus as the Man who fulfils the divine plan and enables others to do so too.

Even though 'the Son of man' is not used as a title, therefore, the ideas linked with it are important. Narrowing Christological investigation down to a consideration of titles is clearly bound to distort our understanding of the way in which our New Testament authors understood Jesus. And if we ask *why* this term was not used as a title for Jesus, then the answer may be partly because Jesus himself had not used it as a title, but rather employed it as a way of describing his mission, and partly because it seemed inadequate for expressing all that the early Church now wanted to express about the status and authority of the one who had, by the resurrection, been made Lord and Christ (Acts 2:36).

The Use of Narrative

Towards the end of the twentieth century, New Testament scholars placed increasing importance on what they termed 'narrative theology', and though Paul's letters do not set out to tell a story, we can see that underlying his theology there is a story about God's purpose for the world he had made. This is most clearly seen in Romans, which speaks of human sin, which has corrupted the world (1:18-32), of God's promises to his people Israel (4; 9:1-5; 11) and the gift of the Law (7), or his redemption of Jew and Gentile alike in Christ (3:21-31), which reversed what had happened through Adam (5:12-21), and of the final, hoped for restoration of all creation (8:18-39; 11:25-36; cf. 1 Cor 15:20-8).

The use of narrative as a way of 'doing theology' is, of course, much clearer in the Gospels. The evangelists' aim is to write 'gospel' – 'good news' – not biography, and in their presentation of Jesus, the so-called 'historical Jesus' is already fused with the 'Christ of faith'. The developing concern of the Christian community with Christological definitions inevitably affected the way in which the evangelists wrote their stories. John, as we have seen, makes his meaning clear by placing Christological claims into the mouth of Jesus. But *all* the evangelists tell their stories in such a way as to spell out the significance of the one whom they believe to be 'Jesus Christ the Son of God' (Mark 1:1).[7] All of them have 'prologues', which spell out the significance of who Jesus is, using Christological terms such as 'Messiah', 'Son of God' and 'Lord' (Matt 1-2; Mark 1:1-13; Luke 1-2; John 1:1-18), and they clearly expect this revelatory material to inform the way in which the stories that follow are read. Although, in the Synoptics, Jesus so rarely speaks about himself, all four evangelists arrange their material in such a way that the reader's attention is focused on him. They use narrative to spell out their under-standing of who Jesus is.

We have a good example of this in Mark's Gospel, in the passage where he describes how Jesus taught the people in parables, beginning with the parable of the Sower, which is introduced and concluded with the injunction to listen (Mark 4:3, 9). The response of the hearers to Jesus' teaching is clearly of vital importance, and the interpretation that follows explains that what they are being asked to respond to is 'the word' (4:14). The word spoken by Jesus concerns the Rule of God, which is at present invisible, but which will be given to those who respond to Jesus' message and enjoy the harvest (4:11, 26, 30). Yet it is clear that for Mark, those who respond to Jesus' message respond to Jesus himself, and that 'the word' is, in effect, the word – the Gospel – about *him*. It is his followers – 'those who were around him, with the Twelve' – who are given the secret of the Kingdom (4:10-11). Moreover, Mark has positioned this group of parables immediately after the story of how opinion concerning Jesus divided the community: on the one hand, the scribes who accused him of working under the control of Satan, together with the members of his own family who believed that he was out of his mind, had clearly *rejected* the word; on the other, those who were around him and who did God's will had *received* it. Immediately *after* the parable collection, we have the story of Jesus stilling the storm, which leads the disciples to ask 'Who then is this?' This is the question with which Mark, by his arrangement of the material, continually confronts his readers, leaving them to supply the answer. At the same time, he reminds them that the truth is hidden from those who have no eyes to see it (4:12).

It is the failure of Jesus' own people to perceive the truth that is stressed by Matthew in *his* arrangement of the tradition, since he not only introduces the parables with the story of the refusal of Jesus' own family to acknowledge his authority, but concludes them with an account of how he came to his home town and was rejected there. Though Jesus speaks of a prophet being rejected in his own country, the implication of this story is that he is far greater than any prophet. For Matthew, too, the parables confront the reader with a choice about how they respond to Jesus himself.

All our evangelists have chosen to shape their narratives in ways that help to demonstrate the truth of the good news about Jesus the Messiah. Matthew, for example, includes far more teaching than Mark, and we might assume at first sight that his aim is simply to preserve the teaching of Jesus. But when we look at the way in which he introduces the first block of teaching material in chapters 5-7, we realize that he is deliberately present-ing Jesus as greater than Moses (Matt 5:1, 17, 21-2 etc.). The 'Sermon' ends by pointing to the choice which faces all who hear Jesus' words: will they act on them or ignore them? The decision they take is crucial (7:24-7).

Luke, also, arranges material in such a way as to point to the truth of Jesus' identity. In 4:16-21, Jesus announces that in him, the words in Isaiah 61 have been fulfilled: he is bringing good news to the poor, the recovery of sight to the blind (4:18). He then records various stories of healings and his version of the Sermon (6:17-49): Jesus is seen proclaim-ing good news to the poor (6:20) and healing the sick. When John's dis-ciples come to enquire whether he is 'the one who is to come' (7:19), Jesus makes no direct reply, but tells them to report to John what they have seen and heard: 'the blind receive their sight, the lame walk, the lepers are cleansed, the deaf hear, the dead are raised, the poor have good news brought to them' (7:22). Luke leaves us, his readers, in no doubt as to the correct answer to the question.

John's method is to arrange his material around the great Jewish feasts (John 2:13; 5:1; 6:4; 10:22; 11:55); each of his 'signs' is linked with a dis-course which brings out its meaning, and the themes of the discourse are appropriate to the festival with which it is associated (2:1-11 and 13-22 with 3:1-21 and 4:1-26; 4:46-54 and 5:2-9 with 5:19-47; 6:1-14 and 16-21 with 6:25-59; 9:1-12 with 8:12-59 and 9:13-41; 11:1-53 with 10:1-39. Jesus teaches openly about his relationship with the Father (10:22-38), and about his coming death and glorification (12:23-33).

It is clear that all our evangelists consider the truth about Jesus to be plain to those with eyes to see and ears to hear. Although Jesus may not make explicit claims for himself, his words and actions are evidence enough for those who believe. Others, moreover, whether intentionally or not, declare the truth. This often leads to irony, as in the Markan passion narrative. It is the high priest who speaks of Jesus as 'the Messiah, the Son of the Blessed One' (14:61), Pilate - together with the Roman soldiers - who declares him to be 'the King of the Jews' (15:9, 18, 26), and his executioner who declares him to be 'Son of God' (15:39). The evangelist thus uses the story of Jesus' death to reveal the truth about him, and also stresses the fact that obedience, suffering and death are all integral to Jesus' Messiahship. It is only because he refuses to save himself that he is able to save others (15:30-1). It is only because he does not come down from the cross that he is the true Messiah and King of Israel (15:32).

The Origins of New Testament Christology

In using narrative, our New Testament writers were following in the tradition of the Old Testament, where God consistently reveals himself by what he does - in creation, in history, and in what is said and done by his prophets. When Moses catches a glimpse of God's glory on Sinai, this proves to be a revelation of God's steadfast love for his people (Exod 33:18-23; 34:4-7). And when the Son reveals the glory of God, he reveals, by his death, God's love for the world (John 3:16; 12:23-8; 13:31-2). If biblical theology is about how God reveals himself to men and women, then Christology must be about how he is revealed in Christ. It is essentially about the way in which God acts.

In spite of the fact that the New Testament consists of documents written by different authors in very different circumstances, so that they describe who and what Jesus is and does in such different ways, there is an underlying consistency in their Christology: they present Jesus as the one who is sent by God, and who acts with the authority of God - the one through whom God is working. They give him the name of God himself - 'Lord' (Rom 10:9; Phil 2:11; John 20:28). At the same time, they insist that Jesus is obedient to his Father (Rom 5:19; Phil 2:8; John 5:30), and that he is our representative, the model of what men and women should be. Behind their very different presentations of Jesus there lies the conviction that God created men and women in his likeness, intending them to be 'sons of God'; that Israel was called to fulfil this purpose; and that now, in Christ, it is possible for men and women of all races to become God's children by trusting in Christ, who is the pattern of what men and women should be, since he is 'the image of God' himself.

One of the formative elements in the development of New Testament Christology appears to have been the discussion of Christ's relation to the Law. On Sinai, God had revealed his will in the Law; it was impossible that God could have made a mistake, or changed his mind. But Jewish Christians found themselves increasingly isolated from their fellow Jews, while the influx of Gentile Christians into the Church raised questions as to whether or not the Law was binding upon them. Different answers were given, according to the situation, but underlying them all is the conviction that Jesus is the fulfilment of the Law: that is, that through him, the *intention* of the Law is fulfilled. For Matthew, in conflict with fellow Jews, this seems to mean continuing to obey the Law, but going beyond its literal demands (Matthew 5). For the Fourth Evangelist, it seems to imply that now that God has spoken fully in Christ, the Law is no longer necessary (1:17-18). The author of Hebrews makes a similar point (Heb 1:1-4); for him, there is no need for the sacrifices set out in the Law, since Christ, our high priest has offered a sacrifice that requires no repetition (Heb 9-10). For Paul, too, Christ seems to have replaced the Law: the Law points forward to him (Rom 10:8), but what the Law promised has now been achieved by God through Christ (Rom 8:3). Instead of living by the Law, Christians now live by 'the law of Christ' (Gal 6:2).

It is hardly surprising, then, that we find signs of the influence of the so-called 'Wisdom Christology' in at least three of our New Testament books: John 1:1-18, Col. 1:15-20 and Heb. 1:1-4; cf. also Matt 11:19, 25-30). All seem to be drawing on the interpretation of the Law found in the Wisdom literature. The Law is identified with God's word, and since God created the world by his word (Gen 1:1-3), this word is personified as Wisdom, God's master-workman (Prov 8:22-35; Wisd 7:22-6; 9:1-2).

It is surely significant that it is in these passages, which attempt to spell out how God reveals himself through Christ, that we find some of the most exalted language about Christ himself. Although the concerns that shaped the theology of our New Testament authors were very different from those that led the Fathers of the Church to produce the creeds, we can understand how, building on what the New Testament says about him, they would wish to define him in terms both of 'God' and of 'Man'.

Notes

1. The translation of this verse is notoriously difficult: does Paul mean that 'God was in Christ, reconciling the world to himself', or that 'in Christ, God was reconciling the world to himself'? Whichever way we translate these words,

it is clear that the reconciliation that took place through Christ's death and resurrection was understood by Paul to be the work of God.

2. Many modern translations obscure Paul's logic, by choosing to use politically correct language and substituting 'children' for 'sons'; Paul's point, however, is that men and women all become like him; for him, the term 'sons' was inclusive, not exclusive.

3. Once again, Paul's term is meant to include women as well as men, a point he specifically spells out in v. 28, where he makes it clear that race, gender and status are all irrelevant 'in Christ'. His insistence that women had equal standing with men in the new people of God is remarkable, in view of the cultural assumptions of his day.

4. The phrase is usually translated 'to me', but the normal meaning of the Greek preposition used by Paul here is 'in'; For Paul, the revelation on the Damascus Road was far more than an apparition; it was a call to reveal God to the Gentiles; cf. Acts 9:15; 22:15; 26:16-18.

5. Once again, modern translations which opt for political correctness disguise the significance of the Hebrew, which speaks in v. 4 of 'man' and of 'son of man'.

6. As in Ps 8:4, 'man' and 'son of man' are used in parallel.

7. The words 'the Son of God' may or may not belong to the original text of 1:1, but certainly represent Mark's views; cf. 1:9; 9:11; 15:39.

References

Bowman, J.W., *The Intention of Jesus* (London: SCM, 1945).

Bultmann, Rudolf, *Theologie des Neuen Testaments* (2 vols; Tübingen: Mohr Siebeck, 1948-53). ET *Theology of the New Testament* (2 vols; New York: Scribner, 1951-55). References are to the English version, vol. 1.

Caird, G.B., *New Testament Theology* (ed. L.D. Hurst; Oxford: Clarendon, 1994).

Hahn, F., *The Titles of Jesus in Christology* (ET London: Lutterworth, 1969).

Hooker, M.D., Is the Son of Man problem really insoluble?', in Ernest Best and R. McL. Wilson (eds), *Text and Interpretation, Studies in the New Testament presented to Matthew Black* (Cambridge: Cambridge University Press, 1979), pp. 155-68.

Vermes, Geza, *Jesus the Jew* (London: Collins, 1973).

Chapter 6

Does a Theology of the Canonical Gospels Make Sense?

Luke Timothy Johnson, Atlanta

I begin this essay in honor of Robert Morgan in a mood of mild resistance and of modest experimentation. I don't resist joining in the celebration of Robert Morgan, who has done so much to chart the progress and possibilities of biblical theology. Like others who have benefited from his great good will, generosity and spirit of collegiality, I gladly celebrate his life and work. But I resist the topic which has been assigned to me, as these things are, by the editors of this volume. And here is where the mood of modest experimentation comes to my assistance. I have cast my topic in the form of a question, and have asked whether the topic even makes sense. I hope to show that it might, but my expectations are low, as yours should be as well: the title of the chapter indicates my tentative approach to the assigned topic, 'the theology of the canonical Gospels'.

My mood of resistance is mild, for I have grown fond of taking on odd titles and topics as a way of stretching the mind a bit. I am encouraged in this by remembering how much of Greek philosophy grew, like a mighty forest from small seeds, from a handful of pithy statements. So although I have real difficulties generally with 'biblical theology' to which I will turn immediately, I am fascinated by the possibility of thinking well about the problems and possibilities of connecting 'canonical Gospels' with 'theology' and, in particularly, asking whether the preposition 'of' is the best way to link them.

The Problems with Biblical Theology

Although I have sometimes been described as a 'biblical theologian', especially by those who do not think me much of a historian or linguist, my discomfort with the enterprise called biblical theology has persisted over many years. I do not think that I have encouraged the designation 'theologian' by attaching that word to the title of any of my books. The reason is partly autobiographical. Entering professional biblical scholarship from the side of Benedictine monasticism, I had from the start a difficult time putting together the sort of thinking with and on and about the texts of Scripture that happened in the Divine Office and in Lectio Divina – which surely was a sort of theological thinking – and the sort of thing I read in books called 'New Testament theology' (and, for the rest of this chapter, I will confine myself to the New Testament (NT) rather than to the Bible as a whole).

For a long time, I thought that the problem lay mainly in the historical character of the discipline and in the necessary selectivity involved in trying to construct a unitary 'theology of the New Testament'. I found that abstraction was impossible to avoid, and that the voices of NT witnesses were invariably suppressed or distorted in service of some unitary principle or other. In my own work, I tried to resist such pressure toward unification and abstraction by focusing on the diverse 'theological voices' of the canon, seeking ways of hearing those voices in all their plurality. But I have come to acknowledge that such efforts, even when carried out with considerable literary sensitivity and theological imagination, do not entirely avoid the same problem of abstraction. There is still a large gap between 'reading Luke's Gospel theologically' and 'the theology of Luke'. The process of isolating and describing even salient features of a narrative is a stage removed from engaging a narrative. Similarly, when trying to hear the 'theological voice' of a Pauline letter, identifying and discussing the elements of Paul's argument requires a step of abstraction from actually following that argument. Even the most adequate analysis necessarily selects what fits the analysis, and thereby also necessarily excludes what does not fit it. The issue is not whether hearing Luke-Acts as radical prophecy is superior to hearing it as ecclesiastical propaganda, or whether reading Romans as a fund-raising letter is superior to reading it as an attack on works-righteousness. The issue is, rather, that making one or the other case means stressing some evidence and diminishing other evidence, simply because it is required to make any 'reading' at all.

Slowly, I have come to realize a more fundamental reason why books called 'theology of the New Testament' seem to have so little to do with theology or the New Testament, and why they do not give rise to theological thinking with and about the writings of the New Testament, why, in fact, they do not give rise to a vigorous theological conversation so much as they seem to close a conversation, and that is because they are books. They are books, moreover, written by scholars for other scholars (whatever their protests to the contrary) and therefore bristling with learning. This points us to the larger problem of thinking theologically about Scripture, which has to do with the mode and social location of such thinking.

The writing of books requires fixed choices that, once made, remain fixed. When New Testament theology is done in the form of books, it is necessary to be more highly selective in subject and source, more definite in conclusion, than if one were speaking with others *viva voce* about the meaning and implications of the New Testament writings. The writing of books demands and reinforces the problems inherent in the doing of New Testament theology: it remains a description of the past, it exists at the level of abstraction, and it stays fixed – at least until a future edition! That New Testament theology appears in the form of books, in turn, reminds us that this odd subdiscipline of New Testament studies has existed for its entire history, and ever increasingly, within the social context of the academy rather than of the church. Scholars may say that they are writing for the church, but the level of their prose, the character of their imagined readers, and the weight of their footnotes, argue that they are writing primarily for academic colleagues. I do not mean to suggest that this shift in social location and mode of discourse is entirely unfortunate or has not led to some interesting and occasionally even important insights. I simply mean to propose that the activity of writing books within the academy – even if their subject is called theology – should not be considered either inevitable or ideal.

It is in fact possible to think about theology in quite another way. We can think of theology in terms of a living conversation within the church, a conversation that arises out of and is directed to the practices of faith: liturgy, prayer, social action, discernment and decision making. Within such conversation, the New Testament plays a role that is far more flexible and vital, far more dialogical – not only between the texts and the faithful but also between the faithful themselves on the basis of the texts – and far more open and corrigible, than is possible within the static universe of publications. Those who are expert in Scripture and also committed to the shared practices of faith can probably best serve theology within the church, not by writing books called the theology of the New Testament, but by enabling and participating in the practices and joining in the conversation, *viva voce* and vulnerable, together with other, less learned but perhaps holier, fellow believers.

Set against this second way of imagining the use of the New Testament in the church's theological conversation, the assigned topic for the present chapter, 'the theology of the canonical Gospels,' would seem to represent everything that is wrong about the standard academic approach to biblical theology. What could be more static, abstract and artificial, than defining *the* theology of four such disparate literary narratives? Even if it were possible to find their common characteristics, could we then suppose what was common to them was what was most important in each? What would we necessarily leave out in the effort to find what could be said about them together? And even if we were successful in achieving a 'good' summary, what purpose would it serve? What value for the church's conversation about its life would such an exercise have?

The Heuristic Value of Canonical Clusters

I suspect that there is some real value in playing with clusters of canonical compositions if such clusters are temporary, tentative and heuristic. By temporary, I mean that we gather the compositions together only for a time before letting them return to their respective individual status as discrete witnesses. Otherwise, the clustering has the effect of diminishing the voice of each composition in favour of an overall apprehension that does not correspond to any of the compositions while simultaneously blocking a clear view of each composition's character. The classic example is the cluster commonly called 'the Pastoral letters'. So fixed and permanent has this cluster become that it is almost impossible to find a clean reading of any one of Paul's letters to his delegates Titus and Timothy. Closely linked to temporary is tentative: the clustering should retain an open and experimental character; the characterization must not become so fixed and final as to preclude other combinations being put into play. Such tentativeness is connected, in turn, to the purpose of the clustering, which is heuristic: what can such temporary clusters of canonical texts enable us to see that we might not otherwise notice, if we read them separately? The effort will have been worthwhile only if it gives us deeper insight into elements that are truly present in each composition, but whose presence may have gone unnoticed or under-appreciated if they had not been brought together in this fashion.

Such clustering of compositions can, in short, enable us to set up something of a conversation among the New Testament witnesses through a process of comparison and contrast, and this conversation can enable us better to appreciate both what they have in common and how they differ. By seeing them together, it is sometimes possible to see each of them more clearly. The benefit is obvious in the case of Paul's letters, which fall into natural groups (1 and 2 Thessalonians, 1 and 2 Corinthians, Galatians and Romans, Colossians and Ephesians). A close comparison of Romans 4 and Galatians 3 can lead to a deeper appreciation of the distinctiveness of the argument concerning Abraham in the respective chapters. We learn from this that there is more to be learned when the compositions are close enough to enable meaningful comparison, yet distinct enough to also enable contrast. More venturesome temporary and tentative clusters among the Pauline letters could yield considerable benefit. Much could be learned, for example, if 1 Timothy, 2 Timothy and Titus were not always read together, but put individually in conversation with other Pauline letters. A comparison between 1 Timothy and 1 Corinthians reveals a striking similarity of situation and issue in the two compositions, even as it also shows disparate modes of response. Similarly, 2 Timothy appears in a new light when we observe how not only its setting but also its mode of argumentation, closely resembles that in Philippians. The challenge in such exercises remains that of characterizing without caricature, of discerning elements of genuine commonality that are also essential to the respective compositions, without suppressing the evidence that does not fit.

The Canonical Gospels: Two Exercises in Comparison

In the case of the canonical Gospels, we are able to get a sense of what 'theology' might be associated with them as a group by means of a double comparison, the first between the Synoptics and John, and the second, between all four canonical Gospels and selected apocryphal Gospels. The first comparison is helped by the fact that, despite their many significant differences that enable them to be truly distinct witnesses, the literary interdependence among the Synoptics gives them a sufficiently stable shared profile to allow a genuine comparison to John. I agree with the majority of scholars who conclude that John has no direct literary contact with the Matthew, Mark or Luke, although the Fourth Gospel clearly shares some common traditions with the Synoptics.

The Synoptics and John in comparison

The differences between John and the Synoptics are obvious and for this exercise, require only a quick reminder. The length of Jesus' ministry differs: it is one year in the Synoptics and three years in John. The place of Jesus' ministry is distinct: in the Synoptics, it centres in Galilee, in John, Jesus works mainly in Judaea, with short trips to Galilee. The placement of events differs: in John, the cleansing of the temple occurs at the start of Jesus' ministry rather than at the end; in John, Jesus' eucharistic words occur after the feeding of the multitude, not at the last supper. Even the date of Jesus' death is different: in the Synoptics, it takes place on Passover, in John on the day of preparation for the Passover. The roles played by disciples differ: in the Synoptics, Peter is the chief spokesperson; in John, Peter retains that role, but important speaking parts are given as well to Nathaniel, Thomas, Philip, and especially 'the disciple whom Jesus loved'.

Far more intriguing are the ways in which the characteristic deeds and words of Jesus are dissimilar. In the Synoptics, Jesus' words often take the form of short aphorisms, or the punch-lines of *chreiai*, in which the objections of interlocutors are quickly demolished by an authoritative pronouncement. His longer discourses, like the Sermon on the Mount (or Plain) seem clearly cobbled together by the evangelists out of such shorter (and originally free-floating) *logia*. Most of all, Jesus in the Synoptic Gospels speaks in parables; his remarkable narrative analogies subvert reader expectations and awaken insight. In John's Gospel, by contrast, Jesus tells no parables; his few *paroimiai* in that Gospel do not at all resemble the parables of the synoptic tradition.

Jesus' characteristic speech in the Fourth Gospel, moreover, is quite unlike the patterns we find in Matthew, Mark or Luke. Here, Jesus confronts opponents, it is true, but he does not crush them with a single saying. The controversies instead go on and on, stretching in one case across several chapters (John 7–10). And instead of speaking discourses that are obviously constructed by the evangelist out of smaller units, Jesus in John's Gospel moves from controversies into long, self-revealing monologues, justifying the report of the temple police who had been sent to spy on him, 'no one has ever spoken like this!' (John 7:46). Unlike the pattern of speech in the Synoptics, in which Jesus addresses by turns the crowds, his opponents and his disciples – providing the last group positive instructions on power and prayer and possessions – John's Jesus gives no teaching to his disciples until the last supper, and then it is by way of answering their questions, before elaborating his final and most solemn monologue.

Finally, we note how different Jesus' characteristic actions are in John and in the Synoptics. For Mark, and to a lesser sense also Matthew and Luke, Jesus' exorcisms serve as the prime demonstration that the rule of God has come upon humans. Remarkably, John has no exorcisms at all. John reports a small selection of healings and a resuscitation, which, although transmuted, clearly resemble versions in the Synoptic account. John also shares the sequence of the 'nature wonders' found in the Synoptics: the multiplication of the loaves and the walking on the water. And John adds still another miracle of the same sort, the changing of water into wine. What distinguishes all these wonders in John, to be sure, is that they are designated as 'signs' that reveal Jesus as the bearer of God's glory.

So great are these dissimilarities that we cannot link the four canonical Gospels at the obvious level of plot line, sayings or deeds. It is for this reason, even more than its supposedly more 'dogmatic' character, that the quest for the historical Jesus began by dismissing John from consideration, and continues to disregard John's witness to the humanity of Jesus. But there are ways in which we can speak of theological perceptions that join the four Gospels that exist at a deeper and more implicit level.

First, all four Gospels are realistic narratives. By this, I do not mean that they are lacking the miraculous, but that their stories take place in real time and space, with characters who interact with each other in specific places and in a genuine temporal sequence. Characters are born, live and die, including Jesus, who is born in a specific place of specific parents, has brothers, and dies violently by a specific means in a specific city. The theological significance of this is fairly obvious: that divine revelation takes place through bodies rather than apart from bodies not only affirms the worth of bodies, but also of time, since time is simply the measure of bodies in motion. As realistic narratives set in a specific time and place, moreover, all four Gospels implicitly affirm the compatibility of God's self-disclosure and real human existence within history.

Second, all four Gospels have specific historical roots in first-century Palestine. Despite differences in locating specific events, the canonical Gospels share the placement of their stories in the verifiable circumstances of Roman rule, Hellenistic culture, and above all, the complex Judaism of Galilee and Judaea in the time of Pontius Pilate. One of the most remarkable aspects of the extensive archaeological discoveries of the past century, in fact, is that no important aspect of the canonical Gospels' report concerning those historical circumstances has been disconfirmed, and every important aspect concerning Judaism in that place has been confirmed. So profound and pervasive is this grounding in first-century Palestinian Judaism – and so surprising, given the circumstances of the development of the Gospel tradition – that the Jesus of the canonical Gospels is literally unimaginable outside that world.

Third, all four Gospels explicitly connect the story of Jesus to that of Israel, using the texts and symbols of Torah to express the identity and role of Jesus. They do this differently; the distance between Matthew's formula-citation of Scripture, and John's subtle appropriation of the imagery associated with Jewish feasts is real. Yet for both – as also for Mark and Luke – Jesus is to be understood within the framework of Torah, and, in turn, Torah is to be understood as pointing to Jesus. Indeed, John and Matthew are perhaps closest in this, that one imagines Jesus as the Word made flesh, and the other images Jesus as Torah made human. The intertextual links between the Jewish Scripture and the canonical Gospels are so intricate and extensive that the story of Jesus appears overwhelmingly as the continuation of the story of Israel told in Torah.

Fourth, all the canonical Gospels emphasize the way humans respond to Jesus. Despite the insignificant differences in terminology, the canonical Gospels all show a human drama of challenge and decision. Other characters beside Jesus matter, and they do more than pose questions to him. They enter into genuine relationships with Jesus, whether of opposition, or friendship, or discipleship. The Gospels thereby support the perception of humans as capable of making such choices. They are free to decide for or against the revelation of God in Christ. Not least among the many surprising elements in the Gospels is the amount of space given to the rejection of the message and the messenger.

Fifth, all the canonical Gospels emphasize the passion of Jesus. The dominant position of the passion is most obvious in Mark, to be sure. But the attention to the suffering and death of Jesus is not less in the other three canonical Gospels; it is simply that in them the attention to Jesus' ministry is greater. Like Mark, Matthew and Luke each anticipate the actual account of Jesus' passion by formal prophecies made by Jesus, which has the effect of the end of the narrative overshadowing everything that precedes it. John also, with his distinctive language about the hour and glorification of Jesus, creates a sense, early in his narrative, that everything before Jesus' passion and death is a prelude to the main event. The portrayal of Jesus as a suffering Messiah, executed under Roman authority by crucifixion, is not only found in all four Gospels, it is the part of the story on which they most agree. If we add this emphasis on suffering to the previously noted traits of body, time, space, historical location, immersion in Torah, and the human interaction of subsidiary characters, we are stating in more detail that the four canonical Gospels are realistic narratives. But we are also observing that everything asserted about God's revelation in these Gospels involves the physical world.

Sixth, the canonical Gospels share an understanding of the resurrection of Jesus that is continuous with his human existence and sustaining of the relationships formed in his human ministry. In one fashion or another, the appearance of the risen Jesus to his disciples serves to empower them to continue his mission through witnessing to him. The resurrection does not, in these Gospels, become the occasion for the revelation of new and secret truths about Jesus or the cosmos. The modest predictions in John 21 concerning Peter and the Beloved Disciple are the partial and illuminating exception: they concern the mortal destiny of the disciples. In Luke, the resurrection revelation of Jesus concerns the way properly to understand his human existence in light of Scripture.

Seventh, the canonical Gospels, despite their many differences concerning the forms of Jesus' words or his precise actions, agree in their portrayal of Jesus as a human sent from God for the sake of other humans, and who speaks and acts as God's representative, even as he is also radically obedient to God. The nuances of this portrayal are, to be sure, what most distinguish each individual Gospel, so this level of agreement is broad and non-specific. Certainly, John's Gospel elevates the perception of Jesus as the very revelation of God. But at the same time, John places no less stress on Jesus doing and speaking only what he receives from the father. Likewise, Luke's Gospel portrays Jesus in perhaps the most 'life-like' terms, crafting his story in terms most like Hellenistic biographies. Yet Luke also regards Jesus as God's 'son' in a manner distinct from other characters. Another common feature of the canonical Gospels as realistic narratives is that their Jesus has a real human character (*ethos*), which is recognizable in each of the four portrayals despite the distinct rendering of Jesus by the respective evangelists. In all four Gospels, Jesus is first someone totally defined by radical obedience to God. He is motivated not by human ambition or human respect. He seeks to please only God. But equally, Jesus in all four Gospels is the one who shows that obedience to God by giving of himself in service to others. His lack of self-seeking is expressed in his seeking the good of those around him. His obedience to God is articulated by his self-donative pattern of life. His death, in all four Gospels, is at once the supreme expression of his obedient faith in God and his love for others.

Eighth, in all the canonical Gospels, God is at once the father of Jesus and the God of Israel. Stated negatively, the canonical Gospels drive no wedge between the God of Jesus and the God of creation. One of the corollaries of these Gospels' deep enmeshment in the world of Torah is that readers perceive Jesus' 'father' to be continuous with the creating, revealing, judging and saving God of whom the law and prophets spoke. This, perception, to be sure, is entirely consistent with the character of the Gospels as realistic narratives in which bodies, time and history, not to mention human freedom, are valorized.

Ninth, in the canonical Gospels, God's final triumph is still in the future. This note is struck most emphatically in the Synoptic tradition, to be sure, with its explicit future eschatology stated by Jesus himself, and its vision of the coming of the Son of Man on the clouds of heaven. And John's Gospel certainly shifts the emphasis to a 'realized eschatology' in the ministry of Jesus: already in his coming there is judgement in the world. But even in John, there is the clear statement of a future resurrection and judgement, and the disciples are told that the future paraclete has a distinctive work to accomplish, and that they also will need to endure tribulations.

Tenth, despite remarkably different shadings in their portraits of the disciples as characters in the narrative, the canonical Gospels agree that discipleship means following in the path of radical obedience to God and service to others demonstrated by Jesus. The distinctive portraits of the disciples must be acknowledged: in Mark, they are stupid and faithless; in Matthew, they are faithless but intelligent; in Luke, they are the prophets-in-training who will carry on Jesus' prophetic programme; in John, they are the friends who will experience the hatred of the world as Jesus has. Precisely these differences in characterization – fitted to the purposes of the respective evangelists – makes more impressive the fundamental agreement on the character (*ethos*) of the disciple. In John as in the Synoptics, we find no trace of a triumphalistic understanding of discipleship, which would position Jesus' followers above others, or ensure their worldly success and safety. Just the opposite: their radical obedience to God is to lead in them, as it did in Jesus, to the service of others. And this service of others involves a certain way of using power and possessions, both supremely worldly realities. Discipleship in the canonical Gospels is not, in short, a matter of intelligence or understanding, but a matter of moral disposition.

These 10 points of commonality are all the more impressive because of the manifest diversity of the four Gospels in terms of specific literary structuring, portrayal of Jesus, use of Torah, depiction of the disciples and opponents, understanding of the end-time. They are also the more impressive because John is not in a literary relationship with the Synoptics, but in all these points, represents a genuinely independent theological voice.

The next question that must arise concerns the distinctiveness of this cluster of compositions and cluster of theological perceptions that they share despite their surface differences. It might be fruitful at this point to enter into a comparison with non-Gospel canonical writings (Paul's letters, for example), but the process of comparison would be complicated by the simple fact that the other New Testament writings have such an obviously different literary character. The more interesting and illuminating approach might be to compare these canonical witnesses to other compositions from early Christianity that are designated in one manner or another as 'Gospels'. Such comparison might enable us to discern whether what is shared by the canonical Gospels is also essential in the canonical Gospels, or whether much of what they share is simply consequent on writing a Gospel rather than a letter.

Canonical and apocryphal Gospels in comparison

There are many apocryphal Gospels from early Christianity that we cannot adequately compare to the canonical Gospels because they are fragmentary or because they witness to only one element of the story found in the canonical Gospels. It would be wonderful, for example, if we had complete versions of the so-called 'Jewish-Christian' Gospels, such as the *Gospel of the Hebrews* or the *Gospel of the Ebionites*, but we do not; we have only a handful of fragments. Similarly, if the *Gospel of Peter* were extant in more than its present truncated form, it could provide a more useful comparison to the canonical versions. For different reasons, the infancy Gospels of James, Thomas and Pseudo-Matthew offer slender basis for comparison. Their theological tendencies are not obscure, they are right on the surface. But their restriction to the birth and infancy gives them a distinctive character that is difficult to bring into conversation with any portion of the canonical tradition apart from the infancy accounts in Matthew and Luke. The same difficulties apply to the Gospels that we term Gnostic as well, since, with some exceptions, they tend to focus on post-resurrection revelations rather than on the pre-resurrection ministry. In the comparison that follows, therefore, I will use the shared characteristics that I have discerned in the canonical Gospels, and ask whether and in what manner, the same characteristics occur in the apocryphal Gospels.

1. *The Gospels as realistic narratives*. None of the Gnostic Gospels take the form of narrative. Rather, they focus entirely on Jesus as revealer, and take the form of discrete sayings or *chreiai* with no narrative framework (*Gospel of Thomas*), or revelatory discourses in response to questions (*Gospel of Mary, Dialogue of the Saviour*). Two of the most important Gnostic 'Gospels' (*Gospel of Truth, Gospel of Philip*) take the form of teaching *about* Jesus rather than any sort of story. Many of these Gospels, therefore, are not narratives at all. Of those that take narrative form, we can say that the *Gospel of Peter* clearly comes closest to the canonical Gospels in its 'realistic' character, while the infancy Gospels tend toward the legendary and fantastic. As a consequence, neither the body nor time are given a positive valence in the Gnostic or infancy Gospels.
2. *The Gospels as rooted in Palestinian Jewish realities*. On this, the canonical Gospels are distinctive. The *Protevangelium of James* and *the Gospel of Peter* try, but clearly have no real knowledge of Judaism or its relations with the larger political order.
3. *The Gospels as connected to the story of Israel*. The infancy Gospel called *Pseudo-Matthew* imitates the canonical Matthew in using specific formula citations to connect incidents in Jesus' infancy with Scripture. Apart from this exception, the apocryphal Gospels arc noteworthy for the absence of this element.
4. *The Gospels as showing human responses to Jesus*. The point of this category is that characters other than Jesus matter and are

shown making decisive choices. Certainly the infancy Gospels of James and Thomas show some significance to the decisions made by Joseph (*Thomas*) and Mary (*James*). And *The Gospel of Peter* highlights the response of Herod and 'the Jews'. In the Gnostic Gospels, however, the role assigned to other characters is that of asking questions of Jesus. Without a narrative, to be sure, it is difficult to play a narrative role.

5. *The Gospels as emphasizing the passion of Jesus.* The canonical Gospels are impressively, even overwhelmingly, consistent in their attention to the suffering of Jesus. The extant apocryphal Gospels are almost equally consistent in their avoidance of that human suffering. The *Gospel of Peter*, to be sure, corresponds in part to the canonical passion narratives, but does not share their focus on Jesus' actual suffering. The Valentinian *Gospel of Truth* has some beautiful ways of expressing the suffering and death of Christ, but does not touch on the specifics of that suffering. The other apocryphal Gospels simply avoid the subject.

6. *The resurrection as continuous with the human ministry of Jesus.* On this point, the Gnostic Gospels provide the most pertinent comparison. Those that make the resurrection the *mise-en-scene* (as do *Pistis Sophia*, *Questions of Barnabas*, *Gospel of Mary*, *Dialogue of the Saviour*) also make it the occasion for substantially new revelations of Jesus that are intended either to supplement or replace those delivered to the 12 during Jesus' human ministry.

7. *The understanding of Jesus.* The canonical Gospels, we have seen, have an extremely complex presentation of Jesus, at once fully human and enmeshed in the physical world, and representing God in a manner superior to any other figure; defined by complete obedience and submission to God, as well as by self-sacrificing service to others. Insofar as the apocryphal Gospels can be said to have an 'understanding of Jesus,' it is invariably less complex than that in the canonical Gospels. The infancy Gospels are entirely focused on the miraculous, with Jesus either the occasion or the cause of a transcending of natural processes. The *Gospel of Peter* shows Jesus as simply passive. The Gnostic Gospels (including the Coptic *Gospel of Thomas*) emphasize Jesus as divine revealer. In none of them is obedience towards God or loving service to humans part of the character of Jesus, much less its essential note.

8. *Jesus and the God of Israel.* Just as the apocryphal Gospels in general do not portray Jesus in terms of Torah, to an equal degree they avoid the issue of the God whom Jesus represents. The relation of Gnosticism in all its diversity toward the Scriptures of Israel is notoriously

complex, but it is a safe generalization that the Gnostic Gospels are at the very least ambivalent towards those texts as well as the God of whom they speak. Insofar as the God of Israel is the God who creates the material world, the Gnostic texts resist that God. A Gnostic sensibility that finds the world to be a corpse, and blessedness in detachment and solitariness (see the Coptic *Gospel of Thomas*), is far both from the sensibility of Torah and of the canonical Gospels.

9. *God's final triumph is in the future.* Insofar as the apocryphal Gospels tend to diminish the significance of bodies and time, they also diminish the significance of the future as public event. So far as I can determine, there is nothing like the canonical Gospels' future expectation in the apocrypha.

10. *The nature of discipleship.* As with the *ethos* of Jesus, here also we find the sharpest difference between the canonical and apocryphal Gospels. The infancy Gospels do not offer any image of discipleship. Nor does the *Gospel of Peter.* As for the Gnostic Gospels, the emphasis is certainly on knowledge, both of Jesus and of the truths that he reveals. In the case of the Coptic *Gospel of Thomas*, it is properly called self-knowledge. The apprehension of discipleship in the *Gospel of Truth* and the *Gospel of Philip* is certainly more complex, with some sense of outreach to the neighbour through sharing enlightenment. The sacramental language of the *Gospel of Philip* even implies that, to some degree, material things have value as spiritual signs. But the emphasis on the uses of power and possessions as modes of service to others is absent. Nor do we find an understanding of discipleship as following in the path of suffering obedience and service exemplified by Jesus.

The reader, will, I hope, excuse the clumsiness of this set of comparisons, which are offered for their heuristic and experimental value. Although individual apocryphal Gospels resemble the canonical Gospels on one point or another, it can be said that, as a whole – and as we now have them – they represent theological emphases quite other than the canonical ones. On one side (the Infancy Gospels) there is an emphasis on wonderworking and physical purity. On the other side (the Gnostic Gospels) we find an emphasis on saving knowledge, asceticism and rejection of the created order. We simply do not find in them realistic narratives, enmeshment in the world of Torah, affirmation of body, time and history, relationships among humans, an expectation for the future, or a Jesus as obedient to God and servant of humans. The effect of the comparison of canonical and apocryphal Gospels has been to reinforce the perception of what the canonical Gospels distinctively share.

What Theology do the Canonical Gospels Enable?

These comparisons have involved a considerable degree of abstraction. In order to affirm these points of similarity and dissimilarity, I have had to eliminate considerations of all the wonderfully detailed ways in which each composition – apocryphal as well as canonical – escapes such reduction as was necessary to this task. If this list of qualities were to replace reading of the specific compositions, and replace the process of transformation that all serious literary engagement invites, in favour of a neat set of descriptors, then the effort has moved in the wrong direction. The only justification for the exercise is that – while remaining tentative and temporary – it also proves to have heuristic value. I think that in the present case, the exercise has enabled us to see things that are shared by the canonical Gospels and are simply not found in anything like the same degree in any other single apocryphal writing, or in them all collectively. It has also enabled us to detect, beneath the clear diversity to be found on the surface of the four canonical Gospels, genuinely common elements that we might miss if we had only a single Gospel before us, or if we were to read only the Synoptics and not John, or if we were in ignorance of the apocryphal compositions.

Now we are able to ask the question of the best way to relate the terms 'theology' and 'canonical Gospels'. I resist the term 'theology of the canonical Gospels', because it suggests that the qualities I have isolated either represent what the Gospels are about, or adequately summarize any one of them individually, or all of them together. This would be, I think, an inappropriate and inaccurate reduction.

A better question is, 'what theology does the canonical tradition support, and with what theology is it incompatible?' Asking the question this way does not force us to 'find' a theology in the actual compositions, but enables us to think about the theological premises and perceptions out of which the compositions arise and to which they give support, or, conversely, what theological premises and perceptions they would, taken individually or collectively, fail to support.

It is clear, I think, what sort of theology the canonical Gospels would utterly fail to support. A dualistic rejection of the creator God and of his Torah, of the body and of history and of community, in favour of a disembodied revelation concerning esoteric realities beyond those available to this present physical world, would find no support in the canonical Gospels. Neither would an understanding of Jesus purely as thaumaturge or sage, without reference to his obedient suffering in service to others, or an understanding of him as a divine revealer, removed from the passions and problems of embodied humanity. Nor could any support be found in the canonical Gospels for an understanding of discipleship as consisting in a detached and ironic posture – given by revelations available only to the few – superior to the ignorant sufferings of the many. One would need to read the apocryphal Gospels to find support for such a theology.

It should be equally clear what sort of theology the canonical Gospels enable and support. By implication, a realistic narrative of God's revelation through a human person affirms the value of the body, of time, and of history; it supports and enables an incarnational theology. The specific setting of this revelation in the symbolic world of Torah and the social realities of first-century Palestinian, in turn, supports an understanding of revelation that is in continuous with the story of Israel, and therefore affirms the validity of that earlier story even as it claims to continue it in a distinctive fashion. The rendering of secondary characters as important for the relationships they form and the choices they make supports a positive understanding of human freedom and the value of relationship and community.

The portrayal of Jesus as suffering as other humans do supports an understanding of incarnation that is complete, and an understanding of God as participating fully in the human condition even to the experience of suffering and death. The emphasis on resurrection as continuous with Jesus' human ministry further affirms the value and the future of the human person with whom God has associated Godself in the humanity of Jesus. As Jesus' body had a future that was not utterly discontinuous with his human identity, so, we might think, other humans can look forward to an embodied existence that, however changed, is also not utterly discontinuous with their present bodily being. The expectation of God's triumph as future works against any sort of realized eschatology that rests in the perfection of the individual, and therefore works for the effort to realize God's kingdom through the transformation of communities and social realities. The understanding of discipleship as consisting in radical obedience to God, demonstrated by loving service to others supports an understanding of discipleship as not measured by human expectations but God's will, and not measured by individual accomplishment but by the building up of the human community.

It will come as no shock to readers of this volume that the theology enabled and supported by the canonical Gospels bears the strongest possible resemblance to the theology found in Christianity's rule of faith, eventually elaborated as the Apostles' Creed and the Nicene-Constantinopolitan Creed. These creeds take the form of a narrative with past, present and future. They profess faith in one God who is also the father of Jesus Christ, who was born of a specific woman and crucified under a specific historical ruler, who suffered, died and was buried, was raised on the third day, and is expected to come again as judge of the living and the dead. The classic creeds of Christianity, in short, represent a version of theology that finds its best support in the canonical Gospels.

An answer, finally, to the question that has directed this chapter. I think that sense can be made of a 'theology of the canonical Gospels', but only when it is understood as a theology that is enabled and supported by the canonical Gospels.

Chapter 7

Paul in New Testament Theology: Some Preliminary Remarks

Leander E. Keck, Yale

The subject matter of this chapter is not as innocent as its title implies, for both 'Paul' and 'New Testament theology', being modern constructs, are unstable and controversial. Robert Morgan has shown, from his magisterial 'Introduction' to *The Nature of New Testament Theology* (1973) to his 'New Testament Theology' (1995), that the controversies that have swirled around New Testament (NT) theology are essentially theological, not merely methodological. Morgan's own command of the history of modern theology has enabled him to both understand NT theology in its wider historical context and to grasp its *theological* significance. The scope of this chapter, however, is more modest: it will first clarify both parts of the subject matter (I) before looking at Paul's theology (II), and then at some aspects of its place in NT theology as a whole (III).

I

New Testament theology has not fared well in recent decades. On the one hand, the disintegration of the theological milieu in which NT theology was central (represented by Barth and Bultmann, for instance), has left NT theology more or less stranded. On the other hand, NT theology lost its pre-eminence within NT scholarship itself, partly because new interests invoked other disciplines (e.g., sociology or rhetoric), and partly because the emphasis on NT theology as a historical discipline turned it into the history of ideas in the highly diverse 'Jesus movement' (a protean surrogate for 'church'). Consequently, 'NT theology' has become a misleading label for something that is not really *theology*. (Wrede might well say, 'I told you so!')

No one will deny that our historical understanding of the discrete early Christian theologies has become more precise; nor will anyone call for halting the historical and sociological investigations that situate them in burgeoning early Christianity in Greco-Roman society. Still, such work is not to be confused with studying NT theology as *theology*. Indeed, NT theology *as theology* cannot be pursued simply by extending, correcting or refining the history of early Christian theologies, even when limited to those in the NT. Rather, NT theology proper is a historically informed theological discipline that asks its own questions and answers them in its own way. Appropriately, the historian of early Christian thought looks for origins (especially the origin of Christology) and sequences, infers influences, and emphasizes differences in order to reconstruct the past; the historically informed NT theologian looks for the logical relationships between the ideas generated by root premises in order to grasp the subject matter of the NT. Each discipline has its own integrity and value; each complements the other.

As viewed here, NT theology makes explicit the *rationale* of the Gospel (the salvific import of the Jesus-event) and its variously expressed logical, moral and communal entailments in the NT as a whole. Moreover, because the theology of the NT is not simply 'there', waiting to be exposed like a vein of ore, every statement of NT theology is an interpretive construct by an interpreter who is as historically conditioned as the texts. What one 'sees', as well as how one says what is 'seen', reflect one's sense of what is important and why it is important – as true of the scholar who asks only historical questions as of the one who is concerned with theological consistency and consequences. Consequently, it is as necessary to ask, whose historical reconstruction? as to ask, whose NT theology?

'Paul' too is a modern construct. The same cluster of historical-critical methods that exposed the diverse theologies in the NT not only disclosed the diverse 'Pauls' in the canon, but also insisted that 'the real Paul' is found only in his undoubtedly genuine letters (commonly limited to seven, though some say eight, nine or ten; rarely are all 13 deemed to be from Paul) and not in the Paul of Acts. But even the seven-letter Paul is not problem-free, for some letters may be composite, having been compiled by an unknown editor (notably 2 Corinthians, possibly Philippians, and perhaps Romans if its chapter 16 was originally sent to Ephesus). Besides, some of the letters may contain non-Pauline passages inserted later (so Walker 2001). Consequently, ignoring a possible interpolation can have the same distorting effect on 'the real Paul' as treating a deutero-Pauline letter as if it were genuine. And since Paul's letters respond to particular issues, deconstructing composite letters into their original components increases the number of situations addressed, making the coherence of Paul's theology even more elusive than it already is. Moreover, the reconstructions of the situations have differed widely for virtually every letter. But it is one thing to recognize that specific situations elicited and shaped Paul's responses, another to assume that he had not thought about the subject matter before the situations arose. In any case, here too one must ask, whose Paul?

It is not surprising that this outcome has encouraged the reluctance, and sometimes refusal, to speak of Paul's theology at all, especially as a reservoir of ideas on which he drew to address varying situations. In the Pauline Theology Group, which met for a decade (beginning in 1986) during the Annual Meeting of the Society of Biblical Literature and published four volumes called *Pauline Theology*, many participants spoke instead of Paul's theology as an 'activity' (one suggesting that sometimes Paul, rather like a modern author, 'discovered where he wanted to go during the act of composition rather than prior to it'). But it is a long step from recognizing the contingency and variety of Paul's letters to the conclusion that, lacking a system of carefully calibrated 'doctrines', his theology had neither a defining starting point, persistent rationale nor characteristic content, for Paul himself refers to what he teaches 'everywhere in every church' (1 Cor 4:17). Nonetheless, the current emphasis on the adaptability of Paul's theology has shown the degree to which it is intensely personal, reflecting *his* reading (or misreading) of the situations addressed as well as expressing his unique experience and apostolic self-understanding (repeatedly defended). In this sense, our topic really does refer to *Paul* in NT theology; still, his theology must be distinguished from the man himself if one is to grasp it as his *theology*.

Robert Morgan (1995, p. 117) noted that 'the temptation to substitute history for theology, historical reconstruction for theological reflection on NT texts, is strongest in relation to Paul'. Historical criticism has in fact concentrated on the man's history, whether by emphasizing the continuing legacy of his pre-Christian life as a Pharisee, the impact of his 'conversion' experience on his thought, his alleged 'development', his interpretation of Christian traditions, or some combination of all these factors. Essential as such factors are for understanding the influences on his theology (a historical matter), not even a full theological biography of the Apostle would explain his thought as theology, a consistent grasp of a determinative subject matter whose stated consequences varied because differing situations prompted him to continue thinking about it.

Grasping the theology of the seven-letter Paul, then, requires discerning the rationale, the logos, which links its various expressions to the determinative subject matter; it requires seeing how, in Paul Achtemeier's formulation, 'the generative conviction begets a further network of coherent beliefs' (Achtemeier 1991, p. 36). To see both the begetting and the begotten, we must see *what* Paul saw by looking at it *with* him, while recognizing that what is seen is the interpreter's vision of Paul's vision.

II

For Paul, the determinative subject matter was not a new idea but an event – the resurrection of the crucified Jesus by God. For the Apostle, the reality of that event was beyond doubt because he experienced its happenedness (not the event itself!) in his own life, for he claimed that the resurrected Lord appeared also to him as he had to Peter (1 Cor 15:3–8), or as expressed in Gal 2:15–16, that God 'revealed his Son' to him. This disclosure was not solely cognitive. So compelling was it that it turned a persecutor into a propagator who was convinced that God's action in Jesus' resurrection was, and must continue to be, ratified in his own life and in that of the churches. Paul's whole theology, then, both in its conceptual and in its experienced content, is *ex post facto* theology. That is, it is both logically thinkable only subsequent to the resurrection event and materially contingent on that event because for him it was the transforming break-through of the really real into the presently distorted real. When Jesus' resurrection is construed as his resuscitation or as the disciples' awareness of Jesus' on-going impact, it becomes impossible to think with Paul. Understanding him, therefore, requires one to imagine what it was like to understand Jesus' resurrection as he did. It does not require agreeing with him. In fact, understanding him might make it more difficult to agree with him.

Already as a Pharisee, we may assume, Paul understood 'resurrection' (whether of all the righteous as their reward or of everyone so they could receive either reward or retribution at the Judgement) as one of the events in the scenario that some Jews expected to occur at the transition from the current state of affairs ('this age') to the future state ('the age to come') when God will make everything as it should be. We may also assume that the Pharisee Paul regarded the first believers' claim that Jesus, and only he, had been resurrected as ludicrous if not blasphemous because everything in 30 CE had certainly not been made as it should be. But once convinced by God's intervention in his own life that God *had* resurrected Jesus, he could not avoid concluding that though the

New Age is not here, it has been *inaugurated*, and that its full actualization would inevitably follow. Paul's whole theology, then, spells out, in various circumstances and with varying concepts, the consequences of Jesus' resurrection, understood in light of the two ages. While we cannot trace the steps by which Paul reached his conclusions, we can discern the logical impact of the happenedness of Jesus' resurrection, first on *how* Paul thought, and then on *what* he thought.

Consistent with two-age thinking, Paul thinks holistically. Two-age thinking divides the whole of reality into the past accumulated into the present and the fundamentally different future. What matters is what determines the character of each age, what makes it an 'age'. The very language – 'this age' and 'the age to come' – shows that each is characterized *vis-à-vis* the other. Further, by definition the expected coming age will not be a new phase of Jewish or Roman history destined to be replaced by yet another, nor will the New Age simply improve the Old, for its arrival brings a radical change in the realities that determine the present as a whole. Therefore Paul shows no interest in making distinctions within 'this age' (e.g., between better or worse rulers, grosser or lesser sins). What matters in two-age thinking is grasping what is determinatively wrong in 'this age', why it is wrong, and what keeps it wrong. And that requires viewing it holistically, and for Paul that meant viewing it in light of an the inauguration of the New Age. Because he does not view 'this age' in light of an idyllic Eden before Adam's sin, he does not regard the New Age as Eden restored. His eye is on the inaugurated future.

He expressed his holistic grasp of present 'age' in various ways, in accord with the particular issue he is discussing. Seen ontologically, the whole created order has been 'subjected to futility' (Rom 8:20, restating Gen 3:17); seen morally, it has become 'evil' (Gal 1:4); viewed mythologically, it is subject to the tyranny of cosmos-wide powers, sin and death (Rom 5:12–14); seen religiously, there is no distinction between Jew and Greek, because all 'all have sinned' (Rom 3:23), with or without the law; viewed epistemologically, the wisdom of this age (or 'world') is futile for it does not know who God really is, though it thinks it does (1 Cor 1:12; Rom 1:18–23). The inauguration of the New Age begins to transform each of these aspects of the present malaise, though only those who believe the announcement that Jesus has been resurrected know that 'if anyone is in Christ, there is new creation [= New Age]: the old things have passed away; see, they have become new' (2 Cor 5:17, my translation). So Paul emphasizes the contrasts between the believer's former life and the new life in Christ, for there are no shades of grey between enslavement to sin and liberation from it.

Because all Christians believed that God had raised Jesus from the dead, Paul was not the only *ex post facto* theologian in earliest Christianity. But apparently he was the first to think through, with relentless rigor, the import of that event and to express it holistically in assertion, argument and admonition. Moreover, the results of doing so show that he grasped two logical consequences of thinking *ex post facto* about the pivotal event. First, since by definition the coming of the New Age leaves nothing and no one unaffected but transforms everything and everyone, word of the inauguration of the New Age is the same salvific good news for everyone everywhere, though its particular import for Gentiles is not the same as for Jews. Consequently, the inauguration of the New Age implies that both the meaning of Israel's election and scripture must be rethought in light of what has happened. While the circumstances in which Paul came to these conclusions are biographically interesting, more important is the theological rationale that produced them. Second, since it was *Jesus'* resurrection (not just anybody's) that was the inaugural event, Jesus himself is inseparable from it and its entailments. Making sense of the good news, therefore, required explaining who Jesus was and now is. Thus Paul's *ex post facto* Christology is theocentric, for it was God who acted decisively through Christ; conversely, Paul's theology is Christomorphic because also his understanding of God is reshaped by the Christ-event. Because Paul is consistent in thinking holistically, his Christology too is holistic. His letters show no interest in the particular incidents in Jesus' mission because what is theologically significant is the character of the Christ-event as a whole, seen from its result – Jesus' resurrection as the New Age-inaugurating act of God. Paul's Christology, then, is the result of thinking through the implications of Jesus' resurrection as the act of God by which the salvific import of the New Age is now begun.

Since the logic of those implications, the rationale of his Christology, is largely assumed in his letters, it must be inferred if we are to understand that Christology, though only its rudimentary elements can be noted here. (a) Since for Paul, God's righteousness/rectitude/moral integrity is axiomatic, God's resurrecting Jesus could not be an arbitrary, amoral act but one that disclosed decisively the character of God's rectitude. That is, Paul assumes that *whom* God resurrects definitively reveals *who* God really is. Therefore the lived life of Jesus which led to the cross is inseparable from the disclosed character of God. (b) Seen holistically, the determinative quality in Jesus' life was obedience (Rom 5:19; Phil 2:7–8), or his faithfulness, to God (Rom 3:22, 25). The correlation between Jesus' obedience and God's rectitude implies that what Christ did and what God did are two sides of the same event. Consequently Paul could assert that '*God* proves his love for us in that while we still were sinners *Christ* died for us

(Rom 5:8). (c) To express the *identity* of Christ, and so point to the ground of Jesus' obedience, Paul calls him 'Son of God', in accord with the ancient assumption that the son represents the father and actualizes the father's will. The Son of God is the self-expression of God, and so is also the agent of creation (1 Cor 8:6). It follows, then, that since the agent of creation became the agent of salvation, the completion of what the Christ-event inaugurated is the unqualified sovereignty of God (1 Cor 15:24–8). (d) To account for the *occurrence* of the Christ-event as God's act in history, Paul says 'God sent his Son' (Gal 4:4) – not meaning that God inspired Jesus to leave Nazareth but that God's self-expression brought the Son from eternity into human existence in time. (Because the Son is the self-expression of God, there is no substantive tension between saying that *God* sent the Son and saying that the one 'equal to God . . . emptied *himself* . . . humbled *himself*' in Phil 2:6–8; see also Gal 2:20.)

Since Paul saw that the salvation begun is inseparable from the one whose resurrection began it, his reasoning exemplified a fundamental principle of Christian theology – that Christology makes event-based soteriology possible, and conversely, that event-based soteriology makes Christology necessary. He also saw that according to the logic of soteriology, the cure must fit the disease; therefore soteriology is consistently correlated with anthropology, the human plight. Accordingly, when Paul views the human plight as the *dilemma* of being accountable for a wrong relation to God, he speaks of rectification (justification) or reconciliation (Rom 3:21–6; 5:9–11; 2 Cor 5:19). When Paul has in view the forementioned ontic consequences of living in 'this age' as a *condition* of being subjected to the inevitability of death, of being mortal, he does not envisage salvation as release of the immortal soul from the mortal body (that would impugn the Creator); nor does he speak of forgiveness. Instead, he argues that salvation from that condition requires participation in a reality not subject to death. Accordingly, he points out that those baptized 'into Christ' are made participants in Christ, who 'being raised from the dead, will never die again; death no longer has dominion over him' (Rom 6:9).

Not to be missed is the logical connection between being a baptized participant in the ongoing Christ-event (the parousia is still to come) and the kind of existence that results from participating in the inaugurated New Age. Because the New Age is not yet fully here, the baptized are not yet immortalized, for that will occur only when 'this mortal body puts on [acquires] immortality' (1 Cor 15:54). Until then, the baptized are participants in Christ's death, a death 'he died to sin' (the ultimate cause of mortality according to Rom 5:12) and so are also 'dead to sin' and freed to 'walk in newness of life' (Rom 6:4). In other words, the already/not yet of the New Age is recapitulated in the already/not yet of the baptized believer, whose new mandated *moral* life is to be no longer 'conformed to this age' (Rom 12:2), but, having been freed from enslavement to sin, is rather to anticipate the future transformation into *immortal* life (Rom 6:22–3). In short, the inaugurated indicative generates the appropriate imperative. Further, the Spirit is the experienced power whose presence is a pledge that the future transformation will surely occur: 'If the Spirit of him who raised Jesus from the dead dwells in you, he who raised Christ from the dead will give life to your mortal bodies also through his Spirit that dwells in you' (Rom 8:11). In the meantime, during the 'not yet', the Spirit empowers the believers to live the new life which is cele- brated and nurtured in the church, the beachhead of the New Age.

III

If NT theology is an interpretive act that makes explicit the rationale of the news of God's salvific act in Jesus and its entailments, it follows that discussing Paul's place in NT theology too is an interpretive construct involving the interpreter's own theological sensibility. That construct is neither apologetic (defending the unity and historical accuracy of the NT) nor primarily historical (detecting Paul's influence and influences on Paul), but is itself theological because it seeks the (theo)logical relation- ship between Paul's letters and other parts of the NT. Focusing now on the Synoptic Gospels, we ask, are Paul's and their theologies consistent, complementary, compatible, or contradictory? Interestingly, the NT itself gives us clues to the answer.

It is appropriate to note that in the NT Paul's voice is pre-eminent because of (a) the sheer quantity of texts (13) claiming him as their author, (b) his paramount role in Acts, (c) the placement of his letters, and (d) their current order (it originally varied). Although Romans prob- ably was Paul's last letter, it now heads the Pauline letter corpus, which immediately follows Acts. Acts reports that while under 'house arrest' in Rome, he was 'proclaiming the kingdom of God and the things about the Lord Jesus Christ [not 'the facts' as REB has it] with all boldness' (Acts 28:31, my translation). Consequently, the NT reader who passes from Acts to Romans is encouraged to think that what Paul was teaching *in Rome* can be found in what he had written *to Roman* believers previously.

Although Peter was the initial and most prominent leader in the first church in Jerusalem, the placement of the Pauline corpus puts Paul's letters ahead of those claiming to be from Peter (and those claiming to be from James and John). Nonetheless, this ordering does not really demote Peter, for according to Acts, Paul's message basically repeated that of Peter (compare Acts 2:14-40; 3:12-26 with 13:16-41), and Peter's conversion of the Gentile Cornelius set the precedent for Paul's mission to Gentiles (Acts 10; 15:1-11). The many details by which Acts links Paul to Peter and the earliest church are well enough known that there is no need to repeat them here. More important is noting that when the NT is viewed as a whole, Acts' insistence on the continuity between Peter and Paul is underscored by the fact that three Gospels report that Jesus himself singled out Peter as the key figure in the coming church (Matt 16:13-18; Luke 22:32; John 21:15-17). Thus in effect Paul's link to Peter also links Paul to Jesus.

Moreover, just as historians shape the future by the way they present the past, so the way Acts looks back at Paul is designed to secure his role in the future (the author's own time). Not surprisingly, then, in Acts 20:29-30, Paul himself foresees that after his death 'savage wolves' will enter the Christian flock, 'distorting the truth in order to entice the disciples to follow them', implying thereby that the later church will be engaged in a struggle to remain faithful to Paul, the implied norm (as 2 Pet 3:15-16 later confirms: 'the ignorant and unstable twist' the letters of 'our beloved brother Paul'). Indeed, Acts reports no dissensions within Paul's churches during his lifetime, implying that conflicts arose only later. In short, between the portrayal of Paul in Acts and the placement of the Pauline letters, the NT implies that when the church is faithful to Paul it is faithful to the earliest church, which in turn was faithful to Jesus. Not accidentally does Acts have Paul say that he had preached 'the whole counsel [NRSV: purpose] of God' (Acts 20:27).

Seen historically, however, Paul is more pre-eminent in the NT than he was in the Christianity of his lifetime. His letters show that he was a controversial figure even in his own churches, and that he knew he was unwelcome to many believers in Jerusalem (Rom 15:30-1; after his confrontation with Peter [Gal 2:11-14], probably in Antioch as well). Acts itself acknowledges that there was intense antipathy to Paul in Jerusalem (though for the wrong reasons, Acts 21:17-24) and reports no effort by the Jerusalem believers to come to his aid after he was arrested. Indeed, one might propose that Acts emphasizes both Paul's continuity with Peter and Paul's continuing Jewishness in order to oppose the idea that Paul had turned the church away from its roots (a misunderstanding Paul himself had tried to correct in Rom 9-11). In any case, does the present location of Acts - between the Gospels and the Pauline corpus - imply that we are to read the Gospels in light of Paul? And if so, what would that mean theologically?

The import of these questions becomes evident when we note that, Acts aside momentarily, four narratives about Jesus are followed by a quite different type of discourse: explanations of Jesus' significance that rely on concepts like sacrifice, God's righteousness, grace, or Jesus' faithfulness. How, then, are the two modes of discourse related theologically (not historically: What did Paul know of the Jesus traditions?)? Probing the theological relationship requires thinking as a hermeneutical theologian who detects both consistencies beneath the diverse concepts in the texts (e.g., the kingdom of God in the Synoptics is consistent with God's rectifying rectitude in Rom 3:26), and the conceptual differences between surface similarities (e.g., Son of God in the Synoptics differs from the pre-existent Son in Paul). Especially important is whether the rationale in Paul's concept-using theology is consistent with the rationale of the Gospel narratives.

It is instructive to note that frequently Paul's holistic thinking about the Christ-event is distilled into various brief soteriological statements. In addition to Rom 5:8 already cited, Gal 4:4 declares that 'when the fullness of time had come, God sent his Son, born of woman, born under the law, in order to redeem those who were under the law'; likewise 1 Cor 1:30 says that Christ 'became for us wisdom from God, and righteousness and sanctification and redemption'. The assertion in 2 Cor 5:19 that 'in Christ God was reconciling the world to himself, not counting their trespasses against them' is followed by another: 'For our sake he [God] made him [Christ] to be sin who knew no sin, so that in him we might become the righteousness of God' (2 Cor 5:21). Comparable statements appear also in Heb 2:9; 1 Pet 1:21; 1 John 2:1; 3:8.

Significantly, in addition to the cup sayings at the Last Supper (Matt 26:28; Mark 14:24; Luke 22:20), similar varying, brief soteriological statements are found also in each of the four Gospels, where they appear on the lips of Jesus: 'I have come to call not the righteous but sinners' (Matt 9:13). In Mark 10:45 Jesus declares, 'For the Son of Man came not to be served but to serve, and to give his life a ransom for many', and in Luke 12:49-50 he says, 'I came to bring fire to the earth. . . . I have a baptism with which to be baptized'. In John such statements are pervasive. For example, 'I came into this world for judgement so that those who do not see may see, and those who do see may become blind' (John 9:32), or 'I [the good shepherd] lay down my life for the sheep' (John 10:15). What matters here is not the specific ways in which the soteriology is stated but the significance of the appearance of such statements in both Paul's letters and the Gospels.

In the Gospels, these statements formulate the soteriological significance of the whole narrated Jesus story. In the narratives they are addressed to Jesus' hearers, but they also function to guide the readers' understanding of the whole story, while, conversely, the whole narrative supports the assertions of the statements. Moreover, even though each Gospel's story line runs *toward* Jesus' cross and resurrection, the salvific significance of Jesus in light of cross and resurrection is the unstated theological starting point *from which* each evangelist writes his forward-moving narrative. Theologically, the evangelists begin where their narratives end. Otherwise, they would not have written the Jesus story at all.

In short, the Gospels' soteriological formulations, while differing from each other conceptually, are theologically consistent with each other *and* with Paul's statements, though his concepts also differ from each other and from those in the Gospels' statements as well. And since Paul's statements are amplified in the letters, it follows that the consistency between his statements and those of the Gospels implies that his letters overall are also consistent with the Gospels' narratives.

This relationship – consistency in diversity – implies that theologically, Paul's statements interpret the narratives, and conversely, that the narratives portray the Christ whose significance Paul explains with concepts like Christ's obedience or faithfulness, or self-giving (Gal 2:20). Theologically, what the Gospels recount, Paul explains. Thus when the Gospels are read in light of Paul, their narratives are accounts of the one whose life and death are an intrinsic part of the event through which God acted salvifically. The Synoptics' narratives, even without their soteriological statements, would still have soteriological significance, but it would not address the human plight as a flawed ontic condition, bondage to mortality. Since the Synoptics do not envisage the human plight this way, they lack also the appropriate solution: participation in a reality that has overcome death; for them, the solution to the human plight is repentance as discipleship. Since 'consistency' itself assumes that differences remain, we can say that the Synoptics are nonetheless consistent with Paul, for what they say about discipleship can be read as making concrete what Paul means by life 'in Christ'. Reading the Synoptics in light of Paul draws them into the orbit of his Gospel without eclipsing their real differences.

Given the implication of 'consistency', we return to Acts, whose portrayal of Paul and Peter emphasizes the continuity, not only the consistency, of the Gospels they preached. Are the two as continuous as Acts claims? If not, are they nonetheless theologically consistent? These questions surface in light of Acts 3:19–21, where Peter, preaching at the temple, calls for repentance 'so that your sins [particularly the rejection of Jesus, 'the Holy and Righteous One'] may be wiped out, so that times of refreshing may come from the presence of the Lord, and he may send the Messiah appointed for you, that is, Jesus, who must remain in heaven until the time of universal restoration' [the *apokatastasis panton* = the

New Age]. According to Peter, the 'already' inaugurated by Jesus' post-resurrection Ascension has two phases: the current 'times of refreshing' and the following New Age, which will begin when the Messiah comes from heaven (which Paul calls the *parousia*). Thus the 'times of refreshing' is the time of the church, during which the Gospel is preached *before* the New Age arrives. For Paul, on the other hand, the Gospel announces the inauguration of the New Age and its current salvific effects for those in Christ; the newly restored creation does not follow a phase between Jesus' resurrection and the parousia; instead, the parousia completes what is already begun.

Important as it is to ask the historical question, what accounts for Peter's view? (e.g., Luke's reliance on old traditions or Luke's own view that reflects the delayed parousia), what matters theologically is how the rationale in Peter's view is related to that in Paul's. Looked at in this way, Peter's view turns Paul's present dialectical already/not yet into the temporal succession of two distinct eras, now and then. While the difference is real, and significant, the two are neither mutually exclusive nor simply continuous; they are, however, theologically consistent because in both, the goal of salvation remains contingent on the parousia, which both expect. The fact that Paul could say that 'salvation is nearer to us now than when we became believers' (Rom 13:11) implies that, although he expected its arrival to be imminent, he too reckoned with a temporal phase between the inauguration and the consummation of the Christ-event; Acts, written decades later, understandably extended that intervening phase. Indeed, until existentialist theology transformed the temporally future into the futurity of existence, Christian theology has been closer here to Peter than to Paul, while at the same time it has sometimes looked more to Paul for understanding the current import of the inaugurated New Age as life 'in Christ'.

If NT theology makes explicit the rationale of the Gospel in the NT as a whole, one cannot ignore real differences between Paul and other parts of the NT. Best known, perhaps, is the contrast between Paul's positive view of Rome in Romans 13 and the negative view of Rome in Revelation 13. And while Paul said that non-Christian Jews do not submit to God's (rectifying) rectitude and instead seek to establish their own because their zeal for God lacks knowledge (Rom 10:2–3), he did not say that none of them keeps the law (John 7:19), and would not have said that their 'father' is the devil, 'the father of lies' (John 8:44). While historical criticism has, with considerable success, accounted for such explicit differences by tracing them to circumstances, the logical disparities remain. In fact, it is by emphasizing differences that history-dominated study has isolated diverse theologies within the NT. Still, further reflection is in order, lest the undeniable differences be hastily magnified into incompatible theologies.

First, bearing in mind that Paul's letters, were written largely to correct the readers' wrong inferences from the Gospel they had already accepted, the Apostle's silences should not be converted into evidence of significant tensions with the Gospels. For example, from his reference to Jesus' burial (part of the received tradition) one may infer that he also assumed that the tomb was emptied, though he never mentions it (why should he have?). The Gospels themselves recognize that its emptiness is ambiguous and must be interpreted before it can be a sign of Jesus' resurrection. Second, bearing in mind that it is the Galatian situation that prompted Paul to say that God sent the Son to 'redeem those who were under the law' (Gal 4:4), one must also ask just how different theologically is his claim in Rom 10:4 (Christ is the *telos*, goal, of the law) from Matt 5:17, where Jesus says he came to fulfil the law. Analysing such assertions theologically often discloses a consistency in diverse concepts. Third, genre is important. Bearing in mind also that 'What if ...?' is a an endless game with no winners, it is nonetheless heuristically useful to ask what sort of Gospel narrative Paul might have written, and what sort of letter Matthew might have sent to the Corinthians.

Nonetheless, because each text deserves to be heard in its own right, basic differences that shape the whole should not be glossed over. For instance, although Matthew's Jesus insists that the gate is narrow and the road leading to life is found by few (Matt 7:13–14), they can do what is necessary; but Paul insists that one does not, and cannot, do what the law requires because sin uses it to awaken precisely what it forbids (Rom 7:7–12) – an insight absent from Matthew. Nor do Paul's letters even imply that the Spirit is the interpreter of Jesus (John 16:13–14). What matters for NT theology as *theology*, however, is whether such differences preclude the consistency necessary for a theology of the NT as a whole. As Morgan (1995, pp. 126–7) noted, 'even partially conflicting theologies are compatible with a unity of faith', not to be confused with 'a unitary doctrinal system'.

Paul's pre-eminence in the NT does not silence these other voices. Rather, the Apostle's pre-eminence, while not giving him the right to speak *for* everyone in the NT, does give him the right to speak *to* them. Conversely, the NT's inclusion of differing voices gives *them* the right to speak to Paul, and obligates them all to listen to one another – i.e., to correct, as well as complement, each other. In this light, the co-existence of differences and consistencies summons the interpreter concerned with the NT as a whole to become a hermeneutical theologian, not to harmonize disparities but to discern whether, and to what extent, the rationale of the Christ-event is expressed consistently and convincingly in each, as well as to decide which is the more adequate conceptually as well as appropriate for a given situation. In making these judgements, the interpreter assumes responsibility for the NT theology constructed as a result. We may infer that Paul himself would agree, for he wrote, 'Let two or three prophets speak, and let the others weigh what is said' (1 Cor 14:29). Besides, he had already admitted that he did not know everything but only 'in part' (1 Cor 13:12). His fellow contributors to the NT would have agreed. And in forming the NT as we have it, the church also agreed. And so does Bob Morgan. That is why he is a pre-eminent, responsible, theologian of the New Testament.

References

Achtemeier, Paul J., 'Finding the way to Paul's theology. A response to J. Christiaan Beker and J. Paul Sampley', in Jouette M. Bassler (ed.), *Pauline Theology. Vol. 1: Thessalonians, Philippians, Galatians, Philemon* (Minneapolis: Fortress Press, 1991), pp. 15–36.
Morgan, Robert, *The Nature of New Testament Theology* (London: SCM Press/ Naperville, IL: Alec R. Allenson, 1973).
Morgan, Robert, 'New Testament theology', in Steven J. Kraftcheck, Charles D. Myers, Jr. and Ben C. Ollenburger (eds), *Biblical Theology: Problems and Perspectives. In Honor of J. Christiaan Beker* (Nashville: Abingdon, 1995), pp. 104–30.
Walker, William O. Jr., *Interpolations in the Pauline Letters* (JSNTSup 213; Sheffield: Sheffield Academic Press, 2001).

Chapter 8

The Contribution of Reception History to a Theology of the New Testament

Ulrich Luz, Bern

Introduction: Reception History and Theology of the New Testament

Depending on the definition of what a 'theology of the New Testament' might be, the question posed by the title of this chapter will be answered differently. If a 'theology of the New Testament' is conceived as a 'history of theology of the documents of the New Testament' or as a 'history of theology of earliest Christianity', then naturally reception history does not contribute anything to it. Reception history of the Bible is the history of the reception of biblical texts in periods subsequent to New Testament times. Reception history then seems significant for Church history and not for a theology of the New Testament. In this way Gerhard Ebeling said in a famous and influential article: 'Church history is the history of the exposition of scripture' (Ebeling 1968, p. 28). 'Exposition of scripture' was for him what we call 'reception history' today and was understood by him in a very broad sense: it included interpretations of the Bible in non-verbal media such as art, music, dancing, prayer; it also included receptions of the Bible in political actions, wars, peace-making, suffering, institutions etc. One even could go beyond Ebeling's concept and say that history beyond Church history is also reception history of the Bible, or at least that the reception history of the Bible is a very important part of the whole history of Europe, North America and other so-called Christian parts of the world.

If the question implied by the title is answered positively, then a 'theology of the New Testament' must be conceived differently: it must be a contextual 'theology of the New Testament for today', giving at least guidelines that explain what is theologically important in the New Testament for today. Only then can the question how we or others have received the New Testament in our history be a relevant question. There are few New Testament theologies of this type on the market today[1] and none of them reflects the theological importance of reception history. That is the reason why a positive answer to the question implied by the title can only be given in a preliminary way: I want to give an answer to the question what kind of contribution reception history can give to the question how we can interpret the New Testament in a theologically meaningful way for today.

Reception History and 'Wirkungsgeschichte'

Reception history is in vogue today in biblical studies. This is evident not so much through the numerous monographs about the history of interpretation or reception history of specific biblical texts, but even more through the project of the 'Blackwell Bible Commentaries' that started publication in 2004.[2] In Germany, the already venerable and voluminous 'Evangelisch-Katholischer Kommentar' (EKK), with its emphasis on 'history of interpretation', is its older brother.[3]

In German theological circles, including the EKK, it has become customary to speak about 'Wirkungsgeschichte' while others speak about 'reception history'. Why this difference? Is it not just one more case where Germans use their own, somewhat mystery-laden, terms that make it sometimes difficult for other people to understand exactly what they mean? The term 'Wirkungsgeschichte' is due to Hans Georg Gadamer's influential work *Truth and Method* (Gadamer 1989). It can be translated in different ways: either by 'effective history' or by 'history of effects'. The latter would have been much closer to 'reception history', only with the difference that the term 'reception history' is formulated from the standpoint of the receivers and the term 'history of effects' from the standpoint of the original events or texts. However, it seems to me that 'effective history' is a translation which corresponds much more closely to what Gadamer meant. In this case 'Wirkungsgeschichte' is not the same as 'reception history'.

What is the difference? Gadamer[4] opposes the principle of historical objectivity that is satisfied with the reconstruction of the 'historical horizon' of a text of the past only. Being satisfied with this means to try to examine a text in a scholarly way like a professor examines a candidate or a doctor examines a sick person. What the examiner does not realize is his/her own connection with history: the examining scholar is at the same time part of the history she/he examines. Therefore objectivizing history is impossible because doing so would catapult him/her out of that history. Gadamer's interest rather is the interrelation of the historian or the interpreter with the past. Neither history nor texts of the past are simply objects of research: rather, they belong to the stream of history which also carries the boat of the interpreter. Gadamer's term 'effective history' wants to shed light upon this interrelation: history is 'effective', because it is a basic foundation which carries our life. I think that the merit of Gadamer is that through his philosophy he gave us back to history. History is for him the basic element that enables our life. History is effective, because we owe to it almost everything we are: our culture, our language, our questions and our worldviews. This idea of our indebtedness to history is much more than mere traditionalism. It is for me something very fundamental in our postmodern culture which is in danger of becoming merely individualist and subjectivist.

What is the relation of reception history to this concept of 'effective history'? Gadamer explicitly rejects the idea that 'effective history' should develop into an independent ancillary discipline of the human sciences (Gadamer 1989, p. 300). His idea would not have been the project of a Bible commentary oriented towards reception history, and surely not the idea of Bible commentaries that are twice as voluminous as normal commentaries because they also treat reception history.[5]

The main question for us who work on reception history is therefore: Why are we doing this? What is reception history good for? Is it more than just a possibility to write dissertations and to fill bookshelves or commentaries with additional historical material? My thesis is that the study of reception history is an excellent tool to regain what we might call the 'consciousness of effective history'. It is an important instrument, because both in Europe and in North America we have widely forgotten our own history. It was a very frequent experience when I was writing my commentary on Matthew (Luz 1985–2002) that readers, pastors, priests, teachers etc. told me that the sections about reception history in my commentary were absolutely fascinating because all this was so new for them! The history over centuries the Bible has had with us, during which it formed and shaped our culture and our churches, has become unknown for most so-called 'educated' people of today. We do not know any more where we come from! The effective history of the biblical texts has become widely unknown to their recipients of the twenty-first century. But without knowing what we owe to history and why we have become what we are – spiritually, ecclesiastically, culturally – not least through the effective history of the Bible, no consciousness of our inter-relation with history and our indebtedness to history – and that means consciousness of effective history – is possible. The study of reception history of eminent texts like the biblical texts is an important help to regain this consciousness and to clarify our own relation to the texts of the past we study.

In the following sections I want to reflect about possible ways how reception history can help towards a 'consciousness of effective history'.

No Naive Simultaneity with the Text

Both the reconstruction of the original historical horizon of a biblical text and the study of its reception history prevent a naive simultaneity with the biblical text. They do it in a different way: the reconstruction of the historical horizon of the text, its world, its first readers, their situation and the author's intention, distances the text from present-day readers. Its effect is something like an 'ugly ditch' of an insurmountable distance between past text and present reader: Paul did speak to the Corinthians in their situation, in their culture, with their background. All of this is unique and unrepeatable. Through the reconstruction of the historical horizon the text gains its own contextuality, but it is a contextuality of the past which has now gone. Our own context is different: it is just *because* Paul (or another author) has spoken so clearly in a specific context of the past that he cannot speak any more directly to us. This is what I mean by a 'ditch' of the temporal distance. In the history of Protestant reading of the Bible the experience of this ditch created through the influence of Enlightenment and historical criticism was very painful and met a lot of resistance – understandably enough because it prevented Protestants from founding their churches, their faith, their morality and their piety *directly* on the Bible.

Preoccupation with reception history shows that this historical dis-tance between then and now is not an ugly ditch, but a highly diverse landscape with a lot of ups and downs, unexpected views, side-valleys, plains and viewpoints and with a wealth of wonderful and sometimes very strange flowers. Study of reception history makes it difficult to condemn and deplore all this, as Protestants like to do because they tend to reject tradition and to take later receptions of the biblical texts as aberrations or decline. Study of the reception history of the Bible shows that it is difficult to condemn all later interpretations as 'unbiblical' simply because they were different from the biblical texts. Reception history shows that *every* interpretation is different! Study of reception history shows that all interpretations of the Bible are based on later traditions, not only those of the others, but also our own. For Protestant exegesis it was always easy to concede this for Catholic interpretations, because Catholics themselves made an important point out of it. It was also easy to concede that fundamentalists by no means interpret the biblical texts directly and are obedient to them only, but rather they depend on a view of the biblical texts which has its roots in Protestant orthodoxy of the late sixteenth and early seventeenth century. However it was rather difficult for them to acknowledge the ways in which their own 'liberal' views of the Bible were shaped and biased by their own reception history of the Bible. In all cases the study of reception history opens the eyes of Protestants to the importance and unavoidability of tradition in the sense of Roman Catholic theology. It opens the eyes to the fact that biblical texts are something like the roots or the stem of a tree with many different branches, little twigs, leaves and fruits on it. It makes it difficult, if not impossible, to reject any of these branches, particularly because they, the Protestants, belonged to the heap of branches that were rejected and cut off by others. The study of reception history makes it difficult, if not impossible, to say that this or that interpretation of a biblical text is clearly and definitely false!

All this sounds rather negative, not only for many pious people, fundamentalists and others, who read the Bible directly as God's word and try to apply the message of biblical texts directly to their lives. Historical criticism has taught us that the Bible speaks not with one voice; rather it is a library of many different voices recorded in one book. Reception history has added to this the insight that every biblical text gives life to many different receptions and seems to contain a very rich potential of different meanings. This makes very urgent the question whether there is a limitation to this variety, whether it is possible to distinguish between legitimate and non-legitimate receptions of biblical texts, or whether the Bible is ultimately nothing else than a basis of unlimited pluralism. I leave this question for the moment unanswered because I want to turn to the positive effects that the study of reception history can provide. Two are important for me.

That reception history makes the distinction between true and false interpretations difficult is only one side of the truth: there is also another. The study of reception history opens the eyes to receptions of the Bible in other churches, in other cultures, by people with different theological views, by so-called heretics or unbelievers. Their interpretations of biblical texts are not more and not less than receptions, just as our own interpretations are. The insight into the contextual character of every reception of a biblical text reinforces this. In this way, the study of reception history strengthens tolerance and mutual understanding.

My other point is of a quite different character. The study of the rich landscape of reception history between us and the original meaning of the texts and their original witness to Christ leads to the insight that no view about this original meaning and about Christ is possible without this landscape. Let me compare the original meaning of a text with a high mountain peak visible at a great distance. As a Swiss living in Berne, I know that no view of the summit of a distant high mountain like the 'Jungfrau' is possible without looking at all the hills, valleys and smaller mountains in the foreground. Even more: it is only this foreground, the frame of the surrounding landscape, which makes the beauty of the high mountain visible. A 'naked' Jungfrau would be ridiculous. In the same way a 'naked' biblical text, not viewed from a specific point of view and not 'framed' by a specific reception history, would be meaningless. It is the tradition that shapes our own place from where we look at the text and which makes the text to be meaningful. Without the tradition in and through which we live there is no meaningfulness. Only the surrounding landscape makes an *image* of the distant mountain possible which is not isolated. In the same way the effective history which becomes visible in the reception history of a text is a precondition for its *meaningful* interpretation.

Effective History, the Interpreter and the Hermeneutical Situation

'Consciousness of being affected by history [*Wirkungsgeschichte*] is primarily consciousness of the hermeneutical situation' (Gadamer 1989, p. 301). This quotation of Gadamer is applicable to reception history in a double sense. First, study of the reception history of biblical texts in our own ecclesiastical and cultural tradition shows what we have become through them as Christians, theologians, Protestants, Catholics, Orthodox, Europeans, Africans, as modern people and as individuals in our personal biographies. It shows what we owe to the texts. It helps us to understand why we interpret a text – as Catholics, Orthodox, Lutherans, Europeans – in the specific way we do. In this way, the study of the reception history of a biblical text in our own tradition introduces *us* into the process of interpretation. It helps towards recognizing and laying open the determining role of the interpreter in the process of interpretation. It is a contribution to overcoming the distance to the texts which is necessary in any historical or synchronic analysis, but which prevents understanding a text for today. It helps towards de-objectivizing the process of interpretation.

Second, studying recent and contemporary reception history helps even further in that it is an excellent instrument to illuminate what Gadamer calls the 'hermeneutical situation'. Let me take the reception history of the passion narrative in the twentieth century as an example. It is evident that the traditional Reformation interpretation, with its emphasis on the atoning death of Jesus, has lost its influence in Protestant Europe almost completely – and this not only because it is exegetically wrong and was mainly an 'eisegesis' of Pauline theology into the passion narrative of the Gospels. The reading of the passion narrative that dominated in the Late Middle Ages, where contemplation of the figure of the suffering Jesus used as a basis for a piety of compassion was in the foreground, remains in a certain way more influential today. However, the process of an identification of the reader with the suffering Jesus has become a different one: Jesus is no more a suffering God but a suffering human being. Whereas in the eighteenth and nineteenth centuries, the suffering human Jesus was mostly interpreted as a model of a 'noble death', it has become different in the twentieth century: Jesus' death reflects all the despair and hopelessness of humanity in the past century.'Jesus wasn't more than a human ... He has cried out his agony: this is why I like him, my friend', says Albert Camus (Camus 1993, p. 120, my translation). The depth of this despair is that Jesus has lost even the consciousness of God's presence (Matt 27:46):'My God, why have you forsaken me?' This seems to be the key question of modern people in Western Europe when they are confronted with the passion narrative. The absence of God is mirrored again and again by modern interpretations of the passion narrative particularly in literature and art.[6] This is what I call our 'hermeneutical situation' vis à vis the passion narrative. It includes a specific way of looking at a text and a specific way of posing questions to a text. In this way the study of reception history helps towards a contextual exegesis.

To understand a biblical text without introducing the interpreter and without a clear consciousness of the hermeneutical situation is like looking at a distant mountain without taking into account the surrounding landscape. The mountain peak then will stand like an isolated triangle in the void.

Reception History and Holistic Interpretation

The study of reception history includes non-scholarly interpretations of the Bible in prayers, hymns and all kinds of pious literature. It includes also literature: poems, novels etc. Beyond this, the interpretation of the Bible in visual arts, music, dance, private or political activities, wars and peace, ethics, institutions and institutional texts, suffering and martyrdom is the object of studies of reception history. Reception history reminds theologians that they are not the only, and not the most important, persons who interpret the Bible. The study of reception history encourages theologians to take up a dialogue about the Bible with artists, musicians and politicians. It is a reminder for theologians to take the biblical interpretations of so-called 'ordinary people' seriously. Theologians tend to isolate themselves from other people, particularly in Europe and North America with their high-level universities. Reception history can be used as a remedy against this.

Through reception history theologians become aware of the possibilities and opportunities of biblical interpretation in media other than language. Particularly important for me has been the visual arts. Paintings require a holistic interpretation which includes senses, feelings and actions. This is evident for instance in late medieval religious art: many paintings seek to evoke and strengthen a piety of compassion. They want to evoke deep feelings of sorrow and compassion. Paintings are used in meditation and stimulate the spectators' readiness to accept their own suffering. Since the Renaissance, religious art has become more and more decontextualized; it has widely lost its function for piety and has become 'pure art' that can be looked at in museums and churches that have become museums. As a reaction against this, the literary theorist Hans Robert Jauss, in an important essay about aesthetic experience (Jauss 1972), has emphasized the important cognitive function of modern art. Particularly important for him is the innovative power of surprising and even shocking new 'inventions' of old subjects by artists. For Jauss art must neither be isolated from cognition nor from society – contrary to the aesthetics of 'pure art' and the purity of 'judgements of taste' in European history of aesthetics before and after Kant's *Critique of Judgement*. New, sometimes provocative and even shocking inventions of artists create a 'space of freedom' which leads spectators to a new vision of traditional stories, questions their well-accustomed way of life and leads to new actions. This is particularly true for new artistic 'creations' of old, seemingly well-known biblical stories.

The Ecumenical Impact of Reception History

The study of reception history confronts us with receptions of biblical texts in other churches. It shows us what Roman Catholics or Orthodox,

Pentecostals or secular people, African women, monks or Anabaptist peasants became through the Bible. Here it is not a matter of becoming conscious of our own interpretative horizon, but of widening our horizon by opening it up to others' horizons. In this way, effective history opens the eyes for the otherness of meanings of New Testament texts in other traditions. Used like that the study of reception history aims not primarily at self-understanding but at a better understanding of other people and other churches in the spectrum of the biblical texts. The texts are theirs as well as ours! Only indirectly is it also an exercise in self-understanding, in that we understand what we are not, but might become. In this way the study of reception history provides correctives to our own readings. It shows in exemplary manner what we could become by means of the texts by showing what others have become by means of the texts.

Studying reception history of the Bible in other ecclesiastical traditions does not only lead to a deeper understanding of how biblical texts were interpreted in these churches, but also to a deeper understanding of their hermeneutics. It leads, for example, Protestants to a deeper understanding of the Roman Catholic concept of interpretation guided by the 'rule of faith' and of the Orthodox understanding of the Bible as a book read and celebrated *in* the church. In a similar way, it leads Orthodox or Catholic interpreters of the Bible to a deeper understanding of the Protestant concept of the Bible as a fundamental vis à vis the church: it is the Bible *before* the church which has enabled Protestants to realize the critical and self-critical potential of the Bible in a remarkable way.

Studying reception history of the Bible includes the interpretations of the Bible in other cultures. Africans with their deep sensitivity for community and social justice, or Japanese with their deep sensitivity for ambiguity and beauty, have discovered other potential meanings of biblical texts which were widely overlooked by white European readers.

Studying reception history widens the interpreter's horizon even beyond the borderlines of the churches: the Bible is not only the book of church-members, but also the book of those considered to be heretics by other churches. I can personally attest to having learned a great deal from the interpretations and actualizations of those who have been consigned to the scrap heap of heresy. In the case of the Gospel of Matthew, for instance, I am thinking of the Arian *Opus Imperfectum* (Banning 1988) preserved under the protection of its being attributed to John Chrysostom, or of the testimonies of persecuted Anabaptists in the Swiss Emmental, which holds a special interest for me as a Bernese citizen. They understood the Sermon on the Mount definitely better than their contemporary Reformed preachers in the city of Berne.

Beyond this, reception history studies the reception of the Bible by non-Christians as well. The Bible has become a cultural heritage of Europe and the world, which is precious and influential far beyond the churches: people like Mark Chagall, Mahatma Gandhi, Milan Machovec or Nikos Katsantsakis understood the Bible in a much deeper way than most of their Christian contemporaries. The study of reception history considers *all* the receptions of the Bible. It treats them with the same basic principle of sympathy as Christian interpretations. Quite possibly, they will reveal something of the truth of biblical texts just as well!

To conclude: the study of reception history opens up narrow horizons and leads into an ecumenical and universal dialogue. This dialogue is much broader than most ecclesiastical dialogues, because the effective power of the Bible transcends the borderlines of the churches. It questions basic models of life and offers possibilities of what we could have become and still could become through the Bible. It provides us with 'different eyes' through which we can look upon our own texts in a new way.

Reception History Presents Good and Bad Receptions

Biblical texts effected love and hatred, peace and wars, segregation and tolerance, androcentricsm and female piety, fraternal fellowship with Israel and anti-Judaism, justification by faith alone and self-legitimation, triumphalism and humility. Heikki Räisänen has proposed reserving the term 'effective history' for the legitimate and good effects of biblical texts; for the rest one should not speak about effects of the texts, but about abuse (Räisänen 2001). But complex reality does not permit such a simple distinction. Can we distinguish between good and bad fruits so easily? Many interpretations and realizations of biblical texts are ambiguous, in some respects good, in some bad. And what about the biblical texts themselves? There are texts that deserve criticism – texts like the woes of Matt 23, texts full of God-produced cruelties like in the Apocalypse, or texts condemning so-called heretics with insulting words like 'dogs who turn back to their own vomit' (2 Pet 2:22). Is it possible to take a text as a good text when it produced only or predominantly bad fruits in its reception history?

Be it as it may, the question how we can distinguish between good and bad texts and their good and bad fruits is unavoidable for any theological interpretation. Theological interpretation of a biblical text includes its application; it includes a responsible human answer to its claim. Robert Morgan says: 'The very openness of literary study to all kinds of interpretations means that the question of truth, which is always central to theology, can disappear from view' (Morgan and Barton 1988, p. 289). Whatever literary critics might say to this, for theology Morgan's remark is very true. The quest for truth is the essence of theology; theology cannot get rid of it. If theology is *only* descriptive it is a blunt sword and useless for anybody. Theology *has* to evaluate and to judge interpretations.

But this task is very difficult! Theology has to distinguish, but at the same time it has to propose its distinctions in a non-imposing, non-imperative, non-absolute and argumentative way. Theology cannot distinguish without discussing carefully a great variety of criteria for distinction between true and false interpretations. Here once more the indispensability of the study of reception history of the Bible becomes obvious: reception history offers such criteria for discussion. Reception history teaches how they functioned in history and what were their results and failures. It invites us to compare the different criteria, to discuss their biases and to confront them with the Bible itself. In this respect reception history offers materials for the theological question for truth.

Reception history shows also that not only are interpretations of the Bible contextual, but also every criterion of truth is contextual. There are no 'abstract heavens of truth'[7] which are not affected, changed, used and abused in history. A student of reception history in the wide sense of the word will be sceptical about merely doctrinal criteria of truth. He/she will be inclined to propose criteria of truth which encompass the full reality of life which is the territory of holistic interpretations and applications of the Bible. Such a criterion was proposed by Augustine in the first book of his four volumes *About Christian teaching*: 'Whoever believes to have understood the divine Scriptures or any part of them without building up through his insight the twofold love to God and to the neighbour, has not yet understood them'.[8] This is a criterion that considers the totality of life into which any authentic interpretation of a New Testament text is embodied.[9] But with this, our study of reception history has led us in the midst of a theological discussion of how a New Testament theology should be construed that focuses the message of the New Testament into our life and our society today.

Notes

1. Most New Testament theologies that are available today are histories of New Testament theology with some afterthoughts. Maybe Childs (1993) has the strongest claim to be a biblical theology for today, in spite of the fact that it hardly contains any explicit reflections on today's hermeneutical situation and little on reception history – for obvious systematic reasons.

2. The series is edited by John Sawyer, Christopher Rowland and Judith Kovacs. The first NT volumes: Kovacs and Rowland 2004; Edwards 2004.
3. Founded by Eduard Schweizer and Rudolf Schnackenburg in 1970.
4. The following draws on the section 'The principle of history of effect' (Gadamer 1989, pp. 299–306).
5. This is what seemed to happen with the EKK!
6. For details I refer to the passages on reception history in vol. 4 of my commentary on Matthew (Luz 1985–2002); cf. particularly the interpretations of Matt 26:36–46 and 27:45–50. (The English edition of the commentary will come out in 2005 in the *Hermeneia* series.)
7. I owe the formulation to Miguez-Bonino 1975, p. 88.
8. Augustine, *De Doctrina Christiana* 1.40.
9. This is the main reason why I am hesitant about Robert Morgan's proposal to give preference to the study of the literary framework of the biblical texts over the study of the historical framework (1988, p. 286). Only the study of the historical horizon opens up the original life-context of a text!

References

Banning, J. von (ed.), *Opus Imperfectum in Matthaeum* (CCSL; Turholt: Brepols, 1988).
Camus, A., *La chute* (Paris: Edition folia, 1993).
Childs, B.S., *Biblical Theology of the Old and New Testaments* (Minneapolis: Fortress Press, 1993).
Ebeling, G., *The Word of God and Tradition* (ET London: Collins, 1968).
Edwards, M., *John* (Oxford: Blackwell, 2004).
Gadamer, H.G., *Truth and Method* (2nd rev. edn; New York: Continuum, 1989).
Jauss, H.R., *Kleine Apologie der ästhetischen Erfahrung* (Konstanzer Universitätsreden 59; Konstanz: Universitätsverlag, 1972).
Kovacs, J. and Rowland C., *Revelation* (Oxford: Blackwell, 2004).
Luz, U., *Das Evangelium nach Matthäus* (4 vols; EKK I; Neukirchen/Düsseldorf: Neukirchener/Benziger, 1985–2002).
Morgan, Robert, with Barton, J., *Biblical Interpretation* (Oxford: Oxford University Press, 1988).
Miguez-Bonino, J., *Doing Theology in a Revolutionary Situation* (Philadelphia: Fortress Press, 1975).
Räisänen, H., 'The "Effective History"' of the Bible: a challenge to biblical scholarship', in *idem, Challenges to Biblical Interpretation* (Leiden: Brill, 2001), pp. 263–82.

Chapter 9

Women in Early Christianity: the Challenge to a New Testament Theology

Margaret Y. MacDonald, Nova Scotia

While there are many areas of New Testament research where the concerns of New Testament theology are either bracketed or deliberately avoided, this does not generally hold true for the study of women in early Christianity. The relationship between research on early Christian women and theology has two central facets to be discussed below. First, perhaps more than any other aspect of the study of early Christianity, investigations of early Christian women have been taken up by contemporary theologians, especially feminist theologians. Second, while this is not always the case, several interpreters of early Christian texts dealing with women have framed their discussion with explicitly theological interests.

After an initial discussion of these two aspects of the relationship between research on early Christian women and theology, this chapter will consider four challenges to a New Testament theology emerging from the study of early Christian women. In an effort to illustrate these challenges, the essay will culminate in an analysis of Eph 5:22–33 – a text which has been viewed as problematic for women on many levels.

Feminist Theology

The publication of two of the most recent collections of essays on
feminism and theology offers an illustration of the first facet of the
relationship between theology and the study of early Christian women
as described above. Both designed to provide a broad overview of the
field in an accessible format, Susan Frank Parsons (ed.), *The Cambridge
Companion to Feminist Theology* (2002) and Janet Martin Soskice and
Diana Lipton (eds), *Feminism and Theology* (2003) bear witness to the
importance of feminist work on the New Testament for the emergence
of Christian feminist theology. The latter work in particular includes
numerous essays on various New Testament texts and themes, as well as
on the treatment of women in post-New Testament texts and the precious few indications of women's authorship and voices in the literature
of the early church. In these works and others, the study of biblical
women and early Christian women acts as, if not the foundation, then at
least as a very important component of feminist theology.

    At a time when theologians might be expected to pay only passing
interest to highly technical and sometimes overtly anti-theological scholarship on the New Testament, there are indications of precisely the
opposite tendencies in relation to the study of early Christian women.
Robert Morgan's insights into the nature of New Testament theology may
help us to understand why this is so. In discussing the influence of the
nineteenth-century scholarship of William Wrede who sought to define
New Testament scholarship as a historical discipline without reference
to the interests of Christian theologians, Morgan (1973, p. 21) sets out
the distinction between the historical and theological perspective in a
manner that to a large extent rings true even today:'The worst crime that
the historian can be accused of is modernization; theology, looking for a
contemporary meaning in the sources, continually tempts him in this
direction'. Theology tempts the historian of early Christian thought with
engagement with the concerns of the modern Christian church and,
more broadly, with the concerns of modern society. It is precisely this
type of 'engagement' that often appears in scholarship on biblical and
early Christian women that is celebrated by theologians, however much
it might be frowned upon by some fellow specialists on ancient texts.

    It is interesting to compare Morgan's assessment to Janet Martin
Soskice's (2003, p. 4) rationale for speaking about theology rather than
religious studies in the introduction to her edited collection:

> Religious studies is concerned with the phenomena of religiosity, while
> theology is a first-order engagement with a community of faith. Whereas

the feminist sociologist of religion looks at changing patterns of worship, the feminist theologian asks about the pain or exasperation that excludes women from organized religion and asks if it need be so. Needless to say, there is an important overlap with theologians drawing on insights of social scientists, but the theologian retains her engagement with the faith community, even where she finds herself operating at a critical distance.

Perhaps more than any other type of recent biblical scholarship, feminist work on the Bible and early Christianity has been taken up and used by faith communities. One prime example of this is Carol A. Newsom and Sharon H. Ringe (eds), *The Women's Bible Commentary* (1992). The relationship between this book and faith communities is actually dialectical for not only has it been frequently taken up for discussion in faith communities, but also the authors acknowledge the influence (both positive and negative) of faith communities and theology upon their work. For example, in the introduction to the volume, the editors report on Claudia Camp's acknowledgement of the influence of a church women's Bible study group for her commentary on 1 and 2 Kings. In contrast, Jane Schaberg (1992, p. xvi) has expressed the relationship between church experience and her commentary on the Gospel of Luke in more problematic terms as '. . . written from a position of anguished, stubborn membership in the Catholic church, whose official leaders currently uphold patriarchal values and resist egalitarian, democratic trends in contemporary society'. For Carol Newsom's (1992, p. 130) commentary on Job, it is the issues raised by feminist theology which guide her reading such as 'the significance of personal experience as a source of religious insight' and 'the relationship between human existence and the whole of creation'.

As Schaberg's comments illustrate so well, feminist interpreters of biblical and early Christian texts have often been forthright about their particular perspectives and social locations. In fact, social location becomes for some scholars one of the critical tools for reading texts. As one of many Jewish women interpreters of early Christian texts, Adele Reinhartz challenges readers from a Christian background both theologically and ethically. She brings her identity as a Jew and as a feminist to the forefront of her writing. Her literary analysis is especially well suited to raising many theological questions, with her Jewish perspective acting as a valuable lens for indicating who is included and who is excluded by the perspective of the text. As a 'resistant reader', Reinhartz (1994, p. 597) places herself '. . . in the subject position of the Johannine Jews, who dispute the christological claims of the text, dismiss its christological interpretation of scripture, and discount its claims of authority'. But as

Reinhartz is careful to point out, 'resistant reading' does not always involve negativity for there is much in the text that she finds helpful for her life as a woman in her own faith community:

> . . . even though I am a resisting Jew, this text speaks to me directly, through the persons of Martha and Mary. While these sisters have made a faith choice that I do not emulate, their role in the community is not unfamiliar to me. The choices they made set them apart from the larger Jewish community, yet they continued to reside within it and related themselves to it. They derived support from their community in time of grief and, if they were indeed apostles, worked for transformation and change from within. . . . Similarly, Mary and Martha can encourage those of us who belong to faith communities in which women still struggle for equality and in which feminist theology is taboo, to remain within, enjoy what we can, and work for transformation.

Although she stands outside of the Christian tradition, Adele Reinhartz offers us here a fine example of the second aspect of the relationship between research on early Christian women and theology mentioned above: several interpreters of early Christian texts dealing with women have framed their discussion with explicitly theological interests.

Adele Reinhartz' Jewish perspective is one of many examples of the diversity of perspectives and social locations which have characterized work on early Christian texts concerning women and feminist theology alike (Ruether 2002). In both of these overlapping domains, Jewish scholars and representatives of various Christian communities are working alongside scholars who no longer identify themselves with religious communities at all and, especially in the case of historical investigations of early Christian texts, sometimes come to the study of religion from secular backgrounds. Moreover, increasingly the task of interpretation is viewed as a global exercise, involving not only North American and European scholars, but also African, Asian and Latin-American scholars.

Four Challenges

In considering the diversity of scholarship on early Christian women and feminist interpretation of early Christian texts, the work of Jewish feminist scholars has been so important that it must be singled out as offering one of the most important challenges to a New Testament theology (e.g., Levine 1991, Kraemer 1992, Reinhartz 1994, Tanzer 1994). These scholars have challenged simplistic assumptions about Jewish women in the bibli-

cal world, and historical inaccuracies whereby Jewish women are sometimes viewed as foils for the liberating position of Jesus or the rise of
early Christianity (Kraemer 1999a,b). Such findings obviously have important consequences for a New Testament theology, not only because they
render claims of superiority problematic; but, more subtly, they also
require the theologian to exercise great caution in putting forth a background for a message of 'liberation', and in arguing for distinct features
of the New Testament world. In helping us to arrive at an accurate understanding of women's involvement in religious groups in this era, perhaps
no scholar has been more influential than Ross S. Kraemer with her
broadly comparative work, *Her Share of the Blessings: Women's Religions
Among Pagans, Jews, and Christians in the Greco-Roman World* (1992).
Drawing extensively upon the work of classicists and ancient historians,
Kraemer does not gloss over the particularities of groups. Yet, she also
allows one to see evidence with a broad comparative lens and to identify
repeating patterns in the treatment of women by ancient authors and
evidence for the roles (including leadership roles) they played in the
ancient Mediterranean world.

More recently, scholars drawing upon the extensive work on the
Roman family (e.g., Osiek and Balch 1997, Balch and Osiek 2003, Osiek
and MacDonald forthcoming), have filled out our understanding of the
daily lives of early Christian women and have drawn attention to the
shared experiences between early Christian women and other women
in the Roman world; not only is it appropriate to think of a good deal of
commonality between Jewish women and women in emerging Christian
communities, but an understanding of the lives of pagan women also has
much to contribute to our knowledge of early Christian women. Work
on house churches and the familial context of early Christianity offers
its own kind of challenge to theology for it makes us take the domestic
context of Christianity seriously and shatters any illusion of a New
Testament born in some type of rarefied 'academic' environment isolated
from the concerns of daily life (e.g., caring for children and the sick,
management of meals, hospitality). As will be discussed further below in
relation to Ephesians 5, if New Testament theology is to include an ecclesiological component, it must consider how the presence of women in
the household shaped the sacred space of New Testament communities
and must allow the influence of women to be acknowledged as an important aspect of the religious symbolism and ethical discourse of the New
Testament.

The second challenge to a New Testament theology arising from work
on early Christian women has been presented by feminist scholars to
their colleagues in early Christian studies generally, but it has special

significance for theological work on the New Testament. It is what has been termed above as 'engagement' with the concerns of the modern church and/or society. A vivid example of this engagement with respect to church life can be seen in the introduction to Karen Jo Torjesen's, *When Women were Priests* (1993, p. 7): 'Understanding why and how women, once leaders in the Jesus movement and in the early church, were marginalized and scapegoated as Christianity became the state religion is crucial if women are to reclaim their rightful, equal place in the church today . . . It is high time that the church, which claims to embody his [Jesus'] good news to the world, stop betraying its own essential heritage of absolute equality'. In my work on the early Christian women, *Early Christian Women and Pagan Opinion* (1996, p. 24), the focus is less on contemporary church issues and more broadly upon how the values encoded in early Christian texts and Greco-Roman reactions to early Christian women can lead to critical reflection about the patterns of behaviour in our own society:

> . . . I hope that this study will cause the reader to reflect upon the trans-historical survival of expectations concerning female behaviour which continue to shape the lives of women in various ways. I hope that my study will raise questions about why the violation of stereotypes can elicit violent reaction within societies. I also hope that this window into the lives of women, who risked relations with their families to enter a new religious group, will lead to a further appreciation of the challenges faced by all women who strive to lead 'multi-dimensional' lives.

In both of these examples (and many more could be added), one detects an attempt to grapple with the political functions and ethical consequences of ancient texts in their historical contexts, but also to raise questions about the ramifications of these texts in contemporary contexts. Careful historical work is highly valued, but there is an attempt to draw implications from the results of this historical work for life today. Such efforts are in keeping with the general suspicion in feminist work of claims of value neutrality, as if deliberate bracketing of modern concerns, presuppositions and values leads to a more accurate understanding of the ancient Mediterranean world. According to some feminist New Testament scholars, however, such aspirations are not only illusory, but also contrary to what should be the ultimate goals of biblical scholarship.

A critique of positivism, objectivity and value-neutrality has occupied a central place in the theoretical reflections of a pioneer in feminist theological analysis of the New Testament, Elisabeth Schüssler Fiorenza.

No scholar has been more influential in presenting early Christian women as a challenge to New Testament theology. As the title of her ground-breaking work, *In Memory of Her: A Feminist Theological Reconstruction of Christian Origins* (1983) – a book that must be counted as one of the most important works in New Testament studies in the twentieth century – makes clear, Fiorenza has explicitly defined her historical work in relation to theological purposes.[1] In fact, in her various publications, Fiorenza argues that historical reconstruction for its own sake is not enough. While valuing many of the new methodologies and approaches as key to the interpretative enterprise, Fiorenza sees the New Testament scholar as ethically bound (1988) to comment on the ethical and theological significance of the text. For example, in setting forth her fourfold methodology for rhetorical-critical analysis of 1 Corinthians, Fiorenza (1987, p. 389) describes a fourth stage where the essence of rhetoric as political discourse leads to critical assessment:'New Testament rhetorical criticism, therefore, cannot limit itself to a formalistic analysis of 1 Corinthians, nor to an elucidation of its historical-social context; rather it must develop a responsible ethical and evaluative theological criticism'. Fiorenza's own exegetical approach includes a combination of feminist hermeneutics and rhetorical analysis, and her detailed theoretical discussions of her approach and of exegetical methods in general (1984, 1992) are of great value for delineating and reflecting upon the potential of a New Testament theology. By asking (1992, p. 47) what a reading of the Bible does to those who submit 'to its world of vision' and by rejecting claims of value-neutrality in favour of explicit articulation of theoretical, religious and socio-political frameworks, Fiorenza's work creates opportunities for rapprochement between New Testament scholarship and theology: '. . . the transformation of the scientific-positivist ethos of biblical studies into a rhetorical-ethical one creates a theoretical space in which feminist and other liberation theologies can participate in the center rather than on the margins of biblical interpretation'.

While they have not always escaped criticism, Fiorenza's theological concepts have seemed bold and empowering to many. The limits of space prevent detailed discussion, but it is valuable to consider at least one example, her concept of the *ekklesia* of women. In the following excerpt (1983, pp. 322–3) she discusses the Markan community:

> Despite the extraordinary fear for their lives the women disciples stood with Jesus in his suffering, sought to honor him in his death, and now become the proclaimers of his resurrection. They preserve the messianic identity of the crucified and resurrected Lord which is entrusted to the circle of the disciples. Despite their fear and flight the good news of the

resurrection is carried on. The Markan community still experiences this fear of Mary Magdalene and the other women. Like Peter, the community is tempted to betray Jesus in order to avoid suffering . . . It struggles to avoid the pattern of dominance and submission that characterizes its social-cultural environment. Those who are the farthest from the centre of religious and political power, the slaves, the children, the gentiles, the women, becomes paradigms of true discipleship.

Against those who see her *ekklesia* of women as naive or idealistic, Fiorenza (1992, pp. 6–7) has pointed to a tension (visible in the above citation) between the 'already' and 'not yet' of the *ekklesia* of women. Against those who argue that her construct inevitably privileges believers over non-believers, Fiorenza acknowledges that she is writing as a Christian theologian, but argues that she is neither encouraging women to remain within biblical religions nor even recommending that they should read the Bible: 'Rather I seek to work out a process and method for a feminist political reading that can empower women who, for whatever reasons, are still affected by the Bible to read "against the grain" of its patriarchal rhetoric'. However much it might be related to a New Testament vision of the discipleship of equals, the *ekklesia* is also clearly a modern and variegated assembly with a specific 'political' agenda: '. . . I seek simultaneously to destabilize the center *and* the margins of "malestream" biblical studies by constructing the *ekklesia* as a feminist counter-public-sphere from which a feminist biblical rhetoric can speak'.

As is evident in Fiorenza's comments about the Markan community, feminist analysis of early Christian texts has brought the voice of women to the centre of interpretation. The recovery of women's voices in fact constitutes the third central challenge to a New Testament theology arising from work on early Christian women. This challenge involves two interrelated parts: the recovery of alternative voices within the biblical text itself and the questioning of the boundaries of the canon of Scripture to allow for consideration of material which is of central importance to women's experience (then and now), but which was marginalized by the process of canonization and the evolving 'orthodoxy' of the church.

Shortly after the publication of Fiorenza's *In Memory of Her* (1983), Bernadette Brooten published a seminal essay (1985) where she called for an approach to the history of early Christian women, which brings women to the centre of investigation. Brooten highlighted the inadequacies of earlier tendencies to study women largely in terms of male views on women (e.g. Paul's views on women compared to Philo's views on

women), calling for an approach to the study of early Christian women
that would draw upon a full knowledge of the lives of women in the
ancient world and focus on the women themselves. In the case of the
evidence from the Pauline letters (1985, pp. 80-1), for example this
would mean that '. . . one would be locating women like Junia and Prisca
in the continuum of Jewish women's history, which includes the
Therapeutrides, Jewish women who were synagogue leaders, and
Beruriah [a learned Palestinian Jewish woman of the early second
century]'. This focus on women led Brooten to make some penetrating
remarks about the women associates of Paul (1985, p. 82). Just because
they were Paul's associates, we can by no means be certain that these
women were in agreement with his theology, Christology, or views on
women. With respect to a text like 1 Cor 11:2-16, Brooten called for a
new type of analysis: 'Rather than taking Paul's views on women as an
accurate reflection of early Christian women's reality, one would analyze
Paul's system of thought on its own terms and in the context of male
thinking of the time and then ask how women in antiquity were affected
by and, in turn, how they affected Paul's views'.

Antoinette Clark Wire's book, *The Corinthian Women Prophets: A
Reconstruction Through Paul's Rhetoric* (1990), went some distance
in addressing Brooten's call for a new type of analysis. Her work is
particularly important for this chapter because of its deliberate focus on
the theology of the Corinthian women. In her book, Wire engages in
rhetorical analysis, seeking to elucidate the rhetorical situation created
by Paul's arguments. But in contrast to the many studies of 1 Corinthians
where Paul's thought remains at the centre of interpretation, she seeks
to recover other voices, leading to discussion of the implications of texts
for women in the community even where women are not specifically
named. The result is a rhetorical commentary which aims to bring the
perspective of the Corinthian women prophets to bear on every part of
Paul's letter.

Wire's work challenges New Testament theology to take minority or
marginalized voices (even those who were clearly in opposition to the
dominant voice of authoritative texts) in the Bible seriously as theological
possibilities. In contrast to so many New Testament scholars who have
presented Paul's response to the pneumatic excesses of the Corinthians
as theologically superior, Wire has undertaken a type of reversal in her
argumentation, seeking to understand 'the other side' on its own terms.
It is the 'theology of the spirit' of the Corinthian women prophets that
Wire (1990, p. 185) presents as a challenge to Paul: '. . . the Corinthian
women prophets claim direct access to resurrected life in Christ through
God's spirit. Being thus filled, rich and ruling, they take part in Christ's

joyful meal and God's word goes forth from them to each other in ever-widening circles'. Robin Scroggs (1992, p. 547) has called Wire's work, 'the most striking defense of the Corinthian theology against Paul's theology of the cross'.

Wire's investigation (1990, p. 9) rests explicitly upon the presupposition that 'the women prophets in Corinth's church have a place in the group Paul is addressing, some role in the rhetorical situation'. Reviewers have critiqued Wire for exceeding the evidence by assuming that the women prophets of Corinth are always on Paul's mind and for giving these women prominence when it is not warranted by the sources.[2] But by forcefully reminding the reader of the problematic nature of the assumption that women are absent from Paul's purview (given that the history of women frequently involves failure to acknowledge the presence and influence of women), Wire has opened up new theological potential for 1 Corinthians. It is not only possible to read the letter with Paul as a guide, but also with the Corinthian women prophets who, as women, are representatives of the group previously described by Fiorenza as central to the vision of the *ekklesia* of women: those who are the farthest from the centre of religious and political power. Rather than being simply misguided women who irreverently removed their head covering during worship, they too can serve a paradigm of discipleship.

As an example of the recovery of alternative voices within the biblical text itself, Wire's work hints at re-evaluation of the authority of scripture and the boundaries of the canon. In fact, the notion of a 'canon within a canon' frequently appears in theoretical discussion of feminist work on the Bible. In the type of feminist biblical hermeneutics which is best described as 'liberationist feminism' (Osiek 1985) the focus is clearly upon those biblical texts which challenge or transcend androcentric and patriarchal structures and encode a vision of liberated humanity. In her highly influential reconstruction of Christian origins Fiorenza (1983, p. 30), for example, makes clear choices about what should be considered revelatory in the New Testament and what should be rejected: 'Biblical revelation and truth are given only in those texts and interpretative models that transcend critically their patriarchal frameworks and allow for a vision of Christian women as historical and theological subjects and actors'.[3] In her conclusion to this work (1983, p. 334), she clearly distinguishes between texts which reveal 'integral parts of Jesus' "alternative" praxis of agape and service' and other texts which do not: 'While – for apologetic reasons – the post-Pauline and post-Petrine writers seek to limit women's leadership roles in the Christian community to roles which are culturally and religiously acceptable, the evangelists called Mark and John highlight the alternative character of the Christian community, and therefore accord women apostolic and ministerial leadership'.

Given that Robert Morgan (1990, p. 690) has written that a New Testament theology hinges on its view of revelation, it is important to note that such 'selective' reading and assessment in feminist biblical scholarship has been critiqued precisely for setting forth an overly restrictive basis for a theology of revelation; what is revelatory and what is authoritative appear to be equated too simplistically and whatever does not fit certain fairly narrow criteria is rejected as non-revelatory (Osiek 1985). Writing about the liberationist hermeneutic in feminist work on the Bible in general, Carolyn Osiek (1985, p. 104) has observed: '. . . this narrow criterion of revelation leads the liberationist method to eulogize the prophets, Jesus, and sometimes Paul while writing off other, particularly later, New Testament writers who do not meet the liberation criterion, thus forming a type of "canon within the canon" on very slim foundations'.

In 1992 (p. 149) Fiorenza wrote that 'the question of scriptural authority has taken center stage in the discussions of a feminist theological hermeneutics'. Within feminist research itself, there still remains no consensus on the authority of the Bible and the role of the canon. The question can be posed in deceptively simple terms, but for many the answer seems far from straightforward: How does one reconcile the presence of oppressive, androcentric and patriarchal texts with liberating elements and material which appears to have lasting and universal value? Feminist scholars are to be commended for addressing these issues head on, for they arise so frequently in the public forum, whether in churches, classrooms, and cultural exchanges of various kind (with the recent great interest in Dan Brown's *The Da Vinci Code* offering a good example of renewed interest in 'alternative' sources). Yet even if there remains no consensus on the issue of scriptural authority among feminist thinkers, there is broad consensus on the inadequacy of the canon as a theological norm that is revealed first in the task of uncovering the voices which have been neglected or even condemned in the Bible itself, but most obviously in the openness to extra-canonical sources as a wellspring of women's experience and potential empowerment.[4]

Perhaps the clearest example of this openness is the inclusion of various extra-canonical texts in the edited work of Elisabeth Schüssler Fiorenza, *Searching the Scriptures: A Feminist Commentary*. In her introduction to this work (1994, p. 5), Fiorenza is explicit about her desire to highlight the exclusionary function of the canon. She states that '. . . the historical silencing and textual marginalization of women are by-products of the so-called patristic kyriarchal selection and exclusionary canonization process'. In setting commentaries on canonical New Testament works alongside commentaries on a variety of works written within a few centuries of the New Testament, new opportunities are created to witness women's authorship and story-telling, women's various experiences in early Christian communities, and the revelation of divine Sophia/Wisdom. Among the texts of particular interest to early Christian women are numerous so-called apocryphal and Gnostic writings, including *The Gospel of Mary Magdalene*, *The Infancy of Mary of Nazareth* (also know as *The Proto-Gospel of James*), *The Passion of Perpetua and Felicity*, and the *Acts of Thecla*.

For a better understanding of how Fiorenza's commentary highlights the exclusionary function of the canon, we might consider the case of the *Acts of Thecla*. The inclusion of this work (viewed by some early Christians as part of the canonical scriptures) is in keeping with significant scholarly interest in the work as a counter-voice in relation to the New Testament Pastoral Epistles. While the connection between the *Acts of Thecla* and the experience of real ascetic women has recently been questioned (Cooper 1996, pp. 62–3), the theory of Dennis MacDonald (1983; cf. Burrus 1986, McGinn 1994) concerning the relationship between the Pastorals and the *Acts* remains influential: the *Acts* reflects the oral story-telling of celibate women (cf. 1 Tim 4:7; 2 Tim 3:6) which seems also to have been popular among the widows exhorted in 1 Tim 5:3–16 and to have promoted asceticism in the community (1 Tim 4:3). The challenge to a New Testament theology created by the emerging portrait of early Christian women involves reading the Pastoral Epistles in tandem with the *Acts of Thecla*, seeking to counterbalance the author of the Pastoral's restrictive stance with the openness to women's roles in the *Acts*, and raising critical questions about the attitudes to the created order inherent in the competing visions. Moreover, despite its legend-like quality, the *Acts of Thecla* has much to contribute on its terms, including how faith can challenge such central societal institutions as the family and lead to great courage in the face of adversaries.

A discussion of how the study of women in early Christianity can offer a challenge to New Testament theology would not be complete without consideration of some of the most cautionary statements concerning the nature of the evidence coming from feminist biblical scholars and historians of religion in antiquity alike. The European scholar Lone Fatum (1989, 1991, 1994), for example, has been critical of some feminist reconstructions of Christian origins as being overly optimistic in light of limited evidence and an overtly patriarchal legacy. In her article on 1 Thessalonians (1994, p. 250) she makes her point forcefully in the first line: 'Involving oneself as a feminist theologian in the interpretation of 1 Thessalonians is like forcing one's way into male company, uninvited and perhaps unwanted'. To those who would view her conclusions as pessimistic, she replies that it is vital to confront the sociosexual discrimination which is at the very heart of the Christian tradition. According to Luise Schottroff (1998, p. 203), however, Lone Fatum's deconstruction of patriarchal texts goes too far for it has the potential of rendering '. . . invisible the history of women's resistance and of their liberation that may lurk behind even such texts.'

Few scholars seem to go as far as Lone Fatum in their views concerning the possibilities of historical reconstructions of the lives of early Christian women, but there is a clear discernible trend in the direction of greater pessimism with respect to the possibilities of reconstructing the lives of early Christian women and detecting traces of women's influence. This greater pessimism is resulting especially from more sophistication in literary and rhetorical analysis, and a growing awareness of the representation of women in order to further the agenda of male authors in various ways. This means that studying early Christian women has moved beyond issues of historical construction as they had previously been conceived to include demands for careful attention to how the representation of women is affected by genre, metaphor, novelistic tendencies and ancient *topoi* (e.g., Cooper 1992, 1996, Kraemer and Lander 2000, Lieu 1998). Sophisticated analysis of the representation of women is, therefore, emerging as a fourth challenge to a New Testament theology. For a New Testament theology, however, this can also lead to new opportunities for understanding the importance of women for theological constructions. The appeal to women on a symbolic level, as symbols of the communal and the divine, is part of New Testament tradition with the role of the wife/woman church in the famous marriage teaching of Ephesians offering a particularly good case in point.

The Bride of Christ

At the outset, it is important to note that Ephesians contains the most detailed reflection on the meaning of marriage (including unmistakably theological reflection), and the role of wives in the New Testament. This reflection takes place within the broader framework of the household code of Eph 5:21–6:9 which, like other New Testament codes, is generally viewed as highly conventional teaching. It is generally accepted that the New Testament household codes draw their origins from the traditional moral expositions on household management (involving the three pairs: husband-wife, parent-child, master-slave) found in the teaching of various philosophers, moralists and political thinkers from Aristotle (*Politics* 1.1253b.1–14) onward. A distinctive feature of the code in Ephesians, however, is its detailed treatment of marriage in Eph 5:22–33, which seems so deliberately to build upon the brief treatment of marriage in the Colossian household code (cf. Col 3:18–4:1). Thus, many scholars have attached great significance to this segment of the letter with some even seeing the text as the key to unlocking the purpose of the work as a whole.

Feminist commentators have drawn attention to the hierarchical and patriarchal features of the teaching on marriage in Ephesians, and many have offered categorically negative assessments based on what has seemed as a Deutero-Pauline departure from some of Paul's most important theological concepts. Elizabeth Johnson (1992a, pp. 341–2), for example, writes: 'The result for women is thus a retreat from the initial freedom promised them in Paul's preaching and a reassertion of conventional patriarchal morality'. In keeping with the tendencies highlighted above, Johnson includes an assessment of the challenges to contemporary Christians for whom Ephesians continues to be scripture, including the challenge 'to appreciate the letter's many significant contributions to Christian theology aside from its rather unfortunate view of human marriage'.

For many critics the problematic nature of the teaching concerning wives and marriage in Eph 5:22–33 extends beyond its linkages with household code material to include the manner in which women are inscribed within its symbolism. In Eph 5:25, the author moves from a command for husbands to love their wives to begin a theological exposition of the identity of the church and its relationship to Christ, with human marriage serving primarily in 5:25b–27 as an analogical tool for discussing the human–divine relationship (Tanzer 1994). Here we find language recalling biblical notions of sanctification tied to God's appropriation of Israel, and reflections of the ancient theme of the *hieros gamos* or 'sacred marriage'. With the use of this recurring motif from ancient Near Eastern literature, the author draws the attention of readers to sexual union and especially to the sexual purity of the bride (Osiek 2003) that serves as such an apt metaphor for dissociation of the *ekklesia* from a corrupt society. While the effect is perhaps mitigated at least for modern readers by the presence of scriptural allusions and citations (Eph 5:26 [Ezek 16:9]; Eph 5:28 [Lev 19:18]; Eph 5:31 [Gen 2:24]), we are nevertheless confronted in Eph 5:22–33 by the image of a bride's prenuptial bath and the suggestion of a purity inspection conducted by the bridegroom-Christ who eventually takes her as his own (5:26–7).

Drawing especially upon the work of literary critics on simile and metaphor, Carolyn Osiek (2003, p. 35) has uncovered the sexual undertones of the metaphorical language of Ephesians 5:

> . . . the ideal shy, pure, therefore inexperienced, virgin bride who submits her body to the waiting bridegroom and is reserved for his pleasure alone, for him to initiate her into the joy of sex in whatever way he would like. I do not mean to titillate, but I think all of these undertones are there, especially in the highly unusual suggestion that the bridegroom is the agent of the bride's prenuptial bath and purity inspection. The metaphor comes close to asserting that female biology is destiny. However, it is typical of the kind of projections of the feminine that are based solely on the women's sexual status in the male world: virgin, mother, or whore.

Osiek notes the irony in the fact that so much has been made of Jesus' celibacy in history, when the glorified Christ of Eph 5:22–33 is presented as the bridegroom preparing for the bridal chamber. Offering a good example (2003, p. 35) of the engagement with concerns of the modern church and/or society that is typical of feminist scholarship, she comments: "'It's only symbolic,' we say. Yet there are other elements of the metaphor that are taken with complete seriousness, like the need to conform gender symbolism in eucharistic presidency to reflect the sacred marriage of Christ and the church'. Osiek does not mean to suggest that either the biblical writer or most subsequent theological commentators have taken the metaphor to refer to actual physical union, nevertheless this metaphor has been so influential precisely because the suggestions of sexual union evoke primordial energy. In addition to the explicit engagement with contemporary theological concerns, her work is in keeping with recent feminist scholarship, drawing especially on literary analysis, which problematizes symbolic discourse on women and gender and highlights the extent to which women's identity is used in order to further the agenda of male authors and leaders.

Often read in relation to the Canticle of Canticles, the theology of the sacred marriage of Christ and the church in Ephesians 5 has had a great impact not only on ecclesiology, but also on Mariology and the theology and spirituality of religious life (Osiek 2003). Despite the fact that it seems to have spoken to so many about the mysteries of the relation between the human and the divine, there has been a consensus among scholars working on early Christian women that the metaphor ultimately remains problematic both in the New Testament and in its interpretative legacy across the ages (MacDonald 2000). The problems ultimately stem from the fact that in this theological construct, it is the husband who is understood as representing God or Christ and the wife is the symbol for the human *ekklesia*. When the metaphorical nature of the language is forgotten, possibilities for abuse are created: male impunity comes to overpower female fallibility and ultimately God seems more and more like the ultimate male, leaving no room for feminine imagery for the divine (Osiek 2003, Johnson 1992b).

Perhaps more than any other New Testament text which has been examined by scholars working on early Christian women, Eph 5:22–33 brings the problem of scriptural authority sharply into focus. On the one hand, there are aspects of the text which have been recognized as having timeless value (MacDonald 2000) and could occupy an important place in a theology of the New Testament, even a feminist theology of the New Testament: the transformative power of love, the importance of using life 'in the Lord' as a means of discerning how to treat others, the value assigned to marriage/physical partnership – sometimes forgotten in a church eager to embrace celibacy. But on the other hand, an awareness of the highly problematic nature of the text and its legacy can easily lead to the conclusion that the bride of Christ metaphor should be abandoned altogether (Osiek 2003). At the very least, scholarship on early Christian women suggests that a New Testament theology cannot ignore the problematic nature of the text. But one approach that is in keeping with previous feminist work on the New Testament is to allow the problematic features of the text to be considered in relation to other perspectives and voices reflected in the text of Ephesians itself and reconstructed on the basis of ancient evidence for the lives of wives in the Roman era.

The hierarchical and conventional features of the text need to be read in relation to textual indications of resistance to the dominant social order. As has been noted by commentators, it is somewhat ironic that the highly conventional Ephesian household code is presented within the context of teaching which ultimately sets believers apart from the Gentile world (Tanzer 1994). Ethical teaching directing church members on how to live in a manner distinct from the Gentiles begins at Eph 4:17 (with Eph 5:21 acting as a transition into the household code material) and is resumed again at Eph 6:10. The sentiment of believers being set apart – a recurring motif in Ephesians as a whole – actually also surfaces within the metaphorical exploration of marriage as a reflection of the relationship between Christ and the *purified* church.[5]

Textual indications of resistance to the dominant social order are also being brought to light in recent studies of Ephesians which use Roman Imperial ideology as an interpretative grid (e.g., Faust 1993, MacDonald 2004, Ubieta 2001) and this has significant bearing upon our understanding of Eph 5:22–33. Eph 2:11–22 has figured prominently in these discussions and is increasingly being recognized as having political overtones (e.g., propaganda for imperial peace [the *Pax Romana*] vs. the peace of Christ, Eph 2:14-18). It is particularly relevant for our study that in Eph 2:11-22 the household code teaching is anticipated by means of a merging of civic and familial concepts; believers are described in Eph 2:19 as 'fellow-citizens with the saints and members of the household of God'. As recent work on the Roman family has illustrated (e.g., Dixon 1991), a juxtaposition of familial and civic concepts is in keeping with the widespread interest in demonstrating the concord of the family in the empire – especially the concord of the married couple – using a range of media as a vehicle for social comment and political propaganda. Such analysis, therefore, invites us to view the emphasis on the unity of the married couple in Ephesians as encoding the political stance of the community: personified as wife, the *ekklesia* stands purified and united with her one true husband Christ as manifestly distinct from society (MacDonald 2004). In other words, by setting Eph 5:22-33 within the broader context of the letter, we need to consider how a vision of a unified and recreated cosmos (Eph 2:11-22) is being projected onto the micro-cosmos of the family. Ironically, what is in many ways highly conventional marriage teaching may encode messages of resistance and subversion within a first-century community context which are all but lost upon modern listeners.

Even granted that the teaching concerning marriage in Ephesians may have been framed by certain elements of resistance to the dominant social order, recent feminist analysis demands that we deal with a crucial question: by means of a potent combination of ethical exhortations calling for subordination to their husbands and symbolic idealizations of their bodily purity to define the community, are women being represented primarily in order to further the agenda of male authority figures? Are the symbolic associations between wives and the distinct identity of the *ekklesia* simply a strategy to control the women of the community? That the development of the New Testament household codes has frequently been understood as arising from a need to offer apologetic responses to society and the fact that the codes are consistent with prime assertions of masculinity in the Roman world (Osiek and MacDonald, forthcoming) would suggest this. But ultimately these are difficult questions to answer for there are some features of the life of women within the familial context of the *ekklesia* in the Roman world that at least qualify an affirmative answer to these questions.

First, it is important to recognize that Eph 5:22-33 is an idealization of familial relationships in the *ekklesia* and the lived reality of families was more complicated and included a myriad of conventions and values which remain unspoken in the text. For example, it was probably the case (Seim 1995) that the audience to which Ephesians was addressed included wives whose husbands were non-believers (mixed marriages involving believing men and non-believing women are possible, but virtually unheard of in the literature) and who may have interpreted the instructions as a call to remain married no matter what the circumstances. From one perspective this seems to prepare the way for the abuse of women, but from another angle, the presence of these women without their partners is itself subversive, going against cultural expectations concerning the authority of husbands in religious matters (MacDonald 1996).

The complexity of the family life underlying Eph 5:22–33 also comes into sharper focus when one considers the significant work which has been accomplished on wives in Roman family studies. In her work on Roman mothers, for example, Suzanne Dixon (1988) has argued that the weighty authority of the Roman *paterfamilias* (so clearly reinforced by the household code), should not be taken at face value. While mothers clearly lacked this kind of formal, legal authority, they nevertheless had considerable influence based on convention. By way of illustration, she points to evidence of mothers and widows involved in administering their children's affairs, including finances, and their frequent active participation in the arrangement of marriages. In calling us to look beyond the letter of the law and the inflexible rule of authority figures, Dixon's work raises important doubts about the limited influence of the unnamed wives of Eph 5:22–33.

Dixon's conclusions in fact complement recent anthropological discussions of women and gender in modern Mediterranean societies. Anthropologists such as Jill Dubisch (1986) have noted the close association of family integrity and purity with women's bodies that is also clearly discernible in the teaching on marriage in Ephesians. But they also have drawn attention to features of this association that might not be immediately obvious given the focus on the control of women's physicality in Mediterranean value systems: women's bodies function symbolically in the maintenance of household, group and societal boundaries, and in the *mediation* between realms. We do not know if wives ever felt empowered by being associated with the woman-church, but there is clear evidence for their role as mediators in early Christian texts; wives who entered the church without their husbands were mediators between the realm of the church and the realm of the world (cf. 1 Pet 3:1–6; 1 Cor 7:12–16). Mothers evangelized other family members including children (cf. 2 Tim 1:5) and in the household setting of early church meetings, wives played a vital part in creating the infrastructure necessary for group survival (MacDonald 2000).

Conclusion

Throughout the history of Christianity, women have frequently been denied a theological voice and have been defined and confined by theological argumentation appealing to biblical texts. It is not surprising, therefore, that scholars studying early Christian women have generally kept theological concerns at the forefront of the interpretive task. Like other specialists in Christian origins, they have drawn upon the latest findings of historical, literary and social-scientific analysis. But they have not allowed a focus on context, genre or underlying sources to overshadow the question of the relevance of the text for life's most profound questions either in New Testament times or today. This engagement with church and/or society is shared with feminist theologians generally, as is openness to a diversity of interpretative voices, and honesty about the impact of various perspectives and social locations on interpretation.

While the list is by no means exhaustive, I have aimed in this chapter to isolate four central challenges to a New Testament theology emerging from work on early Christian women that might be summarized as follows: the challenge posed by Jewish feminist scholarship for accurate description of the lives of Jewish women in the biblical world in discussions of the teaching of Jesus and the development of early Christianity; the challenge of explicit engagement with concerns of modern society in the interpretation of New Testament texts as opposed to (often implicit) claims of value-neutrality; the challenge to recover female and other marginalized voices within the biblical text itself and in extracanonical sources; and the challenge to consider how the representation of women and various gendered theological constructions are influenced by literary style, genre and conventions. It goes without saying that these challenges are disclosed in the writings of scholars working on early Christian women to varying degrees and debate continues on many important issues, including scriptural authority and the extent to which the reconstruction of the lives of early Christian women is even possible. Yet, it is appropriate to speak about broad consensus on a number of issues including commitment to theoretical discussion of the ideological presuppositions inherent in particular approaches and methodologies, determination to uncover alternative voices that have been marginalized by the dominant structures of power in ancient society and beyond, and insistence upon self-conscious reading of texts.

By way of illustrating some the challenges raised by the study of early Christian women for a New Testament theology, I have discussed Eph 5:22-33. This is a text which has been identified as highly problematic on account of both its ethical and theological content, but which also holds out an invitation to reconstruct the lives of the unnamed wives whose lives were viewed by the author of Ephesians as mirroring the identity of the *ekklesia*. Perhaps what an examination of this text illustrates above all is the growing complexity of the picture of early Christian women which is emerging from scholarship in this area. In the end, the challenge of early Christian women to a New Testament theology is to reflect this complexity. With respect to Ephesians 5 this means serious consideration of the limits of gendered reflection about God, Christ and the church. But in my view, it also means recognizing how new insights about early Christian women and textual representation of them in the form of metaphor and ethical discourse can contribute to a New Testament theology in the twenty-first century. The unnamed wives of Ephesians 5, for example, have something significant to teach not only about the importance of activities and commitments which are often devalued as mundane or conventional, but also about the potential of these activities and commitments as a source of revelation and inspiration.

Notes

1. On the significance of Fiorenza's work (including detailed discussion of theological significance) see especially Matthews *et al.* (2003). This work includes a complete bibliography of Fiorenza's publications. On the contribution of Fiorenza and others (with a special focus on German scholarship) to feminist interpretation of the Bible see also Schottroff *et al.* (1998).
2. See reviews of Wire's book by Robert H. Gundry, *JAAR* 61 (1993), 392-5; Beverly Gaventa, *Interpretation* 66 (1992), 412-13; Barbara E. Reid, *CBQ* 54 (1992), 594-6; Robin Scroggs, *JBL* 111 (1992), 546-8.
3. It should be noted, however, that in subsequent work Fiorenza (1992, pp. 138-50) gave detailed attention to the issue of biblical authority and the problem of a canon within a canon.
4. At the extreme end of this openness, we have what Fiorenza (1992, pp. 148-9) describes as a hermeneutical strategy which '. . . proposes that women-church must create a feminist *Third Testament* that canonizes women's experiences of G-d's presence as a new textual base'. Fiorenza herself notes, however, that she would not want this material to be assigned, 'fixed canonical status' alongside the canonical First and Second Testaments.
5. Among the Pauline letters, Ephesians arguably displays the most intense call to separate from the Gentile world. See MacDonald 2000, 2004.

References

Balch, D.L and Osiek, C., *Early Christian Families in Context: An Interdisciplinary Dialogue* (Grand Rapids MI/Cambridge UK: Eerdmans, 2003).

Brooten, B.J., 'Early Christian women and their cultural context: issues of method in historical reconstruction', in A.Y. Collins (ed.) *Feminist Perspectives in Biblical Scholarship* (Chico, CA: Scholars Press, 1985), pp. 65–91.

Burrus, V., *Chastity as Autonomy: Women in the Stories of the Apocryphal Acts* (Studies in Women and Religion 23; Lewiston/Queenston: Edwin Mellen Press, 1987).

Cooper, K., 'Insinuations of womanly influence: an aspect of the Christianization of the Roman aristocracy', *JRS* 82 (1992), 150–64.

Cooper, K., *The Virgin and the Bride: Idealized Womanhood in Late Antiquity* (Cambridge, MA: Harvard University Press, 1996).

Dixon, S., *The Roman Mother* (London: Croom Held, 1988).

Dixon, S., 'The sentimental ideal of the Roman family', in B. Rawson (ed.), *Marriage, Divorce, and Children in Ancient Rome* (Oxford: Clarendon Press, 1991), pp.99–113.

Dubisch, J., *Gender and Power in Rural Greece* (Princeton: Princeton University Press, 1986).

Fatum, L., 'Women, symbolic universe and structures of silence: challenges and possibilities in androcentric texts', *Studia Theologica* 43 (1989) 61–80.

Fatum, L., 'Image of God and glory of man: women in the Pauline congregations', in K.E. Borresen (ed.), *Image of God and Gender Models in Judaeo-Christian Tradition* (Oslo: Solum Forlag, 1991), pp. 56–137.

Fatum, L., '1 Thessalonians', in E.S. Fiorenza (ed.), *Searching the Scriptures: A Feminist Commentary* (New York: Crossroad Books, 1994), pp. 250–62.

Faust, E., *Pax Christi et Pax Caesaris: Religionsgeschichtliche, traditions-geschichtliche und sozialgeschichtliche Studien zum Epheserbrief* (Fribourg/Göttingen: Universitätsverlag/Vandenhoeck & Ruprecht, 1993).

Fiorenza, E.S., *In Memory of Her: A Feminist Theological Reconstruction of Christian Origins* (London: SCM Press, 1983).

Fiorenza, E.S., *Bread Not Stone: The Challenge of Feminist Biblical Interpretation* (Boston: Beacon Press, 1984).

Fiorenza, E.S., 'Rhetorical situation and historical reconstruction in 1 Corinthians', *NTS* 33 (1987), 386–403.

Fiorenza, E.S., 'The ethics of biblical interpretation: de-centering biblical scholarship', *JBL* 107 (1988), 3–17.

Fiorenza, E.S., *But She Said: Feminist Practices of Biblical Interpretation* (Boston: Beacon Press, 1992).

Fiorenza, E.S., (ed.), *Searching the Scriptures: A Feminist Commentary* (New York: Crossroad Books, 1994).

Johnson, E.A., 'Ephesians', in C.A. Newsom and H.R. Ringe (eds), *The Women's Bible Commentary* (Louisville, KY: Westminster/John Knox, 1992a), pp. 338–42.

Johnson, E.A., *She Who Is: The Mystery of God in Feminist Theological Discourse* (New York: Crossroad Books, 1992b).

Kraemer R.S., *Her Share of the Blessings: Women's Religions among Pagans, Jews, and Christians in the Greco-Roman World* (New York: Oxford University Press, 1992).

Kraemer, R.S., 'Jewish women and Christian origins: some caveats', in R.S. Kraemer and M.R. D'Angelo (eds), *Women and Christian Origins* (Oxford: Oxford University Press, 1999a), pp. 35-49.

Kraemer, R.S., 'Jewish women and women's Judaism(s) at the beginning of Christianity', in R.S. Kraemer and M.R. D'Angelo (eds), *Women and Christian Origins* (Oxford: Oxford University Press, 1999b), pp. 50-79.

Kraemer, R.S. and Lander, S.L., 'Perpetua and Felicitas', in P.F. Esler (ed.), *The Early Christian World* (vol 2.) (London and New York: Routledge, 2000), pp. 1051-8.

Levine, A.J. (ed.), *'Women Like This': New Perspectives on Jewish Women in the Greco-Roman World* (Atlanta: Scholars Press, 1991).

Lieu, J.M., 'The "attraction of women" in/to early Judaism and Christianity: gender and the politics of conversion', *JSNT* 72 (1998), 5-22.

MacDonald, D.R., *The Legend and the Apostle: The Battle for Paul in Story and Canon* (Philadelphia: Westminster Press, 1983).

MacDonald, M.Y., *Early Christian Women and Pagan Opinion* (Cambridge: Cambridge University Press, 1996).

MacDonald, M.Y., *Colossians and Ephesians* (Sacra Pagina 17; Collegeville, MN: Liturgical Press, 2000).

MacDonald, M.Y., 'The politics of identity in Ephesians', *JSNT* 26 (2004), 419-44.

Martin Soskice, J. and Lipton, D., *Feminism and Theology* (Oxford: Oxford University Press, 2003).

Matthews, S., Johnson-DeBaufre, M. and Kittredge, C.B. (eds), *Walk in the Ways of Wisdom: Essays in Honor of Elisabeth Schüssler Fiorenza* (Harrisburg, PA: Trinity Press International, 2003).

McGinn, S.E., 'The Acts of Thecla', in E.S. Fiorenza (ed.), *Searching the Scriptures: A Feminist Commentary* (New York: Crossroad Books, 1994), pp. 800-28.

Morgan, R., *The Nature of New Testament Theology: The Contributions of William Wrede and Adolf Schlatter* (London: SCM Press, 1973).

Morgan, R., 'Theology (New Testament)', in R.J. Coggins and J.L. Houlden (eds), *A Dictionary of Biblical Interpretation* (London: SCM Press, 1990), pp. 689-91.

Newsom C.A., 'Job', in C.A. Newsom and H.R. Ringe (eds), *The Women's Bible Commentary* (Louisville, KY: Westminster/John Knox, 1992), pp. 130-6.

Newsom C.A. and Ringe, H.R. (eds), *The Women's Bible Commentary* (Louisville, KY: Westminster/John Knox, 1992).

Osiek, C., 'The feminist and the Bible: hermeneutical alternatives', in A.Y. Collins (ed.), *Feminist Perspectives in Biblical Scholarship* (Chico, CA: Scholars Press, 1985), pp. 95-105.

Osiek, C., 'The bride of Christ (Eph 5:22-33): a problematic wedding', *BTB* 32 (2003), 29-39.

Osiek, C. and Balch, D.L., *Families in the New Testament World: Households and Housechurches* (Louisville, KY: Westminster/John Knox, 1997).

Osiek, C. and MacDonald, M.Y., *Women and House Churches in Early Christianity*. (Minneapolis: Fortress Press, forthcoming).

Parsons, S.F. (ed.), *The Cambridge Companion to Feminist Theology* (Cambridge: Cambridge University Press, 2002).

Reinhartz, A., 'The Gospel of John', in E.S. Fiorenza (ed.), *Searching the Scriptures: A Feminist Commentary* (New York: Crossroad Books, 1994), pp. 561-600.

Ruether, R.R., 'The emergence of Christian feminist theology', in S.F. Parsons (ed.), *The Cambridge Companion to Feminist Theology* (Cambridge: Cambridge University Press, 2002), pp.3-22.

Schaberg, J., 'Luke', in C.A. Newsom and H.R. Ringe (eds), *The Women's Bible Commentary* (Louisville, KY: Westminster/John Knox, 1992), pp. 275-92.

Schottroff, L., Schroer, S. and Wacker, M.T., *Feminist Interpretation: The Bible in Women's Perspective* (Minneapolis: Fortress Press, 1998).

Scroggs, R., 'Review of Wire, *The Corinthian Women Prophets*', *JBL* 111 (1992), 546-8.

Seim, T.K., 'A superior minority: the problem of men's headship in Ephesians 5', in D. Hellholm, H. Moxnes and T.K. Seim (eds), *Mighty Minorities? Minorities in Early Christianity - Positions and Strategies* (Oslo/Copenhagen/Stockholm/Boston: Scandinavian University Press, 1995), pp.167-81.

Tanzer, S.J., 'Ephesians', in E.S. Fiorenza (ed.), *Searching the Scriptures: A Feminist Commentary* (New York: Crossroad Books, 1994), pp. 325-48.

Torjesen, K.J., *When Women were Priests: Women's Leadership in the Early Church and the Scandal of their Subordination in the Rise of Christianity* (San Francisco: Harper, 1993).

Ubieta, C.B., '"Neither *Xenoi* nor *paroikoi, sympolitai* and *oikeioi tou theo*" (Eph 2:19). Pauline Christian communities: defining a new territoriality', in J.J. Pilch (ed.), *Social-Scientific Models for Interpreting the Bible* (Leiden: Brill, 2001) pp. 260-80.

Wire, A.C., *The Corinthian Women Prophets: A Reconstruction through Paul's Rhetoric* (Minneapolis: Augsburg Fortress, 1990).

Chapter 10

Deutero-Paulinism, Pseudonymity and the Canon

John Muddiman, Oxford

As I was preparing to write the Black's commentary on Ephesians, I happened to mention to Robert Morgan the idea I was toying with, that Ephesians is an expansion of an earlier original. He instantly identified its pedigree reaching back to H.J. Holtzmann in 1872, and added that I would not find his *Kritik der Epheser- und Kolosserbriefe* in the Bodleian but only in the John Rylands Library, Manchester. The incident illustrates for me why it has been such a privilege to be one of Bob's colleagues in the Oxford Theology Faculty. His main research and publications have been in the fields of New Testament theology and biblical interpretation, but his knowledge of the history of exegesis, especially in Germany, is unrivalled. For his (early) retirement volume I offer him with gratitude an essay on the effects for New Testament theology of the presence in the canon of writings falsely attributed to the apostle Paul.

Apart from the letters that Paul himself wrote between the years 51 and 60 CE, all the remainder of the New Testament could be called Deutero-Pauline in the temporal sense, i.e. post 70 CE. The term may also be appropriate to describe the enduring influence of Paul's Gospel and mission on those who came after him, including obviously the authors of Luke-Acts and the pseudo-Pauline epistles but also arguably those of the Petrine epistles and Hebrews and the evangelists Mark and John. There is, in other words, a theological continuity between Paul and the rest of the New Testament in the emphasis on faith and grace, on the gift of the Spirit and being in Christ. But is there also theological discontinuity? Does 'Deutero-Pauline' literature witness to a fundamental change in the structure of Christian belief, to a move away from imminent end expectation to a timeless mystical ascent (from the horizontal to the vertical), to a move away from charismatic egalitarian community to hierarchy and subordination, to a move away from the freedom of the Spirit to the imposition of Church dogma and the regulation of the sacraments, to a move away from faith as existential encounter with Christ to faith as a set of creedal propositions requiring intellectual assent? If an affirmative answer is given to these questions, then the concept of a single theology of the New Testament becomes highly problematic. It will either be reduced to the few common factors that survive the transition; or else it will be divided into two (at least) contradictory New Testament theologies: Paulinism and Deutero-Paulinism.

I will argue in this essay that the letters that falsely claim authorship by Paul are not Deutero-Pauline in this negative sense; indeed that they point rather to a neglected aspect in the move towards early Catholicism (so-called) which throws into doubt the other characteristics listed above and that this neglected aspect may open up a new possibility for an integrated theology of the New Testament as a whole.

Scepticism about the authorship of several of the Pauline letters arose particularly with the Tübingen school of F.C. Baur and his followers. It was based chiefly on a particular theory of doctrinal development in early Christianity, an initial clash between Pauline Gentile Christianity and Petrine Jewish Christianity, eventually resolved in the synthesis of second-century Catholicism. The Pauline texts were read in a minimizing, anti-Catholic way and conversely the other texts, chiefly Luke-Acts and the pseudo-Paulines, were read tendentiously in a catholicizing way. In the wake of the Tübingen theory the argument about Pauline authorship of the disputed letters has moved into other territory; linguistic, literary and historical factors have mounted up and led scholars who had no particular theological axe to grind to conclude against their authenticity, especially of Ephesians and the Pastorals.

This is not the place to rehearse the arguments in full, but, for instance, the vocabulary of the Pastorals is highly idiosyncratic compared with the rest of the corpus, with 175 *hapax legomena* out of a word pool of 850 (viz. 20 per cent of the total). The *Gattung* of a personal letter conflicts with the content especially of 1 Timothy and Titus which are really forms of church constitution. And the historical setting of the Pastorals does not fit with what we know of the final stages of Paul's career from Romans (cf. Rom 15:23) and Acts (chapter 28).

Similarly in the case of Ephesians, the style of the earlier chapters at least is distinctively different, more measured and liturgical, than that of the undisputed Paulines. The letter is apparently addressed to the Church at Ephesus where Paul stayed for about three years in the mid-fifties, yet

Paul has no first acquaintance with his addressees (1:15) nor they of him (3:2). The lack of specifics is remarkable: Ephesians reads more like a sermon. Its similarity with Colossians is so close (see the virtual doublet, Eph 6:21-2; Col 4:7-8) as to require, if both are genuine, the same place and date of composition. But the overall emphases of the two letters are then strangely divergent: in Colossians cosmic Christology (Col 1:15-20) is used against a Jewish Christian mystical asceticism (2:8-23); in Ephesians a cosmic ecclesiology (1:22-3 etc.) is set against pagan darkness (2:1-4; 4:17-18) with a much more positive evaluation of Christianity's debt to Judaism (see 2:12 and 17). If Paul wrote both of these letters from his final imprisonment in Rome, we would need to ask which of them represents his mature thought. But the problem of the historical setting is compounded by the links between Colossians and Philemon. The latter is universally accepted as a genuine Pauline composition, but it implies that Paul expects to be released from prison shortly and to visit his correspondent (Phm 22). This is the basis for a theory of a spell in prison in Ephesus c. 54 CE, but then Colossians and Ephesians would also be drawn into that setting, and in terms of the development of Paul's thought, it is very difficult to read these letters coherently in sequence between the Corinthians correspondence and Galatians/Romans.

It is linguistic, literary and historical factors such as these that have perpetuated the debate. Doubts have also been raised against other letters, chiefly Colossians and 2 Thessalonians, but the arguments are less conclusive. If the author of Ephesians used Colossians as his model and basis,[1] then he at least must have believed it to be genuine. And if 2 Thessalonians is not by Paul, then it represents a particularly pernicious and flagrant type of pseudepigraphy, seeking to discredit the very letter (1 Thessalonians) on which it is based (see 2 Thess 2:2 and 3:17). Other explanations are therefore more plausible: that 2 Thessalonians is Paul's own correction of a misreading of his earlier letter, and that Colossians is basically Pauline but has in places been edited along the same lines as Ephesians (cf. esp. Col 1:18 and 2:19, on Christ as head of the Church).[2]

It is of course far easier to list the problems with the letters that are under suspicion than to offer a convincing alternative explanation of their origins. This is no doubt why the conservative option of ascribing Ephesians and the Pastorals to Paul himself, despite all the arguments against them, still attracts even critical scholars.[3]

The collecting of the Pauline corpus is lost to us in the murky period prior to Justin Martyr and Marcion. The citations and allusions to them in the earlier apostolic fathers are unable to settle the question of the extent or text form of the corpus. Famously, E.J. Goodspeed proposed that Ephesians was intended as a preface to the collection which the author himself had made, but that suggestion has received little support in recent times.[4] In 1994, David Trobisch argued that Paul began the collection of the four *Hauptbriefe* himself by keeping copies (Trobisch 1994), but that seems unlikely. 2 Corinthians is pretty obviously a later compilation, and when Paul discusses food sacrificed to idols in Romans (chs. 14 and 15) he does not have to hand his answer to the Corinthians on the same subject (1 Cor 8 and 10) but tackles it afresh. More generally, what purpose could such an archive possibly serve, with time running out before the day of the Lord? Paul did not even send duplicate copies of his letters to Colossae and Laodicea (Col 4:14) but expected them to swap.

The more likely hypothesis is that the letter collection grew gradually through exchange between the major urban centres with a Christian presence (so von Campenhausen 1972). For this purpose, smaller letters would have been copied in the first instance into minimal scroll length texts, and then put together wither into two maximum length scrolls or else already into a codex.[5]

The significance of this is clear: the Pauline corpus has gone through at least one, possibly several, stage(s) of editing; and the manuscripts that survive, from the third century and later, are all indebted to this recension. There is therefore no 'pure Paul' to be had, uncontaminated by the Church's preservation technique, though the extent of alterations and interpolations in the undisputed letters will inevitably remain a matter for debate. The non-authenticity of the pseudo-Paulines is, in other words, only a matter of degree, not of kind. It was this realization that led me to propose that the writer of Ephesians had edited and expanded Paul's original letter to the Laodiceans.[6] I will not rehearse here all the supporting arguments for this suggestion, but only make a general preliminary point, before examining the claim that Ephesians and the Pastorals are Deutero-Pauline in the negative sense. Pauline pseudepigraphy is not to be understood as the (mis)use of the Apostle's name to introduce new doctrines with the stamp of his authority; it is rather at root an act of conservation. We should not expect, nor do we find, theological innovations. The writers of Ephesians and the Pastorals were effectively encouraging their readers to pay attention to Paul's teaching not only in these but also in his other letters.

The three distinguishing features of Deutero-Pauline early Catholicism, as outlined conveniently by James Dunn,[7] are (1) the fading of parousia hope, (2) increasing institutionalization and (3) the crystallization of faith into set forms. How do the pseudo-Pauline letters fare when judged against these criteria?

There are in Ephesians many more references to hope for the arrival of the new age than in several of the undoubted Paulines – Galatians is the prime example where there is no hint of the idea. Dunn concedes six,[8] but nevertheless claims that 'otherwise the expectation is wholly lacking'. He further claims that the author envisages a much longer period for the church on earth lasting several generations, citing 2:7; 3:21 and 6:3. But 'the ages to come' at 2:7 is surely not earthly ages but has the same meaning as the age to come of 1:21, i.e. post-parousia heavenly existence. 'From generation to generation' at 3:21 is just a stock biblical expression meaning 'for ever'; and 6:3 only promises longevity for the dutiful child, in accordance with scripture, but for the human race as such. The (relative) reticence about the imminence of the second coming is what we should expect from a second-generation writer aware that initial hopes had failed to materialize but the reticence is diplomatic, not dogmatic. For the writer of Ephesians, the End could still come at any moment.

Increasing institutionalization is alleged against Ephesians in its use of *ekklesia* exclusively to refer to the universal Church. This is a very odd accusation. It is the local church, even in Paul's day, that has to develop institutions for the regulation of its common life. When the author imagines the glorious destiny of the church as the bride of Christ, he is as far away from institutionalization as you can get. Marriage may be an institution, but the union of Christ and the Church is 'a great mystery' (5:32). Not even the reference to the various ministries in 4:11 can be called in to support the allegation, for these are emphatically gifts of the ascended Christ (4:10) and not earthly offices, and, moreover, priority is given – even in the second-generation terminology, to those exercising a missionary function as evangelists.

On the criterion of the crystallization of the faith into set forms in Ephesians, Dunn is, correctly, silent. There are no grounds for such a charge. The formula repeated at 2:5 and 2:8 'saved by grace through faith' is as accurate a summary of Paul's own understanding as one could wish for, from someone determined to give the essence of Paul's teaching stripped of its polemical colouring. Even the quasi-creedal chant at 4:4-6, with its reference to one faith that comes between one Lord and one baptism is not spelled out in dogmatic propositions, In context, it probably means that faith in the Lordship of Christ expressed in baptism is one because it is the only route to salvation for Jews and Gentiles alike, which is indeed Paul's own understanding of the matter. In sum, Ephesians is not Deutero-Pauline or early Catholic on any of these criteria.

The Pastoral epistles, though we normally treat them as a set, are a rather mixed collection. 2 Timothy stands apart from the others; it has all the warmth of a personal letter that the others conspicuously lack. Paul is in prison facing martyrdom while in the others he is still at liberty. There is little about organizing the church and much more about Timothy's own calling. Furthermore, there is a whole series of circumstantial details at the beginning and end of the letter that, unless they are pure flights of fancy on the part of an author who is more usually rather pedestrian, must surely be derived by whatever route from Paul and/or Timothy himself. They cannot be explained by and at certain points are at odds with the evidence of Acts and the genuine Paulines.[9] It seems to me likely that 2 Timothy has a similar origin to that of Ephesians, as an expansion of an original personal letter to Paul's chief assistant in Ephesus into something resembling a 'last will and testament'. The testamentary form justifies the pseudepigraphy. Paul at the moment of death is granted special foreknowledge of what his people would be facing later.

In contrast to 2 Timothy, 1 Timothy and Titus are not personal letters at all, but general rules for church life and warnings against the danger of heresy.[10] There is little, apart from Tit 3:12–13, that demands any other explanation than *de novo* pseudepigraphy. Titus is a close shadow of 1 Timothy and it is not at all clear what the point of this duplication might be. Perhaps it serves to indicate that Paul gave the same instructions to the uncircumcised Titus (see Gal 2:3) as to the circumcised Timothy (see Acts 16:3), thus dealing even-handedly with Jewish and Gentile members of the church.

Applying the criteria for Deutero-Paulinism, how do the Pastorals fare? On eschatology, 2 Timothy in particular frequently refers to 'that Day' (1:12, 18; 4:8) and the same distinctive expression for the parousia, the 'epiphany of our Lord Jesus Christ' occurs in all three (2 Tim 4:1; 1 Tim 6:12; Tit 2:13). Dunn claims that 'clearly in 2 Timothy 2.2 the perspective has perceptibly lengthened' (Dunn 1977, p. 346). This is the passage where Timothy is told 'to pass on to reliable people what you have heard from me, so that they may in turn be able to teach others'. But Dunn's comment fails to reckon with the rhetorical situation of a pseudepigraphical text. The instruction to Timothy, back in 60 CE, refers forward to the present situation of the readers, not to any long drawn-out future there might be.

On institutionalization, any mention it seems of the word bishop (*episkopos*) excites the suspicion of early Catholicism (in spite of Phil 1:1). But the underlying assumption operating here, that the original Pauline congregations were charismatic egalitarian communities that had rejected the 'old Jewish distinctions between priest and people' (Dunn 1997, p. 114),[11] is pure romanticism. Paul's own authority as apostle stands, when necessary, over against the communities he had founded.

There is remarkably little instruction in the Pastorals about the powers or even the functions of a bishop or deacon, only about the moral prerequisites for their appointment. Furthermore the reference to the ritual act of laying on of hands at 2 Tim 1:6 must be read in context: 'I remind you to rekindle the gift (Greek *charisma*) of God that is within you'. Ordination is not necessarily uncharismatic! In any case the Pastorals are inconsistent on the source of authorization. In this passage it is Paul himself but elsewhere (1 Tim 1:18 and 4:14) ordination is by the word of the prophets and the laying on of hands by the whole body of the presbytery.

Finally, do the Pastorals represent 'the strongest evidence in the New Testament to an early Catholic attitude to tradition' (Dunn 1997, p. 361)? There is admittedly frequent reference to sound tradition but what exactly is its content? The hymnic sections of 1 Timothy send out contradictory signals: 1 Tim 2:5 summarizes the Pauline gospel in terms of the oneness of God and the unique mediatorship of the man Jesus made effective through the cross. But 1 Tim 3:16 defines the 'mystery of our religion' in a way that could almost be mistaken for docetism ('revealed in the flesh, vindicated in the spirit').

Conversely the references to heresy in the Pastorals do not give a coherent picture of what is being attacked. On the assumption of historicity we should expect Titus to be addressed to a different situation (in Crete) to that of the letters to Timothy (in Ephesus); but this is not the case. References to 'Jewish myths' – presumably Jewish mystical speculations – appear in all three: Tit 1:14; 1 Tim 1:4; 4:7; 2 Tim 4:4. But 1 Timothy seems to have simple Torah observant Judaism in its sights, and yet the 'contradictions of knowledge falsely so called' at 1 Tim 6:20 sounds like an attack on the anti-Jewish gnosticism of Marcion. At 2 Tim 2:17 the erroneous assertion that the resurrection has already taken place sounds more like the over-realized eschatology of Paul's opponents in Corinth. We are left not knowing whether asceticism or libertinism is the real threat. The 'heresy' in other words is a compendium of all heresies and not anything in particular. So much for 'crystallization'. For the actual content of the 'sound teaching' the Pastor wishes to commend, he presumably expects his readers to consult the weightier letters of Paul.

In conclusion, the pseudo-Pauline letters in the canon are not Deutero-Pauline according to the negative definition of that term. But they are early Catholic in another, neglected sense. They represent the 'scripturalization' of Paul. Perhaps the German scholarly tradition failed to take note of this aspect of second-century Catholicism because it thought of 'scripture' as an essentially Protestant principle. But scripture has been and still is a central feature of the Catholic synthesis, and the pseudepigraphical texts in the New Testament tacitly testify to the fact. As I wrote in the commemorative volume for the 150th anniversary of the Oxford movement, edited by Bob Morgan:

> The pressing imminence of eschatological hope is the main feature that distinguishes canonical from post-canonical literature. Despite what must have been a strong temptation to abandon hope when it failed to materialize and to rewrite its foundation documents, Christianity nevertheless insisted on retaining its original vision. It did this by lowering the status of the interim period, the post-apostolic church, and marking off the time of the first generation with a 'scriptural boundary'. The same could be said of 'institutionalization' and 'crystallization' (see Muddiman 1989, pp. 131–2).

The scripturalization of the Christian faith enshrines permanently in an authoritative text the always existing tension between proper order and the freedom of the Spirit. A theology of the New Testament is a theology of a particular corpus of texts acknowledged as scripture by the Christian community. It is not merely a historical enquiry into the character of earliest Christianity, but rather a discipline that interrogates the texts for the truth claims that they make and that reads the texts in the light of their impact through a variety of interpretations on the later history of the Church. If Paul did actually write Ephesians, then as a measured summary it would trump all his other letters: that he did not means that Paul is also allowed to speak for himself. If Paul did actually write the Pastorals, then their socially conservative attitudes (not least towards the place of women in the church) would eclipse everything he had written on the issue before: that he did not means that Paul is also allowed to speak for himself. The presence in the canon of pseudo-Pauline texts, far from muting or distorting the authentic voice of Paul contributes towards his 'scripturalization' and thus to his continuing influence.

Notes

1. The consensus view: see e.g. Lincoln 1990, pp. xlvii–lviii.
2. So also Weiss 1959, p. 684: 'It has not yet been settled whether the author of Ephesians is not the same person as the collector of the Pauline corpus. Certainly his spirit, perhaps also his hand, makes itself perceptible, not only in the editing of Colossians, but also in the editorial closing doxology of the Epistle to the Romans, 16 25ff'.
3. E.g. Johnson 1986; cf. also Johnson 2001.
4. Goodspeed 1933 and 1956. For critique see Muddiman 2001, pp. 12–14.

5. Approximately three metres, which is precisely the length of 2 Corinthians, the Macedonian letters, the Asiatic letters and indeed the Pastorals. See further Trobisch 2000.
6. Johannes Weiss also recognized this possibility when he wrote 'The author of Ephesians [expands] the material before him, the Epistle to the Colossians *or Laodiceans*' [My emphasis] (Weiss 1959, p. 684).
7. Dunn 1977, p. 344, following the classic discussion of Käsemann 1969.
8. Dunn 1977, p. 346: Eph 1:14, 18, 21; 4:4, 30; 5:5, but not, strangely, 6:12: standing firm 'on the evil day'.
9. Why, for example, would a pseudepigrapher set out to blacken the character of Demas, who, when he was last heard of in the Paulines (Phm 24 cf. Col 4:14), was a loyal companion?
10. They have the same genre as the *Didache*.
11. Were the Diaspora synagogues not models of charismatic egalitarianism (for their male members at any rate)?

References

Campenhausen, H. von, *The Formation of the Christian Bible* (London: A. & C. Black, 1972).

Dunn, J.D.G., *Unity and Diversity in the New Testament* (London: SCM, 1977).

Goodspeed, E.J., *The Meaning of Ephesians* (Chicago, University of Chicago Press, 1933).

Goodspeed, E.J., *The Key to Ephesians* (Chicago, University of Chicago Press, 1956).

Johnson, L.T., *The Writings of the New Testament* (London: SCM, 1986).

Johnson, L.T., *The First and Second Letters to Timothy* (AB 35A; New York: Doubleday, 2001).

Käsemann, E., 'Paul and early Catholicism', in *New Testament Questions of Today* (London: SCM, 1969), pp. 236-51.

Lincoln, A.T., *Ephesians* (Dallas: Word Books, 1990).

Muddiman, J., 'The Holy Spirit and inspiration', in R. Morgan (ed.), *The Religion of the Incarnation* (Bristol: Bristol Classical Press, 1989), pp. 119-33.

Muddiman, J., *The Epistle to the Ephesians* (London: Continuum, 2001).

Trobisch, D., *Paul's Letter Collection: Tracing the Origins* (Minneapolis, Fortress Press, 1994).

Trobisch, D., *The First Edition of the New Testament* (Oxford: Oxford University Press, 2000).

Weiss, J., *Earliest Christianity: A History of the Period AD 30-150*, vol. 2 (New York: Harper and Row, 1959).

Chapter 11

Towards an Alternative to New Testament Theology: 'Individual Eschatology' as an Example

Heikki Räisänen, Helsinki

Nature of the Enterprise

One of the many valuable services of Bob Morgan to the community of scholars is his translation and evaluation of a pivotal article by William Wrede (1859–1906) (Morgan 1973). As early as 1897, Wrede sketched the programme of a 'History of Early Christian Religion (and Theology)' (from now on 'ECR') as an alternative to 'New Testament Theology' ('NTT'). He complained that too close a relationship to dogmatics had prevented the discipline of NTT from becoming truly historical and claimed that it is not the task of the exegete to serve the needs of the church. Consequently, the biblical canon (which is a result of church decisions) must have no significance in a critical synthesis of scholarly findings. A NTT constructed on such a basis would in no respect differ from an ECR.

Wrede died young. As the theological climate changed in the aftermath of the First World War, it took nearly a century until efforts were undertaken to carry out his programme.[1] There is room for further experiments.

For some time now I have been working on a 'Wredean' overall account of early Christian ideas. It will be *religionswissenschaftlich* in orientation and has no ecclesiastical concern, being addressed to a wider readership.[2] This means in practice that:

- the work is not limited to the New Testament canon, but deals on equal terms with all material down to the middle of the second century, and casts a glance at even later developments;
- it makes no distinction between 'orthodoxy' and 'heresy' (except as historical notions);
- it pays attention to the roots of early Christian ideas in their cultural and religious environment;
- it is not focused on 'doctrines', but on the formation of ideas in interaction with the experience (largely social experience) of individuals and communities;
- it concentrates on great lines and main problems, opting for a topical organization;[3] thereby full justice must be done to the diversity of early Christianity;
- it acknowledges intellectual and moral problems in the sources;
- it contains hints at the reception and influence of the ideas, thus helping to build a bridge to the present.

Without denying the legitimacy of other options, I have decided to start with (collective) 'eschatology'. A draft of this first chapter has been published elsewhere.[4] Here I shall illustrate the approach by way of an abridged draft of the next chapter in which the 'last things' are considered from the perspective of the individual.

First, however, attention is to be called to the specific points where the difference of a 'Wredean' account from current NTTs actually comes to expression.

The NTTs practically limit their *source material* to the New Testament – sometimes even to key writings within it (many NTTs give a special position to Paul[5]). In my draft, too, Paul does get a lot of attention, but he is not treated as anything like a norm. The *Gospel of Thomas* and other Nag Hammadi writings are treated on the same level as canonical writings. Patristic authors are also given consideration.

The *roots* of early Christian ideas on the destiny of the individual in *Israelite and Greco-Roman traditions* get little attention in most NTTs. My draft tries to point out the crucial connections.

I treat the issue 'resurrection or immortality' as a major conceptual problem. Most NTTs pay little attention to it.[6] I also dwell on self-contradictions or ambiguities of Paul. Some NTTs do discuss them, though tending to do away with the problem in the final analysis.[7] Moral problems arising in connection with the depictions of post-mortem punishments are largely evaded. The judgement is mostly mentioned when one emphasizes that people are *not* judged in a particular way (say, according to 'works').[8] Hell in particular is absent in the picture.[9] Presumably this is because the authors of NTTs also want to preach a message, and in a present-day sermon hell has no place. It follows that the dire *Wirkungsgeschichte* gendered by the texts concerned with hell is passed over in silence.

Acknowledging the importance of the reception and influence of early Christian ideas, I offer here and there brief comments on present-day matters. While they indicate my sympathies, they are not prescriptive; unlike the NTTs, 'Christian truth' is not taken for granted as the point of departure. I just wish to point out some connections (sometimes slightly surprising: see the two last paragraphs of this chapter) between the past and the present, and to stimulate the reader to think for herself or himself what these ancient attempts to make sense of life and experience might mean today.

Some concrete differences with regard to NTTs will be noted along the way (see p. 184 nn. 15, 18, 21, 22). It goes without saying that the difference is sometimes one of degree only. Some NTTs (Bultmann[10] and Strecker in particular) have long sections which do not differ from an ECR at all.

From the World of Shadows to Heaven and Hell

Few Israelites ever thought that death would be the end of everything. Care was devoted to dead ancestors and relatives; food and drink was offered at their graves. Obviously, a distinction between the body and something that might be called soul or spirit (but was never defined) was current in Israel, as well as elsewhere in the ancient world.

The 'Yahweh-alone-movement', that gained ground from the sixth century on, banned not only the worship of other gods and goddesses, but also the veneration of ancestors as inherently pagan: 'orthodox Israelites no longer defined themselves in relation to their ancestors but exclusively in relation to their national God' (McDannell and Lang 1990, p. 10f.). The existence of the dead in Sheol, the netherworld, came to be conceived of as an existence of shades, void of vitality and joy. A state of equal misery awaited all who died.

Such ideas of Sheol were close to old Greek conceptions. According to Homer, the dead spent their time in Hades as feeble shades. A common destiny awaited all, apart from a few notorious cases. Yet gradually the view spread that different post-mortem destinies awaited normal mortals as well. In death, souls separate from bodies and are transferred to Hades where they face judgement; the good are rewarded, the bad punished. Plato tells the tale of Er who returns from the netherworld to report the judgement of the dead. The souls pass through an interim period of reward or punishment, after which they return to the earth and are reincarnated in new bodies. In the Hellenistic and Roman period 'a strong strand of belief in a differentiated fate for different souls' (see Lehtipuu 2004, ch. 6) is attested.

Apart from the reincarnation, the tale of Er might have struck a familiar chord in many Jewish minds. In Israel, too, there was a development towards differentiation of fates. *1 Enoch* 22 contains a famous vision of different post-mortem destinies. The souls of the sinners and the righteous respectively are allocated to different places 'in the west', though it is never told how it came to the separation.[11] The righteous will enjoy a long life in the 'blessed land' (25:6). In its midst is an 'accursed valley' for 'those who will be accursed for ever' (27:2). A similar differentiation is envisaged in the '*Animal Apocalypse*' (*1 Enoch* 90).

The conception of Sheol has thus undergone a change: it has become a waiting place where the dead are assembled until their fate is confirmed. Finally it becomes the place of punishment. Depictions of it are enriched with the image of fire, derived mostly from the notorious Valley of Hinnom (*Ge-hinnom*, hence 'Gehenna') where offerings had once been burnt to foreign gods.

If the souls that now are in the waiting chambers are to participate in the last judgement, a resurrection – the reunion of soul and (some kind of) body – must take place. The *Animal Apocalypse* gives a hint of this: all those who had been 'destroyed and dispersed', reassemble (*1 Enoch* 90:33). Those redeemed will enjoy a new life on the earth, albeit in the pristine paradisal form of existence (90:38). The elect are not merely resuscitated, but transformed to a different mode of life.

The notion of the souls waiting for the judgement is due to a combination of different eschatologies, the result being that *two* judgements seem to be envisaged: an immediate one at death, and the great collective event on the last day. An interim period makes sense in the Platonic scenario, in which the souls return to the earth for reincarnation in *another* body. In a Jewish context it seems somewhat awkward, as the *same* judgement will apparently be pronounced twice. But there is a point: the judgement of the mighty oppressors must take place publicly. The prospect of a day of judgement is a cause of joy for ordinary pious people.

'On that day, they shall raise one voice, blessing, glorifying, and extolling in the spirit of faith . . .' (*1 Enoch* 61:11).

While the *Animal Apocalypse* apparently has a renewed earthly life in view, the *Epistle of Enoch* (*1 Enoch* 91–105) transfers the vindication of the righteous to heaven: they 'will shine like the lights of heaven . . . and the gate of heaven will be opened to you . . . for you will have great joy like the angels of heaven . . . (104:2–6). 'This is not the Greek idea of immortality of the soul, but neither is it the resurrection of the body. Rather, it is the *resurrection, or exaltation, of the spirit* from Sheol to heaven. The bodies of the righteous will presumably continue to rest in the earth' (Collins 2000, p. 124, emphasis added).

Resurrection of some individuals – of the martyrs and their persecutors – is envisaged in Daniel 12. Despite a contrary trend in recent research, it would seem that this resurrection life will be lived on this earth. 'The wise' will shine like the stars of heaven; if they are the leaders of the community, it is natural to take this to refer to their eminence in an earthly kingdom of God. The destiny of those wicked who are resurrected is 'shame' and 'contempt'; such expressions are easier to connect with a pitiful existence in the world than with a punishment in hell. But the wording of Dan 12:2f is open to a more spiritual interpretation as well.

The new beliefs spread, displaying a fair amount of variation. Some texts (e.g. 2 Macc 12:39–45) presuppose a general resurrection at the turn of history, while others (e.g. *Ps. Sol.* 3:10–12) speak of a resurrection of the righteous, apparently implying the extinction of the impious. Some are explicit on their annihilation.[12] This version of the punishment theme continues the tradition of divine destruction of the people's enemies on the 'day of Yahweh', yet even 'wicked' Israelites have come to be included among those punished. What matters is to belong to the right group. Typically (in contrast to the usual Greek view) only *two* groups and two kinds of fate are envisaged.

The judgement could become fearful even for those to whom it had been a cause of comfort, as the story (from the second-century CE?) of Johanan ben Zakkai on his death-bed illustrates: the pious rabbi wept, knowing that two ways would be before him, and he did not know which way he would be led (*bBer.* 28b). We also hear of attempts to mitigate the harshness of the judgement. Intercession of the righteous was thought to move God to mercy; to Rabbi Aqiba is ascribed the view that the punishment of hell will last 12 months only.

The physical character of resurrection is emphasized in *2 Maccabees*. A martyr expresses the hope to receive his hands and tongue back from

God (7:10f); another, preferring suicide to capture, tears his entrails from his dying body 'calling upon the Lord of life and spirit to give them back to him again' (14:46). According to the *Fourth Sibyl*, history ends with a fire, but God 'will again fashion the bones and ashes of men, and he will raise up mortals again as they were before' (181–2). The resurrection is physical and earthly – and this very combination makes sense. The Pharisees confessed belief in bodily resurrection in Jesus' time, but the issue remained open to different interpretations.

Indeed the restoration of the present body was never the sole, perhaps not even the dominant concept. The Greek way of thinking inevitably had an influence on Jewish conceptions of afterlife. Greek philosophy could not accommodate anything like a resurrection of the body; yet neither was the soul conceived of as wholly immaterial. 'The *psyche* in archaic Greece was conceived of as a material substance, very fine and akin to air and aether, but *material* nonetheless' (Riley 1995, p. 28). To be sure, by the time of Plato the soul had come to be viewed as superior to the body and the body as a distraction for the soul. Plato was persuaded that the soul was uncreated and immortal, the true vehicle for human identity. The body can corrupt the soul; therefore the soul must separate itself from the body as far as possible.

In the Greco-Roman period most philosophers spoke of the soul 'as if it were composed of some substance that we would consider "stuff"' (Martin 1995, pp. 8f. 115, etc.). Being of a fine fire-like substance, complete with its mental and spiritual faculties, it was the whole person, but for its expression in fleshly material, which had become devalued as a hindrance to the real person. The Greco-Roman dead kept their recognizable form and appearance apart from their bodies because the surviving soul bears the 'image' of the body. In stories, the disembodied souls even bore the marks of the death wounds of the persons. The categories spiritual and physical were not mutually exclusive: the soul itself was a kind of material 'body'.

In Alexandrian Judaism, in particular, the resurrection is understood as the immortality of the soul. Philo never mentions bodily resurrection (nor judgement for that matter). All references to resurrection found in the traditional literature are understood by him as figurative references to immortality. There is a strong emphasis on the superiority of soul to body which dissolves with death. Yet the soul is, even for Philo, *not* immaterial, but composed of small particles (Riley 1995, pp. 42f, n. 106). *4 Maccabees* for its part conceives of the immortality of souls as a prize conferred by God for victory in the conflict endured by the pious.

In the *Testament of Job*, the children of Job are caught up to heaven at death, and the soul of Job himself ascends in a shining chariot, driven by angels, while his body lies in the grave (ch. 52). But even writings which do not resort to this conception (e.g. *Slavonic Enoch*) can speak of post-mortem ascent, paying attention to the reward and the punishment of the dead, but being silent of a general resurrection. The focus on individual afterlife is compatible with the Greek belief in the immortality of the soul, though it is expressed in a different idiom.

Judgement and Punishment in the Jesus Movement

The notion of an imminent, final judgement played a larger role in the Christian communities than in other groups of the time. Various Jewish visions were taken over and reapplied. Some texts suggest that the unrighteous will not survive at all. If they are alive when the end comes, they will perish. If they are dead, they may not be resurrected, or they will rise only to be judged, and disappear for ever. The *Didache* (16:7) explicitly states that 'there will be the resurrection of the dead, but not of all'.

In two passages on the parousia Paul, too, seems to assume the resurrection of the righteous only: the dead *in Christ* (1 Thess 4:16) or 'those *of Christ*' (1 Cor 15:23) will rise; it is the resurrection of Jesus that makes possible the resurrection of his devotees in the first place. Apparently non-believers will *not* be resurrected, though it is not clear how this fits with the notion of judgement of all according to their deeds which Paul puts forward elsewhere (Rom 2:13-16; 3:19). Paul's allusions to the eschatological events cannot be combined to a consistent whole; his interest is focused on the salvation of the believers.

Luke 20:35 suggests that only those who are 'worthy' may gain the 'resurrection of the dead', meaning that there is a resurrection of the just only – a view confirmed by Luke 14:14, but contradicted by Acts 24:15, where Paul assures that there will be a 'resurrection of the just *and the unjust*'.[13]

A more common notion is that of a judgement which will divide mankind into two groups, whose destinies are sealed for ever. A universal judgement is widely presupposed (Acts 17:31, John 5:28-9, Heb 6:2, Rev 20:11-15), though it is often in tension with other notions found in the same writings.

If the wicked *are* judged, what will their fate be? Paul is rather reticent, but the odds are that he favours the idea of extinction (Bernstein 1993, pp. 207-24). The assertion that eventually God will be 'all in all' (1 Cor 15:28) speaks for this alternative; nothing that opposes God will remain in existence. The Gospel of John lacks the notion of eternal torment. The unbelievers are 'condemned already' (John 3:18). 'This is not a theory of eternal punishment . . . The excluded are destroyed, or annihilated' (Bernstein 1993, pp. 225, 227).

In Matthew's famous portrayal of the last judgement (Matt 25:31-46), 'all nations' are brought before the tribunal of the Son of Man. Yet it is not nations that are being judged, but individuals; they are rewarded or punished according to what they have (or have not) done to Jesus' 'least brothers'. The judgement is final, and the punishment in hell of those condemned will be very painful. In disregarding the needs of the little ones they have offended the divine majesty of the King (v. 34) who now takes vengeance.[14]

While the 'wailing and gnashing of teeth' of the damned is a favourite phrase of Matthew, who repeats it *ad nauseam*, he was not the first to introduce the fires of hell into the Jesus tradition. The threat of impending judgement has a conspicuous place in the Synoptic Gospels and probably stems from Jesus himself. While the coming of the kingdom was in focus in Jesus' message, judgement was the other side of the coin. The threatening character of much of Jesus' proclamation should not be explained away. It is better to lose a member than have the whole body thrown to hell (Mark 9:43ff par).

The motif of the day of judgement is elaborated in Q (Luke 10:13ff par, 11:37ff par) and given great prominence in Matthew. In Q the judgement falls mainly on Israel who has rejected Jesus. Matthew partly changes the emphasis, addressing many warning words also to the Christians. It is not only the 'others' who will be condemned; the day of judgement will bring bitter surprises. A disciple of Jesus must bring good fruit. Those who correspond to the weeds or to the bad fish in the Matthaean parables are thrown into the furnace of fire (13:41f, 13:49f). The prospect is terrifying: though many are called, few will be saved (22:14). The parable of the 10 virgins (25:1-13) suggests that half (!) of the members of the congregation might fail the test. The *Didache* (ch. 16) states in the same vein that the whole time one has lived in faith is useless if one is not 'made perfect' in the end-time, when many will fall away and perish.

Rev 20:14f states that everyone whose name is not found in the book of life is thrown into the pit for eternal torment.[15] The terror of the fire is underlined in many other texts. With it, Heb 10:26f threatens apostates and Ignatius (*Eph* 16:2) those who teach bad doctrines or listen to them.

Whereas Matthew and Revelation are relatively reserved in their visualizations of hell, the *Apocalypse of Peter* (early second century) revels in depictions of the horrendous punishments. These correspond to the transgressions: the blasphemers will be hung up by their tongues, etc. This kind of literature takes much of its descriptions of torture from

Greek mythology, but omits the Greek idea that the punishments are temporary and therapeutic. It has had an immense influence on Christian exhortation in sermons, church paintings, psalms and tractates.

This history is not without irony. At an early stage the notion of a final judgement was apparently meant to encourage little people who could expect their oppressors to get their due in the end; eventually the judgement came increasingly to be the source of fear for just such ordinary people.

The judgement of all people who have ever lived generates an obvious problem: how will those be treated who have never heard of Christ? An obscure section in 1 Peter caught the imagination of subsequent Christians. 1 Pet 3:19ff may have in view an occasion after the resurrection on which Christ preached (with whatever outcome) to the generation of the Flood, regarded as the worst sinners ever. 1 Pet 4:6 seems to envisage proclamation to those who had died before Christ. Interpreters speculated that Christ had descended to Hades in order to save the saints of old Israel. The problem remained that the great poets and philosophers of antiquity seemed doomed to everlasting torment – an intolerable notion for sensitive Christians. A solution was achieved by postulating a special compartment in hell, called limbo, for those who had lived good lives but had not known Christ. They suffered no torment, but enjoyed no bliss either.

In other ways, too, hell could become an emotional and moral problem. In Revelation 14 the Lamb seems pleased with the sight of the fate of the unrighteous. Tertullian expresses joy over the prospect of watching the calamity of the persecutors (and, above all, of the Jews). By contrast, Aristides (*Apol.* 15) displays some compassion in stating that the Christians weep bitterly at the death of a sinner, knowing that he will be punished.

For some Christians the current notions of hell were incompatible with God's nature. Following philosophical traditions, Clement of Alexandria and Origen conceived of the punishments as pedagogical and therapeutic and thus as temporary; hell became a kind of purgatory. While the deterrent value of the biblical description of penalties was to be appreciated, Origen makes it clear, when addressing the 'advanced', that the fire is a metaphor and that the punishments serve the eventual well-being of those punished. Why should God's mercy come to an end when a person dies? The final goal is *apokatastasis*, the restoration of all.

While Origen had important followers, his view faced opposition. Augustine came to represent a decisive milestone. Taking his cue from Matt 25, he was determined to postulate eternal, unchangeable destinies in heaven or hell. For a millennium and a half, the view of Origen was the loser. Today, however, mainstream theologians take a metaphorical view of hell to the point of explaining it away: we can hope, it is said, that hell will not become a reality for anybody (Kehl 1986, pp. 294, 297). This reticence is visible in the NTTs which confuse the historical task with a theological-kerygmatic one.

Another line of development in a milder direction is due to the feeling that a mere dichotomy is simply too rigid. For this reasons Christians gradually developed the less offensive belief in purgatorial punishment.

Resurrection or Immortality?

Resurrection of the flesh?

The phrase 'resurrection of the *flesh*' in the second-century Roman creed reminds one of the Maccabean martyrs. Second-century Christian spokesmen for the idea, such as Tertullian, were likewise deeply concerned with the bodies of *martyrs*.

The phrase is first found in Justin (*Dial.* 80:5), but the notion that 'this very flesh' will be resurrected appears in several second-century writings. Tertullian claimed that what is raised is '*this* flesh, suffused with blood, built up with bones, interwoven with nerves, entwined with veins . . .' (*De Carne Christi* 5). God would put in place again even the tiniest bit of each person's body, down to the last finger-nail. Resurrection of the body is necessary, since 'the soul alone, without solid matter, cannot suffer anything' (*Apol.* 48).

Not only in Zoroastrian eschatology (see Hultgård 2000, pp. 56–60), but also in many early Jewish conceptions bodily resurrection was connected with an *earthly* expectation. Possibly this was the case also with Jesus. It is hardly accidental that Justin, Irenaeus and Tertullian, the stern defenders of the resurrection of the fleshly body, were all enthusiastic millenarians.

The risen Jesus as a model

Tertullian and the Roman creed stand at the end of *one* line of development. For long, the nature of the post-mortem existence was a bone of contention between Christians. Debates concerning the resurrection were closely connected with debates concerning the appearances of the risen Jesus, who was conceived as the model. Some accounts of these appearances (Luke 24, John 21) stress their bodily character: Jesus has flesh and bones, he eats, he presents his arms and feet for touching.[16] The stories of the empty tomb also presuppose that the very body that was buried rose from the dead (even if it may have undergone changes in the event). Yet both Luke and John also narrate scenes in which the disciples do *not* recognise Jesus, implying that his resurrected body was different from his previous body (Luke 24:16, John 21:4-12).

'The impression given in some accounts is of a figure who has been resuscitated to a fully physical, visible and tangible state, and in other accounts of one who is not immediately recognizable . . . While the risen Christ of Luke moves towards ascension, the ascended Christ of Matthew stays with men until the end of the age, but not as the bodily risen one' (Evans 1970, p. 129f). The Easter stories as we have them are relatively late. How the early witnesses would have described and interpreted what they saw is a matter of educated guessing.

In many gnostic writings Jesus does *not* appear in the human form which the disciples would recognize. He emerges as a luminous presence or transforms himself into multiple forms. These interpretations are found in relatively late texts, but they agree with Acts' account of Paul's encounter with Jesus (the light) and to some extent also with those Gospel stories in which Jesus is first not recognised. Nor are they very far from what can be inferred from the hints dropped by our earliest witness, Paul.

Paul expected that Jesus would, in the parousia, 'change our lowly body to be *like his glorious body*' (Phil 3:21). Consequently, Jesus must have appeared to him in a transformed 'spiritual body' (1 Cor 15:44).[17] Paul's testimony is supported by the vision of Stephen (Acts 7:55f) and by that of John of Patmos (Rev 1:13-16). A development from the intangible towards the tangible in the interpretation of the appearances seems much more likely than a development in the opposite direction.

Whatever the visions may have been like, many of those who heard and accepted the preaching of the resurrection did *not* conceive of it in 'fleshly' terms. They were guided by the popular philosophy of the time.

The beginning of the spiritual trajectory

As we have seen, Greek thought held that the soul itself was a kind of material 'body'. Some of the physical activities claimed for the post-Easter Jesus were common religious inheritance for the post-mortem soul. Souls could appear to the living, still bearing the recognizable form of the body and the death wounds of the person, pass through closed doors, give preternatural advice, and vanish. To Christians trained in such ideas – including even many Christians with a Jewish background – 'resurrection' meant 'that the soul was raised, without the flesh' (Riley 1995, p. 41).

Some members of the Corinthian congregation held a view which evoked a lengthy digression from Paul in 1 Cor 15. Paul's wording in v. 12, and especially his polemic in vv. 29ff suggests that they denied all post-mortem life. Yet it is difficult to understand why such people would have joined the congregation in the first place; v. 29 (baptism for the dead) shows that Paul actually knew about post-mortem hope among them. Vv. 35ff. entail an attack at a position for which the problem was not the survival of the self, but the notion of *bodily* resurrection. So one may assume that these Corinthians did not wish to deny eternal life, but interpreted it differently from Paul. Probably they held the standard educated Greco-Roman view of the immortality of the soul (thus also Bultmann 1952, p. 169).

Before we trace the further course of this trajectory it is appropriate to discuss Paul's relation to it – for his view differs less from that of the Corinthians than one might have thought.

Paul

In 1 Cor 15:35ff. Paul speaks of the parousia and of bodily resurrection. Yet instead of showing interest in any post-parousia events on the earth, he is concerned with the *transformation* of the believers, for 'flesh and blood' cannot inherit the kingdom of God (v. 50). Deceased Christians (as distinct from those living at the parousia) will rise in a *different* body. The earthly body they once had was mortal, perishing and 'soulish'; what will rise is a '*pneumatic body*' (v. 44). The earthly mortal body which we have carried is the image of the earthly man, but the glorious resurrection body amounts to the image of the 'heavenly man' (v. 49).

Paul is anxious to emphasize the true corporeality of the resurrection body, yet his 'stress is all on the *difference* of the new "spiritual" body from the old, perishable mortal body' (Wedderburn 1999, p. 31). Consequently Wedderburn asks '*why this resurrection existence should be described as bodily* at all' (Wedderburn 1999, p. 118, my emphasis). Paul is speaking in terms which actually resemble the Greco-Roman view of the immortal, but *material, soul*. His language also reminds one of those Jewish visions which are characterized as 'resurrection of the spirit from Sheol' by modern scholars.[18]

Ultimately, the division is less between body and soul than between 'flesh' and (some kind of) 'body'. Paul's battle for the resurrection of spiritual bodies against the survival of souls (with somatic qualities!) seems largely a battle about words. Paul might have looked more kindly on his Corinthian opponents, 'had not his upbringing made the resurrection of the body a shibboleth for him' (Wedderburn 1999, p. 119).

In 2 Cor 5:1–10[19] Paul resumes some of the language he used in 1 Cor 15, such as the image of putting on new clothes. The passage does not make the nature of his hope any clearer, however. Paul's thought fluctuates between traditional and novel notions – between the public event of the parousia and the ascent of the individual self – without relating these notions to each other in any way. The emphasis, however, lies on 'individual eschatology'. It seems as if one could reach the state of being 'with the Lord' immediately at death, when the 'earthly tent we live in is destroyed' and we may 'put on our heavenly dwelling' (vv. 1–2). Paul's gaze is fixed on the invisible world (2 Cor 4:18). While he, in his clothing metaphor, uses language familiar from 1 Cor 15, there is little in this passage that would suggest transformation of the earthly body. *Dis*continuity between the earthly and heavenly forms of existence is in focus (correctly Strecker 1995, p. 116): Paul has the desire to leave his earthly body (the wretched appearance of which has been criticized in Corinth!), to change it for a heavenly 'dwelling' or 'garment'; he even suggests that this 'dwelling' is pre-existent in heaven, waiting for the believer to gain it (5:1) There is a decisive contrast between 'being away' from the Lord and 'being at home' with him (v. 8), and bodily existence belongs to the phase of being away (v. 6); however, Paul 'would rather be away from the body and at home with the Lord'. Having left the earthly body behind, the individual Christian[20] may appear before the judgement seat of Christ (v. 10); an immediate private judgement (of the deeds done 'in the body' which now obviously belongs to the past) seems envisaged. Having stood the test, he or she will then stay with the Lord in this new form of existence.

Paul's reflections in Phil. 1:20–26 go in the same direction.[21] 'Dying is gain' (v. 21), because it is a direct way of gaining a union with the Lord. The author of this passage would seem to agree (willy-nilly) with those 'deniers of resurrection' he had attacked; yet though he dropped the 'body language' with regard to the believers' heavenly existence, he could not bring himself to use current Greco-Roman language about the 'soul'. Attentive readers must have been left in confusion, as they are today. But then many Jewish notions of resurrection existence were never very clear either.

Developments after Paul

Mark, followed by Matthew and Luke, lets Jesus silence the Sadducees with a 'demonstration' of the reality of the resurrection: God is the God of Abraham, Isaac and Jacob, and he is not God of the dead (Mark 12:25–7 par). Luke makes the point even clearer by adding the clause 'for all live to him [God]'. Taken literally, such statements presuppose a (spiritual) 'resurrection' at death. Luke, at least, leaves no doubt that this is his own view as well.

Luke speaks of resurrection in the traditional way in some places, but his own emphasis lies on an immediate post-mortem retribution (see Lehtipuu 2004). In Luke 23:42f. Jesus will 'arrive' in the Paradise on the very day of the crucifixion, and the robber next to him will join him there at once – certainly not in a resurrected body. As in the story of Dives and Lazarus, there seems to exist a direct route to the beyond.[22] In neither case is an act of judgement envisaged; people just get to the right place (as in *1 Enoch* 22). When Stephen sees the heaven open, he asks the Lord to 'receive his spirit' (Acts 7:55-6). His body remains in the earth, as the mention of the burial (8:2) makes clear.

Clement, too, speaks of Peter and Paul as having departed straight to 'the holy place' (*1 Clem.* 5:4-7), finding there a multitude of martyrs and saints (50:3). Polycarp was known to have already received his 'crown of imperishability', while his body was being burnt (*Mart. Pol.* 17-18).

The fact that the *Gospel of Thomas* (51) refutes the conception of an eschatological resurrection is reflected even in the formulation of the question posed by Jesus' disciples: 'When will the *repose* of the dead come about?' The desired state of the individual, both in the present and in the future, is one of repose of the soul. Logion 21 presents an allegory: the disciples 'undress' in death which releases them from the 'field' of the material world. This would seem to mean the removal of the body at death, and the ascent of the soul. Yet Thomas can 'also conceptualize future salvation in terms of bodily existence and describe the replacement of the earthly body with a new asexual body'; in logion 22 entering the kingdom entails putting on a new 'image' (body). Here Thomas comes near to the Pauline view of the resurrection body (Uro 2003, p. 75f).

Some writings in the 'gnostic Christian' trajectory use even Pauline language. The *Dialogue of the Saviour* holds that 'repose' is something the Christian has reached (1), but it will only be definitely realized when one is liberated from the burden of the body and puts on the promised *heavenly clothes*. 'You will clothe yourself in light and enter the bridal chamber' (50-2). The disciples 'wish to understand the sort of garments we are to be [clothed] with, [when] we depart the decay of the [flesh]'; the Lord answers that these are not temporary, transitory garments, but 'you will become [blessed] when you strip' (84f). Such statements sound rather similar to what Paul had said about putting on the heavenly garment. What is different is the notion of the heavenly *origin* of the soul (also stressed in the *Gospel of Thomas*), so that its journey to heaven is actually a return.

The Valentinian *Treatise on Resurrection* suggests that, in the ascension after death, 'the living [members]' within the person will arise, covered by a new, spiritual 'flesh' (47.4-8, 47.38-48.3).[23] The resurrection is spiritual (45.40); it is spoken of by means of symbols and images (49.6-7). But it is not an illusion, as the post-mortem appearance of Elijah and Moses in the Transfiguration episode proves (48.3-11). There is, then, between the earthly and the risen person a continuity 'furnished by the inner, spiritual man and a spiritual flesh which retains personally identifiable characteristics'. Though the author goes beyond Paul's anthropology in a dualistic direction, his might be considered a more faithful interpretation of Paul's conception of the resurrection body than that of many church fathers who affirmed a literal identity between the physical body and the resurrection body (Peel 1970, p. 160).

The denial of 'fleshly' resurrection was not limited to Christians with 'gnostic' leanings. Polycarp (*Phil.* 7) complains that the claim that there is 'no judgment nor resurrection' is the vanity of the *majority*. Tertullian admits not only that almost all heretics accept the salvation of the soul, but also that a great many Christians claim that resurrection is going out of the body itself, i.e. the ascent of the disembodied soul.

Origen developed a mediating reinterpretation: the bodies in which the saints rise will be identical with their earthly bodies as regards their 'form', but their 'material substratum' will be different. In the eyes of critics this was no real resurrection at all. Yet surely Origen's was a reasonable attempt to make sense of 1 Cor 15.

A basic tension

In summary, the idea that the flesh should survive the grave was abhorrent to many. Christians in Paul's Corinth, Christians of the Thomas tradition and many others both within and without the mainstream church during many centuries denied it. Even Paul's stance seems to be closer to their view than to the doctrine of the resurrection of the flesh which came to be established as orthodoxy.

The boundary between spiritual and material is imprecise in any case. If one is of the (common) opinion that Paul's view serves to maintain the identity of the person in the afterlife, it is hard to see why the Valentinian view in the *Treatise on Resurrection* would not. The same is true when the specific value of Paul's position is found to consist in its emphasis on the goodness of creation and the significance of interpersonal relationships and social communication. It is difficult to see why the idea of the immortality of the soul (which, in the Greek view, did have somatic characteristics) would be any more incompatible with these goods than is Paul's vague notion of corporeality. In fact it is the 'crude' view of the resurrection of the flesh in an earthly kingdom (whatever *its* problems!) that best safeguards the values connected with corporeality. Again, if the point of bodily resurrection is found in the idea that only so can the restoration of God's people take place, then it would be logical to posit the (renewed) *earth* as the place of the resurrection life. But precisely at this point Paul is (at best) quite vague.

The notions of resurrection and immortality are conceptually different. The resurrection logically belongs to the collective expectation of an earthly kingdom, the survival of souls to the expectation of a direct transfer to heaven. The natural location for resurrected bodies is a space-time world. On the other hand, it would seem natural that the souls which have reached heaven would stay there, no longer needing to return to the earth.

One attempt to remove the inconsistency is to postulate, in accordance with many Jewish writings, an interim state in which the souls find themselves between death and resurrection, waiting for the last day. The writings of Paul and Luke were open to interpretations which later went in this direction. In the theology of the church the notion of the judgement of the individual soul at death became crucial, and the conception of an active interim existence of the souls emerged. Speculations concerning the interim state helped to create the notion of purgatory which supplies the interim with a meaning (and mitigates the problem of eternal hell).

The notion of interim is coherent, if the waiting place is located in the netherworld, in which case the last day would actually bring about an improvement in the existence of the saints. But when it is assumed that the souls of the righteous go to *heaven* immediately at death, an awkward scenario results. Now the soul ascends, if not to the very throne of God, then at least to a pleasant waiting chamber; when the last things start on earth, it will go back, unite with the body, and get the reward it had already enjoyed – in order to eventually return to heaven. If set in the overarching framework of immortality, resurrection of the body inevitably becomes a dispensable 'appendix' to individual eschatology.

In modern theology the notion of an interim has not fared well. Protestants have often resorted to the notion of a 'total death': resurrection amounts to a *creatio ex nihilo*. This view is partly based on the mistaken idea that 'total death' is the original 'biblical' idea. In Catholic theology, by contrast, something of a consensus (based on the thought of Karl Rahner) has emerged: one speaks of a 'resurrection at death' which concerns the whole person (soul and some kind of transformed 'body', defined in the vaguest of terms; the fleshly body will rest in the grave). This is the only 'resurrection' envisaged (e.g. Kehl 1986).

This seems a complete victory of *one* early Christian line of thought (in a modernized version) over another. But the tables are now turned, and the result amounts to a tacit vindication of the Valentinian interpretation of Paul.[24] Nor does the paradox end there. If we have interpreted at all correctly the position of those Corinthians who claimed that 'there is no resurrection of the dead', then this modern view, disseminated in books with papal imprimaturs,[25] serves to rehabilitate *their* position as well.

Notes

1. Berger 1995 and Theissen 1999 refer explicitly to Wrede's programme; see now above all D. Zeller's succinct account of earliest Christianity: 'Die Entstehung des Christentums' and 'Konsolidierung in der 2./3. Generation', in Zeller 2002, pp. 1–222. Of course critical historical work on the New Testament and its environment was being done throughout the twentieth century. The point is that the atmosphere often changed dramatically, when scholars moved from special studies to overall accounts or to programmatic statements.

2. On the programme see Räisänen 2000; for a comprehensive discussion see Penner and Vander Stichele (forthcoming).

3. Opting for a topical organization is a personal decision which departs from Wrede's vision.

4. Räisänen 2003–4. A draft of the chapter on Christology, entitled 'True Man or True God?', appears in 2005 in a volume dedicated to the memory of K-J. Illman.

5. In the NTTs by Lutheran scholars Paul tends to get the lion's share, but even a Catholic finds that it is Paul who presents 'the New Testament doctrine of general resurrection' in a forceful way (Schelkle 1974, p. 83).

6. For instance Stuhlmacher 1992–99, who pays thorough attention to the resurrection of *Jesus*, has nothing to say on the resurrection or immortality of individuals according to 1 Cor 15 and 2 Cor 5. Conzelmann 1987, p. 357ff., has a five-line note on the topic. Hahn 2002, p. 776 dilutes the problem.

7. Bultmann 1952, p. 346 does note contradictions, but lets them just prove how little difference different images make. A comprehensive discussion which includes cautiously critical comments, ending up with a conclusion similar to Bultmann's, is found in Schelkle 1974, pp. 79–91. Conzelmann 1987, pp. 206–212 gives an existential analysis, underlining the contradiction between what Paul says and what he means. Strecker 1995, p. 116ff. makes acute observations on individual points.

8. See e.g. Conzelmann 1987, p. 73 on Matt 25:31ff. On the punishment depicted he has nothing to say.

9. Exceptions: Guthrie 1981, pp. 888–92; Schelkle 1974, pp. 112–16.

10. On the mixture of religio-historical and overtly theological elements in Bultmann's work see Räisänen 2000, pp. 47–53.

11. The idea of a forensic judgement can be traced back to the Egyptian notion of weighing the souls of the dead; in Egypt, for the first time, a happy after-life seems to have been connected with the moral quality of the person's earthly life.
12. E.g. *T Zeb*. 10:2: 'the Lord shall bring down fire on the impious and will destroy them to all generations'.
13. Still other Lukan passages contradict the notion of a resurrection altogether; see below.
14. The *NTTs* tend to underline the positive side of the judgement only, e.g. Stuhlmacher 1999, p. 165; Hahn, 2002, pp. 785, 795; Gnilka 1994, p. 185. The reader learns nothing of the fate of the condemned.
15. In his *NTT*, Stuhlmacher does not discuss judgement at all in connection with Revelation. Gnilka 1994, p. 417f. notes correctly that the judgement is described as punitive, but concludes that the idea of salvation predominates. He omits to mention the lake of fire.
16. Differently, however, John 21: do not touch!
17. Therefore it is logical to infer from 1 Cor 15 (with, e.g., Wedderburn 1999, p. 87) that Paul may well have thought that Jesus' 'former body remained sown in the ground', for 'so great is the stress upon the newness and the difference of the resurrection existence'.
18. There is little on the pneumatic body *in the NTTs*. Stuhlmacher, for instance, does not mention it at all. Strecker 1995, p. 116f infers that the body will not rise from the grave. Conzelmann 1987, p. 207, notes a conflict of Paul also with himself – and eventually makes a virtue out of this necessity (p. 210). Bultmann 1952, p. 192 claims that Paul, misled by his opponents, here uses *soma* in a non-characteristic way.
19. For a thorough analysis of this passage see Lindgård (2005) who gives due attention to its internal discrepancies.
20. The generalizing words *pantas* and *hekastos* show that Paul is not thinking just of himself here.
21. In his *NTT*, Bultmann 1952, p. 346 notes the contradiction with the resurrection doctrine. Hahn 2002, p. 776 harmonizes the different notions.
22. Luke 23:42f is typically missing in many *NTTs* altogether, e.g. in those of Strecker, Stuhlmacher, Conzelmann, Hübner 1990–95 and Lohse 1974; Luke 16:19–31 in those of Strecker, Stuhlmacher, Hübner and Lohse. Conzelmann 1987, p. 25 mentions it on one line.
23. To be sure, the interpretation of the passage is debated.
24. Kehl 1986, p. 266 admits that in patristic time his position would have been considered gnostic.
25. It is not, of course, a Catholic view only.

References

Berger, K., *Theologiegeschichte des Urchristentums* (Tübingen & Basel, 1995)

Bernstein, A., *The Formation of Hell* (Ithaca, NY, 1993).

Bultmann, Rudolf, *Theologie des Neuen Testaments* (2 vols; Tübingen: Mohr Siebeck, 1948-53). ET *Theology of the New Testament* (2 vols; New York: Scribner, 1951-55). References are to the English version, vol. 1.

Collins, J.J., 'The afterlife in apocalyptic literature', in A.J. Avery-Peck and J. Neusner (eds), *Death, Life-after-death, Resurrection and the World-to-come in the Judaisms of Antiquity* (Leiden, 2000).

Conzelmann, H., *Grundriss der Theologie des Neuen Testaments* (UTB 1446; Tübingen, 1987).

Evans, C.F., *Resurrection and the New Testament* (London, 1970).

Gnilka, J., *Theologie des Neuen Testaments* (Freiburg, 1994).

Guthrie, D., *New Testament Theology* (Leicester, 1981).

Hahn, F., *Theologie des Neuen Testaments* 2 (Tübingen, 2002).

Hübner, H., *Biblische Theologie des Neuen Testaments* 1-3 (Göttingen, 1990-95).

Hultgård, A., 'Persian apocalypticism', in J.J. Collins (ed.), *The Encyclopedia of Apocalypticism 1* (New York, 2000).

Kehl, M., *Eschatologie* (Würzburg, 1986).

Lehtipuu, O., *The Afterlife Imagery in Luke's Story of the Rich Man and Lazarus* (Dissertation, University of Helsinki, 2004).

Lindgård, F., *Paul's Line of Thought in 2 Corinthians 4:16-5:10* (Tübingen, 2005).

Lohse, E., *Grundriss der neutestamentlichen Theologie* (Stuttgart, 1974).

Martin, D.B., *The Corinthian Body* (New Haven, 1995).

McDannell, C. and Lang, B., *Heaven: A History* (New Haven, 1990).

Morgan, Robert, *The Nature of New Testament Theology. The Contribution of William Wrede and Adolf Schlatter* (London: SCM Press, 1973).

Peel, M., 'Gnostic eschatology and the New Testament', *NovT* 12 (1970).

Penner, T. and Vander Stichele, C. (eds), *Prospects for a Story and Programme: Essays on Räisänen's 'Beyond New Testament Theology'* (forthcoming).

Räisänen, H., *Beyond New Testament Theology* (London, 2000).

Räisänen, H., 'Last things first: 'Eschatology' as the first chapter in a synthesis of early Christian thought', *Temenos* 39-40 (2003-4).

Riley, G., *Resurrection Reconsidered* (Minneapolis, 1995).

Schelkle, K.H., *Theologie des Neuen Testaments* IV/1 (Düsseldorf, 1974).

Strecker, G., *Theologie des Neuen Testaments* (Berlin/New York, 1995).

Stuhlmacher, P., *Biblische Theologie des Neuen Testaments 1-2* (Göttingen, 1992-9).

Theissen, G., *A Theory of Primitive Christian Religion* (London, 1999).

Uro, R., *Thomas* (London, 2003).

Wedderburn, A.J.M., *Beyond Resurrection* (London, 1999).

Zeller, D. (ed.), *Christentum* I (Die Religionen der Menschheit 28; Stuttgart, 2002).

Chapter 12

'Action is the Life of All' New Testament Theology and Practical Theology

Christopher Rowland, Oxford, and Zoë Bennett, Cambridge

Introduction

Robert Morgan's selection from the work of William Wrede and Adolf Schlatter sets the scene for an understanding of New Testament theology which juxtaposes a historical approach with a theological approach. Put another way: what we have in the works which he introduces represents the characteristic debate about New Testament theology in modernity, in which the setting of the New Testament in the ancient history of religions is contrasted with an equally historical approach, but one which is more sensitive to the way in which theology has emerged in the life of the church down the centuries. The form and content of New Testament theology has often involved a debate between these two positions. The late twentieth century has witnessed a different perspective emerging, albeit one with many antecedents within Christian history. This involves an understanding of theology as an activity which is not primarily confined to the intellectual debates of either historian or theologian but is rooted in the active participation in commitment to God and an understanding of the form and content of that theology which arises out of that commitment. In this engagement with the Bible scriptural texts have been used imaginatively to engage with life and experience.

This approach is touched on by Robert Morgan who suggests three levels on which the task of 'New Testament theology' takes place: the purely historical, as exemplified by the work of Wrede, whose primary concern is the history of the Christian religion in its socio-historical context in antiquity. Here there is no need to confine our sources to canonical texts. Compared with this, which is primarily an exercise in the history of religions, there is a form of historical work which explicates the theological presentations made in the New Testament itself – what one may term a descriptive theological task. Finally there is a constructive theology, whose primary engagement is with the New Testament, which is not controlled solely by historical considerations and is attentive to the dogmatic tradition of the Christian church.

Elsewhere Morgan uses the highly suggestive image of a web, which opens up a connection with the kind of interaction between the New Testament and practical theology which is the key to our chapter (1973, pp. 39–40, 60):

> Theological construction is a matter of weaving the pattern of one's own convictions with the various threads of the tradition in the web of one's own experience. A person's historical situation influences what thread he receives, and the structure of his own life has some effect upon what in the tradition makes Christian sense to him (1973, p. 40).

He goes on to write about the process of listening to the tradition, thereby selecting and criticizing according to one's 'current apprehension of Christianity', thus modifying one's picture by taking new elements of the tradition seriously. In this process there is a mutual critique of faith understanding and tradition, and an appeal both to the tradition as a whole and to contemporary experience:

> The theological interpreter must make choices within the tradition and defend his choice by reference to his understanding of the tradition as a whole, and to the apprehension of reality that provides the web in which threads of tradition are woven to represent a theological pattern corresponding to his apprehension of the Christian revelation. (1973, p. 60).

For anyone interested in practical theology it is the image of the web which is of most importance. In several respects this at least qualifies and perhaps even challenges the hierarchy implied in Morgan's 'level' or 'layer' analogy. In the latter there is an implicit primacy given to the historical, whose fundamental character is seen as a way of preventing the theological construction falling into error. This way of relating the New Testament to the theological task has been questioned, not least by

Nicholas Lash in two seminal articles, both of which are of importance for this chapter. Lash's recognition that Scripture is something to be performed, lived and acted upon and not just analysed, challenges a widespread assumption among New Testament exegetes that they are engaged in a scientific task providing the basic data for those theologians who wish to engage in theological construction. Not only does Lash challenge the philosophical naiveté of this kind of position but he also questions whether any exegesis is adequate which goes no further than describe what the text meant (Lash 1986).

There is an implicit recognition of this in Robert Morgan's work. In the tasks of doing New Testament theology there is an interweaving of the threads of tradition into the web of one's own experience, so the structure of one's own life affects what makes sense in tradition.

The character of New Testament theology as an objective and primarily historical discipline has often been questioned. Indeed, in memorable words in the introduction to the second edition of his Romans commentary, Karl Barth asked: 'Why should parallels drawn from the ancient world be of more value for our understanding of the epistle than the situation in which we ourselves actually are and to which we can therefore bear witness' (Barth 1933, pp. 2–15).

Much theology can often seem remote from ordinary life. In contrast, practical theology has its starting place, not in detached reflection on Scripture and tradition but the present life – for example, in liberation theology the lack of basic amenities, the carelessness about the welfare of human persons. The meaning of faith is illuminated at the same time as engagement takes place with the concerns of the commitment to the poor and vulnerable which is the context and motor of theological reflection, not a consequence of it. Thus practical discipleship becomes the dynamic within which theological understanding takes place. Understanding of God and the world comes about and is altered in a life of service to those who are the least of Christ's brothers and sisters. It means interpreting everyday life by means of the Bible rather than the study of the Bible being an end in itself cut off from involvement in everyday living and the exegetical insights which they offer to the theological task. This way of doing theology, therefore, is not primarily the accumulation of, or learning about, a distinctive body of information, detached from the understanding of the impact of the Bible on people's lives. In some ways, it harks back to the method of an earlier age when worship, service to humanity and theological reflection were more closely integrated and when the conduct of the Christian life was an indispensable context for theological reflection. One can only learn about theology by embarking on practice.

Developing the Metaphor of the 'Web' in the Light of Practical Theology

Robert Morgan's metaphor of a web to describe the work of theological interpretation and construction provides an excellent starting point for consideration of the task of the practical theologian, whose work involves the engagement of contemporary life, experience and context with the theological tradition – here specifically that theological tradition which is mediated to us in the texts of the Bible. Morgan envisages the theologian making sense of the threads of tradition through the web of his own experience, and through his sense and apprehension in relation to judgements about that which is Christian and about revelation. He acknowledges that the structure of one's own life affects what makes sense in the tradition, and that the historical situation influences what threads are received. The constructive theologian is a weaver of tradition and experience, contextually influenced and personally implicated in his own work.

This insight from a New Testament theology perspective resonates strongly with recent discussions in practical theology about the nature, meaning and structure of interpretation. Such discussion concerns both the texts for interpretation and the nature of the act of interpretation itself. In the 1930s Anton Boisen set the agenda by insisting that education for practical and pastoral action and understanding in the church should pay attention to the study not only of texts but also of 'the living human document' (quoted in Miller-McLemore 1996, p. 16). Boisen himself suffered acute mental health problems, and it was from this experience that he advocated the need in pastoral theological education for interpretation of living human realities in engagement with the realities of the faith tradition. It is important to note that this was not just a study of external realities, but implied a reflexive move on the part of the practical theologian, a consideration of the historical situation of the interpreter and of her life structure, sense and apprehension. Such a hermeneutical approach to the work of practical theology has been continued and developed in the work of Capps, Gerkin and Farley (Capps 1984, Gerkin 1984, 1997, Farley 2000). The implications of full attention to context implied by such a hermeneutical approach have been developed in the social and communal, contextual paradigms of practical theology (Couture and Hunter 1995, Patton 1993). Specifically in recent feminist practical theology the metaphor of the 'web' has explicitly surfaced as a way of moving beyond the need to listen to the 'living human document' towards a method of doing theology which listens to multiple voices of both tradition and experience. Bonnie Miller-McLemore writes

> Many in pastoral theology have traditionally harkened back to Anton Boisen's powerful foundational metaphor for the existential subject of pastoral theology – *'the study of living human documents rather than books'* . . . Today, the 'living human *web*' suggests itself as a better term for the appropriate subject for investigation, interpretation and transformation (1996, p. 16).

> We cannot predict what difference other stories and traditions will make to general formulations in the field or in pastoral practice. When we admit that knowledge is seldom universal or uniform, and that truth is contextual and tentative, we discover a host of methodological, pedagogical, and practical problems . . . Pastoral theology's trademark of empathy for the living human document is confounded by the limitations of empathy in the midst of the living human web (1996, p. 21).

This chapter seeks to develop one specific element in that weaving of tradition and experience identified by Morgan as a key moment in theological construction, and by contemporary writers and practitioners as central to the task of practical theology. That element is the part of the pattern which develops when the Bible is woven with the experiences, sense, judgement and response of the practical theologian reading the text in context.

Roger Walton, in a recent article based on research in a context of ecumenically diverse British theological education (Walton 2003), identifies 'seven distinct types or ways in which students used the Bible and the Christian tradition' as follows (quotations from pp. 136–47). In the *Links and Associations* strategy, student practitioners 'make an instant, often single link between an experience and a scriptural passage'. Such links may act as 'orientation, legitimation or reassurance' or may give 'some kind of critical distance'. In *Prooftexting*, student practitioners draw, normally uncritically, on the texts of the tradition to 'indicate what they should do or justify what they have done'. The biblical texts are expected to answer 'cognitive or affective questions posed by an experience or issues' and 'to provide an authoritative statement to justify or guide response'. Walton's third category, *Resonance and Analogy*, is the category we wish to develop and explore in this chapter. He describes it thus: 'Here students see in a Bible story or other Christian text many points of connection with their own experience and then use various aspects of the text to draw out significance, meaning and insight for their own experience.' *Exploring a Theological Theme* involves using a theological theme, such as incarnation, self-giving love or death and resurrection, as an interpretative tool for experience. This 'becomes a way of making meaning and formulating a response'; for example one student examined the themes of sacrifice and stewardship in relation to the foot-and mouth crisis. *Taking an Extrapolated Question to the Tradition* is a common way of trying to weave the threads. An example would be deriving questions about community from experience in a deprived urban setting and then taking those questions to the Christian tradition, asking what is meant by community in the New Testament and drawing this into a discussion of the role of the church in nurturing community in the contemporary setting. A *One-Way Critique* uses the resources of the Bible to assess practice; A *Mutual Critique* 'operates in a more sophisticated and dialectical fashion' being 'both a critique of the practice by theology and a critique of theology by practice and experience'.

While Walton is clear that his ordering of the types in no way implies a hierarchy of value, he does 'discern a difference in criticality between the first three and the second four'. Given the value placed on criticality in the Western academic and educational context, it is inevitable that strategies of 'weaving' which imply higher criticality should be more highly regarded and rewarded. Furthermore, in contemporary practical theology there is a dominant model of 'critical correlation' in which questions are put to the world from the faith and to the faith from the world, or to tradition from experience and to experience from tradition. This is further developed in Stephen Pattison's influential model of practical theology as 'conversation' (Pattison 2000). These models fit well with Walton's 'mutual critique' and reinforce its value.

Possibilities for critical power, however – for questioning both one's own position and the more widespread *status quo* – do not only arise from cognitive/argumentative critical questioning. Such possibilities also arise from seeing something or hearing something in a fresh way, from seeing the 'stranger's' perspective, looking 'aslant'. To change the metaphor and return to Walton's language, resonance and analogy are potentially fruitful ways of describing and exploring the act of weaving experience and text in freshly illuminated constructive theological understanding.

Walton explicates the 'resonance and analogy' method of weaving text and experience primarily in two areas. First he writes of the 'extended and explored story' where analogies between text and experience are used 'as a sounding or springboard for a more extended discussion between theology and experience'. His examples here are a discussion of bereavement in engagement with the Emmaus story in Luke 24 and a discussion of worship in engagement with the Jew–Gentile tension 'at the heart of Paul's ministry'. Here texts were used which appeared to 'mirror or parallel experience'. Second he discusses a way of using resonance and analogy which takes more the form of a meditation, and is used in 'interpreting and nurturing . . . spirituality'. Scriptural stories of change, healing and growth in the Gospels are used in one example to reflect on an unfolding pattern of personal story.

These ways of relating text and experience are common in practical theology – in professional practice, in educational contexts, and in the practical discipleship of the 'whole people of God'. It is therefore important to develop a sophisticated theoretical understanding of this method of interpreting the Bible, and of this basis for Christian theology and practice. It is a method of interpretation which can be, and often is, used naively; it is our contention that it is in fact a method rooted in Christian tradition and indeed in the Scriptures themselves, which has the potential to be developed in a sophisticated way, and as such deserves extended attention.

Walton explicitly refers in his analysis more to 'analogy' than to 'resonance', whereas the latter is the category which has most captured our imagination. We affirm what comes out in Walton's treatment of this type of reflection – a way of getting a new perspective, of encouraging complexity of exploration, of attending to the meditative and contemplative in theological work, of making connections and patterns – and want to take his work further, particularly by developing the metaphor of *resonance*. We propose to demonstrate that this is as critical as the much-valued 'critical correlation' (mutual critique) and to indicate its equal claim to fruitfulness, and to an honoured position in that web which is constructive theology in engagement with the Scriptures.

'Resonance' is a musical metaphor. It is the 'sound produced by a body vibrating in sympathy with a neighbouring source of sound' (*Collins English Dictionary*). In terms of practical theology and the Scriptures, the metaphor opens up the idea that an interpreter, or a community of interpreters, in reading the Scriptures, find themselves moved ('vibrating') as what they read sets off in them emotions, actions, thoughts and perspectives which have connections with what is read sufficient to respond, but which are expanded and activated by that reading. In turn the Scriptures themselves 'vibrate' with freshly understood meaning.

'Resonance' as a way of reading the Scriptures is imaginatively engaging. It opens up possibilities of various different ways of being both constructive and critical theologically. The key point is to expand the imagination, to allow the imagination to play, in ways which maximise the engagement between the Scriptures and contemporary life, action and culture. 'Resonance' invites the contemplative, the artistic, the visual and the musical into theological reflection and interpretation. Thus new ways of seeing are opened up which invite new ways of action.

It is important to stress both the imagination and the action. The image of resonance throws light on the example of liberation theology given above; the struggle of the oppressed in their everyday living resonates with the stories and the values found in the Scriptures. This example shows clearly how resonance is not only about thought and emotion but also inevitably about action, about bodies. This point is well brought out in an article by Nicholas Lash whose thesis is germane to the thesis of this chapter (Lash 1986). He rightly points out that while musicology can provide the best possible text, that music has still to be performed, has still to be, as it were, translated from the page into lived lives of those who adhere to this body of texts and claim that they are life giving. That latter quality can only be apprehended by those who seek to embody its life-giving possibility in the way in which the words on the page are turned into living words. In this they imitate the Divine Word who became flesh and in whom God has now spoken (John 1:18; Heb 1:1).

Walton's category, *Resonance and Analogy*, suggests a way of exploring analogies between text and experience 'as a sounding or springboard for a more extended discussion between theology and experience'. It is important not to see these examples from contemporary practical theology as merely naive engagement with the scriptural text devoid of a critical awareness. The very process of engaging in analogical imagination itself opens up critical possibilities of the one engaged in it. Unlike 'prooftexting', for example, the juxtaposition of differences makes possible critical reflection. Resonance and analogy not only describes how New Testament writers related texts, tradition and action, but also closely parallels the hermeneutical insight into an aspect of Latin American liberationist hermeneutics as set out by Clodovis Boff (Boff 1987 and Sugirtharajah 1991, pp. 9–35). Boff's 'correspondence of relationships' method, which sees the Bible read through the lens of the experience of the present thereby enabling it to become a key to understanding that to which the scriptural text bears witness about the life and struggles of ancestors in the faith and which in turn casts light on the present, is very similar. Two things are important about Boff's model. First, this is not only about thought but also about action, about the lived lives of people seeking to embody the way of God in faithful struggle for justice. Secondly, this method does not presuppose the application of a set of principles based on a theological programme or pattern to modern situations.

We need not, then, look for formulas to 'copy' or techniques to 'apply' from Scripture. What Scripture will offer us are rather something like orientations, models, types, directives, principles, inspirations – elements permitting us to acquire, on our own initiative, a 'hermeneutic competency' and thus the capacity to judge – on our own initiative, in our own right – 'according to the mind of Christ', or 'according to the Spirit', the new unpredictable situations with which we are continually confronted. The Christian writings offer us not a *what*, but a *how* – a manner, a style, a spirit (Sugirtharajah 1991, p. 30).

What we have been expounding is a mode of such 'hermeneutical competency'. It is a mode whose shaping metaphors are those of 'web' and of 'resonance'. Both metaphors, as we have expounded them, imply complexity, embodiedness, relationship and attentive responsiveness. They implicate the interpreting subject. It is important to note that such a mode of hermeneutical competency has epistemological implications. The philosopher Hegel wrote of the impoverished kind of knowledge which adopts '*only a historical attitude* towards religion', putting the theologian in the position of a counting house clerk who counts out other people's wealth (Hegel 1984, p. 128). True knowledge is participative knowledge, not available to the detached observer. Knowledge and knower are inseparable. Resonance, sympathetic vibration, implies this.

Furthermore, the act of understanding is part of the 'practical art of living rightly' (Bennett Moore 1997, p. 39). This applies as much to the understanding of the Scriptures as to anything else. Martha Nussbaum, writing about this practical art in *The Fragility of Goodness*, draws out Sophocles' words about 'thinking on both sides':

> The Sophoclean soul is more like Heraclitus's image of *psyche*: a spider sitting in the middle of its web, able to feel and respond to any tug in any part of the complicated structure . . . The image of learning expressed in this style . . . stresses responsiveness and an attention to complexity; it discourages the search for the simple and, above all, for the reductive (1986, p. 69).

Within the web of the interpretation of Scripture – that web of tradition, experience, historical situation and subjective apprehension – the interpreter is like a spider and the act of interpretation requires responsiveness to tugs in all parts of the web. The interpreter is an agent embedded in circumstances, whose attentiveness and responsiveness to both text and context needs to be intentional action.

Understanding is thus impossible to divorce from action. This is not only because a key purpose of understanding is to further right action, but also because understanding itself comes through that co-inherence of feeling tugs and giving tugs which is known in practical theology as the model of action/reflection. The impossibility of splitting understanding from action is given a particular post-modern philosophical underpinning in the centrality of practice as disclosive of truth (Graham 1996); it is from the start inscribed in the very heart of Christianity, in which the central doctrinal/theological assertion that God *is* Love is complemented by a central ethical/practical imperative *to* love God and neighbour.

The evidence from the examples from students' work in practical theology reflects the pattern of using the Bible in theological reflection down the centuries. So, within the New Testament letters we can find 'Links and Associations' (Heb 6 on Melchizedek), 'Prooftexting' (1 Cor 1:19 and passim – this is the favourite way of using Scripture in the early church), 'Resonance and Analogy' (1 Cor 10), 'Exploring a Theological Theme' (Abraham in Gal 3-4 and Rom 4), 'An Extrapolated Question to take to the Tradition' (1 Cor 9, especially 9:8-9, 14-15 on the issues of payment of apostles), and 'A One-way Critique' (the use of Gen 15 as the key to understanding the significance of Abraham in the light of the experience of the gentile Christians). A 'Mutual Critique' is less evident, for the simple reason that 'the new has come' and has relativized the old, suggesting that we, as modern readers, might relativize the position of Christian Scripture by reference to experience just as Paul relativized the Old Testament in the light of his Christian experience of the Spirit.

We now offer examples of the way in which practical theologians have engaged in resonance and analogy in their own interpretation of Scripture as it opened up in contexts of their active, theological practice.

Gerrard Winstanley: 'action is the life of all'

Between 1648 and 1652 Winstanley wrote more than 20 politico-religious tracts, many arising from his participation in a community, the Diggers. Winstanley and the Diggers were convinced that a moment had come in history when the promises for God's kingdom on earth were about to be fulfilled. The hostility of local landowners ensured no communities survived for long. They saw themselves as agents of its coming at 'the acceptable time' and sought to improve the lot of the hungry and landless through the cultivation of the common land and to create the kind of society they believed had existed before the Fall. They believed the earth to have been originally a 'common treasury' for all to share, with the practice of buying and selling the land, which allowed some to become rich and others to starve, constituting the Fall of Adam from which humanity, severally and corporately, stood in need of redemption.

Winstanley stresses the priority of experience over what he calls 'book-learning', and like many of his radical predecessors the importance of visions as vehicles to discern the underlying state of things:

Many things were revealed to me which I never read in books nor heard from the mouth of any flesh, and when I began to speak of them, some people could not bear my words and amongst these revelations this was one: that the earth shall be made a common treasury of livelihood to the whole of mankind, without respect of persons; and I heard a voice within me bade me declare it all abroad which I did obey, for I declared it by word of mouth wheresoever I came. Then I was made to write a little book called *The New Law of Righteousness* and therein declared it: yet my mind was not at rest, because nothing was acted, and thoughts ran in me, that words and writings were all nothing, and must die, for action is the life of all, and if thou dost not act, thou dost nothing. With a little time I was made obedient to the words in that particular, for I took my spade and went and broke the ground upon George Hill in Surrey thereby declaring freedom to the creation and the earth must be set free from entanglements of law and landlords, and that it shall become a common treasury to all as it was first made and given to the sons of men. ('A Watch-Word to the City of London, and the Army', Bradstock and Rowland 2002, pp. 131–2).

Typical features of Winstanley's use of Scripture are that he reads Scripture through current events and in turn current events are viewed through the lens of scriptural types and illuminated by them. The struggle between the Dragon and Christ is now linked to the struggle between the oppressive political powers which kept the common people in thrall. Winstanley used the imagery of the book of Daniel and Revelation, particularly the references to the beasts arising from the sea, to comprehend the oppressive character of the state. The Book of Revelation itself takes up the idea of the Beast of Daniel and relates it to the experience of oppression and state power exercised by the state in John's own day (Bradstock and Rowland 2002, p. 133).

Winstanley was an advocate of what one might term a realized eschatology in which future hope is not only a present possibility but also the very condition of the life he lived. His was a conviction, however, that the coming of the Kingdom was dependent on human repentance rather than an inevitable and inexorable divine action (cf. Acts 3:19). The Second Coming takes the form of Christ 'rising up in sons and daughters' and drawing them back into a spirit of true community. The new heaven and earth is something to be seen here and now, for royal power is the old heaven and earth that must pass away. The New Jerusalem is not to be seen only after one dies: 'I know that the glory of the Lord shall be seen and known within creation, and the blessing shall spread within all nations'. God is not far above the heavens; God is to be found in the lives and experiences of ordinary men and women. The perfect society will come wherever there takes place 'the rising up of Christ in sons and daughters, which is his second coming'.

Winstanley's position is typical of many radicals down the centuries in believing that the Spirit who opens up the meaning of the letters of Scripture to the eye of faith and leads God's people in ever new ways. It has long been a feature of liberation theology, for example, that knowing God is rooted in commitment to the poor and outcast and action in solidarity with them. Indeed, it is something of a commonplace in studies of Mark's Gospel that the journey to Jerusalem with Jesus, on the way, is the necessary framework for understanding, even if it does not guarantee it.

It is that 'embodied character of exegesis' that Winstanley's words 'action is the life of all' capture so well. Exegesis, therefore, is to continue that process initiated by the Word become flesh who offers an 'exegesis' of the unseen God. As already mentioned, John 1:18 (and Heb 1:1–4 also) points to a practical demonstration of meaning in the living out of the meaning of the biblical words. This is, if anything, more important.

William Stringfellow: 'the practice of the vocation to live as Jerusalem in the midst of Babylon'

William Stringfellow was an early civil rights activist and protestor against the war in Vietnam. He turned his back on a distinguished legal career, and worked in East Harlem where he was an early advocate of the theology of the 'principalities and powers' and their contemporary social reality. In *An Ethic for Christians and Other Aliens in a Strange Land* William Stringfellow seeks to write a book which is geared to enabling his audience, to read America biblically, 'rather than allow the United States of America, its culture and values to determine the way the Bible is read' (Stringfellow 1973). At the heart of his method is this conviction that the Bible, and particularly the Apocalypse, can assist one to understand a particular moment of time because it enables an enhanced vision of the reality that confronts one (Stringfellow 1973, p. 152). For Stringfellow, the Apocalypse does not offer a timetable about the end of the world but a template by which one can assess the theological character of the world in which one lives, that reading itself catalysed by the experience of the Vietnam war. Stringfellow follows in a long and distinguished tradition in which Babylon and Jerusalem are types of two different kinds of religious communities.

Stringfellow does not expect to go to the Scriptures as if to a self-help manual which will offer off-the-shelf solutions. Nor is he interested in abstract principles or grand theories to apply to human situations. For him the ethics of biblical people concern events not moral propositions:

'Precedent and parable, not propositions or principle' (Stringfellow 1977, p. 24). There is no norm, no ideal, no grandiose principle from which hypothetical, preconceived or carefully worked out answers can be derived because there are no disincarnate issues. The Apocalypse's stark contrasts offer an interpretative key to understand the cosmos under God and the situation of his nation in the 1970s and 1980s. Like the great Donatist interpreter Tyconius, he considers the images of Babylon and Jerusalem are not only eschatologically future images, but assist readers in their understanding of reality here and now. Babylon is a description of every city, an allegory of the condition of death, the principality in bondage to death in time, the focus of apocalyptic judgement. Jerusalem is about the emancipation of human life in society from the rule of death. It is a parable he says of the church of prophecy, an anticipation of the end of time (Stringfellow 1973, p. 21).

Stringfellow's work has many affinities with Latin American liberation theology, particularly as it is reflected in the life of the Basic Ecclesial Communities. Stringfellow's work explores those areas of life in action, where one is confronted with the limits of compromise, what to protest about and what to keep quiet about, how to act prophetically, and how to avoid just taking the line of least resistance. For him, there is that ongoing need to emphasize the particularities of every situation. For Stringfellow, it is an ongoing, contextual task for which there are no simple answers from the Scriptures but a resource to inform the struggle to interpret the particulars. For Stringfellow, the Bible furnishes no answers:

> The ethics of biblical politics offer no basis for divining specific, unambiguous, narrow, or ordained solutions for any social issue. Biblical theology does not deduce 'the will of God' for political involvement or social action. The Bible – if it is esteemed for its own genius – does not yield 'right' or 'good' or 'true'; or ultimate' answers. The Bible does not do that in seemingly private or personal matters; even less can it be said to do so in political or institutional life.
>
> . . . The impotence of any scheme of ethics boasting answers of ultimate connotation or asserting the will of God is that time and history are not truly respected as the context of decision making. Instead, they are treated in an abstract, fragmented, selective, or otherwise, arbitrary version hung together at most under some illusory rubric of 'progress' or 'effectiveness' or 'success'. From a biblical vantage point as much from an empirical outlook, this means a drastic incapacity to cope with history as the saga in which death as a moral power claims sovereignty over human beings and nations and all creatures. It means a failure to recognize time as an epoch of death's worldly reign, a misapprehension of the ubiquity of

fallenness throughout the whole of creation, and in turn, a blindness to imminent and recurrent redemptive signs in the everyday life of this world (Stringfellow 1973, pp. 54–5).

The Practice of New Testament Theology: a Contemporary Example

A contemporary example of the practice of New Testament theology that appropriates and implements Paul's theology – centred in the embodied exegesis of Jesus Christ – may be found in the practices of the Center for Faith in the Work Place (San Antonio, Texas). The Center promotes a Christological ethic that emphasizes imaginative and contextual discipleship in daily life. Its weekly practice of small group spiritual discernment provides participants with the opportunity to think with the 'mind of Christ' (see 1 Cor 2:10–16; cf. Phil 2:4–5) and to 'clothe themselves with Christ' in all of their daily actions (see Gal 3:27; Rom 13:14).[1]

The Center's small group spiritual discernment practice always begins in one of two ways with reflection on the daily experience of a participant. First, a person may describe a recent experience and identify particular human actions that may have somehow shaped that experience. The group then collectively attempts to interpret the experience and conduct through the lens of Scripture (this is very similar to the methods of resonance and analogy described earlier). Using one or more scriptural characterizations of Jesus, they seek to discern the revelation of Jesus Christ that may have taken place through the embodied exegesis of one or more of the participants in the encounter (see 1 Cor 1:6–8). As group members reflect on *past* conduct and experience, they attempt to connect these individual acts of embodied exegesis of Jesus Christ with community experiences of God's life-giving power (see, e.g. 1 Cor 1:4–9; 12:4–7). In this practice group members reflectively 'prove through testing' what appears to be God's will in that given context (see Rom 12:1–2). This, in turn, helps group members imaginatively envision a range of *future* Christ-conforming actions through which God's life-giving power might also be experienced anew in community life.

Alternatively, a group member may describe a present web of relationships and invite the group to assess the situation with the 'mind of Christ'. The group seeks to illuminate prophetically what it might look like for the participant to be 'clothed with Christ' in his future engagements in the particular context. The group turns to specific Scripture texts to try to illuminate the situation by analogy.

For example, a group member at the Center recently described a meeting he would be attending that involved a dispute over the construction of a building. The building contractor had caught the building owner's site representative in the act of making a misrepresentation about how the building should be constructed. The contractor threatened the owner with a lawsuit over the increased costs resulting from the misrepresentation. The parties agreed to meet to discuss the claims. The Center's group member was to attend the meeting in his role as lawyer for the building owner.

The lawyer invited the discernment group to help him envision how he might 'clothe himself with Christ' in the upcoming meeting. To illuminate the situation by analogy, the group read and reflected on John 8:2-11 – the story of the woman caught in adultery. Group members imaginatively cast themselves in the role of Jesus and how he responded to the angry crowd about to stone the woman for her violations of the law. The group began to think analogically about how the lawyer might similarly respond. As a result of the group's conversation, the lawyer imaginatively envisioned possible actions that might constitute his embodied exegesis of Jesus Christ in the circumstances.

The next week the lawyer returned to the group to report his experience of the meeting. Just like the story in John 8, the meeting began with the contractor angrily stating that he had caught the owner's employee in the act of making misrepresentations and demanding the lawyer's agreement that the contractor was entitled to damages from the owner.

Having imaginatively 'clothed himself with Christ' after reflecting on John 8, the lawyer did not immediately respond. He remained silent and took notes while the contractor continued angrily to repeat his claims. Finally, after the contractor had exhausted his complaints, the lawyer responded. He patiently but firmly pointed out the contractor's complicity in the situation: the written contract expressly prohibited the owner's employee from giving such instructions on the jobsite. The lawyer also confronted the owner's employee, instructing him clearly not to give any further directions about construction details. The tension among the parties abated, their differences were reconciled, and the project proceeded to completion without further conflict. Moreover, according to the lawyer, he experienced a deep connection with Christ through his embodied exegesis in the context.

At the Center for Faith in the Workplace, participants engage in the practice of spiritual discernment and seek to 'clothe themselves with Christ' in all of their daily actions. They grow to understand that embodied exegesis of Jesus Christ is the pathway to experiences of God's life-giving power that transforms communities. In the process, they discover that 'action is the life of all'.

Some Theological Reflections

To approach New Testament theology in the ways sketched in this chapter is to do something which is fundamental to the nature of the New Testament and its formation. A major thread throughout historical scholarship of the New Testament has been to question whether the major New Testament writings are in any sense pieces of systematic theological reflection. Rather, they are occasional pieces, which may draw on the thought forms and genres of the day but are entirely contingent pieces conditioned by the pressing demands of nascent groups struggling to make sense of life, experience and new religious conviction. So, it has become axiomatic in modern historical study of the New Testament to stress the importance of circumstances as a motor of doctrinal development (Moule 1982, pp. 163–99, Becker 1980). The theological implications of this have not been fully explored, for they involve the reversal of much traditional doctrinal understanding in which beliefs become the basis for application in certain circumstances. When circumstances determine doctrine then it is the subtle mix of the two with the contingent conditioning thought which produces the peculiar doctrinal formulations in particular circumstances. This should not surprise us. While Paul is capable of appealing to tradition (e.g. 1 Cor 7:10; 9:14; 11:23; 14:35) and Scripture (1 Cor 10; Galatians 3), especially in circumstances (such as those in Corinth) where realized eschatology played down the relevance of the past and the future, Paul's theology was rooted in a conviction that the living Christ met him moment by moment and thereby became the motor of theology and ethics. The practice of New Testament theology, therefore, is one which, to quote Kenneth Leach, 'abandons its "purity" and lives in interaction and dialectical engagement both with other disciplines and with the concrete struggles of people' (Leech 2001, p. 126). To do this is to go with the grain of the character of the New Testament writings, contingent and context-bound writings that they all are.

Circumstances dictated the content and approach of the Pauline letters. In no case can it be said that Paul is offering a systematic presentation of his views. It is an exegetical commonplace to say that our approach to Paul's letters must at all times be controlled by the context in which the particular ideas are formulated and addressed. It is apparent that there was something important about the practice of faith guided by the divine Spirit which was important for Paul which had to take priority over the attempt to try to be in continuity with the past. Paul's letters are imbued with the conviction that the experience of God was what mattered most, provided that this was something which was in continuity with the Christ whose presence Paul as an apostle (Gal 2:20) and the various communities embodied (1 Cor 12). The past had to be viewed afresh, with its meaning determined by the experience of the love of Christ. Engaging with Scripture means trying to get at what the Bible might point to about conformity to Christ rather than be preoccupied with what its literal demands might be or what the text might have meant in the first-century CE.

Recent approaches to Paul have tended to stress continuity with the Torah. Nevertheless any reading of Romans or 1 Corinthians leaves one with the impression that there is a thinly disguised fault line between the life in Christ mysticism and the demands of communal and political order. In the extraordinary language of 1 Cor 2:9–16, Paul claims that life in the Spirit enables a person to have the mind of Christ and to understand the things of God. In Romans 8, life in Christ places the Christian beyond any written code, though here in Romans Paul makes more of the continuity of that ethical life with the Law: 'the law of the spirit of life has set me free from the law of sin and death'. Paul needs no external guide, for the Christ inhabits him prompting and directing: 'it is no longer I but Christ' (Gal 2:20). His is the kind of embodied exegesis which we considered in the context of our discussion of Winstanley: 'action is the life of all'.

What one finds in this use of Scripture is something which is altogether less precise in its exegesis. The text becomes a catalyst for interpreting, a gateway to new understanding. What is demanded of the reader is imaginative participation, to explore the ambiguities, tensions and problems that the text offers. As Blake perceptively put it:

> The wisest of the ancients consider'd what is not too explicit as the fittest for instruction, because it rouzes the faculties to act. . . . Why is the Bible more Entertaining & Instructive than any other book? Is it not because they are addressed to the Imagination, which is Spiritual Sensation and but mediately to the understanding or reason'. . . . ('Letter to Trusler', Keynes 1972, p. 793).

The 'rouzing of the faculties' leads to new and different understandings of the meaning of the original text as the texts function as a springboard for new understanding. The outcome is a relationship to earlier Scripture which is oblique. Stringfellow, for example, allows the imagery of the Apocalypse being juxtaposed with the interpreter's own circumstances, whether personal or social, so as to allow the images to inform understanding of contemporary persons and events and to serve as a guide for action. In such imaginative and ethically orientated readings, the biblical text is a springboard, a creative frame of reference for the world which confronts the interpreter. It suggests a rather different approach to the practical theological engagement, in which anecdote and analogy all contribute to the pursuit of truth. Like the parables of Jesus, which have consistently refused to be tied down to one particular meaning, it offers a mode of moral reasoning which prompts and tantalizes in ways which are unpredictable in their effects and may offer those who persevere a means of understanding reality and thereby of illuminating the action and commitment on which they are already embarked.

Human experience opens up perspectives on Scripture which a narrowly analytical approach would miss. Such experiences have their origin in an approach to texts in which the pursuit of the meaning of the text is not a detached operation but may involve the interpreter, who thereby becomes a recipient of insight rather than one whose rational powers search out meaning from the text. Such meditative practice in previous ages of the Christian life opened up the gateway to a network of allusions and personal context to effect a memory of Scripture which yielded an elaborate and existentially addressed meditative 'lectio' (Caruthers 1990, 1998). But this is not just about an engagement with Scripture in which the body is at rest but active in the service of the Son of man who meets us in the poor, the hungry and the despised, and through which activity the promptings of the divine spirit may be discerned.

A Christian practical theology which is rooted in the New Testament will be a curious mixture of genres. If it is to be true to a New Testament theology, what it will not do is function according to the structure of logical argument. The reason for this is that the attempts to discern logic in even the most supposedly systematic parts of the New Testament, such as the Pauline epistles, have invariably foundered on the fact that, despite the best endeavours of modern interpreters, determined to find a careful structure, the case for a logical flow almost invariably breaks down. But in looking for rational argument we have been looking for the wrong thing. The practical theology in the New Testament functions differently. If we consider the New Testament Gospels, Christianity's foundation texts, their contribution to practical reasoning is to assert the importance of the aphoristic and the anecdotal, the telling of a story to illuminate a theological concept like the Kingdom of God: 'with what may we compare the Kingdom of God?' The genre of all the biblical books, in both the Old and New Testaments, is never a philosophical treatise but collections of stories, often with a story line, visions and oracles. The story telling, the experiential rather than the abstraction, is the stuff of which New Testament theology is made.

Conclusion

> The theological interpreter must make choices within the tradition and defend his choice by reference to his understanding of the tradition as a whole, and to the apprehension of reality that provides the web in which threads of tradition are woven to represent a theological pattern corresponding to his apprehension of the Christian revelation (Morgan 1973, p. 60).

We have made our choices. Our primary choice is that 'action is the life of all', and that specifically the understanding of the Christian Scriptures is an activity and a discipline inseparable from that activity and discipline known as practical theology. We have defended that choice through examination of the Scriptures themselves, and through examples both historical and contemporary of interpretation of the Scriptures, in all of which the resonances between the text and the context – the Scriptures, experience and action – are the living and moving motor of ongoing belief and action.

The 'apprehension of reality that provides the web' in which the various threads of this chapter are woven together has many facets. Of these the most crucial are: that action is epistemologically fundamental; that what happens in this world, most especially to 'the least of these who are members of my family' (Matt 25:40 NRSV), is theologically fundamental; and that imagination is fundamental to the nuanced and complex business of the interpretation of texts and of living according to the Spirit of God in this world. These correspond to our 'apprehension of the Christian revelation', in that exegesis of the meaning of God's self-revelation in Jesus Christ comes through our resolve to do the will of God and through our capacity to extend our imaginative grasp of God's action in the world (John 7:14–24).

Notes

1. This approach to community life and discipline is grounded in biblical exegesis of Paul's letters by the Center's founding director, John G. Lewis, one of Robert Morgan's recent Oxford doctoral students. Publication of the fruits of Lewis' doctoral work are forthcoming from T. & T. Clark (April 2005) in

the JSNT Supplement series under the title *Looking for Life: The Role of 'Theo-Ethical Reasoning' in Paul's Religion*. Lewis contributes this portion of the present article in grateful appreciation for Robert Morgan's important and enduring work in New Testament theology.

References

Barth, K., *Epistle to the Romans* (Oxford: Clarendon, 1933).
Becker, J.C., *Paul the Apostle. The Triumph of God in Life and Thought* (Edinburgh: T. & T. Clark, 1980).
Bennett Moore, Z., 'On copy clerks, transformers and spiders: teachers and learners in adult theological education', *British Journal of Theological Education* 9.3 (1997/8), 44.
Blake, W., *The Complete Writings* (ed. G. Keynes; Oxford: Oxford University Press, 1972).
Boff, C., *Theology and Praxis: Epistemological Foundations* (New York: Orbis, 1987).
Bradstock, A. and Rowland, C., *Radical Christian Writings: A Reader* (Oxford: Blackwell, 2002).
Carruthers, M., *The Book of Memory* (Cambridge: Cambridge University Press, 1990).
Carruthers, M., *The Craft of Thought: Meditation, Rhetoric, and the Making of Images, 400-1200* (Cambridge: Cambridge University Press, 1998).
Capps, D., *Pastoral Care and Hermeneutics* (Philadelphia: Fortress Press, 1984).
Couture, P. and Hunter, R. (eds), *Pastoral Care and Social Conflict* (Nashville: Abingdon Press, 1995).
Farley, E., 'Interpreting situations: an inquiry into the nature of practical theology', in James Woodward and Stephen Pattison (eds), *The Blackwell Reader in Pastoral and Practical Theology* (Oxford: Blackwell, 2000).
Graham, E., *Transforming Practice: Pastoral Theology in an Age of Uncertainty* (London: Mowbray, 1996).
Gerkin, C., *The Living Human Document* (Nashville: Abingdon Press, 1984).
Gerkin, C., *An Introduction to Pastoral Care* (Nashville: Abingdon Press, 1997).
Hegel, G.W.F., *Lectures on the Philosophy of Religion Vol. 1 Introduction and The Concept of Religion* (ed. Peter C. Hodgson; Berkeley: University of California Press, 1984).
Lash, N., *Theology on the Way to Emmaus* (London: SCM, 1986).
Leech, K., *Through Our Long Exile: Contextual Theology and the Urban Experience* (London: Darton, Longman and Todd, 2001).
Miller-McLemore, B.J., 'The living human web: pastoral theology at the turn of the century', in Jeanne Stevenson Moessner (ed.), *Through the Eyes of Women: Insights for Pastoral Care* (Minneapolis: Augsburg-Fortress, 1996), pp. 9-26.
Morgan, R.C., *The Nature of New Testament Theology* (London: SCM, 1973).

Moule, C.F.D., 'The Influence of circumstances on the use of Christological terms', and 'The influence of circumstances on the use of eschatological terms', in C.F.D. Moule, *Essays in New Testament Interpretation* (Cambridge: Cambridge University Press, 1982), pp. 163–99.

Nussbaum, M., *The Fragility of Goodness: Luck and Ethics in Greek Tragedy and Philosophy* (Cambridge: Cambridge University Press, 1986).

Pattison, S. 'A vision of pastoral theology: in search of words that resurrect the dead', in S. Pattison, *A Critique of Pastoral Care* (London: SCM, 2000), pp. 217–53.

Patton, J., *Pastoral Care in Context: An Introduction to Pastoral Care* (Louisville: Westminster/John Knox Press, 1993).

Sabine, G., *The Works of Gerrard Winstanley with an Appendix of Documents relating to the Digger Movement* (Ithaca: Cornell University Press, 1941).

Stringfellow, W., *An Ethic for Christians and Other Aliens in a Strange Land* (Waco: Word, 1973).

Stringfellow, W., *Conscience and Obedience* (Waco: Word, 1977).

Sugirtharajah, R.S. (ed.), *Voices from the Margins: Interpreting the Bible in the Third World* (London: SPCK, 1991).

Walton, R. 'Using the Bible and Christian tradition in theological reflection', *British Journal of Theological Education* 13.2 (2003), 133–51.

Chapter 13

Theory of Primitive Christian Religion and New Testament Theology: An Evolutionary Essay[1]

Gerd Theissen, Heidelberg

'In secular culture some theory of religion is always necessary ... in order to connect believers' talk of God with the generally acknowledged reality that can be investigated by anyone. Theologians choose a theory of religion and reality which does not deny the reality of their religion's transcendent referent. This general theory of religion is then joined by a theological judgement, specific to the religion concerned, about where revelation is located – which in the Christian case includes a view of how it is related to the Bible' (Morgan 1988, p. 189).[2] Robert Morgan was one of the first to call for a link between exegesis and the theory of religion in order to understand the Bible. My own *Theory of Primitive Christian Religion* (Theissen 1999) is an attempt to pursue this programme.

What distinguishes a theory of primitive Christian religion from a theology of the New Testament? Using the categories of general religious studies, a theory of primitive Christian religion analyses the belief, the rites and the ethos of primitive Christianity on the basis of all canonical and non-canonical extant sources. It is useful for gaining academic knowledge, not for building up a religious identity. A theology of the New Testament is, by comparison, the normative exposition of a religion through an interpretative summary of its canonical texts. It is done by people with a Christian identity and aims to facilitate Christian belief. There is a clear distinction between religious studies with an open identity and identity-bound theology. But each of these two great traditions contains great diversity in itself. In the theology of the New Testament there are existential approaches, salvation-historical approaches and apocalyptic approaches. Religious studies can consider religion as an autonomous phenomenon, as part of culture or as a product of nature, so here we find phenomenological, cultural and evolutionary approaches side by side. This chapter will set out some alternatives within the framework of religious studies. And it will finally outline an attempt to integrate them and link them to a theological perspective.

Today when primitive Christianity is analysed as *religion*, consciously or unconsciously, the phenomenological tradition in religious studies is often pursued. According to this tradition, religion is an autonomous area of human life that is determined by a specific experience of the sacred: through *Anschauung und Gefühl des Universums* (a view of and feeling for the universe) (Schleiermacher 1799) or through a *mysterium fascinosum et tremendum* (Otto 1917). The sacred is regarded here as an objective 'phenomenon' that becomes apparent; it is not merely a human construct (Gantke 1998). For some, such a theory of religion is theology in disguise, even if it treats all religions equally. This is because a phenomenological approach to religion is fundamentally open to transcendence and compatible with religious belief even if it strictly adheres to the phenomenological tradition and withholds any judgement regarding the reality of its subject. Whether one speaks of phenomena that become apparent or of 'revelations' makes little difference for those who see a human construct in religion. In this framework it is the task of a theory of primitive Christian religion to bring out the specific religious experience reflected upon in the texts of the New Testament.

A newer (and today predominant) trend in religious studies understands religion as an aspect of *culture* (Sabbatucci 1988, Kippenberg and v. Stuckrad 2003). Culture, as distinct from nature, is everything that we produce ourselves. Religion is examined here as a sign system produced by human beings. This sign system can be semantically related to an objective dimension of reality. To the extent that religious studies adopts this position, it is closely connected with religious phenomenology. However, religious studies can also see the meaning of signs in their pragmatic application – without their having to relate to something objective. It then becomes cultural studies. In a theory of primitive Christian religion leading questions in this second approach would be: What contribution has it made to our culture (or lack of culture)? How has it coordinated human action? What stimuli did it give for a change

of world-view and for human self-exploration? Much that for a phenomenological approach to religion belongs to the context of religious manifestations, turns here into its 'core'.

A third trend in religious studies considers religion not only as a cultural creation of humankind but also as a product of *nature*. It explains
the appearance of religion through its evolutionary benefit: in prehistoric
times people with religious ways of behaving had advantages for survival:
religion promotes the cohesion of its own group, stimulates hostility
towards outside groups, justifies internal authority, strengthens altruistic
behaviour or suppresses egoistic tendencies, and promotes bodily and
mental health (Euler 2004, p. 67f.). The advantages for reproduction
achieved through religion explain why religion is universally widespread.
This approach bore fruit above all through the integration of cognitive
evolutionary psychology (Boyer 1994, 2001, Andresen 2001, Pyysiäinen
2001, Pyysiäinen and Anttonen 2002, Söling 2002, Voland and Söling
2004). The filter of selection has embedded in human beings genetically
established mechanisms for data processing that become productive in
religion. According to this approach, a theory of primitive Christian religion should show that the primitive Christian world of belief was based
on these cognitive-processing mechanisms that were once responsible
for the appearance of religion at all. It should show too that this world
of belief met the needs of evolutionary survival.

We can thus distinguish four theories: naturalistic, cultural, phenomenological and theological approaches. It is an open question whether
they can be understood as 'layered explanations', i.e. as complementary
interpretations that do not contradict each other. Rembrandt's art can be
researched, for example, through chemical analyses as *nature*, historically
as part of the Dutch *culture* of the seventeenth century, aesthetically as
intimate *realism*, theologically as an expression of Protestant *piety*. None
of these levels of analysis contradicts any other. With religion it is more
difficult. When a religion is explained through its advantages for survival,
for example, it is at best a productive illusion. A phenomenological and
theological interpretation then becomes superfluous.

The Starting Point in a Naturalistic Theory of Religion

Naturalistic theories of religion are still at an experimental stage. In
recent times, however, they have reached a high degree of differentiation
and maturity. The theory developed by the philosopher E. Voland and
the theologian C. Söling based on evolutionary cognition psychology
(2004) merits discussion. Their theory sees evolutionarily developed

dataprocessing mechanisms at work in four areas of religions: in mysticism, myth, ethos and rite. I take their reflections further at some points but overall I am basing myself on their ideas.

Religious *experience*[3] interrupts daily life through extraordinary occurrences full of immediacy, clarity, certainty and joy. Such experiences are anthropomorphically interpreted in religion so that people can apply their social intelligence to them; they have learnt how socially interacting beings can be influenced. The anthropomorphic interpretation of religious experience is based on the fact that, owing to an innate perceptivity, people assume intentionality in remarkable appearances; they have an innate 'intentionality detector' at their disposal. This is deeply rooted within us because when in doubt it is more advantageous (temporarily) to consider something inanimate as animate, rather than something animate as inanimate, which could end up being fatal in an encounter with some animals. That is why, time and time again in interpreting religious experiences, we violate the familiar categories of our 'intuitive everyday ontology' through 'counter-intuitive ideas' by mixing animate with inanimate (Pyssiäinen 2002): everything is determined by intentions and purpose. The world becomes the expression of active deities. With this interpretation, we cope with the dimensions of reality that are inaccessible to us. The evolutionary advantage consists in contingency processing through categorizing reality and through faster discrimination.

Myth consists of stories of events transcending space and time in which the world was created just as it is now. Myth gives it legitimacy. It is based on the intuitive ontology of religion and shows how this ontology is typically endangered, through impurity, through the tireless search for happiness, through striving for status and rank, through clashes with relatives and partners. A myth has a narrative form. A story changes the situation that existed at the beginning of it. Thus chaos and ambiguity are often overcome in myths. The evolutionary advantage of myth corresponds to the advantage of every language. Language makes it possible to communicate individual experiences and is the most important social bond of human beings. Among all linguistic forms of expression myth is special in creating a collective identity and in differentiating between the in-group and the out-group. Above all through its story structure it can change experiences: founders of religions each shape the myth of their community anew and thus tie the social bond that binds people together (and separates them) in a new way.

Ethics are also grounded in religion. All religions emphasize reciprocity of action. The Golden Rule is disseminated in almost all of them (Philippides 1929) or is prescribed in all. It is based on an innate sensitivity for mutuality – an ability to put oneself inside another, as if one was standing in his or her place. The fact that reciprocity is demanded everywhere does not, however, mean that it is always practised. Often there is too little opportunity to give something in return. Often people are willing to receive benefits but do not want to share the costs. They take advantage of the ethos of the group. It is thus vitally important for the functioning of an ethos to track down rule-breakers. Fraud detectors are imperative for social cooperation. Human beings are made sensitive to this through innate cognitive mechanisms that are strengthened in religion through the idea of the omniscient God and Judge of people, through the connection between conduct and state of health, and through oath. The evolutionary benefit is evident: cooperative groups have more chances of survival than others, even if in every group the group morale is manipulatively exploited by some.

Rites are stereotyped repeated actions that have a communicative sense beyond their utilitarian aim: in a rite, washing is no longer used for cleansing but to make people fit for worship and for community. Houses are no longer used for living in but for the worship of gods. In all rites there is an effective cost-raising mechanism: rites are extravagant: temples and churches testify to an investment that goes well beyond any cost of living. As the largest buildings of a place, they are a demonstration of a waste of resources! Religions demand sacrifices. Cost-raising mechanisms have the same evolutionary benefits as fraud detectors: they frighten off the free-riders of morality. Anyone who sacrifices a lot for a community will not deceitfully exploit its solidarity.

Religion presupposes innate data-processing mechanisms: intentionality detectors, a sense of mutuality, fraud detectors, cost-raising mechanisms. It intertwines the four areas we have mentioned. Experience and myth, ethos and rite all belong to each other: religious experiences are interpreted through an intuitive ontology, any threats to which are overcome by myth. Ethos demands solidarity: any threats to this are combated through rites. We find a similar underlying structure in all parts of religion: myths depict the transition from an unstable to a stable situation (Stolz 1988). The transitions from one phase of life to another are organized in rites (particularly discernible in rites of passage). Through rites people pass through an unstable phase at the threshold between an old and new situation.

Can primitive Christianity, too, be analysed using such categories? Undoubtedly! Many correspondences will be found. In this connection we are above all interested in the phenomena that contradict such a theory. Is myth really the basis for group identity? The Baptist alone shattered his Jewish fellow citizens' consciousness of being chosen. He warned of trusting all too lightly in being the children of Abraham. God is free to raise up children to Abraham from these stones! (Matt 3:8ff.). In Jesus' preaching the myth of the coming of God's kingdom is encountered as a criticism of exclusion: Gentiles (and Jews?) will stream from all directions into God's kingdom, while those who think they possess it will be thrown out (Matt 8:11f.). The beginnings of primitive Christianity are shaken by conflicts about two identity and boundary markers of Judaism: circumcision and laws about food. These are declared non-obligatory in order to be able to receive Gentiles into the community. With the demand to love one's enemy, Jesus' ethic makes it a duty to break through traditional barriers. Admittedly the New Testament texts base the collective identity of the emerging church also on disassociation from others but they also testify to a struggle to overcome boundaries: a universal religion that is open to all peoples is destined to develop out of a religion restricted to one people.

Jesus' *ethic* is only partially appropriate for the coordination of human action. His preaching causes war within families (Luke 12:51–3). His command not to resist the evil doer seems to neglect the ethical task of protecting the weak from their exploitation by the strong. Rather one should react paradoxically to attacks, and if one is struck turn the other cheek as well (Matt 5:39). Even the classic rule of mutual obligation is made almost unrealistically radical: the Golden Rule is found in a positive formulation (Matt 7:12). There are many parallels to this in antiquity. Nevertheless, when positively formulated, they refer only to privileged relationships within the framework of the ethos of a family, friendship or ruler. Otherwise only the negative Golden Rule is valid as a truly universal norm: it is required of everyone that they avoid doing evil to others but the command to do good on one's own initiative is only in relation to certain groups (Theissen 2003). With Jesus, on the other hand, the Golden Rule is positively formulated for all relationships. To do good spontaneously on one's own initiative is required of all in relationship to all.

Finally with regard to *rite*, the preaching of Jesus is characterized by de-ritualization. As a sign of conversion, the Baptist demands a confession of sins *with* baptism. Jesus preached conversion without such a ritual safeguard (Luke 13:1ff.). With him the forgiveness of sins is granted only through prayer (cf. the Lord's Prayer). He does not drive up the price of following him through any extravagant ritual. Admittedly the follower pays a high price in another regard: the step into homelessness and vulnerability. But Jesus was by no means so strict with most people. On the contrary, he was criticized because he ate with doubtful people about whom there was no certainty that they had really been converted (Sanders 1985, pp. 172–211). As far as the cost of rituals is concerned, the central rite of Christianity was markedly simple: only wine and bread were needed. Sometimes Christians had no wine. Because of this the words over the cup (unlike the words over the bread) are: 'Do this, *as oft as you shall drink it*, in remembrance of me' (1 Cor 11:25). Entry into the Christian community costs nothing. The non-material costs of entry (in the metaphorical sense) were nevertheless high – and in this respect the theory outlined above applies: whoever wanted to become a Christian renounced many possible ways of behaving that at the time were taken for granted. Again we find both: a driving up of the 'costs' and their demonstrative reduction.

Some observations confirm the naturalistic theory of religion outlined above, others contradict it. From this one could conclude that there is a cultural clash with the primary functions of religion in primitive Christianity – a mixture of functions that are based on the biological make up of human beings and cultural counter-tendencies that can even steer in the opposite direction of such functions. The question is whether religion is not shaped from the beginning by this mixture: are not the first 'evolutionary' advantages founded upon an interaction of biology and culture? Those who want to interpret them as exclusively biological must assume that religious processing mechanisms have been genetically inherited because their bearers had greater chances of reproduction than others. But was not the anthropomorphic interpretation of the world – the myths of the ancestors, the ethos of the tribe and its rites – always communicated through cultural tradition? Certainly there will be genetic predispositions without which religion in its different forms of expression cannot come about – just as no language comes into being without a natural foundation. But the learning of a concrete language (including its system of rules) remains an act of cultural learning, even when the ability to speak is inherited. In the same way the learning of each religion is a cultural act, even when the ability to be religious has biological roots. This is not contradicted by the fact that what is culturally learnt and handed down can be used to preserve life (also in a biological sense). The knowledge of a function does not mean that the causes for making the practice of that function possible have yet been discovered.

If primitive Christianity (and the early church) is considered from an evolutionary perspective, the question still has to be asked how it can be explained that attitudes were admired and treasured in it that certainly did not increase the chances of reproduction. I am thinking of asceticism and martyrdom. The early Christians trusted so much in the cultural dissemination of their convictions that physical losses through asceticism and martyrdom were of no consequence, for it was precisely through asceticism and martyrdom that they gained the powerful aura that moved other people to convert to them.

In spite of these limitations, the interpretation of cultural creations against the background of biological prerequisites has been indispensable in bringing our findings forward. Religion is a universal phenomenon whose morphology is comparable in many cultures. Religious phenomenology has reduced the profusion of manifestations to a few basic models (see Leeuw 1933). In fact a plausible hypothesis is that genetic predispositions also play a role here. They could explain why, among the many culturally determined variations of ideas and actions, the same patterns prevail in all cultures again and again. Nevertheless we must take the cultural factor (and the variability of religion) much more seriously.

The Need for a Cultural Theory of Religion

The eminent ancient philologist W. Burkert also understands his interpretation of ancient religions as a biological theory. He points to recurring characteristics in them as possible biological functions (Burkert 1998). Nevertheless, his theory is a cultural theory. The functions that he ascribes to ancient religions are social functions. Here too it is a question of 'survival'. But the survival of a society is not identical to the survival of its genetic representatives. Societies also survive, for example, through being sufficiently culturally attractive to assimilate immigrants or to infiltrate peacefully other countries with their culture. 'Genetically' foreign people can become the representatives of their same culture. That can be noted in the ancient world very well. European culture rooted in antiquity was shaped by two peoples who did not belong to the conquerors: Greeks and Jews. The Greeks had to hold their own against the superior might of the Persians, the Jews against the great kingdoms in the South and North. Both were subdued by the Romans. But both managed to win the Romans over to their culture. The Romans became culturally 'Greek'; they took over Greek philosophy, education and literature. They converted to a religion shaped by Judaism, for they took on Christianity. They were changed from inside by the culture of the people they had conquered. But even independently of this (contrary to its own self-understanding), W. Burkert's theory of religion in relation to antiquity can hardly be represented as a naturalistic theory of religion. It is through and through a functionalist social theory. It is true that biology has always been the model for functionalist social theories but sociological functionalism is not biological functionalism. It certainly works with analogies between culture and nature but only to a limited extent with the causal links between nature and culture. Turning now to W. Burkert's concrete analysis of ancient religions: he establishes that people in antiquity needed religion for four reasons – and these four reasons correspond to four functions for the survival of a society:

1. Religion has to justify *authority*. The justification for authority comes about through a differentiation between 'above' and 'below'. The extent to which the differentiation of above and below provides legitimacy is clearly shown by the term 'hierarchy' (= *heilige Herrschaft* or 'holy authority'). Religion has always ascribed legitimacy to rulers and hierarchies.
2. Religion is necessary for the sanctioning of *oaths*. Every ethos can be exploited by swindlers. The easiest form of deception is lying. A society cannot tolerate all lies. In important cases it demands the oath with its contingent self-condemnation – whereby deities are called upon who will punish those who tell lies.
3. Religion is needed to overcome *disaster*. This applies to private as well as collective disaster. Those who were struck by illness and great misfortune could make sacrifices, pray and go to a sanatorium. If the whole society was threatened by disaster, sacrifices and expiatory rites were quickly resorted to, in order to appease the angered gods.
4. Finally, religion ensures the *reciprocity* of gift and counter gift. This reciprocity often takes place later on in time. Parents invest for a long time in their children before the latter take on responsibility for the parents. It is not by chance, therefore, that respect for parents had to be emphasized in all religions. In pagan antiquity they are regarded as the 'second gods', in Judaism only the command about parents contained a positive promise. Particular motivation was needed for it to be carried out (Balla 2003).

In primitive Christianity, it is particularly these four fundamental (social) functions of religion which were made problematic. Let us clarify this for all four tasks and functions:

1. The Jesus tradition challenges authority. The principle of renouncing status occurs in many places and with many variations: 'He who will be first shall be last of all and the servant of all' (Mark 9:35). This maxim is contrasted with the behaviour of worldly rulers (Mark 10:42-4). But even under these rulers we find authority made similarly problematic: the king Antigonos Gonatas gave his son the paradoxical maxim for life that kingly rule should be 'honourable slavery'

(an ἔνδοξος δουλεία) (Aelian, var. 2.20). In all these traditions a humanization and self-limitation of authority is contrasted with actual power relations (Guttenberger 1999).

2. The teaching of Jesus does not serve to justify oaths. On the contrary, he rejects oaths. This is unique in antiquity (Kollmann 1996, Luz 2002, pp. 369–82). All words and promises should be as credible as if they were sworn on oath (Matt 5:33–7), independently of whether it is a matter of promissory assurances or vindicatory declarations of truth. Here the archaic function of religion as a fraud detector is enlarged without limit. Unconditional truthfulness should prevail everywhere. This radicalism concerning truth which cannot really be lived up to – Paul swears quite uninhibitedly in his letters – is in tension with the primary function of religion.

3. There is no doubt that the work of Jesus serves to overcome disasters. Even if early on the miracle stories took on a symbolic sense, their original meaning, the overcoming of illness and need, danger and threats, is not discarded. Nowhere in antiquity do we find so many miracle stories concentrated on a single person (Theissen 1998). It is precisely because of this that the passion story is so impressive: the one who has helped others dies helpless on the cross. The one who is just must suffer. In following him Christians have consciously to risk conflicts and suffering. Paul is not healed but receives the promise: 'my strength is made powerful in the weak' (i.e. the sick) (2 Cor 12:9).

4. The reciprocity of gift and counter gift is also broken in primitive Christianity. The exhortations to renounce violence and to love one's enemy are asymmetrical. They may well hope for the opponent's surrender and by breaking through well-worn reactions create an opportunity for this to happen – but they are certainly not bound to the opponent's symmetrical reaction. They consciously risk it not occurring (see Gemünden 2003).

The four functions of religion named by W. Burkert are applicable to ancient religions but not to primitive Christianity which prevailed in the Roman Empire against the competition of older cults and religions. A theory of primitive Christian religion will (along with W. Burkert) also connect this new religion to a natural basis but in the end interpret it as a cultural phenomenon. Every religion must be compatible with the needs for elementary survival or it disappears from history. But it belongs to culture: it is a sign system produced by people out of beliefs, rites and ethos. In the process, the concrete forms of religion are culturally very varied. This cultural conditioning of religion comes most clearly to light

when it is changed. The emergence of primitive Christianity is connected
to such a change. It is part of a great 'religious change'.

The Plausibility of a Phenomenological
Theory of Religion

This religious change consists in primary religions (that are often called
tribal or primitive religions) being overlaid by secondary religions that
have arisen out of a critique of the primary religions (Sundermeier 1999,
pp. 34–42). The 'world religions' – Judaism, Christianity, Islam, Hinduism
and Buddhism – belong to the secondary religions. Since they are all
based on older tribal religions, the morphology universal to all religions
can be explained as a common inheritance: what religious phenomenology has established as 'cross-cultural' is explained less through a common
genetic predisposition than through a common past history:

> What all religions have in common is not to be ascertained through a
> phenomenological description of certain similar forms of manifestation in
> religions, nor on the basis of a religious term obtained from abstraction,
> or of a connection, however it is to be defined, to transcendence. It is to
> be ascertained on the basis of the historically concrete religious inheri-
> tance common to each religion. This is still most clearly discernible today
> in tribal religions and continues to be present in the different religions not
> as 'remains' but as fundamental experience and structure (Sundermeier
> 1999, p. 239).

A critique and overlaying of primary religious traditions occurs in all
world religions that secondarily enter religious history. These traditions
do not disappear but live on as the underlying layer of religious behaviour and experience. The great religions are thus characterized by a
structural contradiction between a primary religious foundation and its
secondary religious overlaying. The tension dates back in the end to the
great founders and reformers of religions and their critique of the primary
religious traditions they encountered. In this Jesus is an example of
others. We can classify his critique of previous traditions as 'religiously
phenomenological'. In doing so, we must ask what experiences determined this change from the primary to the secondary religion. What
experience of the sacred prevailed here? The following remarks follows
A. Feldtkeller (2002, pp. 46–62).

It is a characteristic of primary religions, as well as of the old religions
of antiquity, that they make the visible world and present-day human
existence sacred. As the foundation of life, the community from which

they descended is made sacred: clan and tribe are sacrosanct. *Time* that is structured in the cycle of the day and year as well as through the course of human life is made sacred. *Space* is made sacred. Sacred times and sacred places make festivals and their ordering possible. Finally the order of life in the *community* is made sacred. It is a natural order that cannot be thought of in any other way. The knowable *world* in general is also made sacred. The deities have concrete relationships to water sources and mountains, thunder and rain, fertility and war. Their transcendence is limited.

The religions based on texts all came into being through a critique of this sanctifying of the world by the primary religions. The religious criticism of their founders and prophets is put down in 'sacred texts' while the everyday life of the primary religious tradition carries on. Secondary religious renewal can thus prevail time and time again in the continuum of the same tradition: the prophets in Judaism, Jesus in primitive Christianity, Mohammed in Islam. But what is criticized in this change from a primary to a secondary religion?

1. The *idea of God* is criticized on the basis of a more radical experience of the transcendent: only now does religion become an experience of the 'absolutely other'. Polytheism is rejected in the monotheistic religions. Judaism began with a radical revolution: it confessed to believing in the one and only God. Some Greek philosophers, too (like Xenophon), arrived at this belief at the same time as Deutero-Isaiah but they allowed polytheistic cults to continue to exist. Only the Jews tried to shape their whole life consistently according to religion. With them religion became a separate sphere for communication. Everything had to be imbued with it. Since this was not the case anywhere else, religion became an autonomous centre that potentially confronted all areas of society. In primitive Christianity the one and only God who devoted himself to Israel became the God who wants to extend his covenant to all people. The image of God thus takes on new attributes in primitive Christianity. Characteristic are the three 'definitions of God' that we find in the Johannine literature. The first is found in the conversation between Jesus and the Samaritan woman: 'God is spirit and those who worship him must worship him in spirit and in truth' (John 4:23). This means that he can definitely not be worshipped either in Jerusalem or in Gerizim, but rather that there are people who worship him all over the world, independently of existing places of worship and peoples. The second definition says: 'God is light and in him is no darkness. If we say that we have fellowship with him and walk

in darkness, then we lie and do not do what is true. But if we walk in the light, as he is in the light, we have fellowship with one another . . .' (1 John 1:6). The one and only God founds a community instead of strengthening already existing communities. The third definition emphasizes this social character of the experience of God: 'God is *love* and he who abides in love abides in God and God abides in him' (1 John 4:16b). The new experience of the holy is the experience of divine love that wants to devote itself to all.

2. In all secondary religions the *practice of worship* is criticized: the prophets criticized trust being placed in ritual sacrifices while at the same time the law was being violated. The Upanishads, Buddhism and Jainism criticized the ineffectiveness of sacrifices for redemption. In primitive Christianity sacrifices are superseded by baptism and the Lord's Supper – through two non-bloody rites that (with Paul) are secretly linked to the death of Jesus: baptism is a dying with Christ; the individual voluntarily undergoes a symbolic death in order to attain a new life now with Jesus. The Lord's Supper is the remembrance of the death of Christ, that is of the death of another for the community. Only those who are baptized are admitted to the Lord's Supper (*Did* 9:5), this means that only those who are ready to offer their life to God as a living sacrifice (Rom 12:1) share in another laying down his life for them: 'God proves his *love* for us in that while we were still sinners Christ died for us' (Rom 5:8).

3. In all secondary religions there is a criticism of the existing *world*, which loses its legitimacy in cosmic expectations of its destruction: Jesus and Mohammed announced that the end of the world was near. A judgement would come upon it. Buddhism too sees the world negatively and critically: for Buddhism redemption is the dissolution of this world. In primitive Christianity this end of the world is celebrated as the beginning of a new world in the present time. In a paradoxical way this double eschatology links the illegitimacy of the world with the legitimacy of life in it. The restored Christians have the judgement already behind them: 'There is therefore now no condemnation for those who are in Christ Jesus' (Rom 8:1). 'Very truly, I tell you, anyone who hears my word and believes him who sent me has eternal life, and does not come under judgement, but has passed from death to life' (John 5:24). The certainty for this existence beyond judgement is, however, love: 'We know that we have passed from death to life because we *love* one another. Whoever does not love abides in death' (1 John 3:14).

4. Finally in all secondary religions the traditional *way of life* is criticized, the Torah in Christianity, the Arabic way of life in Islam, Hindu

asceticism in Buddhism. Cutting across all religions, movements of drop outs, of homeless itinerant monks and of ascetics arise. In primitive Christianity two fundamental commandments taken over from Judaism form a new way of life: the commandments to love and to renounce status. The commandment to love is radicalized into love of the enemy and the stranger. The lifting of barriers in relation to the outside corresponds to a restriction in relation to the inside: Jesus' words demand that his followers break with their families: 'Whoever comes to me and does not hate father and mother, wife and children, brothers and sisters, yes, and even life itself, cannot be my disciple' (Luke 14:26). In the asceticism of Christianity, this a-familial ethos lives on. We can observe something analogous with the renunciation of status: the renunciation of authority is required for relationships inside the community. 'Whoever wishes to become great among you must be your servant; and whoever wishes to be first among you must be slave of all' (Mark 10:43f.) applies here. The willingness to do this reaches its limit when belief is at stake. Then 'we must obey God rather than human authorities' is valid with regard to the outsider (Acts 5:29). That is the end of all 'humility', i.e. the willingness to subordinate oneself. The refusal to obey lives on in the martyrs of Christianity. Ascetics and martyrs show the fundamental tensions between Christianity and the ethos of the home on the one hand and the ethos of the state on the other.

Two levels can thus be distinguished within religions: a primary religious layer and a secondary religious layer. In secondary religions the original religious function of survival is challenged! If, for example, ascetics and martyrs are highly valued a rebellion against the biological need to survive is taking place. If we ask on what this (real or pretended) emancipation from the need for biological survival in Christianity is based, from a phenomenological point of view it can be said that it is based on an encounter with the sacred in which the sacred is experienced as love's centre of energy that grips people, changes them and engages them. This love encompasses extreme behaviour as well: the surrender of the Son of God on the cross and the asceticism and martyrdom of his followers. The decisive changes in the image of God emerge out of this central experience: God is the loving father who exposes himself to the greatest suffering. The ritual order is changed. For love and mercy are more important than sacrifice (cf. Matt 9:13; 12:7; Hos 6:6). The world takes on a different appearance: love among brothers (and sisters) is experienced as the entry into a new world (1 John 3:14). Of course the commandment to love is at the centre of the new way of life. The recourse to a phenomenologically describable experience of the sacred is not, however, theoretically satisfactory, for with it we have abandoned a functionalist analysis: religion is explained neither on the grounds of its evolutionary function through its adaptive value nor through its social function for the survival of a society. It is based on fundamental experiences that themselves contain its truth and its value. Precisely the idea of love can express that: love responds to something that represents a value in itself. The Iraqi mystic Rabi'a al-adawiya (ca. 717–801) expressed this in an impressive thought that the Christian poet K. Marti has rendered thus: (1980, p. 61):

> I worshipped you
> for fear of hell
> for oh I burn
> in hell
>
> I worshipped you
> in hope of paradise
> for oh paradise
> locks me in
>
> But I worship you
> for your sake alone
> then – oh God – wed me
> to your eternal beauty.

Towards a Summary of an Evolutionary Theory of Religion

In the end an outline of an evolutionary theory of religion should be one that looks for the beginnings of religion in biological evolution but interprets the development of religion as the expression of cultural evolution which leads to an intrinsic value of religious experience. There are analogies and differences between both evolutionary phases. The analogies make it possible to speak of a continuous evolution, the differences oblige us to separate the cultural evolution clearly from the previous biological evolution. A principal idea of this outline is that, in different ways, religions code the secret programme of culture – particularly in the elements that lead beyond nature (see Table 13.1).

To what degree are the elements specific to cultural evolution coded in religion? This can be at least briefly demonstrated through biblical religion (cf. Theissen 1984). Culture is based on the passing on of information from generation to generation through tradition. Biblical religion

Table 13.1 Summary of an evolutionary theory of religion

Biotic evolution	Cultural evolution
Gene: Information is passed on from one generation to another through inheritance.	*Tradition:* Information is passed on from one generation to the next through learning: in this way cultural memory has the chance of recording life's failed experiments as well.
Selection: The overall conditions of reality lead to a choice between variants of life forms through life and death: selection means a two-fold decrease in the chances of living: (a) In 'natural' selection death is caused by aggression and illness: it is a matter of survival. b) In 'sexual' selection life is reproduced through attraction and relationship: it is a matter of reproduction.	*Test:* Because of the suppositions it first makes about reality, human intelligence encounters a choice of ideas and behaviour: mistakes are eradicated rather than life, hypotheses are sacrificed rather than people. (a) Learning from (negative) consequences leads to ways of behaviour being eliminated. b) Through learning from positive consequences new ways of behaving are promoted.
Mutation: Chance mistakes in copying and in the combination of genes lead to mutations that are either neutral as far as selection goes, rewarded by selection or repressed by selection.	*Creation:* Creative intuitions, new ideas, learning through insight do not come about by chance but because of a perceived pressure arising from a problem and a conscious effort to find a solution. But they contain an irrational contingency element and in this respect are 'mutations' of consciousness.
Adaptation: Preliminary information in the organism concerning the environment sees to it that there is a life-serving adaptation between the organism and the environment.	*Correspondence:* Correspondence with reality makes it possible for consciousness to live 'in reality'.

turns a specific opportunity for cultural evolution into a duty in *remembrance* (Theissen 1998). The past is remembered in the Bible in conscious distinction from the present – even when it has become distant from and contradicts the present. When Israel is in the Land, it remembers the time in the desert, in the time of the kings it remembers the time of the judges, it dreams in the time of exile of past greatness and after the return it preserves the memory of the exile. In Israel a 'remembrance counter to the present' emerged. This made the remembrance of failure and suffering a duty. Israel had to remember its time in slavery in Egypt in order to treat its slaves humanely. It had to remember the catastrophes of Israel in order to find constant motivation for conversion. Digesting the destruction of the temple and the exile shaped the Jewish religion. The remembrance of a prophet and preacher who failed on the cross is at the centre of the New Testament.

The remembrance of the failed 'variants' of life points to something peculiar to cultural evolution: culture can replace 'hard' selection through unequal 'reproduction' by 'soft' selection of human 'production': with hard selection, self-preservation and reproduction are at stake. Here it is a matter of physical existence. 'Soft' selection on the other hand begins with human production: with people's thoughts, attitudes and ways of behaving. On the basis of a preliminary inner supposition about reality, through our understanding we 'obliterate' in anticipation what collides with reality within us and could be harmful for life. We prefer to let hypotheses rather than people die (Popper). This can be reduced to a common denominator: Human beings strive for 'change rather than death'. Biblical religion took an important step in this direction. One of its most important convictions is that *conversion* (a change of behaviour involving the whole person) can replace death: 'As sure as I am alive', says the Lord, 'the death of the godless does not please me but rather that the godless turns from his path and lives' (Isa 33:11). In the New Testament the symbolic death voluntarily undergone in baptism becomes the gateway to the new life here and now (Rom 6:1ff.). This conversion contains aggression turned inwards: self-accusation and self-criticism. But above all it consists in turning towards God through following Jesus and believing in him.

Culture does not experiment with genetic mutation but with ideas and visions, in order to give new answers to challenges. These ideas are consciously sought. They are innovative *creations* of humankind. And nevertheless our ideas are more than logical consequences of already existing stores of knowledge. Their creation and discovery is also something irrational. It is a question of intuitions that we cannot wholly justify but which nonetheless bring us further. Religion particularly is determined by intuitions of this sort. Here too it is often a question of new combinations of well-known elements. The elements are traditional but their combination makes something new out of them. In religion we call such intuitions 'revelations'. An unbridgeable contradiction seems to exist between their interpretation as human creations and godly 'revelations'. This is made relative when one reflects that new ideas are like instruments that open up new spaces in the environment. The revelations of religion are changes of this sort in human beings. They give people an instrument to see what they have not previously seen. They open in them the 'eye of the heart' (Eph 1:18) so that they experience 'what no eye has seen, nor ear heard nor the human heart conceived, what God has prepared for those who love him' (1 Cor 2:9).

Culture does not seek adaptation but harmony: it does not only want to make possible life that has the chance of survival because it is adapted to the conditions of its environment but a life within reality that is led in accordance with reality. Above all it wants to make possible a life in justice that is led in harmony with God and with other people. The biblical religion sees here a deep disorder in human life. People live 'in falsehood', bypassing reality. They are missing the reality of God and of other people. This is sin, alienation from God. But in the failure of this life biblical religion offers a chance: harmony with the reality of God given as a gift, the justification of life *sola gratia*. The Bible sees here a creative power *ex nihilo* (Rom 4:7), a renewal of creation, as if man was returning to an original harmony out of which he once fell.

A theory of primitive Christian religion can pursue many theoretical approaches. In conclusion we ask how the evolutionary theory of religion selected here relates to the different approaches.

It is not a question of a *purely naturalistic theory of religion*. Nevertheless it reckons with a beginning of religion in the history of nature. Religion is based on cognitive data-processing structures that have offered humankind an evolutionary advantage in the sense of a hard selection. The prerequisites for human beings' speech, tradition, sociality and technology also emerged through such a selection: they increased the chances of reproduction of that man from whom we are descended. The *homo sapiens* was successful at the cost of other living things – on the one hand against competing companions of the same sort whom he drove out, and on the other against other sorts of beings that he understood how to use more and more effectively for himself. But human beings can emancipate themselves from nature. They have strong tendencies such as asceticism and martyrdom that are an obstacle to increasing their advantages for reproduction. Man is the first of creation to be set free. Nevertheless, an 'aura' of naturalism hangs over the whole theory:

for (after the natural emergence of the prerequisites for religion) the cultural history of religion also took its course according to analogous (not according to the same) conditions to life in general: it is a game of trial and error whose outcome is recorded in cultural tradition – analogous to the game of mutation and selection that determines genetic information for all living things. Such an evolutionary theory of religion (that includes nature and culture) reckons with an 'evolution of evolution', a change of important evolutionary strategies with the transition from a biological to a cultural evolution. It emphasizes that the prerequisites for cultural evolution are a production of 'natural' evolution and regards the further cultural evolution that is built upon them as a continuation (if not as a part) of biological evolution. But here something new appears too, running counter to natural tendencies. What is this new element?

The outline of a theory of religion presented here is based essentially on a theory of culture that determines this new element thus: all culture has the task of decreasing the pressure of selection. Culture makes life possible even where under natural conditions it would have no chance. However, with every culture while the means for decreasing the pressure of selection grow, so do the means for increasing it, even to the point of the most unreasonable barbarism that has no recognizable selective function. We can see the contribution of religion to culture as turning culture's programme to decrease the pressure of selection into a conscious task formulated as a commandment, as exposing the failure to do this as sin, and as offering the encouragement and comfort that makes it possible to remain true to this fundamental programme through every crisis. In doing this, two religions rebel most clearly against the hardness of the principle of selection: Buddhism and Christianity. Buddhism does this because it wants to extinguish man's thirst for life – the thirst for life that alone allows us to compete with other people and other living things. Christianity, on the other hand, wants to change the thirst for life into love for the weak – that is into love for other people and creatures that come off badly in the struggle for life. An 'anti-selectionism' is noticeable in both cases, a revolt against the principle of selection. What culture in general favours is thus consciously picked out (in images and symbols) as a central theme in religion.

To what degree is this outline of a theory of religion *phenomenological*? The experience of the sacred has a central meaning in it. Humanity's step beyond biological evolution consists of being able to consider and love a thing for its own sake. As soon as the world and their lives have an end in themselves for human beings, humanity has raised its head out of the stream of life in which it swims with all living things: the sacred is per se absolutely an end in itself. In as far as human beings have incalculable worth (and not only a value that can be exchanged for something else) they are the image or reflection of the holy.

But when does such an evolutionary theory of religion become 'theology'? Theology cancels out the double abstention from judgement of religious phenomenology: abstention with regard to the reality of the holy and neutrality in deciding between different religions. It professes a belief in one form of the holy and brings arguments as *fides quaerens intellectum* in order to make this decision comprehensible. Finally I briefly outline the reason why I think that religious experience is not merely a human construct. Religious experience can be described as an experience of transcendence, contingency and resonance in which we discover a superior reality.

We know that our 'world' is not reality in itself. The world we live in is the apparent world that is interpreted and constructed by us and related to our senses and our brain. Reality in itself eludes us. It remains hidden from us, whether we call it 'God' or 'reality in itself'. We make a necessary distinction between being and appearing. We experience the difference of appearing and being most intensively when our thoughts fail to attain final reality. We feel this failure as the wave feels the cliff it crashes against. In this failure of our thoughts and our lives we have original *experiences of transcendence* right inside the present.

The same transcendence that escapes our knowledge is extremely close to us: we *are*, even if we do not adequately recognize what we really are. This miracle penetrates us at every moment and surrounds even the thought with which we make sure of it. This all-penetrating experience of *contingency* is the second source of religious experience. It is not the contrast between being and appearing that is experienced in it but of being and nothing. Everything that exists could equally well not be. Everything that exists will one day be no more. In experiences of transcendence being eludes us, in experiences of contingency it is nearer to us than we are to ourselves. It shows itself as all determining reality.

The miracle of being and not being 'appeals to us'. We experience the holy as an experience of *resonance* i.e. we discover something in reality that is very deeply related to us and what is related sets us in vibration (Theissen 1978). The order of the world finds an echo in our intelligence, the dynamic of nature in our vitality, the You of the other person in our I. Each time we have an experience of something indisputably objective. Such experiences make us sure that living is of great value. In experiences of resonance we are aware of the unity of being and value. Values are not attributes of material things but are based on an interaction between us and these things: on resonance. Thereby we approach reality with 'intentionality detectors' and experience there something related which, on the basis of this relationship, we can interpret as 'intention'. What is decisive is that it is very deeply related to us: it is reason like our reason, life like our life, suffering like our suffering. Such experiences of resonance are experiences of value. They transcend the material. The difference between being and appearing, being and nothing is joined by the third fundamental difference between to be and should be or between reality and value.

Finally these thoughts are illustrated through the famous parable of A. Flew about the gardener, who does not even exist (quoted from Dalferth 1974, p. 84). Two explorers come across a garden in the jungle but find no gardener. Through fences, bloodhounds and electric snares they refute the assumption that he is invisible. One of the explorers is religious. He is convinced that the gardener is insensitive to electric shocks, that he can climb through fences unhindered and that dogs cannot smell him. The other is an agnostic. He sees no difference between an invisible, intangible and constantly elusive gardener who is forever escaping and a gardener that does not exist. The parable was invented in order to express an agnostic position. What I find inconsistent in this parable is that not only the sceptic but also the believer act deeply irreligiously. Both build barbed wire, set the hounds going and lay electric snares. That God evades their methods says less against him than against these methods. How would religious people react to the discovery of the garden? They would organize a festival because they had found order and meaning in the jungle – and moreover as something unexpected and contingent that could just as well not exist, so unlikely is it! They would repeat this festival. In addition they would formulate commandments that make it a duty to maintain and take care of the garden. For in this order they hear a call to maintain it. It is not only given, it is surrendered. It represents a value. They would finally recognize that the order in this garden and the order in their life are the same. Both sound together like melody and accompaniment. The garden is the object of a deep experience of resonance. They will also certainly tell a story of a gardener who made everything, who entrusted the garden to them and created the wonderful harmony between the garden and their needs and possibilities. But this gardener, the final ground of being and of their existence, will always remain transcendent. They will never see him. Again and again they will find allusions to him but again and again they will fail to 'grasp' him. In their search for him they have elementary experiences of transcendence. The story about him is, of course, poetry. It is made up. But with this poetry they make a claim to truth – just as the parable of the gardener contains a truth, even though it is totally made up! It is because religion up to the present day expresses experiences of transcendence, contingency and resonance in poetic language that it is more than a human construct.

Notes

1. English translation of this essay by Wendy Tyndale.
2. With this chapter I express my thanks for all the support and encouragement for which I am indebted to Robert Morgan. I can well remember how he visited me in Bonn in the 1970s. I told him that I had written a small 'Sociology of the Jesus Movement'. While I was making tea in the kitchen, he began to read the manuscript. When I came back from the kitchen, he said: 'I am going to see to it that this manuscript is translated into English'. In his human and congenial way, Robert Morgan has encouraged many young talents and new thoughts. This *Festschrift* should make that a bit apparent to the academic public.
3. E. Voland and C. Söling speak here of 'mysticism'. The term should, in my opinion, be restricted to certain religious experiences. Mysticism occurs as a vision of God that changes one into his being (2 Cor 3:18), as the hearing of a voice that transports one to another state (2 Cor 12:1ff.), as unity with the Deity, that is expressed in reciprocal formulae of immanence (1 John 4:16). The 'prophetic' experience, to be moved by the command of a Deity, is, on the other hand, not a mystical experience but determined by the awareness of a distance and a qualitative difference between human beings and God (Isa 6:1ff.)

References

Andresen, J. (ed.), *Religion in Mind: Cognitive Perspectives on Religious Belief, Ritual, and Experience* (Cambridge: Cambridge University Press, 2001).

Balla, P., *The Child-Parent Relationship in the New Testament and its Environment* (WUNT 155: Tübingen: Mohr, 2003).

Boyer, P., *The Naturalness of Religious Ideas: A Cognitive Theory of Religion* (Cambridge: Cambridge University Press, 1994).

Boyer, P., *Religion Explained. The Evolutionary Origins of Religious Thought* (New York: Basic Books, 2001).

Burkert, W., *Kulte des Altertums. Biologische Grundlagen der Religion* (München, 1998).

Dalferth, I.U., *Sprachlogik des Glaubens. Texte analytischer Religionsphilosophie und Theologie zur religiösen Sprache* (München: Kaiser, 1974).

Euler, H. E., 'Sexuelle Selektion und Religion', in U. Lüke, J. Schnakenberg and G. Souvignier (eds), *Darwin und Gott. Das Verhältnis von Evolution und Religion* (Darmstadt: Wiss. Buchgesellschaft, 2004), pp. 66–88.

Feldtkeller, A., *Theologie und Religion. Eine Wissenschaft in ihrem Sinnzusammenhang* (ThLZ. F 6; Leipzig: Ev. Verlagsanstalt, 2002).

Gantke, W., *Der umstrittene Begriff des Heiligen. Eine problemorientierte religionswissenschaftliche Untersuchung* (Marburg: Diagonal Verlag, 1998).

Gemünden, P.v., 'La gestion de la colère et de l'agression dans l'Antiquité et dans le sermon sur la montagne', *Henoch* 25 (2003), 19-45.

Guttenberger, G., *Status und Statusverzicht im Neuen Testament und seiner Umwelt* (NTOA 39; Freiburg Schweiz: Universitätsverlag and Göttingen: Vandenhoeck & Ruprecht, 1999).

Kippenberg, H.G. and Stuckrad, Kocku v., *Einführung in die Religionswissenschaft. Gegenstände und Begriffe* (München: Beck, 2003).

Kollmann, B., 'Das Schwurverbot Mt 5,33-37/Jak 5,12 im Spiegel antiker Eidkritik', *BZ* 40 (1996), 179-93.

Leeuw, G. v.d., *Phänomenologie der Religion* (Tübingen: Mohr, 1933, 1976).

Luz, U., *Das Evangelium nach Matthäus, 1-7* (EKK I,1; Düsseldorf/Zürich: Patmos/Benzinger/Neukirchener, 2002).

Marti, K., *abendland, gedichte* (Darmstadt: Luchterhand, 1980).

Morgan, R. with J. Barton, *Biblical Interpretation* (Oxford: Oxford University Press, 1988).

Otto, R., *Das Heilige. Über das Irrationale in der Idee des Göttlichen und sein Verhältnis zum Rationalen* (Breslau: Trewendt und Granier, 1917, 1920).

Philippides, L.J., *Die Goldene Regel religionsgeschichtlich untersucht* (Leipzig: Adolf Klein, 1929).

Pyysiäinen, I., *How Religion Works: Towards a New Cognitive Science of Religion* (Leiden: Brill, 2001).

Pyysiäinen, I., 'Religion and the counter-intuitive', in I. Pyysiäinen and V. Anttonen (eds), *Current Approaches in the Cognitive Science of Religion* (London: Continuum, 2002), pp. 110-32.

Pyysiäinen, I. and Anttonen, V. (eds), *Current Approaches in the Cognitive Science of Religion* (London: Continuum, 2002).

Sabbatucci, D., *Kultur und Religion* (HRG 1; Stuttgart: Kohlhammer, 1988), pp. 43-58.

Sanders, E.P., *Jesus and Judaism* (Philadelphia: Fortress, 1985).

Schleiermacher, F., *Über die Religion. Reden an die Gebildeten unter ihren Verächtern* (1799; ed. G. Meckenstock, Berlin/New York: Walter de Gruyter, 1999).

Söling, C., *Der Gottesinstinkt. Bausteine für eine evolutionäre Religionstheorie* (Diss: Gießen, 2002) (http://geb.uni-giessen.de/geb/volltexte/2002/816/pdf/d020116.pdf).

Stolz, F., 'Der mythische Umgang mit der Rationalität und der rationale Umgang mit dem Mythos', in H.H. Schmid (ed.), *Mythos und Rationalität* (Gütersloh: Mohn, 1988), pp. 81-106.

Sundermeier, Th., *Was ist Religion? Religionswissenschaft im theologischen Kontext* (ThB 96; Gütersloh: Kaiser, 1999).

Theissen, G., *Urchristliche Wundergeschichten Ein Beitrag zur formgeschichtlichen Erforschung der synoptischen Evangelien* (StNT 8; Gütersloh: Mohn, 1974, 1998).

Theissen, G., *Argumente für einen kritischen Glauben oder: Was hält der Religionskritik stand?* (TEH 202; München: Kaiser 1978, 1988).

Theissen, G., *Biblischer Glaube in evolutionärer Sicht* (München: Kaiser, 1984; ET 1984/1985).

Theissen, G., 'Tradition und Entscheidung. Der Beitrag des biblischen Glaubens zum kulturellen Gedächtnis', in J. Assmann and T. Hölscher (eds), *Kultur und Gedächtnis* (Frankfurt: Suhrkamp, 1988), pp. 170–96.

Theissen, G., *A Theory of Primitive Christian Religion* (London: SCM, 1999) = (expanded and worked over) *Die Religion der ersten Christen. Eine Theorie des Urchristentums* (Gütersloh: Mohn, 2000, 2003).

Theissen, G., 'Die Goldene Regel (Matthäus 7:12//Lukas 6:31). Über den Sitz im Leben ihrer positiven und negativen Form', *Biblical Interpretation* 11 (2003), 386–99.

Voland, E. and Söling, C., 'Die biologische Basis der Religiosität in Instinkten - Beiträge zu einer evolutionären Religionstheorie', in U. Lüke, J. Schnakenberg and G. Souvignier (eds), *Darwin und Gott. Das Verhältnis von Evolution und Religion* (Darmstadt: Wiss. Buchgesellschaft, 2004), pp. 47–65.

Chapter 14

Does the 'Historical Jesus' belong within a 'New Testament Theology'?

Christopher Tuckett, Oxford

The question posed by the title of this chapter needs to be carefully defined – or rather, the individual terms used in the formulation of the question need careful definition. In one sense (as we shall see: see n. 7 below), the question could be (and has been) decisively answered on the basis of one definition of the terms used in the question. It is too a question which the person to whom this volume is dedicated has contributed an important essay (Morgan 1987), even if the present discussion will (with respect) venture to give a slightly different view.

Two 'definitions', or at least clarifications, are required at the outset: what is meant by 'the historical Jesus' in this context and what is meant by 'New Testament theology'? For the purposes of writing this chapter for the present volume, the first question is much easier to answer than the second! Indeed the issues raised by the second question – what is 'New Testament theology'? – are precisely those addressed in the present volume, and the different contributions here highlight the problems in defining the term. However, the first question is also important if the present essay is not to be misunderstood.

By the 'historical Jesus' I mean (crudely) the life and teaching of the pre-Easter Jesus. Hence I do not mean simply the historicity of Jesus (what Bultmann famously called the '*daß*' of Jesus). However one defines 'New Testament theology' (on which see below), it has almost always been assumed as axiomatic that a theology 'of' the New Testament will involve some exposition of the significance of the figure of Jesus who is assumed to be a historical individual.[1] What is more contentious is how far any concrete substance we might wish to ascribe to this figure (what Bultmann called the '*was*' of Jesus) should have a place within a 'theology of the New Testament'. Few if any would deny that claims about the death and/or 'resurrection' of this figure will play an integral role in any 'theology of the New Testament'. So too claims about the 'incarnation' (however defined or expressed) could be similarly integral.[2] But what of the ma-terial that might (somewhat crudely) be thought of as coming 'between' these two defining 'moments'? How far should the teaching of Jesus (insofar as we can recover it) – his own ideas and beliefs about God, himself or whatever – be part and parcel of whatever it is we mean by a 'theology of the New Testament'?

It is well known that different authors of so-called 'theologies of the NT' have adopted very different positions in relation to this question.[3] Rudolf Bultmann stated famously at the start of his *Theology of the New Testament* that 'The message of Jesus is a presupposition for the theology of the New Testament rather than a part of that theology itself' (1952, p. 3). Others have followed suit.[4] By contrast one might cite J. Jeremias who published his book entitled *New Testament Theology* in 1971. The only part published was devoted exclusively to the 'proclamation of Jesus'. It did also contain the subtitle 'Volume 1': however, no subsequent volume ever appeared (Jeremias died in 1980 and it is unclear if one was ever intended). Clearly then for Jeremias, the teaching of Jesus constituted a major part, if not the essential whole, of a 'New Testament theology'.[5]

The question addressed here is certainly not whether the 'historical Jesus', and information about his life and teaching, is recoverable (with varying degrees of certainty), or whether such a 'quest' for the 'historical Jesus' is an academically justifiable enterprise. Few today would doubt that such a quest is in theory possible even if the results obtained are inherently provisional and incomplete.[6] My question is rather what place, if any, the results of such enquiry should have within a so-called 'New Testament theology'.

Much depends on what we understand to be the nature of a 'New Testament theology'.[7] In his programmatic essay on 'The nature of New Testament theology' (1973) as well as in many other writings, Robert Morgan distinguishes what he calls 'New Testament theology', or theological interpretation of the New Testament, from what might be called the study of the history of early Christian religion. The latter he sees as exemplified above all in the work of William Wrede, and Morgan himself has contributed much clarity and light to an otherwise murky academic and theological landscape, both by translating and publicizing Wrede's programmatic essay on 'The task and nature of "New Testament theology"' for a wider readership and audience (Wrede 1973), and also by his clear and lucid analysis both of Wrede and of his many successors. As is now well known, the 'Aufgabe', or 'task', of Wrede's title in his programmatic essay was for a 'sogenannten' ('so-called') 'New Testament theology'.[8] Certainly Wrede himself claimed (1973, p. 116) that both parts of that phrase – 'New Testament' and 'theology' – were inappropriate for the task he envisaged and outlined: a restriction to the canon of the NT texts, rather than a consideration of all early Christian literature, was not justifiable; and the subject matter of the undertaking should not be restricted to 'theology' (the ideas or concepts) but should encompass the broader spread of 'religion' more widely (hence including more than just abstract ideas). Above all, such analysis should be undertaken as a historical discipline, free from confessional or doctrinal influence.

It may also be noted as a footnote that Wrede regarded it as self-evident that in any such enterprise as he was advocating under the rubric of 'New Testament theology' (so-called), the teaching of Jesus would occupy a prime position: 'the first main theme of New Testament theology is Jesus' preaching' (1973, p. 103), though Wrede was adamant that this was not an 'actual doctrine' in that it could not be abstracted from Jesus' personality and life.

A number of scholars have defended and adopted Wrede's position about the nature of New Testament theology, either implicitly or explicitly. The most notable in the modern era is probably Heikki Räisänen who has defended Wrede's approach and outlined his own proposed 'history of Christian religion' (yet to be completed: but see the programmatic remarks in Räisänen 2000, also his essay in this volume). And it is probably fair to say that, in relation to a large number of studies of individual ('theological'!) themes in NT studies today, many would see their task in very much Wrede-like terms, i.e. aiming to be primarily historical, descriptive and not influenced by contemporary confessional or doctrinal influences.[9] Further, most engaged in any study of the 'history of Christian religion' (whatever phrase is used to describe it), as opposed to 'New Testament theology', would regard it as natural to include a discussion of the historical Jesus.[10]

By contrast, there has always been strong body of scholarly (NT-)exegetical opinion that has regarded the task of NT interpretation in more overtly confessional – or 'theological' – terms. Thus Morgan contrasts Wrede's stance with an explicitly 'theological' approach to the text in the sense of one that refuses to sit on any doctrinal or confessional 'fence'.[11]

This is the approach of scholars such as Bultmann and Käsemann in the modern era, of Schlatter in a previous era, and is clearly the one which Morgan himself wishes to advocate and promote, defending its legitimacy and defining it over against the more historical, religiously detached, approach of Wrede's programme.

In this more 'theological' approach, the exegete is the self-confessed Christian believer, working within the context of the 'church' (broadly conceived) rather than necessarily the 'academy' (though inevitably, in practice, any one individual is likely to occupy a place in both). Such an exegete makes no claim to be 'disinterested' or 'uninvolved' (however disingenuous such a claim might be). Nor does s/he work with any kind of model whereby exegesis produces (value-free?) 'results' which are then handed over to the systematic theologian to do whatever the latter wills with them.[12] One may recall Käsemann's biting complaint about 'a number of exegetes [who] with thoroughly misplaced modesty actually suppose that they merely do the historical donkey work for the systematic theologian' (1969, p. 7): clearly such modesty is not one that Käsemann would wish to endorse or encourage!

Perhaps the classic work of such a theologically committed approach in the modern period is Bultmann's *Theology of the New Testament*, which is simultaneously both a historical description of the thoughts of (some of!) the NT writers, above all Paul and John, and also a claim to provide a normative systematic theology for the contemporary Christian. Thus for Bultmann, 'theology and exegesis – or systematic and historical theology – fundamentally coincide' (1968, p. 239, cited by Morgan 1973, p. 37). Bultmann manages to achieve such a unity in part by claiming that, for theology and history alike, the subject matter is men and women's understanding of their existence – for theology human existence as existence determined by God. Further, for Bultmann's theology, 'God' is the God who addresses human beings through the kerygma, above all the kerygma of Jesus as the crucified and risen one, and it is for this reason that the teaching of the pre-Easter Jesus (the 'historical Jesus' as defined above) has no place in a 'New Testament theology' devoted to an exposition of (this version of) the Christian faith.

> New Testament theology consists in the unfolding of the ideas by means of which Christian faith makes sure of its own object, basis and consequences. But Christian faith did not exist until there was a Christian kerygma, i.e. a kerygma proclaiming Jesus Christ – specifically Jesus Christ the Crucified and Risen One – to be God's eschatological act of salvation. He was first so proclaimed in the kerygma of the earliest Church, not in the message of the historical Jesus, even though that Church frequently introduced into its account of Jesus' message, motifs of its own

proclamation. Thus theological thinking – the theology of the New Testament – begins with the kerygma of the earliest Church and not before (1952, p. 3).

Thus the very definition of 'New Testament theology' adopted here necessarily precludes any inclusion of the teaching of the pre-Easter Jesus as an integral part of it, even though it may allow a place for it in a preface or as a 'presupposition'.

Bultmann's exegetical and theological endeavours have generated a great deal of critical discussion and evaluation. One issue concerns the way in which norms are to be identified and applied in evaluating (historically and/or theologically) the *different* witnesses which form the NT as it is currently formed. It is by now almost universally accepted that the voices of the NT texts speak to a certain extent with different voices.[13] If one is to find a (single!) 'theology' of/in the NT, where or how is this to be located?[14] Bultmann famously found the centre of the NT in the theologies of Paul and John.[15] Other witnesses in the NT were described, but clearly found to be wanting in Bultmann's presentation.[16] But such (theological) value judgements apply not only to the theologies of other witnesses apart from the theological heroes Paul and John. At times Bultmann even claims to be able to criticize Paul himself, to 'know Paul better than Paul knew himself', and to claim that what Paul says is occasionally not true to Pauline theology 'properly' understood (i.e. by Bultmann). Such so-called *Sachkritik* in Bultmann's work is well known and has been described and analysed by many others (see e.g. Morgan 1973, pp. 42–51).

Indeed it is precisely this *Sachkritik*, operating theologically rather than historically, which for Morgan serves to distinguish a historically descriptive approach from that of a committed 'theological' interpretation (1977, pp. 258–9). A non-committed historian might claim the right to say that one writer at times contradicts what s/he says elsewhere and hence wish to make a judgement about what might constitute his/her 'real' thoughts, thus discounting and rejecting what s/he says in one or two places. But a theological critique will claim the right to reject one writer's statements/claims, even his/her whole theological position, on the basis of the *interpreter's* own understanding of Christianity, even though this is derived from other parts of the tradition. As an example, Morgan cites Luther's critique of James, 'not on the basis of James' better thoughts elsewhere but on the basis of his [Luther's] own understanding of Christianity, derived from other parts of the tradition' (1977, p. 259). Part of the structural weakness of Bultmann's theological enterprise, according to Morgan (1973, p. 48), is that Bultmann is seeking to make *theological sachkritische* judgements but presenting them as it they are part of a *historical Sachkritik.*

It is, however, at the level of *Sachkritik* – that is a *theological Sachkritik* – that some appeal to the historical Jesus might be deemed to be both desirable and necessary in any account of what is claimed to be a 'theology of the New Testament', that is, a *theological* interpretation and evaluation of the New Testament texts. (In what follows I am therefore taking the phrase 'New Testament theology' in the sense suggested by Morgan, i.e. to refer to the process of seeking to provide an interpretation of the New Testament from the standpoint of a Christian 'theologian' [broadly conceived].)[17]

It has always been regarded as axiomatic that any genuinely Christian theology must relate integrally and necessarily to the person of Jesus of Nazareth. A Christianity without Jesus would be virtually a contradiction in terms. Hence in turn, any theology not giving central importance to the figure/person of Jesus has been criticized vehemently if it would claim to be 'Christian'.[18] It has always been a constant critique of Bultmann's theology that it is in danger of breaking the link with the person of Jesus, or at least treating the link as effectively superficial if not irrelevant. If faith is primarily in relation to the kerygma and the claims made on human beings by the kerygma, is the specificity – or even the historicity – of the historical figure of Jesus required?[19] Bultmann himself resolutely maintained that the link with the historical Jesus was essential and non-negotiable; but others have questioned how logical this is and whether in fact Bultmann's theology really requires such a historical anchor.

Yet there is another problem as well. Even if it is deemed that the kerygma, or the Christian claims, relate to a historical figure, why should the figure of *Jesus* be the most appropriate figure for the Christian faith? Why, for example, should John the Baptist (who preached a message similar in many respects to that of Jesus, and who died a violent death at the hands of his enemies) not be the focus of the Christian proclamation? What is it that serves to distinguish Jesus from other individuals of his time? Why should Jesus' cross be different from the other (thousands of) crosses which were the means of executing others, some of whom were no doubt as innocent (or guilty) of the crimes of which they were accused as Jesus was?

There is no space to enter fully into all these questions. But it may be at this point that one can begin to stake a claim to say that the historical Jesus (in the sense given above, i.e. the life of teaching of Jesus prior to Easter) may be important in any *theological* evaluation of the witnesses given about Jesus in the pages of the New Testament, i.e. in a 'theological' interpretation of the New Testament, a 'theology of the New Testament'.

It is now almost universally agreed that the different voices of the New Testament witness in different ways to the significance of Jesus (see above). But how is one then not only to describe and highlight these differences (as in a Wrede-type exercise) but also to evaluate them theologically and perhaps claim one (or more) witness as closer to the 'truth' of the Gospel than others?

One way (*not* necessarily the only one) might be to appeal to the teaching of the historical Jesus as some kind of criterion by which to judge competing interpretations of the Gospel and/or the developing Christian tradition. This is in no way to suggest that Christian witnesses to Jesus (in the NT or elsewhere) are to be judged solely by how closely they approximate to a historically reconstructed picture of the teaching of the pre-Easter Jesus. In no sense is Jesus here being proposed as the archetypal Christian preacher! This would, for example, probably rule out of court interpretations of Jesus' death and/or resurrection (since 'historical' reconstructions of Jesus' teaching would regularly attribute many, if not all, of these in the Gospel traditions to later Christians reading such interpretations back into the teaching of Jesus). It would also probably preclude Christian reflections on the 'resurrection' of Jesus (for the same reason), as well as many explicit claims about the uniqueness of Jesus (again for the same reason). It is in this sense that Morgan is probably quite right to reject strongly a model whereby the 'historical Jesus' (or the historians' Jesus) becomes the *sole* criterion of judging competing Christian theological claims about Jesus.[20]

However, Morgan's vehemence appears to be directed against a very one-sided appeal to the historical Jesus as providing the *only* such criterion. He thus talks about the disadvantages, and the (theological) undesirability, of 'replacing' Christian claims about Jesus with historical information concerning Jesus' teaching and of 'substituting' the historical ministry of Jesus for Christology (1987, p. 194), of 'replacing' Christian claims with a 'historical reconstruction devoid of (and so in effect opposed to) Christology'; or of 'substituting' a purely historical for a kerygmatic presentation of Jesus (p. 195). 'Those who place a historical reconstruction at the head of their presentations [of a New Testament theology] are wittingly or unwittingly placing a question mark against all Christian ways of understanding Jesus' (p. 192). A model such as the one apparently presupposed (and rejected) by Morgan would of course lead straight back to the liberal Protestantism of the nineteenth century and the assessment of e.g. Paul by someone such as Wrede as the 'second founder of Christianity'.

Yet one wonders if Morgan's polemic is directed against something of a 'straw man' in relation to contemporary Christian theology and any contemporary 'theological' understanding of the New Testament. Perhaps the critique might be justified against a presentation of 'New Testament theology' that focused *solely* on the teaching of the pre-Easter Jesus, e.g. against a Jeremias-like 'New Testament theology' purged of the reference to 'Volume 1' in the sub-title. But Jeremias did include the 'Volume 1' in the sub-title! And all others who have regarded a presentation of the teaching of Jesus as an integral part of their 'New Testament theology' have put this along *with* other witnesses from elsewhere in the New Testament. Placing a presentation of the historical Jesus at the 'head' of the account, in the sense of being the first topic treated, does not necessarily presuppose anything about the relative importance of what comes after!

Further, in his essay Morgan does concede that historical presentations of Jesus will have an important role to play in 'theological' presentations of the New Testament, and can act at times as a (theological) control. He refers (somewhat paradoxically!) to the 'necessity and the impossibility' of including the historical Jesus within a 'New Testament theology' (p. 190). Thus along with all the reasons (already mentioned) for why the historical Jesus cannot 'replace' or 'substitute for' the theological responses to Jesus (the 'impossibility' side of his dichotomy), Morgan fully accepts that *some* historical information about Jesus is both desirable and theologically necessary in any presentation of the 'theology of the New Testament'. He therefore refers to historical constructions (of Jesus and his teaching) as 'contain[ing] information which a modern Christology *must* include, and may thus be admitted by Christians to contain *part* of the truth about Jesus' (p. 191). There is then some 'historical information which *must* be included' [in a 'Theology of the New Testament'], the only 'problem' being how to do so (p. 197). For example, the very fact that the focus of the Christian kerygma is the historical figure of Jesus of Nazareth means that the reliability of some information about Jesus is essential if any Christian claims about Jesus are to be seen as at least credible (not necessarily 'proven', but at least not definitively disproved). Thus Christian believers 'would admit to some perplexity if it could be shown that Jesus had never existed, or that he was a bad man; or that the post-Resurrection proclamation of the disciples was a fraud, as Reimarus suggested' (1987, p. 190). There are, self-evidently, some 'historical' facts about Jesus which are essential to undergird Christian claims about Jesus, not least the fact that he existed (Bultmann's '*daß*').

But as Morgan implies in the quotation just given, it may need rather more than the simple fact that Jesus existed. He himself says that if it could be shown that Jesus 'was a bad man' (however goodness and badness were to be determined), problems for the Christian kerygma would be acute. But in that case, information about the 'historical Jesus' (in the sense that I have taken the term, i.e. something of the '*was*' of Jesus beyond the fact that he existed) is then necessary to make such a judgement.

All that might be covered by making (with Bultmann) the historical Jesus into a 'presupposition' for a New Testament theology – perhaps a *necessary* presupposition (cf. Dahl 1974, p. 101), but still only a presupposition. Thus in order for the Christian claims about Jesus to be credible, some features of the historical Jesus would be necessary – e.g. that he existed, that he was shown to be 'not a bad man', perhaps even that he was not an atheist! – but the teaching of Jesus would have no place in a New Testament theology itself. Even here, however, one might enter some fairly murky waters. How, for example, should 'we' (or Christians) determine what constitutes a 'good' or a 'bad' man? Many Christians might wish to argue that Jesus himself, the *historical* (i.e. pre-Easter) Jesus, could be an important criterion for determining what is 'good' or 'bad', especially in relation to issues where the ethics concerned are highly disputed. In very general terms, most (Christians and non-Christians alike) would agree that, if Jesus were shown to have killed his mother and raped a 10-year-old girl, that would make him 'bad' and create insuperable problems for later Christian claims about him. But what if Jesus were shown to be a person with a highly active political agenda who planned (and possibly even put into practice) a strategy of violent opposition to the Roman forces in Palestine in the first century? Would this make him 'good' or 'bad'? Or would the very fact that it was *Jesus* who had such a strategy in fact *determine* what should be a contemporary Christian response to the (highly disputed) theological/ethical question of whether active political engagement, including the use of force, is a morally or theologically justifiable – if not required – response in situations of political (and/or economic?) repression?

Morgan does in fact suggest that at times the historical Jesus can and should act as a *criterion* within a theological reading of the New Testament and its varied witnesses. Thus he speaks of Jesus as 'the criterion of the kerygma' (1987, p. 195). He claims that, especially in relation to the Gospels and a discussion of the evangelists' presentation of Jesus, i.e. their 'theologies', it is important not only to describe their contributions but to 'assess' them and that historical information can and should be used in this process of 'critical evaluation': 'For one way in which an evangelist's theology can be criticized [theologically] is by reference to the historical reality of the man the evangelist is seeking to interpret' (p. 198). And at one point in his essay Morgan becomes more specific and spells out how this might operate in practice in relation to particular theological themes or issues:

> Since they [the Gospels] aim to speak Christologically of the man Jesus their interpretations can be criticized by reference to independent information (gained by historical methods) concerning Jesus. Thus John's alleged docetism can be criticized through reference to his astonishing freedom with the tradition, or Matthew's alleged legalism *by denying the authenticity of certain material*. Both these evangelists must be criticized for their treatment of the Jews, and this can be done *by criticizing their history* at certain points (p. 204, my italics).

It is not quite certain if what Morgan says here can be taken at face value, at least in relation to his own terms of reference. He appears to be saying that a *historical* judgement about the authenticity of some parts of the Gospel tradition can serve as the criterion for whether a particular element of the Gospel presentation is *theologically* acceptable (or negatively: a judgement that a feature is inauthentic historically, i.e. does not go back to the pre-Easter Jesus, can be taken as almost sufficient grounds to make a negative theological judgement about its content).

On its own, such a criterion would seem to be potentially dangerous theologically and would open the floodgates to precisely the sort of dangers that Morgan is clearly anxious to guard against elsewhere in his essay. It makes in effect the historical Jesus almost the sole touchstone of what is theologically acceptable in the New Testament (or at least in the Gospels) by rejecting as theologically unacceptable what does not go back to the historical Jesus. There might though well be some things in the Gospels which are deemed to be 'inauthentic' historically (in the sense that they cannot be traced back to the historical Jesus), but which nevertheless could express ideas and/or sentiments which a 'theologian' might deem to be important, theologically 'authentic' and 'valid'.

In practice, the way such a criterion might work would almost certainly involve more than simply an appeal to the issue of historicity, or historical authenticity, as such. For example, the exclusivism reflected in a verse such as Matt 18:17 (where a 'sinner' who refuses to accept demands to 'repent' should in the end 'be to you as a Gentile or a tax collector') would be regarded as historically 'inauthentic' (in relation to the historical Jesus) by most critics. But most 'theologians' would also want to reject such a 'theology' on various grounds. Part of the reason might be that the ideas expressed do not go back to Jesus himself. But more relevant might be the fact that the reason why such a historical judgement is made is that the sentiments implied clash significantly with other parts of the Jesus tradition usually assumed to be authentic which stress Jesus' openness to all (including tax collectors – the issue of Jesus' attitude to Gentiles is more complex!) and his offer of forgiveness and acceptance to all on an unconditional basis. Part of the argument for the historical inauthenticity of Matt 18:17 is also the existence of this tension. But in theological terms, given this tension, it is the openness and forgiveness side that many would wish to affirm theologically as foundational to the Christian Gospel, appealing perhaps too to important other parts of the Christian tradition such as Paul, e.g. his insistence on the significance of the cross and the whole Christ event as bringing forgiveness to the ungodly (cf. Rom 4:5). Thus the sentiments of Matt 18:17 would be criticized theologically not so much by reference to their historical inauthenticity per se, but by reference to the tension the verse creates alongside other parts of the Jesus tradition *and* the broader Christian tradition (both in- and outside the NT itself). The issue would then be not so much that of historical inauthenticity in itself, but the content and substance of the authentic Jesus tradition (even though the two issues are of course interrelated).[21]

Similarly, the 'theology' implied in the tirade against the scribes and Pharisees in Matt 23, or against 'the Jews' in John's Gospel, would be criticized partly because these sections of the Gospels (probably) do not go back to Jesus (at least in their present form), but partly because they conflict fundamentally with other aspects of the tradition – in part Jesus tradition, but also in part other Christian tradition (cf. the far more positive attitude to 'Israel' reflected in Rom 11). Given such a tension, a *theological* value judgement would need to be made, and one might give (theological) preference to the Paul of Rom 11 over the Matthean Jesus of Matt 23 or the Johannine Jesus of John 8.

However, just as important is the fact that there might be parts of the Gospel tradition which are deemed to be 'inauthentic' historically, i.e. they do not go back to the historical Jesus, but which nevertheless one might wish to affirm theologically as expressing something profoundly important about Jesus and/or aspects of the Christian Gospel. I take as an example the parable of the sheep and the goats in Matt 25:31-46, interpreted as advocating an ethic of helping those in need irrespective of their class, colour, creed or whatever. Many would take this parable, especially as interpreted in this way, as not something that could be traced back to the historical Jesus.[22] Nevertheless, the 'theology' (or practical ethic) implied in the parable interpreted this way, viz., the importance of helping the poor of the world today in very concrete, practical terms, is one that many contemporary (Christian) theologians (and preachers) would wish to affirm as powerfully as possible. Further, part of an argument in favour of such a view might be an appeal (in admittedly fairly general terms) to the teaching of Jesus widely thought to be authentic. Thus Jesus may rarely (if ever) have advocated a policy of charitable giving to those in need outside his own social and religious community; but many might wish to see such a policy as the logical corollary of his advocacy of love and of his openness to a wide cross-section of his society. As a (contemporary) 'theological' interpretation of the Gospel tradition, such a use of this parable would be regarded by many as entirely appropriate theologically. The issue of whether or not such an interpretation could be traced back historically to the pre-Easter Jesus might be seen as theologically irrelevant, though a broader appeal to the historical Jesus might be a significant part of the theological evaluation of the tradition and its interpretation here.

Similarly, a saying in the Gospel of John such as John 3:16-17 ('God so loved the world that he gave his only Son, so that everyone who believes in him may not perish but may have eternal life. Indeed God did not send the Son into the world to condemn the world, but in order that the world might be saved through him') expresses a theological claim about God, about Jesus and his significance, and the intended consequences of the Christ event, which many would wish to affirm positively in theological terms, even though one might wish also to affirm that, in all probability, this saying (along with most of the teaching placed on the lips of Jesus in the fourth Gospel) cannot be traced back to the pre-Easter Jesus. But again, part of the argument for the 'theological validity' of the saying might involve relating key elements of the claims made (e.g. about God's 'love' for the 'world', and a desire to 'save the world'), at least in broad and general terms, to things which are arguably more likely to have been said and taught by Jesus himself.

So too many would wish to assert that, in theological terms, the claims of the Johannine Jesus that he 'is the way, the truth and the life' in John 14:6a expresses a profound theological truth about the significance of Jesus which a Christian would want to affirm – even if (crudely) the historical Jesus (probably) never said such a thing.[23]

In instances such as these, then, historical authenticity and theological 'validity' might not go hand in hand – and yet the 'theological validity' side of the balance may be none the worse for that. There can therefore be no neat equation made between the historical Jesus (or material in the Gospels which on historical grounds one would trace back to the pre-Easter Jesus) and what is deemed to be theologically 'valid'; or 'preferable' by a Christian theologian engaging with the New Testament texts.

In this, therefore, the other side of Morgan's argument is fully justified: one cannot equate Christology with Jesus' own teaching; one cannot substitute the historically reconstructed Jesus for Christian claims about Jesus. Indeed it can be argued that, in some respects, a Jesus who is too continuous with later Christian theology could in fact be no longer suit-

able as the focal figure for that theology. A Jesus who had already formulated some ideas about the positive meaning of the cross, who knew
already prior to his death that that death would surely be reversed by
'resurrection', and who perhaps claimed a uniqueness over and beyond
that of any 'normal' mortal, would be a Jesus for whom the agony of
Gethsemane and the cry of dereliction on the cross would be a sham;[24]
it would be a Jesus whom no Christian could claim plumbed the deepest
depths of human despair and godlessness (in Pauline language 'became
sin' cf. 2 Cor 5:21) and who could then be the agent who brought about
'reconciliation' or 'redemption' (or whatever theological language game
is used) in the most profound sense claimed by Christian theology.
(On this see Barrett, 1975, pp. 103–8.)

Certainly within the more restricted area of Christology (as one important part of 'theology' more generally), the relevance of the 'historical
Jesus', in the sense of Jesus' own self-understanding, may be very marginal
for subsequent and/or contemporary Christian Christology. It is certainly
here that the gulf between the historical Jesus and later Christian theology has often been felt to be the widest (and, for some, at its most dangerous).[25] Yet there is no reason why Jesus' views about himself should
be identical with the assertions of others about Jesus. Personal identity
is never solely a result of an individual's self-assessment (see especially
Meeks 1993). People with inflated ideas of their own importance have
often, precisely because of this, been found to be unimpressive by others.
Conversely, true greatness in the eyes of others is often coupled with
very different self-assessment by the individual concerned. A Jesus who
never claimed to be what later Christians claimed for him subsequently
might be a far more appropriate figure as the object for such claims –
perhaps too a more compelling figure religiously – than a Jesus displaying
continuities at every stage of the Christian theological agenda.

The argument of this chapter is not to equate the teaching of the historical Jesus with a 'New Testament theology' without remainder. The
latter (in the sense taken here) will always go beyond the teaching of
the historical Jesus to include reflections by others on the full significance of Jesus, his life, death and 'aftermath'; and in this, the views of the
pre-Easter Jesus (insofar as we can recover them) may well be super-
seded, changed and developed. But in any theological process of doing
more than simply describing the wide range of 'theologies' reflected in
the New Testament, in any process of critically evaluating such differences and seeking to make theological value judgements about them, the
historical Jesus may play an essential role as *part* of that process. In this
sense, therefore, I suggest that the historical Jesus belongs inextricably

within any attempt to engage in a 'theological' interpretation of the New Testament, i.e. to produce a 'New Testament theology'.

Notes

1. Hence, for example, Strauss' attempt to bypass the figure of Jesus has been – and is – described as unacceptable to Christian theology and untrue to the New Testament. (See Morgan 1977.)
2. Morgan has on several occasions insisted on the centrality and fundamental nature of 'the' 'incarnational' claim of Christians, but has left it extremely open-ended as to how that claim might be expressed and/or filled out. E.g. in his 1987 essay: 'in having to do with Jesus we have to do with God' (p. 193), or 'a claim that Jesus represents God finally and uniquely' (p. 197); or '. . . the orthodox Christian claim that in the human, historical, crucified and risen Jesus of Nazareth, we have to do – in as strong a sense as is possible or conceivable – with God himself' (1980a, p. 497).
3. Other brief discussions in Morgan (1973, pp. 20 – where it is called an 'open question'– 63–64), Balla (1997, pp. 171–7), Räisänen (2000, pp. 181–2). The fullest recent discussion I am aware of remains Morgan (1987). See too Perrin (1984), for one of the few other recent attempts to address the question directly at any length. Morgan's claim that the historical Jesus should not be included in a 'New Testament theology' echoes of course M. Kähler's earlier programmatic essay (Kähler 1964, originally 1892) arguing that the basis of Christian faith was the 'Biblical Christ', not the 'Historical Jesus'. Within contemporary Jesus studies, Kähler's general approach is perhaps best seen in the work of Johnson (cf. Johnson 1996).
4. Cf. the works of H. Conzelmann, G. Strecker and J. Gnilka under the title 'New Testament theology'.
5. Others who have included the teaching of Jesus as an integral part of their 'New Testament theology' include L. Goppelt, W.G. Kümmel, G.B. Caird, P. Stuhlmacher. Cf. too the massive recent work of N.T. Wright.
6. I am fully aware too that, in using the tools of historical criticism to seek to recover information about Jesus, one might reach only what some have called the 'historians' Jesus', who might well not be same as the 'real' Jesus, or 'the pre-Easter Jesus', with further big issues about whether these latter two should be equated. (On this see also below.) Cf. the works of those such as Kähler or Johnson (n. 3 above) and others. There is not enough space to enter into those debates here.
7. I leave on one side the 'definition' of a 'New Testament theology' that would restrict attention solely to the writings of the New Testament and hence exclude discussion of the historical Jesus (as well as earlier literary stages of existing NT documents, e.g. Q or other gospel sources) by definition from the outset. (Cf. Morgan 1987, p. 203). If, as will be argued below, a 'theology of the New Testament' is as much a process, involving theological judgements about what is theologically 'valid', or at least desirable, even

within the New Testament itself, the argument of this essay is that at least one precursor to the present NT documents belongs within that enterprise. Whether other pre-literary stages (e.g. Q) do so as well is beyond the scope of this essay: such a question raises broader issues about one's attitude to the process of the canonization of the present NT documents.

8. 'Sogenannten' was not translated in Morgan's translation of the title of Wrede's essay, the force being carried by the inverted commas around the phrase 'New Testament theology'.

9. See the discussion in Morgan and Barton (1988).

10. Räisänen (2000, p. 182), calls it 'self-evident' to do so.

11. For various reasons, such an approach has always been stronger in Germany than in an English-speaking context, partly no doubt because of the strong tradition in German universities of theological faculties being confessionally aligned, unlike the situation in many UK or US universities.

12. The model sometimes associated with the name of K. Stendahl, though whether this is fair to Stendahl is uncertain. Cf. Stendahl's famous distinction between what a text 'meant' and what it 'means'. However, for Stendahl himself this distinction was not to enable exegetes or others to evade hermeneutical questions – it was rather to promote such questions positively, but by allowing the text to have the freedom to speak *to* Christians in the present. See Räisänen 2000, pp. 90–3.

13. For what is now a classic work on the topic in British, and English-speaking, scholarship, see Dunn 1977. Different scholars will inevitably vary in the degree of diversity they acknowledge in the NT, and the extent to which they can claim that there is unity. But few would doubt that any claim to find such a unity has to be established and argued: it can no longer be assumed as axiomatic.

14. For a recent attempt to claim that the 'variety' of NT witnesses has been overplayed and that there is an underlying single centre to the NT, see Balla 1997. However, the attempt is at times very forced: see the brief, but penetrating, critical comments in Räisänen 2000, p. 118. Not dissimilar in one way is Perrin 1984, who claims that the NT writers, apart from Jesus, offer one general viewpoint (on apocalyptic and kingdom language) whereas Jesus offers another, and it is for this reason that Jesus does not belong within a 'New Testament theology'. But whether even the rest of the New Testament can be so easily seen as unified remains doubtful.

15. Hence, despite Bultmann's claim that 'NT theology' starts with the preaching of the early church (cf. above), in fact the preaching of the earliest pre-Pauline churches seems for Bultmann to be as much a 'presupposition' of a 'NT theology' as the teaching of the pre-Easter Jesus! See Räisänen 2000, p. 50.

16. Cf. e.g. Bultmann's famous dismissal of the thought of Revelation as 'a weakly Christianised form of Judaism'.

17. And I am certainly not assuming that there is a single underlying theology in the New Testament.

18. See above on the theology of D.F. Strauss. The general point is made repeatedly by Morgan in his writings.

19. See, for example, Roberts 1976, esp. ch. 3 'The Kerygma'; cf. too Dahl 1974, p. 121: 'I must raise the question whether or not Jesus Christ remains a person in Bultmann's existential interpretation. Is there not a danger that the eschatological event designated by the name Jesus Christ evaporates to a mere occurrence?' Cf. too Morgan 1987, p. 204.
20. This is the main thrust, as far as I can see, in Morgan's 1987 essay.
21. Insofar as *part* of the appeal here might be to the authentic *teaching* of the historical Jesus, my argument would be different from that of Käsemann (1973) who also, at one level at least, makes (formal) appeal to the historical Jesus to act as a possible criterion to assess (theologically) competing claims within the New Testament. However, when it comes to any substance, Käsemann refers only in the most general terms to 'the cross' as providing the necessary criterion, and it is never made clear in his essay (admittedly and self-confessedly only setting out the broad parameters of a possible approach to a 'New Testament theology') how this would work in practice.
22. If the parable does go back to Jesus, the likelihood is that the recipients of the 'charitable' action described in the parable, 'the least of these my brothers and sisters', are meant to be the ('Christian') followers of Jesus, i.e. the parable is about giving aid to Christian missionaries, not to all and sundry. See the commentaries for details.
23. And even if the claims of the next half verse in John 14:6b – 'no one comes to the Father except by me' – would be one which Christians today, acutely aware of the existence of non-Christian faith traditions, might be far more uncomfortable with theologically.
24. As indeed they become in John!
25. Especially for traditional Anglican theology which has traditionally regarded the continuity between Jesus' views about himself and later Christians' claims about him as theologically vital: see Morgan 1980b.

References

Balla, P., *Challenges to New Testament Theology. An Attempt to Justify the Enterprise* (Tübingen: Mohr Siebeck, 1997).

Barrett, C.K., *Jesus and the Gospel Tradition* (London: SPCK, 1975).

Bultmann, R., *Theology of the New Testament 1* (London: SCM Press, 1952).

Bultmann, R., 'The problem of a theological exegesis of the New Testament', in J.M. Robinson (ed.), *The Beginnings of Dialectical Theology* (Virginia: John Knox Press, 1968), pp. 236–56.

Dahl, N.A., 'Rudolf Bultmann's theology of the New Testament', in N.A. Dahl, *The Crucified Messiah and Other Essays* (Minneapolis: Augsburg, 1974), pp. 90–128.

Dunn, J.D.G., *Unity and Diversity in the New Testament* (London: SCM Press, 1977).

Jeremias, J., *New Testament Theology. Volume 1. The Proclamation of Jesus* (London: SCM, 1971).

Johnson, L.T., *The Real Jesus* (San Francisco: Harper Collins, 1996).

Kähler, M., *The So-called Historical Jesus and the Historic, Biblical Christ* (Philadelphia: Fortress, 1964; German original 1892).

Käsemann, E., 'New Testament questions of today', *New Testament Questions of Today* (London: SCM, 1969), pp. 1-22.

Käsemann, E., 'The problem of a New Testament theology', *NTS* 19 (1973) 235-45.

Meeks, W.A., 'Asking back to Jesus' identity', in M.C. de Boer (ed.), *From Jesus to John. Essays on Jesus and Testament Christology in Honour of Marinus de Jonge* (Sheffield: Sheffield Academic Press, 1993), pp. 38-50.

Morgan, Robert, 'The nature of New Testament theology', in Robert Morgan (ed.), *The Nature of New Testament Theology* (London: SCM Press, 1973), pp. 1-67.

Morgan, Robert, 'A Straussian question to "New Testament theology"', *NTS* 23 (1977), 243-65.

Morgan, Robert, 'Günther Bornkamm in England', in D. Lührmann and G. Strecker (eds), *Kirche. Festschrift für Günther Bornkann zum 75. Geburtstag* (Tübingen: Mohr Siebeck, 1980a), pp. 491-506.

Morgan, Robert, '*Non Angli sed Angeli*: some Anglican reactions to German Gospel criticism', in S.W. Sykes and D. Holmes (eds), *New Studies in Theology* (London: Duckworth, 1980b), p. 1-30.

Morgan, Robert, 'The historical Jesus and the theology of the New Testament', in L.D. Hurst and N.T. Wright (eds), *Studies in Christology in Memory of G. B. Caird* (Oxford: Oxford University Press, 1987), pp. 187-206.

Morgan, Robert and Barton, John, *Biblical Interpretation* (Oxford: Oxford University Press, 1988).

Perrin, N., 'Jesus and the Theology of the New Testament', *JR* 64 (1984), 413-31.

Räisänen, H., *Beyond New Testament Theology* (London: SCM, 2000).

Roberts, R.C., *Rudolf Bultmann's Theology: A Critical Introduction* (London: SPCK, 1976).

Wrede, W., 'The task and nature of "New Testament theology"', in Robert Morgan (ed.), *The Nature of New Testament Theology* (London: SCM Press, 1973), pp. 69-116 (German original 1897).

Chapter 15

The Gospel of John and New Testament Theology

Francis Watson, Aberdeen

The Gospel of John is a product of Christian faith. Of course, that is true of all the New Testament writings. Yet the Fourth Gospel is unique in its radical, unremitting focus on the figure of Jesus himself, on his claim to embody in his person and word the life-giving divine gift to the world. Other New Testament texts – whether Gospels or epistles – speak of Jesus only within some kind of context: his Galilean milieu, or Jewish scripture and tradition, or some local difficulty in the churches of Greece or Asia Minor. In the Fourth Gospel, it is as if Jesus generates his own context. Without him it would barely exist.

Take for example the Lukan and the Johannine introductions to the ministry of John the Baptist. Luke carefully dates John's ministry, which began 'in the fifteenth year of the reign of Tiberius Caesar', and provides a range of further information about Pontius Pilate and Herod Antipas, Philip and Lysanias, Annas and Caiaphas. It was within the political and religious context represented by these figures that 'the word of God came to John the son of Zechariah in the desert . . .' (Luke 3:1-2). John's ministry is accorded a degree of autonomy in relation to Jesus, and itself provides the context for the beginning of Jesus' ministry (3:1-22). As he comes to John for baptism, Jesus enters the sphere of John's activity, which is itself set within the realm presided over by the third of the Caesars. As in the case of the genealogy that follows (3:21-38), Jesus is defined in relation to a set of prior coordinates.

In the prologue to the Fourth Gospel, the Baptist is introduced quite differently, as 'a man sent from God whose name was John' (John 1:6). John is not identified by reference to his parentage (as 'John son of

Zechariah') or his own independent activity (as 'John the Baptist') but only in his relation to Jesus: 'He came for testimony, to bear witness to the light . . .' (1:7). Indeed, at this point it is not even clear that 'John' should be identified with John the Baptist: the attribution of this gospel to the Apostle John may reflect an understandable misunderstanding of this passage.[1] Naturally, there is no reference here to the fifteenth year of Tiberius Caesar, or even to the Judean wilderness. In its initial presentation (1:6–8, 15), the testimony of John lacks a time and a place. Even in the more concrete narrative that follows (1:19–37), John's ministry consists exclusively in the testimony to Jesus that leads his own disciples to turn their backs on him in order to follow the one to whom John points: 'Behold, the Lamb of God . . .' (1:29, 36). From the very outset it is the case that 'he must increase but I must decrease' (3:30). And that is also the case throughout the gospel, with everything and everyone. When Jesus cleanses the temple, the 'temple' he subsequently speaks of is that of his own body (2:19–22). Nicodemus simply disappears as the dialogue he initiated turns into a monologue (3:1–21). The whole of reality is redefined by its positive or negative relation to Jesus, losing its autonomous existence in the process.

Does it lose its life in order to receive it back again as eternal life (cf. 12:25)? Or is this relatively late image of Jesus the product of a Christian faith marked by fantasy and fanaticism?

In spite of the high esteem in which it has traditionally been held, the Fourth Gospel has experienced mixed fortunes at the hands of recent critical scholarship. Regarded as central to the New Testament witness throughout the patristic period, and by protestant theologians such as Luther, Schleiermacher and Bultmann, this Gospel has more recently been subjected to a degree of critical suspicion. In part, this has been occasioned by the perceived anti-Jewish bias that comes to expression especially in chapters 5–10, now widely understood as reflecting the situation of the evangelist's community.[2] A broader and perhaps related issue is the sense of unreality often thought to pervade this Gospel. A symptom of this may be seen in its remarkably free handling of the historical realities of Jesus' life. In spite of attempts to argue to the contrary, it is clear that in the Fourth Gospel history is drastically subordinated to dogma. In itself, that need not be a problem – unless one is ideologically committed to a programme of drastically subordinating dogma to history. The problem is rather the air of unreality that, for many contemporary readers, pervades the Johannine image of Jesus. Although the evangelist holds that 'the Word became flesh', he seems chiefly interested not in the flesh *per se* but in the divine glory which shines through it and to which it is transparent (cf. John 1:14). Can a humanity transparent to deity be a real humanity? To modern readers convinced of the full reality of their own embodied, social and material existence, it is hard to answer that question in the affirmative. And so there arises the suspicion that the Fourth Gospel is 'docetic' in tendency. It is not that the humanity of Jesus is formally denied here; on the contrary, it is everywhere presupposed. Yet, arguably, this humanity is for the evangelist a mere vehicle through which the glory of the divine Son is revealed. The point is forcefully made by Ernst Käsemann (1968, p. 9):

> In what sense is he flesh, who walks on the water and through closed doors, who cannot be captured by his enemies, who at the well of Samaria is tired and desires a drink yet has no need of drink and has food different from that which his disciples seek? He cannot be deceived by men, because he knows their innermost thoughts even before they speak. He debates with them from the vantage point of the infinite difference between heaven and earth. He has need neither of the witness of Moses nor of the Baptist. He dissociates himself from the Jews, as if they were not his own people, and he meets his mother as the one who is her Lord. He permits Lazarus to lie in the grave for four days in order that the miracle of his resurrection may be more impressive. And in the end the Johannine Christ goes victoriously to his death of his own accord.

In sum, the evangelist's answer to the Christological question takes the form of 'a naïve docetism' (Käsemann 1968, p. 26). If Käsemann is right, this text will have to be ejected from its normal position somewhere near the centre of the New Testament witness, and banished to the margins.

'A naïve docetism': this celebrated or notorious phrase has generated an extensive discussion about whether and in what sense this Gospel might be described as 'docetic' (see Ashton 1991, pp. 71–4). Here, I shall focus instead on the term 'naïve'. Does the Fourth Gospel present us with a fundamentally naïve 'theology of glory' in which Jesus' divine status is manifested in and demonstrated by marvellous 'signs', accredited by trustworthy eyewitness testimony?[3] If we resist such a claim, finding it to be theologically objectionable, Käsemann might reply that a willingness to acknowledge problematic features of the New Testament texts is an indispensable mark of any genuinely critical scholarship.[4] But the mere fact that Käsemann's interpretation of John is theologically unappealing does not in itself make it plausible – as though by analogy with the 'harder reading' of textual criticism, whose awkwardness is said to reflect its greater fidelity to the original text. To suppose that a theologically negative reading is necessarily superior to a theologically positive one – Bultmann's, for example – is to be deceived by a notably disingenuous piece of scholarly rhetoric.[5] In the following discussion, we shall subject Käsemann's claim to a kind of neo-Bultmannian critique.[6]

The perception that the Gospel of John is a fundamentally naïve text stems in part from the peculiar characteristics of the Johannine miracle stories. Modern critics are understandably unsettled by legends in which water is instantly transformed into wine (wine of the very highest quality) or in which an already decomposing corpse is summoned from its place of rest and restored to its former life. The 'plausibility structure' of modernity makes it natural to regard these tales as naïve, insofar as they claim to inform and persuade us about actual empirical occurrences. This conclusion may conceivably be wrong; there may perhaps be serious philosophical or theological reasons for giving credence to such stories, and for questioning the modern dogma that deity does not disclose itself to the world by such means.[7] For better or worse, however, critical scholarship has sought to interpret these stories in ways that do not assume their empirical veracity. And some commentators on the Fourth Gospel – notably Bultmann – have argued that the evangelist himself adopted a critical attitude towards the stories he inherited from earlier tradition. The evangelist deploys the sometimes naïve traditions at his disposal for their symbolic value and not for the sake of their empirical veracity. Even if he assumes empirical veracity, his real interest in this material lies elsewhere. The problematic naïveté of the miracle stories is displaced from the final form of the text to its prehistory – as belonging to a 'signs source', according to Bultmann and others. Can this hypothesis, or something like it, mitigate the problem that this material poses for critical readers?

The self-critical potential of the Johannine text is dramatized within the text itself. Following Thomas' confession of Jesus as 'my Lord and my God', Jesus replies:'Have you believed because you have seen me? Blessed are those who have not seen and yet believe' (John 20:28–9). The risen Jesus appears to his disciples precisely so that they may see and believe: seeing (and touching), they are not to be unbelieving but believing (cf. v. 27). There is no other rationale for these appearances than to elicit faith. And yet Jesus' words to Thomas imply a criticism of a faith based on sight. There is no suggestion that later believers who do not see are dependent on a report of what was once seen by apostolic eyewitnesses. On the contrary, the blessing Jesus pronounces is nothing less than a critique of the notion of the apostolic eyewitness, most prominent in Luke-Acts but also tacitly present in the Johannine text itself. Thomas is explicitly excluded from Jesus' blessing. He now possesses one of the two qualifications for this blessing, which is believing, but not the other, which is not-having-seen.[8]

Admittedly, Jesus' blessing could be interpreted differently. At the beginning of this story, Thomas is introduced as disbelieving the reports of his fellow disciples (20:24–5), and it is possible that he here represents the situation of later believers who must depend on a report of what others have seen. Jesus' appearance to Thomas would then be an object lesson in how *not* to respond to the apostolic kerygma. Jesus does appear, but he should not have had to; the bare word of Thomas's fellow disciples should have been enough. Thomas is singled out for criticism not as a member of a group whose belief derives from sight, but as representing the sceptical, resisting reader of a text in which the apostolic testimony is authoritatively enshrined. In contrast, those who have not seen and yet believe are the ideal readers of this Gospel, addressed as such in the very next sentence (20:30–1). On this interpretation, Jesus' blessing would imply no criticism of an apostolic faith based on sight, which would be foundational for the faith of those who have not themselves seen.[9]

Plausible though this may seem, it is not a natural interpretation of a blessing that contrasts faith based on sight with faith that lacks sight. It is striking that the verb 'believe' and the adjectives 'believing' and 'unbelieving' occur here in absolute form, without reference to the disciples' message as the occasion of faith or unfaith:

> And he said to them: Unless I see in his hands the mark of the nails and place my finger in the mark of the nails and place my hand in his side, I will not believe. (20:25)

> And he said to Thomas: Put your finger here and see my hands, and put out your hand and place it in my side; and do not be disbelieving but believing. (20:27)

> And Jesus said to him: Because you have seen do you believe? Blessed are those who do not see and yet believe. (20:29)

What Thomas initially disbelieves and subsequently believes is Jesus' resurrection from the dead, but at no point is he criticized for his attitude towards the other disciples' testimony. Jesus does *not* say to him: 'Why did you not believe what was told you by your brethren? Blessed are those who hear and believe!' Instead, Jesus' blessing implies a criticism not just of Thomas but of the very concept of the apostolic eyewitness, who believes on the basis of what is seen.[10]

In the verses that follow, which may have concluded an earlier version of this Gospel, it is said that Jesus performed his signs 'in the presence of the disciples', and that certain of these signs have been narrated 'so that you may believe that Jesus is the Christ, the Son of God . . .' (John 20:30–1). The notion of the apostolic eyewitness is here ostensibly reaffirmed: for belief on the basis of the signs presupposes that the Johannine narration of the signs is itself credible and trustworthy, which it can only be if it derives from the reports of eyewitnesses. That is why it is emphasized that Jesus' signs took place 'in the presence of the disciples'. This motif of the apostolic eyewitness is clearer still in chapter 21, at the conclusion of which the anonymous 'disciple whom Jesus loved' is suddenly identified as the author of the entire Gospel: 'This is the disciple who is bearing witness to these things, and who has written these things – and we know that his testimony is true!' (21:24). Like Thomas, it is earlier said of this disciple that 'he saw and believed' – on the evidence of the empty tomb, however, rather than an appearance (20:8). The credibility of the Johannine signs is here dependent on the apostolic eyewitness, whose own credibility is itself guaranteed by his peculiarly intimate relation to Jesus: the 'disciple whom Jesus loved' is, we are reminded, the one who 'reclined on his breast at the supper and said, 'Lord, who is it who is to betray you?"' (21:20; cf. 13:23–5). The testimony of *this* disciple is, surely, supremely credible and trustworthy. In accepting it as such, the reader aligns him- or herself with the community that confesses, 'We know that his testimony is true' (21:24; cf. 19:35). In its present form, the Fourth Gospel concludes with the strongest affirmation of eyewitness testimony in the whole New Testament. It is, then, all the more striking that, in what may have been an earlier conclusion, those who see and believe are explicitly excluded from a blessing on those who do not see and yet believe. In chapter 20, the blessing is Jesus' final word to his disciples. In chapter 21, Jesus' last word relates to the beloved disciple and leads directly into the affirmation of his authorship of this Gospel. The two conclusions could hardly be more different. In one, the reader's faith is guaranteed by trustworthy eyewitness testimony; in the other, the reader's faith is unsupported by any such guarantee.

In the light of this disjunction, we should look again at the concluding statements that immediately follow the blessing of those who have not seen. By analogy with the Gospel of Mark, we may describe this passage (John 20:30-1) as the Shorter Ending of the Gospel of John, and chapter 21 as the Longer Ending.[11] According to the Shorter Ending,

> Many other signs did Jesus perform before his disciples, which are not written in this book. But these are written so that you may believe that Jesus is the Christ, the Son of God, and that believing you may have life in his name. (20:30-1)

The term 'sign' has previously been used in the singular in connection with the miracle at Cana (2:11), the healing of the royal official's son

(4:54), the multiplication of the loaves and fish (6:14), and the raising of Lazarus (12:18); there is also a reference to 'signs' in the plural in connection with the man born blind (9:16). Elsewhere, the narrator speaks of Jesus as performing a large number of 'signs' which he does not narrate (2:23; 6:2; 7:31; 11:47; 12:37). The term is used throughout as in 20:30-1: certain individual 'signs' are selected for narration out of a much larger number that are referred to but not narrated. This conclusion is entirely in keeping with the summary that concludes the 'Book of Signs':

> Although he had performed so many signs before them, they did not believe in him, so that the word of Isaiah the prophet might be fulfilled, when he said: 'Lord, who has believed our report, and to whom has the arm of the Lord been revealed?' Therefore they were unable to believe, as Isaiah again says: 'He has blinded their eyes and hardened their heart . . .' (12:37-40)

This is simply the converse of the Shorter Ending (20:30-1). Jesus' 'signs' should logically lead to faith among eyewitnesses and readers alike; where this does not take place, an explanation may be found in the mysterious divine dispensation announced through the prophet. The reader, then, is to believe that Jesus is the Christ, the Son of God, on the basis of the remarkable things that Jesus did: turning water into wine, multiplying loaves and fish, raising Lazarus from the dead. It is not Jesus' identity as Son of God that makes the narrated sign credible, as in modern apologetics; on the contrary, it is the narrated sign that makes Jesus' identity as Son of God credible. Can the one who turned water into wine be a mere man? Surely he can only be the divine Son of God? That is the argument that the Shorter Ending apparently ascribes to the entire Gospel – and, from our standpoint, it is a thoroughly naïve argument, requiring a naïve and credulous reader.

What is striking, however, is that the Shorter Ending is utterly unsuitable as a summary of the Fourth Gospel as we now have it. Its reference to the writing of selected 'signs' implies that these are the primary if not the exclusive content of the text that is now drawing to a close. Yet, in the present form of this Gospel, that is simply not the case. If the term 'sign' is defined by events such as the miracle at Cana, it is difficult to see the Passion and Easter narratives of chapters 18-20 as accounts of 'signs'. Still less is this term applicable to the Farewell Discourses of John 13-17, the chapters that form the theological heart of this Gospel. Even in chapters 1-12, far more space is devoted to dialogue between Jesus and others – individuals, authorities, crowds – than to the 'signs' *per se*. Taken at face value, the Shorter Ending seems a remarkably thin and inadequate summary of the contents and purpose of this Gospel. Perhaps it originally formed the conclusion of a 'signs source', an earlier and much briefer text which has been incorporated, in part or as a whole, into the present more extensive text? While this seems a plausible 'diachronic' solution to the problem, it is still appropriate to ask how the Shorter Ending can be re-read within its present literary context. Where a piece of text is transplanted from one context into another, it will retain its connections to its original context but will also acquire a secondary set of connections to the new context. Its meaning will now occur, as it were, on two levels. It is the second-level significance of the Shorter Ending that we must now try to uncover.[12]

According to the Shorter Ending, the text that it summarizes and concludes consists of written signs whose role is to elicit faith. If the term 'sign' is to cover the entire content of the Fourth Gospel, however, its semantic range will have to be greatly extended. It will have to cover not only 'miracles' but also narrations of non-miraculous events such as the cleansing of the temple, the triumphal entry and the footwashing, dialogues with enquirers, opponents or disciples, and the connected account of the passion and the resurrection appearances. On this view, Jesus does not cease to perform signs after the raising of Lazarus: 'signs' of who he is occur at every point in the narrative, no less in his speech than in his actions. 'Signs' must comprehend everything in this Gospel that seeks to elicit the faith that 'Jesus is the Christ, the Son of God' – and that of course encompasses the entire Gospel, without remainder. Furthermore, these signs are said to be *written*: 'These [signs] are written [in this book], so that you may believe . . .' Faith is elicited by the *text*, and not by the manifold actions of Jesus *per se*, most of which are allowed to fade into oblivion. It is only in their textual embodiment that Jesus' deeds and words manifest his true identity as the source of eternal life. In its present context, the Shorter Ending no longer postulates a credulous reader, moved to confess Jesus' divine Sonship by sheer astonishment at the power that can transform water into wine. It envisages a reader for whom the Gospel itself has become 'sign', pointing away from itself to its transcendent origin, the truth of which it embodies and discloses. In the Johannine lexicon, 'sign' and 'testimony' are ultimately synonymous.

The concluding sentence of the Longer Ending has been partially modelled on the Shorter Ending, and serves to clarify further its two-level sense:

Many other signs did Jesus perform [*polla . . . alla sēmeia epoiēsen ho Iēsous*], before his disciples, which are not written in this book. But these

are written so that you may believed that Jesus is the Christ, the Son of
God, and that believing you may have life in his name. (20:30-1)

This is the disciple who is testifying about these things and who has
written them, and we know that his testimony is true. But there are many
other things that Jesus did [*alla polla ha epoiēsen ho Iēsous*], which, if
they were to be written one by one, I do not suppose that the world could
contain the books that would be written. (21:24-5)

Both conclusions focus on the distinction between what has been written
and what remains unwritten, yet develop this distinction in strikingly
different ways. The Shorter Ending emphasizes the sufficiency of what
has been written, and implies the practical irrelevance of what has been
omitted. In contrast, the Longer Ending affirms the eyewitness credentials
of the fictive author, but also asserts the insufficiency of what has been
written. We are presumably meant to attribute the first person singular
statement ('I do not suppose . . .') to the beloved disciple. In spite of the
intrusion of a plurality in the previous sentence ('we know that his testimony is true'), a first person singular utterance from anyone other than
the beloved disciple would be out of place in this context. In a statement
of remarkable naïveté, it is tacitly assumed that the unwritten deeds of
Jesus are indeed writable, in the sense that they are known and have not
faded into oblivion; the problem is just that infinite time and space would
be necessary to record them in full. The unwritten deeds of Jesus are
writable in principle but unwritable in practice. They are writable in
principle in that they are known - but to whom? The answer can only
be that they are known to the beloved disciple, who still recalls the infinite number of deeds that he can never write.[13]

The Shorter Ending points us back to the text we actually possess; the
Longer Ending points us away from that text to the infinite number of
Jesus' unwritten deeds, and also hints at its author's ability to testify to
them. In the one case, Jesus is fully embodied in the text; in the other,
he manifests himself through the text but far transcends any realistic
possibility of textual embodiment. If a 'naïve docetism' is to be found
anywhere in the Fourth Gospel, it is in this final verse, where earlier references to Jesus' 'many signs' (11:47; cf. 7:31; 12:37) are extended to infinity.
In the Shorter Ending, the only signs that matter are the ones that constitute the text itself.[14]

It is true that the Shorter Ending, like the Longer one, assumes the
factuality of the events that the Gospel narrates. The text is not self-
contained and autonomous, it is grounded in the life, deeds and words
of Jesus. Yet, in its present context, the relationship between the text
and the reality to which it testifies has become opaque. Immediately

preceding the concluding references to the unwritten deeds are two sharply contrasting statements:

Jesus says to him, 'Because you saw me have you believed? Blessed are those who do not see and yet believe!' (20:29)

This is the disciple who is testifying about these things and who has written them, and we know that his testimony is true. (21:24)

Eyewitness testimony is subverted in the one case and reaffirmed in the other. In the Longer Ending, eyewitness testimony gives direct access to the historical realities of Jesus' life. In the Shorter Ending, a direct access grounded in sight is marginalized. The blessing is addressed not to those who believe on the basis of what others have seen, but to those whose faith is entirely ungrounded in sight: otherwise the disparagement of those who believed on the basis of what they saw would be inexplicable. Here, the signs that are written in this book, and that constitute the book as a whole, have nothing to do with authentic first-hand recollections of eyewitnesses. We may conjecture that, in the Shorter Ending, the role of the eyewitness is taken over by the Paraclete, who is the Spirit of truth and who leads into all truth. From this perspective, it is the Spirit and not the eyewitness who guarantees the fundamental truth of the Johannine testimony to Jesus.[15]

This contrast between the two endings only comes to light if we accept the distinction *within* the Shorter Ending between the *prima facie* sense it derives from its original context and the secondary sense it acquires from its new context in the final form of the Gospel. The *prima facie* sense is broadly compatible with the concept of eyewitness testimony developed in the Longer Ending. Jesus, we are told, performed his 'signs' or miracles 'in the presence of the disciples' (20:30). Although it is not claimed that one of these disciples is the author of 'this book', a connection between the book and the disciples' testimony is probably implied. In its present context, however, the meaning of these statements shifts. The term 'signs' is extended to cover the entire contents of the Fourth Gospel; eyewitness testimony is marginalized as those who have not seen are blessed at the expense of those who have seen; and the relation between text and truth is ensured instead by the Paraclete. There are, in other words, two versions of the Shorter Ending, an earlier and a later, and it is the second that is so sharply at odds with the Longer Ending. In its final form, then, the text ends not once but twice, and the first ending itself preserves the memory of an earlier text which has now been incorporated into a new context. The two endings both refer explicitly to the text they conclude, and in doing so *they imply fundamentally different perspectives on the Fourth Gospel as a whole.*

The Longer Ending combines a naïve delight in the wonder of Jesus' miracles with an insistence on the veracity of the beloved disciple's testimony, enshrined as it is in the Gospel as a whole. In its own way, it is concerned to assert *historicity*: for a Gospel written by the disciple whom Jesus loved, who lay at his breast at the Last Supper (21:20), will surely be supremely trustworthy and truthful in its account of Jesus' words and deeds. If the Gospel is read from this perspective, then the reader's experience will be one of astonishment at the extraordinary things that Jesus was able to accomplish. This astonishment is articulated within the text by the man born blind, who points out that 'never since the world began has it been heard that anyone opened the eyes of a man born blind' (9:32). That is to be the reaction of the reader (the naïve reader) at every point. Never since the world began has it been heard that anyone converted water into wine, or raised up one man paralyzed for 38 years and another man dead and buried for four days! Amazed and delighted by such occurrences, this reader will also enjoy the Johannine depiction of the authorities' vain attempts to silence the testimony of miracles whose actuality they cannot deny (cf. 9:13-34; 11:45-7; 12:9-11). The naïve reader is totally identified with the protagonist of the narrative; and underlying this identification is the assumption that this narrative gives direct access to prior historical reality, guaranteed as this is by the supremely authoritative eyewitness who is its author.

The Shorter Ending requires a theologically more sophisticated reader, capable of grasping that the faith that leads to eternal life is essentially independent of sight, and that truth is discerned through the ongoing ministry of the Paraclete. This reader will be impressed not by the factuality of the miracle stories but by the symbolic interpretations that often accompany them and that transform them into *parables* of the saving activity of the incarnate Word (cf. 6:35; 8:12; 9:5; 11:25). Yet this reader will find 'signs' testifying to this saving activity at every point in the text, and will not single out the miracle stories for special attention. Thus, Jesus' crucifixion will be understood as the indispensable 'sign' in which his exaltation and glorification is disclosed and enacted (cf. 3:14; 8:28; 12:23, 32-4). Jesus' words will be understood as 'signs' of the eternal life they claim to impart (cf. 5:24, 25; 6:68; 17:1-8). Here, the sign is inherent not in a prior historical occurrence but in the text itself.[16]

These two readings of the Fourth Gospel arise out of the alternative endings. If this dual perspective can be traced throughout the Gospel, that would explain how the same text can both be criticized for its 'naïve docetism' (Käsemann), and regarded as the most profound meditation on the dynamics of the Christian revelation in all early Christian literature (Bultmann). It would explain 'the shift from the elegance and finesse of, say, the farewell discourses to the fairy-tale atmosphere of the resurrection stories' – a shift which, as John Ashton (1991, p. 511) has memorably put it, 'is like finding Hans Christian Andersen hand in hand with Søren Kierkegaard'. Like other sacred texts, the Fourth Gospel is engaged in an ongoing dialogue with itself about its own sense and significance; it does not represent an enforced harmony in which every individual element has been subordinated to the control of a single dominating logic. Here, then, the interpreter is caught up into a dynamic already present within the text itself.

All this is in keeping with the classical Christian assumption that this Gospel represents 'the hermeneutical key to the New Testament', since here above all, and with extraordinary concentration and clarity, Jesus is presented as 'the saving revelation of God' (Morgan 1994, p. 19). Yet, *pace* Bultmann, the New Testament canon preserves not one Gospel but four. This fourfold canonical Gospel is still operative within the Christian community, and its members cannot as it were take up residence within a single Gospel while overlooking or minimizing the others. The gospel itself is not identical with any one of its canonical embodiments, and each of these needs the corrective of the others. As Robert Morgan (1994, p. 23) has written:

> Heirs of second-century catholicism can hardly approve of John's apparent willingness to dispense with the tradition of Jesus' teaching almost entirely. Yet the success of his astonishing strategy of replacing this with disclosure making clear the meaning of Jesus as the decisive revelation of God, and the fascination and power of its modern retrieval by Bultmann, suggest he was in some respects right. On the other hand, second-century Gnosticism alerted the church to the dangerous implication of John's experiment. Had the others not also been included in the canon it might have proved disastrous.

True and important though this is, it may be that there is today a particular need to hear again the gospel in its distinctively Johannine form – according to which Jesus embodies and enacts a definitive divine incursion into the world that occurs 'vertically from above'.

Notes

1. The oldest extant attribution of the Fourth Gospel to John is probably to be found in Irenaeus's statement that 'John the disciple of the Lord, who also had leaned upon his breast, did himself publish a Gospel during his

residence in Asia' (*Against Heresies*, 3.1.1). This statement is apparently dependent on: (1) John 21:20-4; (2) Papias's reference to 'Aristion and the Elder John' as 'disciples of the Lord' who survived into his own lifetime (Eusebius, *Church History*, 3.39.4); (3) the association between 'John' and Asia Minor in Revelation 1-3. Eusebius is probably right to think that Papias's 'Elder John' is the author of Revelation – in which case the subsequent belief that this figure also wrote the Fourth Gospel requires an explanation, which John 1:6-8 may provide.

2. But see Adele Reinhartz's critique of this view in Reinhartz (1998).

3. Käsemann's references to the Johannine 'christology of glory' (1968, p. 26) allude to Luther's attack on the 'theology of glory' in the Heidelberg disputation of 1518 (thesis 21).

4. Compare ibid., p. 8.

5. On this kind of rhetoric in Käsemann, see Matlock 1996, pp. 237-42.

6. Rudolf Bultmann's classic account of Johannine theology is found primarily in Bultmann (1971) and in Bultmann (1955, pp. 3-92). Bultmann is significant for my present argument because of his emphasis on the diversity of theological voices within the text of the Fourth Gospel, and his insistence that the Gospel itself licenses a symbolic interpretation of the 'signs'. In my view, Käsemann's 'naïve docetism' hypothesis is ultimately reductionist. The anti-Bultmannian tendency of Käsemann's reading of John is most explicit in 'New Testament questions of today' and 'The structure and purpose of the Prologue to John's Gospel', in Käsemann (1969, pp. 1-22, 138-67).

7. For a sophisticated (though unconvincing) critique of scholarly 'anti-supernaturalism', see Evans (1996).

8. On this Bultmann writes: 'Thomas's doubt is representative of the common attitude of those who cannot believe without seeing miracles (4.48). As the miracle is a concession to human weakness, so the appearance of the Risen Jesus is a concession to the weakness of the disciples. Fundamentally they ought not to need it! . . . [I]f this critical saying of Jesus forms the conclusion of the Easter narratives, the hearer or reader is warned not to take them to be more than they can be: neither as narrations of events that he himself could wish or hope to experience, nor as a substitute for such experiences of his own, as if the experiences of others could as it were guarantee for him the reality of the resurrection of Jesus; rather they are to be understood as proclaimed word, in which the narrated events have become symbolic pictures for the fellowship which the Lord, who has ascended to the Father, holds with his own' (1971, p. 696).

9. This interpretative possibility is identified by Bultmann, who asks: 'Does the shameful element for Thomas lie in the fact that he did not have faith when the others informed him, "We have seen the Lord"? Does the story teach that faith in the Risen Lord is demanded on the basis of the utterance of the eye-witnesses?' (1971, p. 695). Bultmann rejects this view on the grounds that 'the reproach that falls on Thomas appl[ies] to all the other disciples as well' (p. 696).

10. In these two competing interpretations, it is assumed that Jesus' words imply a rebuke. This has, however, been denied by some commentators (e.g. Bernard 1928, p. 684; Brown 1966, p. 1049).

11. The 'Longer' and the 'Shorter' endings of Mark are the two main attempts to provide a more adequate conclusion to this Gospel than the one provided by the evangelist himself (16:1-8). For discussion, see Metzger (1975, pp. 122-6). Naturally, the parallel between Mark and John here is not exact.

12. Compare Bultmann, who writes: '[I]f the Evangelist dared to use this ending [i.e. the original ending of the 'signs source'] as the conclusion of his book, it shows not only that the *sēmeion* is of fundamental importance for him, but at the same time - if he can subsume Jesus' activity, as he portrays it, under the concept of *sēmeion* - that this concept is more complex than that of the naïve miracle story. Rather it is clear . . . that the concepts *sēmeia* and *rēmata* (*logoi*) both qualify each other: *sēmeion* is not a mere demonstration, but a spoken directive, a symbol; *rēma* is not teaching in the sense of the communication of a set of ideas, but is the occurrence of the Word, the event of the address' (1971, pp. 113-14). To this assimilation of 'sign' to 'word' I would add that the Johannine sign occurs in and through the text, and has no independent reality apart from to the text.

13. As Richard Bauckham (1993) has persuasively argued, the beloved disciple is portrayed in the Fourth Gospel as the 'ideal author' of this text, not as an idealized disciple. Bauckham assumes that the awkward shifts of person in 21:24-5 ('This is the disciple . . . we know . . . I do not suppose . . .') indicate the hand of a later editor. But if the attribution to the beloved disciple is pseudonymous, it is possible to understand this fictive figure as the speaker in v. 24a (cf. 19:35) and perhaps (again in the light of 19:35) even in v.24b. If the beloved disciple is supposed to be the author, then *ex hypothesi* he is in the habit of referring to himself in third person discourse. Having disclosed his identity in 21:24, he is at liberty to venture a single closing utterance in the first person singular.

14. B. Lindars comments that, in the final verse of John 21, the editor drew on 20:30-1 but 'only succeeded in producing an exaggerated literary conceit, which is not to be taken seriously . . . The result is that the conclusion fails to impress. It was a mistake to tamper with John's own conclusion' (Lindars 1972, p. 642). If 21:25 is the utterance of the fictive beloved disciple, however, that fact is more significant than the literary error of judgement.

15. That seems to be the view of the author of the *Apocryphon of James*, who paraphrases John 20:29 as follows: 'Woe to those who have seen the Son of man; blessed will they be who have not seen the man, and they who have not consorted with him, and they who have not spoken with him, and they who have not listened to anything from him: yours is life!' (*Apoc. Jas.* 3.17-25; translation from Robinson, 1984).

16. The distinction between these two readings is closely related to the distinction between literal-historical and allegorical readings, associated especially with Philo of Alexandria and later applied to the interpretation of the Fourth Gospel by Origen. Philo and Origen are both aware that the relationship

between scriptural narrative and prior historical reality is often tenuous, but argue that the true sense of the narrative is to be found elsewhere, in its testimony to the most fundamental realities of the divine-human relationship (which realities Philo and Origen of course understood differently). They also agree that the literal-historical and the allegorical levels correspond to two different readers - the naïve reader who takes scriptural narrative at face value in spite of its evident implausibilities, and the sophisticated reader capable of grasping the existential truths to which the narrative indirectly bears witness. And they agree that readings on both levels are authorized by the text itself.

References

Ashton, J., *Understanding the Fourth Gospel* (Oxford: Clarendon Press, 1991).
Bauckham, R.J., 'The beloved disciple as ideal author', *JSNT* 49 (1993), 21-44.
Bernard, J.H., *St John* (ICC; Edinburgh: T. & T. Clark, 1928).
Brown, R.E., *The Gospel According to John* vol. II (AB; New York: Doubleday, 1966).
Bultmann, R., *Theology of the New Testament, Volume II* (Eng. tr. London: SCM Press, 1955).
Bultmann, R., *The Gospel of John: A Commentary* (Eng. tr. Oxford: Blackwell, 1971).
Evans, C. Stephen, *The Historical Christ and the Jesus of Faith: The Incarnational Narrative as History* (Oxford: Clarendon Press, 1996).
Käsemann, E., *The Testament of Jesus: A Study of the Gospel of John in the Light of Chapter 17* (Eng. tr. London: SCM Press, 1968).
Käsemann, E., *New Testament Questions of Today* (London: SCM Press, 1969).
Lindars, B., *The Gospel of John* (NCB; London: Marshall, Morgan & Scott, 1972).
Matlock, B., *Unveiling the Apocalyptic Paul: Paul's Interpreters and the Rhetoric of Criticism* (Sheffield: Sheffield Academic Press, 1996).
Metzger, B.M., *A Textual Commentary on the Greek New Testament* (London and New York: United Bible Societies, 1975).
Morgan, Robert, 'Which was the Fourth Gospel? The order of the Gospels and the unity of Scripture', *JSNT* 54 (1994), 3-28.
Reinhartz, Adele, 'The Johannine community and its Jewish neighbors: a reappraisal', in F. Segovia (ed.), *'What is John?' Volume II: Literary and Social Readings of the Fourth Gospel* (Atlanta: Scholars Press, 1998), pp. 111-38.
Robinson, James M. (ed.), *The Nag Hammadi Library* (Leiden: Brill, 1984).

Chapter 16

The Theology of the Cross and the Quest for a Doctrinal Norm

Michael Wolter, Bonn

'Christian theology can find and preserve its identity only if it is conceived as a *theologia crucis*.' This principle of controversial theology is rooted deeply in the theological tradition of German Protestantism. It is therefore perhaps appropriate for a German, and Lutheran, friend and colleague of Bob Morgan to honour him by some remarks on this subject. In addition, this thesis is of immediate importance for the project of producing a New Testament theology which the author of this essay has been discussing with Bob Morgan for several years – especially since the term *theologia crucis* is used in German and British New Testament scholarship with completely different meanings. In what follows, I would hope to contribute to a German–British (or Lutheran–Anglican) theological dialogue, a dialogue in which Bob Morgan himself has been engaged for decades. And since he counts Ernst Käsemann among his most important theological teachers, the choice of this subject seems to be all the more justified.

I

The term *theologia crucis* originates with Martin Luther.[1] It appears for the first time in several writings of the year 1518, in which Luther argues against scholastic theology: for him *theologia crucis* is distinguished by the fact that it speaks '*de deo crucifixo et abscondito*' and teaches that *'poenas, cruces, mortem . . . esse thezaurum omnium preciosissimum et reliquias sacratissimas'* (WA 1,613,24-5). Accordingly it recognizes God, not as in scholastic theology *'in gloria et maiestate'*, but *'in humilitate et ignominia crucis'* (WA 1,362,12-3). Luther's concept of a *theologia crucis* is delineated from the very beginning onwards as an antithesis to a *theologia gloriae* (as he called it) which intends to recognize God from the visible things[2] and requires virtuous actions from the believer to correspond to God. Correspondingly he writes in the twenty-first thesis of his *Heidelberg Disputation*: *'Theologus gloriae dicit malum bonum et bonum malum, Theologus crucis dicit id quod res est'* (WA 1,354,21-2). In the corroboration of this thesis, Luther explains that the *theologus gloriae* misses *'Deum absconditum in passionibus'*, because he prefers *'opera passionibus et gloriam cruci, potentiam infirmitati, sapientiam stulticiae, et universaliter bonum malo'* (WA 1,362,23-5). By this he (i.e. the *theologus gloriae*) unmasks himself as belonging to the 'enemies of the cross of Christ' (Phil 3:18), who hate *'crucem et passiones, Amant vero opera et gloriam illorum, Ac sic bonum crucis dicunt malum et malum operis dicunt bonum'* (WA 1,362,26-8). In opposition to this the *theologus crucis 'dicit id quod res est'* (see above): *'Deum non inveniri nisi in passionibus et cruce, . . . crucem esse bonam et opera mala, quia per crucem destruuntur opera et crucifigitur Adam, qui per opera potius aedificatur'* (WA 1,362,28-31).

This means that, for Martin Luther, the 'theology of the cross' is not a mere part or chapter of a theological concept, but is a distinct kind of theology in itself: it is a theological system of signs, which constitutes the structure of an entire theological universe and thereby determines the significance und meaning of every individual theological statement. Moreover, it is important that Martin Luther coined the term *theologia crucis* for his critical and polemical arguments against scholastic theology, because this very use has guided its reception in German New Testament scholarship, in which the adjectives 'polemisch' ('polemical') and 'kritisch' ('critical') have become the most frequently used ones to describe it.

It was Ernst Käsemann who has introduced the term *theologia crucis* into New Testament scholarship.[3] In his article 'The Saving Significance of the Death of Jesus in Paul' (1971), the first paragraph reads as follows:

> The Reformers were indisputably right when they appealed to Paul for their understanding of evangelical theology as a theology of the cross. But this view is no longer generally recognized today, even in the Protestant churches. Generally speaking, and in the Anglo-Saxon countries especially,

it is considered to be a narrowly denominational interpretation or misinterpretation – an attitude which has an unhappy effect on ecumenical conversations. It must be asserted with the greatest possible emphasis that both historically and theologically Paul has to be understood in the light of the Reformation's insight. Any other perspective at most covers part of this thinking; it does not grasp the heart of it (p. 32).[4]

Further, for Käsemann the theology of the cross is essentially 'polemisch' and 'kritisch'. He extends the frontline of this function in two directions: (a) into the present, by allocating the role of 'the enemies of the cross of Christ' (Phil 3:18), which Luther had assigned to scholastic theology, to 'people of other views' (p. 34) among his Christian contemporaries, e.g. Lutheran orthodoxy and pietism, not to forget the theologians in the 'Anglo-Saxon countries'; and (b) into early Christianity, by claiming that Paul has to be interpreted 'historically and theologically' in terms of Luther's theology.

Käsemann filled out this claim by developing a model of interpretation from Martin Luther's struggle with the Roman church on the one side and with the left wing of the Reformation (the so-called 'enthusiasts') on the other: he called this a 'double attack against nomism and enthusiasm' and transferred it anachronistically to Paul (1968b: p. 184).[5] He identifies the former side of this twofold attack with Paul's struggle against the 'the legalistic piety of Jewish-Christian circles' (p. 38) especially in Galatians. The latter he finds in the controversy with the 'enthusiasm of the Hellenistic church' (p. 38) with which Paul is engaged, especially in 1 Corinthians. For Käsemann the theological centre of the Pauline theology of the cross is that the cross makes evident, '. . . who God really is, and who man is' (p. 40):

> The true God alone is the creator who works from nothing. . . . From the aspect of the question of salvation, true man is always the sinner who is fundamentally unable to help himself, who cannot by his own action bridge the endless distance to God, and who is hence a member of the lost, chaotic, futile world . . . (p. 40)

From this, it follows that Paul's theology of the cross has to be understood as an attack against 'the strong and the devout' (p. 39), because the cross of Christ

> exposes man's illusion that he can transcend himself and effect his own salvation, that he can all by himself maintain his own strength, his own wisdom, his own piety and his own self-praise even towards God (p. 40).

II

In recently published German textbooks on New Testament theology, and on the theology of Paul written by Protestant scholars,[6] Ernst Käsemann's work has left behind unmistakable traces.

Leonhard Goppelt (1976) locates Paul's *theologia crucis* in 1 Cor 1-2 and characterizes it like Käsemann as 'polemizing' against two positions: against a 'judaistic' and against a 'sapiential playing down of Jesus' dying' (p. 419). For him Paul has understood the cross as the 'theological cipher for the dying of Christ in its theological meaning' (p. 418), i.e. - as he writes in true Reformation tradition - as 'the symbol, on which the human wish to be self-sufficient fails, through which therefore space is brought about for God as God, viz. as the one who "calls into being things that are not" (Rom 4:17 REB)' (p. 419).

Even more saliently, Jürgen Becker (1993) integrates this approach into his interpretation of Paul's theology. He delineates the Pauline theology of the cross on the basis of 1 Cor 1:18-31. In his opinion Paul distinguishes it here as everywhere in the Corinthian correspondence from the interpretation of Jesus' death as a saving event and lets it become part of Paul's doctrine of God and His relation to the world: the theology of the cross concerns

> the God who elects [the church] in the gospel and God's relationship with the world. The 'word of the cross'. . . reveals how God, contrary to human expectation, chooses what is weak and destroys what is strong. . . . It is thus a way of interpreting God and the world, in that it teaches one to understand everything from the standpoint of God revealed in the crucified One, . . . In the theology of the cross, the cross is not the object of discussion, but through the cross everything simply comes up for new discussion (pp. 207-8).

In texts from the post-Pauline period Becker discovers not only statements about the theology of the cross that are influenced by the Pauline theology of the cross (in Colossians and in the writings of Ignatius of Antioch), but also (in Mark, John and Hebrews) traces of theologies of the cross that are independent of Paul (p. 206).

For Peter Stuhlmacher (1992) too, Paul claims for the cross a 'diacritical impact': 'In the Gospel the message of the cross separates the spirits' (p. 320). With explicit reference to Martin Luther's theology of the cross as it was delineated in his *Heidelberg Disputation*, he characterizes the Pauline theology of the cross as the 'climax and touchstone of every proper theology in general' (p. 322). In the later New Testament writings he finds similar statements about the theology of the cross in 1 Peter (1999, pp. 82–3), in Hebrews (p. 102), and in Mark (pp. 147, 150), whereas he views the theology of the cross in the Gospel of John as not determined by the Pauline antithesis of *theologia gloriae* and *theologia crucis*:

> The offence of Jesus' death on the cross as a curse . . . is dissolved in the fourth gospel by the insight of faith that God has glorified his Son who goes to the cross, and through his death has brought salvation to the world (1999, p. 240).

Hans Hübner (1993) also refers to Martin Luther's interpretation of the cross as that event by which God reveals himself '*sub contrario*' and in which the unbeliever cannot see more than an 'absurd incident' (p. 114). He interprets 1 Cor 1–4 in terms of Rudolf Bultmann's hermeneutics and states: 'Theologia crucis est theologia verbi crucis' (p. 141).

Klaus Berger (1994) points out that the Greek verb σταυροῦν, with the exception of 1 Cor 1:13, never signifies the salvific character of Jesus' death. He therefore interprets the Pauline theology of the cross not as a soteriological concept but something like a 'revolution of values': it 'involves a reversal of the categories of social reputation' (p. 480), and 'Christ crucified is a renunciation of everything that is counted . . . as being honourable' (p. 481).

For Ferdinand Hahn (2002), the Pauline theology of the cross forms the framework of all soteriological, eschatological, ecclesiological and ethical statements (pp. 221, 295). For him 'the message of the cross' (1 Cor 1:18) is a genuinely Pauline idea which had no earlier stages in early Christianity before Paul, and he stresses especially the importance which Paul's *theologia crucis* has 'for the existence of the believers' (p. 261).

Also for Udo Schnelle (2003) in his recently published textbook, Paul interprets the cross not only 'as the historical place of Jesus' death', but also as 'argumentative-theological topos and as theological symbol' (p. 487): by this function the cross symbolizes 'the reversal of all hitherto existing values' and 'God's unexpected action, by which he annihilates human standards' (p. 491):

> The cross radically calls into question every human assertion of the self, and every individualistic attempt to achieve salvation; for it leads in the way of powerlessness and not in power, in wailing and not in rejoicing, in shame not in praise, in the loss of death and not in the glory of ever-present salvation (p. 491).

The last paragraph of this chapter clearly indicates that Ernst Käsemann's interpretation of the Pauline theology of the cross has not lost anything of its influence:

> The theology of the cross is the fundamental interpretation of God, of the world and of existence; it is the centre of Paul's world of being. It enables the reality of God to be understood as the one who is revealed in the crucified one . . . Human values, norms and classifications receive a new interpretation from the cross of Christ, for God's values are the re-evaluation of human values (pp. 491–2).

In addition, three articles may be mentioned which can be viewed as landmarks of how German-speaking Protestant New Testament scholars interpret the 'theology of the cross'.

The article by Ulrich Luz (1974) draws attention to the fact, that 'the theology of the cross' has to be understood in a very restricted way: only a theology, which: (a) views the cross 'exclusively' as the foundation of salvation; (b) treats the theology of the cross not merely as 'part of theology but as theology pure and simple'; and (c) interprets the cross 'as the pivotal point of theology', could actually be called a 'theology of the cross' (p. 116). Accordingly, for him 'the theology of the cross' stands in direct opposition to theologies of glory or resurrection, and in this sense it is 'an extreme theology', and the only New Testament authors to whom it can be attributed are Paul and Mark. His central thesis with respect to the Pauline theology of the cross runs as follows:

> For Paul, the theology of the cross does not consist in the fact that he interprets the cross, but rather that he interprets the world, the community and humanity on the basis of the cross (p. 122).

And:

> A genuine theology of the cross is to be distinguished from an uncritical and unpolemical reflection of faith on the saving significance of the cross by radically calling into question this faith through the cross . . . It is the critical power of the cross which leads not to list the cross as an object of theology alongside others, but rather to develop the whole of theology critically in the light of the cross (p. 139).

The approach by Heinz-Wolfgang Kuhn (1975) starts from a different methodological basis. In his opinion two conditions must be fulfilled before we can speak of a 'theology of the cross': 'where Jesus is distinctively spoken about as crucified, where his cross is . . . mentioned' (Kuhn distinguishes explicitly between statements about Jesus' salvific death in general and his death as a death *on the cross*), and where these statements 'determine the argument . . . theologically' (p. 26). By this he introduces a formal criterion that enables him to ascribe the term 'theology of the cross' also to the letters of Ignatius of Antioch and to the Gospel of John. On the other hand he is against characterizing Paul's theology in its entirety as a 'theology of the cross'. Since the polemical references to the cross and Christ crucified are restricted to very limited contexts, his theology of the cross is 'the critical centre of his theology that appears almost exclusively in altercation' (p. 41).

The final work to be mentioned is the ceremonial address by Wolfgang Schrage (1997) on the occasion of Ernst Käsemann's ninetieth birthday. He engages with Käsemann's interpretation of the Pauline theology as a *theologia crucis* and states at first, following his teacher:

> In all the letters where the word 'cross' occurs, Paul is engaged in dispute with people who threaten his theology, whether enthusiastically from the left, or nomistically from the right (pp. 29–30).

Like Becker, Berger and Kuhn, he points out that 'a soteriological explication of the event of the cross according to the traditional formulae is not undertaken' (p. 30), and again following Käsemann he asserts the Pauline theology of the cross to be

> primarily a theology of controversy intra muros ecclesiae [within the boundaries of the church] which characteristically and sharply distinguishes the spirits and remains purely a stumbling block and criterion, so that it always characteristically has, as well as a critical stance in relation to wisdom and law, a theological-critical function (1997, p. 31).

He parts company from Käsemann's position insofar as he assigns to Paul's statements about Jesus' resurrection and about the hope which is established by it (i.e. the Pauline *theologia resurrectionis*) a certain independence from the apostle's *theologia crucis* – though without allowing them to become an 'illusionary *theologia gloriae*' (p. 33).

If we leave aside the individual emphases, a relatively homogeneous picture results from what we have considered so far: the theology of the cross is a genuine *Pauline* concept that finds its theological distinctiveness in the concurrence of God's salvation with an inversion of human values and norms. Its theological pragmatics are apparent as well: this concept is brought to bear in those situations where access to God's salvation is sought by renouncing or bypassing this inversion.

In contrast to this, and ever since the term has been used by New Testament scholars, it is highly debated whether or not a theology of the cross can be assigned also to the Gospel of John. Ernst Käsemann in his *The Testament of Jesus* (1968a) emphatically denied this: in his opinion for John the cross

> is no longer the pillory, the tree of shame, on which hangs the one who had become the companion of thieves. His death is rather the manifestation of divine self-giving love and his victorious return from the alien realm below to the Father who had sent him (p. 10).

Up to the present day his interpretation has found many followers, e.g. Ulrich Luz (1974, p. 118: 'in John the theology which deals with the cross identifies the cross as a glorious event of salvation', Ulrich B. Müller (1975, p. 69: 'it is not the crucified one who is proclaimed to the community, but the glorified one'; see also idem, 1997), and Jürgen Becker (1991, p. 470: 'it is not the cross that is . . . the basis of redemption, but the exaltation'; see also idem, 2004: 150f., and Straub 2002).

On the other hand a considerable number of scholars take the opposite view. Hans Conzelmann writes:

> In John we find the *theologia crucis* at its sharpest. In Paul, the cross is the saving event; it belongs most closely with the exaltation; we know the Exalted One only as the Crucified One. John goes one step further: the crucifixion is already the exaltation (p. 325).

And Günther Bornkamm (1968/1986) argued directly against Ernst Käsemann:

> John – though he takes a completely different path from the Synoptists and Paul – makes perfectly clear the significance for him of a theology of the cross. The actual concept of glory itself, anchored as it is in this Gospel to the paradox of crucifixion, is in my view sufficient proof of this (p. 88).

Up to the present, this view has found many adherents, especially Kohler 1987, Bühler 1991, Knöppler 1994 and Frey 2002. The latter two concede that there are significant differences between the Johannine interpretation of the cross of Christ and the Pauline theology of the cross, since, as Frey says,

> it is not the cross (as a means of execution and a 'shameful stake'), but the glorified crucified one *in person* who has the central place in Johannine thought (p. 235).

Therefore with regard to the Gospel of John they propose to speak not of a theology of the cross (*'theologia crucis'*), but of a theology of the crucified one (*'theologia crucifixi'*) (cf. Knöppler p. 278; Frey pp. 172-3).

III

If we now ask which traces the term 'theology of the cross' and its meaning have left in British New Testament scholarship of the last 35 years, it becomes immediately clear that among British New Testament scholars the topic plays a much less important role than among their German colleagues, and - if they use this term at all - they ascribe to it a completely different meaning. Neither in Donald Guthrie's textbook on the theology of the New Testament (1981), nor in James Dunn's history of religion of early Christianity (1977/1990) is the phrase 'theology of the cross' mentioned. The recently published *New Testament Theology* by I. Howard Marshall (2004) identifies the cross among the 'theological themes' of Paul's theology only where the individual letters are discussed. He deals with what he calls the Pauline 'message of the cross' in the context of his treatment of 1 Cor 1-4 (pp. 267-70). Here we read:

> Paul sees in the cross the paradigm of the way in which God works by doing something which in the eyes of the world is foolish and weak. . . . Therefore, the effect of the cross is to call into question what human beings regard as powerful and wise (p. 268).

Although Marshall claims that

> Paul's emphasis on the cross as the centre of the gospel in this passage (i.e. 1 Cor 1-4) is significant in itself for the rest of the letter and indeed for his theology as a whole (p. 267),

he never comes back to this insight. This can be seen in the fact that among the 50 pages of his comprehensive chapter on 'The Theology of the Pauline Epistles' (pp. 420-69) no mention of a 'theology of the cross' or at least 'a message of the cross' is traceable, and the same is the case for his final chapter on 'Diversity and Unity in the New Testament' (pp. 707-32).

Among textbooks on Pauline theology, the catchword *theologia crucis* is used by Charles Kingsley Barrett (1994) within the chapter about Pauline ecclesiology, and here in the section dealing with the sacraments.

For Barrett 'Paul makes the connection of baptism and Eucharist with death essential', and therefore they are to be understood as expression of Paul's theology of the cross:

> It is to be emphasized that Paul makes the connection of baptism and eucharist with death essential. For him, these are both parts of the *theologia crucis*, which he found at the heart of the Christian faith. The greatest error (. . .) was to make them part of a *theologia gloriae*, pleasing religious activities by which one might be able to ascend to God. Always for him they were means by which God descends to us, and his descent means nothing less than the cross. These are ways in which he is willing to share it with us (p. 130).

It is obvious that nearly all the attributes that have shaped the understanding of Paul's *theologia crucis* within recent German-speaking New Testament scholarship are missing: the distinction between talking about Jesus' death and about his crucifixion, the critical and polemical impetus, and the idea of the reversal of human values that makes the 'message of the cross' a social offence.

James Dunn in his masterly textbook on Pauline theology (1998) follows a similar line of argument. If we follow the reference given by the entry in the index to 'Cross, theology of', the reader is surprisingly led to a paragraph with the heading 'Paul's theology of atoning sacrifice' (pp. 218–23). That means the 'theology of the cross' is no more than the interpretation of Jesus' death as salvific event. The nearness to German theology increases to some extent if we follow the entry 'Cross, centrality of', because here Dunn points to 1 Cor 1:23 and Gal 3:13 and emphasizes that the Pauline characterization of the cross of Christ is offensive and provocative:

> It was the claim that Jesus had been crucified *as Messiah*, that crucifixion was the heart and climax of Jesus' messianic role, which was so offensive. . . . Already it could be said in Jewish factional polemic that a crucified man was under God's curse. . . . A crucified/cursed Messiah was no doubt for most Jews a contradiction in terms. To make a crucified man the focal point of proclamation . . . was equally foolish to Gentiles . . . since crucifixion was generally regarded as the most degrading and shameful of deaths in the Roman repertoire of execution (p. 209).

However, Dunn does not proceed beyond this statement which is merely guided by a hermeneutics of reception, and he fails to ask about the consequences of this fact for Paul's theology in terms of a hermeneutics of production, i.e. what theological *use* Paul makes of this tension between the evaluation of a death on a cross within the symbolic universe of early Christianity and within the systems of the social values of its Jewish and pagan environments. Consequently, for Dunn too, Paul's theology of the cross is no more than just a linguistic variation of his discourse about the death of Christ:

> This Pauline theology of the cross, then, is somewhat enigmatic. In fact that reflects a repeated feature of most of Paul's theology of the death of Jesus (p. 212).[7]

The distance between the understanding of the term *theologia crucis* in German and in British New Testament scholarship is perhaps marked most clearly in the dissertation by Peter Doble (1996) who tries to assign a theology of the cross even to Luke. Ernst Käsemann (1964) had labelled Luke in particular as representative of early Catholicism in the New Testament, claiming that Luke is no longer founded on the Pauline theology of the cross but argues in favour of a theology of glory.[8] Therefore for Doble it is possible to ascribe to Luke the label 'theology of the cross' only because his understanding of this phrase is completely different from that of German New Testament scholarship. In his opinion 'theology of the cross' means: to 'have a clear, coherent understanding of Jesus' death within God's salvation plan, and not merely as a prelude to resurrection' (p. 3). Although he mentions the fact that Jesus' death on the cross could be viewed as a 'scandal' and as 'shameful', to Luke he ascribes the strategy 'to counter protests that so shameful a death could only be of one cursed by God' (p. 229). The death of Jesus is only 'apparently shameful', but 'actually fulfilled God's saving purposes' (p. 230). With his re-interpretation of Jesus' death by Wisdom's δίκαιος-model, Luke pursues the intention 'to eradicate all suspicion that Jesus' death was ultimately shameful' (ibid.). And finally he writes:

> Luke's *theologia crucis* is that the δίκαιος has died and been raised, so Jesus' followers can be sure that God's plan of salvation is nearing fulfilment (pp. 234–5).

The difference is obvious: in Doble's view Luke's theology of the cross is far from having any critical or polemical function. On the contrary, Luke makes an affirmative use of it:

> Luke probably intended to affirm that Jesus' death stood in God's plan of salvation as *that willing act of faithful response to God's call which*

turned the ages; and that sounds very like a coherent *theologia crucis* (p. 243).

IV

It is easy to describe the place of the theology of the cross within New Testament theology: The term 'theology of the cross' is one of those theological terms and paradigms that are not derived from the sources but are mere scholarly inventions. As such the term is used as a category which scholars do not *discover* in the New Testament writings but *ascribe* to them. Like many other terms 'theology of the cross' does not identify the reality itself, because behind this term lie only more words. Everything depends on how we define the term 'theology of the cross'. In this respect, no single scholar could of course claim the right to determine a given meaning of a term as being compulsory for everybody else's usage. Although the term was coined by Martin Luther we are not forced to use it always and exclusively in a 'Lutheran' meaning.

On the other hand it is highly questionable whether a broad and unsalient use of this term is reasonable: if every theological interpretation of the death of Jesus is designated as a 'theology of the cross', and if we therefore can only speak of different versions of this 'theology of the cross' or even only of a plurality of different 'theologies of the cross', then the term is losing its semantic distinctiveness, and the debate whether or not any of the interpretations I have presented above is working with the proper meaning of the term is futile. In this case the term 'theology of the cross' would be better abandoned.

From this follows that – if we want to retain the term as a useful scholarly paradigm – we have to use it with a very distinct, highly profiled meaning. I would like to try this in what follows without simply adding a further meaning to those that already exist. I suggest starting from what is beyond question, since every scholar whose opinion I have mentioned in the previous sections would agree with it: what Paul wrote in 1 Cor 1:18-25 and in Gal 3:13; 6:14-15 can be called a 'theology of the cross', because it is a theological interpretation of Jesus' *crucifixion* in distinction from a theological interpretation of his *death* as such, i.e. disregarding the instrument by which he was brought to death (as e.g. Rom 3:25; 5:8; 14:15; 1 Cor 8:11; 15:3; Gal 1:4). Although this is a minimal consensus, it is a consensus since nobody seriously denies that in these texts Paul delineates something that can be called a 'theology of the cross'. On the basis of this consensus I want to start by outlining the theological profile of Paul's theology of the cross.

V

For Ernst Käsemann, 1 Cor 1-2 and the Epistle to the Galatians are the texts where Paul fought on two fronts: in 1 Cor 1-2 against the enthusiasts and in Galatians against the nomists.[9]

It can be shown, however, that both texts deal with one and the same conflict; this is shown by the intensive theological recourse made to the cross of Jesus, which supports the line of argumentation in both cases. Thus it is reasonable to assume that both contexts in which these statements appear are based on a coherent perception of the particular situation by Paul. The question is simply: on which level can this coherence be described?

I would like to begin by describing the two situations briefly:

1. In Galatians Paul is engaged with Christians who interpret reality from a Jewish point of view, who make the distinction between Jews and non-Jews dominant, and who conclude that Gentiles who are baptized and believe in Jesus Christ can only belong to God's chosen people and Abraham's offspring by becoming Jews and being circumcized. This demand could be strengthened by appeal to Scripture, with reference to God's covenant with Abraham in Gen 17:1-14, and it can be assumed that the Galatian Christians argued accordingly.

2. 1 Corinthians, however, has a background which can be described in terms of social history: within the Christian community in Corinth, there were considerable differences in social standing between individual house churches. This led to the church as a whole splitting into several warring factions (cf. 1 Cor 1:10-12; also 3:3-4), one of which boasted about its level of 'wisdom' (σοφία)[10] and 'knowledge' (γνῶσις; 8:1, 7). This party obviously not only felt superior to the other community members, but was also scornful of Paul (cf. e.g. 3:3, 18; 4:6ff.). In 4:19 Paul calls them 'arrogant' (πεφυσιωμένοι). Thus in this case the unity within the Corinthian church as a whole is at risk through one group importing the prevalent social structures into the church and creating the factions described by Paul in 1:10ff. Paul's line of argumentation is twofold: on the one hand he deals with the position of this 'knowledge and wisdom' faction (which is probably identical with the 'Apollos party'), and on the other he criticizes the actual formation of factions as such.

One can now see that Paul's line of argumentation in these two cases runs parallel; what unites them is the reference to the cross.

In order to understand the theological significance of the cross within Paul's argumentation we must consider the semantic connotations which were given to a death on a cross in society at the time of early Christianity. Martin Hengel has set out the main points:[11]

> Death by crucifixion was considered – to use the words of Origen – to be a *mors turpissima*.[12] This evaluation was shared by Paul and the early Christians with the non-Christian world of the time. Crucifixion was not only understood as an extremely brutal punishment – Josephus describes it as 'the most despicable way to die'[13] – but it was also a typical punishment for slaves,[14] the *servile supplicium*.[15] The Jewish perception of crucifixion was influenced by the fact that the despicable villain Haman was among those crucified (Esther 7:9ff.). Crucifixion is also attributed this status in the hierarchy of social values by the Jew Trypho who termed it 'shameful and disgraceful' (αἰσχρῶς καὶ ἀτίμως)[16] and by Lucian of Samosata who called the Christians 'crazy' (κακακοδαίμονες) for worshipping a 'crucified sophist'.[17]

(a) In Galatians, Paul argues against the Jewish perception of reality by setting two sets of ideas in confrontation with each other in 6:12–16: on the one hand are σάρξ, κόσμος as well as the distinction between Jews and Gentiles, and on the other 'boasting in the cross of our Lord Jesus Christ' and the 'new creation'. Gal 5:11 can also be included in this confrontation, since here the 'preaching of circumcision' means nothing other than salvation in relation to a perception of reality which draws a distinct boundary between Jews and non-Jews. This, however, is incompatible with the 'foolishness of the cross'. Paul's argumentation gains its specific profile from the way he relates the two sets of ideas to each other and thus attempts to create a paradigm shift: he identifies the distinction between Jews and Gentiles as an element of the world without God, i.e. of the σάρξ and of the κόσμος. The cross forms an irreversible breach with this world. Thus not only the boundary between Jews and Gentiles, but also the impossibility of being able to boast about a cross is identified as a specific characteristic of the σάρξ and κόσμος reality. 'Boasting in the cross' is only possible under the conditions of a new creation, which of course God alone can bring into force, and thus the opposite is also true: that God has opened up a way of salvation through a despicable cross, and thereby has made possible a 'boasting in the cross', can only be rightly understood as the establishment of a new creation. To use the appropriate terminology: God has done away with prevailing boundaries and set up new ones.

This message of the cross in 6:12-16 corresponds to what is said about faith in the other sections of the letter: boasting about a cross, and its perception as the abolition of prevailing boundaries and the setting up of new ones, is only possible because it is not any cross but that of *Jesus Christ*. The same applies to faith: faith which makes non-Jews Abraham's children (3:7, 9), through which God declares man righteous (2:16; 3:8, 11, 24), which imparts the promised Holy Spirit (3:2, 5, 14, 22) and which abolishes the difference between Jews and Gentiles (5:6), does all of this exclusively as πίστις Χριστοῦ (2:16, 20; 3:22), i.e. as faith which focuses exclusively on Jesus Christ (see also 2:16; 3:26).

(b) In 1 Corinthians Paul argues in a similar way: in 1:18-30 he works with semantic opposites which he sets over against each other. He begins with the following:

God	World
Wisdom	Foolishness

For Paul and his addressees it is clear that 'God' and 'wisdom' belong together, as do 'world' and 'foolishness'. It is also virtually a tautology to say that 'God and foolishness do not belong together' and 'world and wisdom do not belong together'.[18] Within the context of these opposites Paul then introduces his 'message of the cross' (1:18), and he does this in such a way that even the representatives of the Corinthian wisdom and knowledge party must agree with him: no Christian (and that means, according to 1 Cor 15:3, everyone who believes that Christ died for our sins) can deny that God has brought salvation through a death on a cross – that salvation comes from a *mors turpissima* which is sufficient for the whole world. According to the standards of the 'world' this is undoubtedly 'foolishness', due to the semantic connotations of crucifixion mentioned above. Two dualistically opposed cognitive positions meet each other here: those who believe that God has brought salvation through a death on a cross are compelled to revise thoroughly their previous perception of reality, in which such assurance has no place whatsoever; thus what is considered 'wisdom' outside the context of faith no longer applies. To those who cannot grasp that the cross is the saving event, Paul's message necessarily must remain foolishness.

This finds support in the second dualistic sequence, which is as follows:

οἱ σῳζόμενοι (18)	(18) οἱ ἀπολλύμενοι
'we' (18)	(23) Jews, to whom the message of the cross is *skandalon*

| οἱ πιστεύοντες (21)

Jews and Gentiles (24)
'you in Christ Jesus' (30) | (23) Gentiles, to whom the message of the cross is 'foolishness' |

Although on each side the terms which comprise the sequences have different meanings, their reference remains one and the same: they represent the distinction between what is inside and what is outside the Christian church.

If we now relate these two comparisons with each other, it is clear what belongs together and what does not: on the one side are 'God', 'wisdom' and the left-hand series above, and on the other 'world', 'foolishness' and the right-hand series above. Thus the counterparts God and world, or wisdom and foolishness, are projected on to the counterparts Christians and non-Christians, and it is the message of the cross at which they coincide. It is of great significance, even though not surprising, that the polarity of Jews and Gentiles appears in both comparisons.

Moreover the cognitive and existential levels merge: 'the message of the cross is foolishness to those who are perishing' (1 Cor 1:18). The response to the message of the cross and its effect coincide: those 'who are perishing' consider the message of the cross foolishness, which leads them to become those who are perishing; on the other hand those 'who are being saved' consider it 'the power of God' and thus appropriate its saving power for themselves. Paul can put it in these terms because the perception of the cross as the saving event and the saving event itself overlap entirely. For this reason he can replace the term σῳζόμενοι with πιστεύοντες in verse 21b.

Within the context of Paul's debate with the factions in Corinth, this means that those who favour wisdom and knowledge can only do so as believers if they understand the cross as the saving event. From a perception of reality outside the Christian faith (which Paul calls 'the wisdom of the world'), this is utterly excluded. This makes it impossible for some Christians to claim cognitive superiority over others, thus allowing paradigms to dominate which are only valid outside the Christian perception of reality and which Paul can only label as 'of man' or 'of the world' (cf. 1:20; 2:5, 6, 13). No one can understand the cross as saving event without having crossed the border from 'foolishness' to 'wisdom', from the 'world' to 'God', and from unbelief to faith in Jesus Christ.

In both texts Paul supports his line of argument in the same way. He does not argue – as Ernst Käsemann claims in his interpretation developed under the influence of Luther – in two different directions, but in one and the same way: in both letters he deals with interpretations of

'Christianity' which are based on an understanding of reality in which the Christian faith and life are not autonomous but are dominated by cultural paradigms which are alien to them. In both letters he engages with Christian positions which do not understand the Christian symbolic universe as a 'new creation' (Gal 6:15) but as mere subordinate parts of other symbolic universes – i.e. of universes which Paul terms 'world' (1 Cor 1:20, 21; Gal 6:14) and 'flesh' (1 Cor 1:26; Gal 6:12, 13). Although the two positions might seem to be different when viewed from outside, for Paul they converge exactly at this point. The fact that he illustrates this common front in both texts by pointing to the significance of the cross of Jesus Christ within the Christian symbolic universe is consistent with this. The significance of Christians ascribing their faith to a death on the cross, or that Christians believe and confess a crucified person to be their Kyrios, indicates a 'fundamental difference' (Dalferth 1994, p. 39) which has a unifying as well as a dividing impact: it *unifies* all those who believe in and confess Christ crucified as their Kyrios – irrespective of their divergent cultural and national identities; and it selectively *divides* all those who believe in and confess Christ crucified as their Kyrios from those who do not – irrespective of their common cultural and national identities. To put it in the words of Dalferth:

> . . . the decisive difference between Christians and non-Christians lies not in diverging ideas about resurrection hope, God, reality, and salvation, or in diverging attitudes to and ways of life, but in the fact that these differences are due to one fundamental difference, which is marked by the cross and which the message of the cross sharply expresses (1994, p. 39).

VI

The distinctive profile of Paul's interpretation of the death which Jesus died on the cross becomes immediately apparent, if we take a brief look at the other New Testament theologies of the cross (or at least the so-called New Testament theologies of the cross). The differences are rather obvious.

Whereas in John, Jesus' crucifixion is given a new interpretation as 'glorification' (e.g. John 7:39; 12:16, 23; 21:19) or 'exaltation' (John 3:14; 8:28; 12:32–4), which is set apart from that of the cultural environment as shameful, Paul uses this very evaluation to explicate the distinctiveness of what 'faith in Jesus Christ' does mean.

In Mark the cross is bridged over by the messianic secret, whereby the demons and the disciples are enjoined not to disclose Jesus' identity as

Messiah and Son of God before his resurrection (Mark 9:9; cf. also 1:34; 3:11-12; 8:29-30). In this respect the messianic secret functions as a literary theory, which enables Mark to narrate the life of the Son of God (i.e. 'The beginning of the gospel of Jesus Christ', Mark 1:1) that ends on the cross. For his readers the darkness of the cross is illuminated from the very beginning of Mark's Gospel by the light of the resurrection. Accordingly in each of the three passion predictions Jesus speaks about his resurrection (cf. Mark 8:31; 9:31; 10:33), but never about his cross. It is reserved for the Jewish inhabitants of Jerusalem, who are influenced by the high priests, to bring the cross into play by demanding Jesus' crucifixion (Mark 15:13). If Mark interprets Jesus' death on the cross as such at all, he uses it to show the guilt of the Jews, and not as a distinct qualification of Jesus' death.

Finally: that the death of a person can bring about salvation, is not only known to early Christianity (Luke included, as we meanwhile know), but also to others at the time.[19] In contrast to Luke's interpretation of Jesus' death and its analogies outside Christianity, Paul's insistence on the cross as the place where Jesus died indicates a fundamental difference: this death that brought about salvation for 'everyone who has faith' (Rom 1:16), and which has therefore become the object of Paul's boasting (Gal 6:14), is by no means a voluntary, heroic, and noble death - it is nothing but a cruel, shameful and despised death.

I return to my starting point. Nobody is obliged by what has been said here to restrict the use of the term 'theology of the cross' to the Pauline interpretation of Jesus' crucifixion. There is no impediment against agreeing to call every theology which interprets Jesus' death as saving event a 'theology of the cross'. The same is true here as in general: meanings of the terms are nothing other than matters of agreement.

Apart from the differences in the use and the understanding of the term 'theology of the cross' which I have described in the first three sections, I am confident that everybody will agree that the Pauline 'theology of the cross', or at least its Pauline version, occupies a special position in the New Testament - or at least among other theologies of the cross - since Paul is the only one who determines the cross as indicating the Christian 'fundamental difference'.

A question hereby arises to which Bob Morgan has devoted a very stimulating article: 'Can the critical study of Scripture provide a doctrinal norm?' (1996). Here he proposed as a doctrinal norm that makes a Christian a Christian: 'Christian groups are identified by their claim to a decisive revelation of God in Jesus Christ' (p. 206). In this respect it is the confession to Jesus' divinity as well as 'the necessity of dogmatically insisting on Jesus' humanity' (p. 213) that could yield a doctrinal criterion of orthodoxy that is sufficiently indeterminate to be unfolded theologically in many ways and yet sufficiently determinate to preserve the identity and *skandalon* of Christianity – its acknowledgment of God in the historical particularity of the crucified Lord (p. 214).

On this very point, discussion of this question can lead to considerable gain in making precise the perception of the issues concerned. The quest for the *differentia specifica* of Christian groups is always presented to the Christian churches as a quest for a balance between cognitive and pragmatic separation from their cultural environment on one hand, and accommodation to it on the other. This was already the case in early Christianity. The same is the case at the beginning of the twenty-first century, and no definition of a Christian doctrinal norm is conceivable which disregards this tension. It is nothing but the diversity of different cultural contexts that determined – and is still determining – the plurality of the Christian churches and Christian theologies. In relation to the situation of the first century, we are still able to observe the results of this culturally determined plurality that was rooted in the tension between separation from, and accommodation to, the social environment of the early communities in the New Testament canon and its internal diversity. Christianity and Christian theology is therefore necessarily multiform; and this fact is not merely unavoidable but is to be welcomed.

The relevance of Paul's theology of the cross against this backdrop is quite obvious: in the texts discussed above he develops a doctrinal norm which, within the New Testament canon, remains restricted to these two literary contexts. However, Paul has taught us that this norm is implicitly present wherever Christians express their Christian identity – even though it is not present on the surface of the texts. All Christian theologies, divergent as they might be, rest upon the fact that the interpretation of the cross of Christ as the integral part of God's salvific turning towards humankind draws a sharp line against accommodation to cultural norms that cannot be passed or bridged over, because it categorically distinguishes the Christian concept of reality from non-Christian ones. This interpretation of the cross of Christ permits and demands theological *Sachkritik* of those expressions of Christian faith and life which seek to integrate norms and conditions from its cultural context into the definition of its own doctrinal and ethical norms, since in terms of every given cultural context the cross indicates that the doctrinal norm which identifies Christianity and distinguishes it from every other symbolic universe remains sheer foolishness. On this basis, I do not want Paul to become the 'centre of Scripture', nor a 'canon within the canon'. That would be a very un-Pauline attempt, since it is not the *littera* which constitutes the doctrinal norm, but only the 'Sache' (substance). Martin Luther, Ernst Käsemann and Bob Morgan have clearly understood that at this precise point, Christian identity has its unique and most distinctive characteristic.

Notes

1. Cf. for the following especially Prenter 1971; v. Loewenich 1976; MacGrath 1990.
2. Accordingly he characterizes Philip's demand, 'Lord, show us the father; we ask no more' (John 14:8), as a request '*iuxta Theologiam gloriae*' (WA 1.362.15).
3. Cf. for the following also Ehler 1986, pp. 300-2.
4. Cf. also: 'The catchword "theology of the cross". . . belongs from the very outset to the controversial theology which Protestant fervour inaugurated through the *particula exclusiva* - the "through Christ alone, through faith alone". This means: *crux sola est nostra theologia*' (p. 34), and: '. . . the catchword about the "theology of the cross" loses its original meaning if it is used non-polemically. It was always a critical attack on the dominating traditional interpretation of the Christian message, and it was not by chance that it characterized Protestant beginnings' (p. 35).
5. Also Käsemann viewed himself as struggling against the same twofold front-line (cf. Ehler 1986, pp. 33-4).
6. In the Roman Catholic 'NT theology' by Gnilka 1994 and 1996 the theme is completely missing.
7. Cf. also p. 232: 'Paul who gave the gospel its focus in the death of Jesus, who stamped the "cross" so firmly on the "gospel"'.
8. Cf. Käsemann 1964, p. 92 on Lukan ecclesiology: 'A *theologia gloriae* is now in the process of replacing the *thelogia crucis*'. See also Luz 1974, p. 120: 'Luke is a prime example of the way in which the cross has been displaced from the centre of theology and has become simply one object alongside others . . . It is just an unfortunate incident, a "low point" in salvation history'.
9. See above p. 265.
10. Cf. 1 Cor 1:17, 19, 20; 2:1, 4, 5, 6, 13; 3:19; 12:8 and Pickett 1997; Konradt 2003.
11. Cf. Hengel 1977.
12. Origen, *Comm. in Mt* 27:22-6 (GCS 38.259.7).
13. Josephus, *War* 7.203.
14. Cf. Kuhn 1982, esp. p. 719ff.
15. Valerius Maximus, *Fact. et dict.* 2.7.12.
16. Justin, *Dial.* 90:1; see also Heb 12:2 with the classification of 'cross' and 'shame' and Heb 6:6.
17. Lucian of Samosata, *Mort. Per.* 13.
18. See also Merklein 1992, p. 171ff.

19. Cf. esp. Origen, *Contra Celsum* 1.31. See also Versnel 1989; Seeley 1990; Bremmer 1992.

References

Barrett, C.K., *Paul. An Introduction to His Thought* (London: Geoffrey Chapman, 1994).
Becker, J., *Das Evangelium nach Johannes* (2 vols; Gersloh: Gütersloher Verlagshaus Gerd Mohn, 1991).
Becker, J., *Paul: Apostle to the Gentiles* (Louisville, KY: Westminster/John Knox Press, 1993).
Becker, J., *Johanneisches Christentum* (Tübingen: Mohr Siebeck, 2004).
Berger, K., *Theologiegeschichte des Urchristentums: Theologie des Neuen Testaments* (Tübingen: Francke Verlag, 1994).
Bornkamm, G., 'Towards the interpretation of John's Gospel', in J. Ashton (ed.), *The Interpretation of John* (Philadelphia: Fortress Press, 1986), pp. 79–98.
Bremmer, J.N., 'The atonement in the interaction of Jews, Greeks, and Christians', in J.N. Bremmer and F.G. Martinez (eds), *Sacred History and Sacred Texts in Early Judaism* (Kampen: Kok Pharos, 1992), pp. 75–93.
Bühler, P., 'Ist Johannes ein Kreuzestheologe?', in M. Rose (ed.), *Johannesstudien, Festschrift Jean Zumstein* (Zürich: Theologischer Vrlag, 1991), pp. 191–207.
Conzelmann, H., *An Outline of the Theology of the New Testament* (London: SCM, 1969).
Dalferth, I.U., *Der auferweckte Gekreuzigte* (Tübingen: J.C.B. Mohr [Paul Siebeck], 1994).
Doble, P., *The Paradox of Salvation: Luke's Theology of the Cross* (Cambridge: Cambridge University Press, 1996).
Dunn, James D.G., *Unity and Diversity in the New Testament* (Harrisburg: Trinity Press International, 1977/1990).
Dunn, James D.G., *The Theology of Paul the Apostle* (Grand Rapids: Eerdmans, 1998).
Ehler, B., *Die Herrschaft des Gekreuzigten: Ernst Käsemanns Frage nach der Mitte der Schrift.* (Berlin: de Gruyter, 1986).
Frey, J., 'Die "theologia crucifixi" des Johannesevangelium', in A. Dettwiler and J. Zumstein (eds), *Kreuzestheologie im Neuen Testament* (Tübingen: Mohr Siebeck, 2002), pp. 169–238.
Gnilka, J., *Theologie des Neuen Testaments* (Freiburg: Herder, 1994).
Gnilka, J., *Paulus von Tarsus: Apostel und Zeuge* (Freiburg: Herder, 1996).
Goppelt, L., *Theologie des Neuen Testaments* (Göttingen: Vandenhoeck & Ruprecht, 1976).
Guthrie, D., *New Testament Theology* (Leicester: Inter-Varsity Press, 1981).
Hahn, F., *Theologie des Neuen Testaments 1 Die Vielfalt des Neuen Testaments* (Tübingen: Mohr Siebeck, 2002).
Hengel, M., *Crucifixion in the Ancient World and the Folly of the Message of the Cross* (London: SCM, 1977).

Hübner, H., *Biblische Theologie des Neuen Testaments 2 Die Theologie des Paulus* (Göttingen: Vandenhoeck & Ruprecht, 1993).

Käsemann, E., *Essays on New Testament Themes* (London: SCM Press, 1964).

Käsemann, E., 'Die Heilsbedeutung des Todes Jesu nach Paulus', in H. Conzelmann, E. Flesseman-van Leer, E. Haenchen, E. Käsemann and E. Lohse (eds), *Zur Bedeutung des Todes Jesu* (Gütersloh: Gütersloher Verlagshaus Gerd Mohn, 1967), pp. 11-34.

Käsemann, E., *The Testament of Jesus* (London: SCM, 1968a).

Käsemann, E., 'Gottesgerechtigkeit bei Paulus', in idem, *Exegetische Versuche und Besinnungen* (Göttingen: Vandenhoeck & Ruprecht, 1968b), pp. 181-93.

Käsemann, E., 'The saving significance of the death of Jesus in Paul', in idem, *Perspectives on Paul* (London: SCM, 1971), pp. 32-59.

Knöppler, Th., *Die theologia crucis des Johannesevangeliums* (Neukirchen-Vluyn: Neukirchener Verlag, 1994).

Kohler, H., *Kreuz und Menschwerdung im Johannesevangelium* (Zürich: Theologischer Verlag, 1987).

Konradt, M., 'Die korinthische Weisheit und das Wort vom Kreuz', *ZNW* 94 (2003), 181-214.

Kuhn, H.-W., 'Jesus als Gekreuzigter in der frühchristlichen Verkündigung bis zur Mitte des 2. Jahrhunderts', *ZThK* 72 (1975), 1-46.

Kuhn, H.-W., 'Die Kreuzesstrafe während der frühen Kaiserzeit. Ihre Wirklichkeit und Wertung in der Umwelt des Urchristentums', *ANRW* 2.25.1 (Berlin: de Gruyter, 1982), pp. 648-793.

Loewenich, W. v., *Luther's Theology of the Cross* (Minneapolis: Augsburg, 1976).

Luz, U. 'Theologia crucis als Mitte der Theologie im Neuen Testament', *EvTh* 34 (1974) 116-41.

MacGrath, A., *Luther's Theology of the Cross* (Oxford: Blackwell, 1990).

Marshall, I. H., *New Testament Theology. Many Witnesses One Gospel* (Downers Grove, IL: Inter-Varsity Press, 2004).

Merklein, H., *Der erste Brief an die Korinther 1* (Gütersloh: Gütersloher Verlagshaus Gerd Mohn, 1992).

Morgan, R., 'Can the critical study of Scripture provide a doctrinal norm? *JR* 76 (1996), 206-32.

Müller, U.B., 'Die Bedeutung des Kreuzestodes Jesu im Johannesevangelium. Erwägungen zur Kreuzestheologie im Neuen Testament', *KuD* 21 (1975), 49-71.

Müller, U.B., 'Zur Eigentümlichkeit des Johannesevaneliums. Das Problem des Todes Jesu', *ZNW* 88 (1997), 24-55.

Pickett, R., *The Cross in Corinth. The Social Significance of the Death of Jesus* (Sheffield. Sheffield Academic Press, 1997).

Prenter, R., *Luther's Theology of the Cross* (Philadelphia: Fortress, 1971).

Schnelle, U., *Paulus. Leben und Denken*. (Berlin: Walter de Gruyter, 2003).

Schrage, W., 'Der gekreuzigte und auferweckte Herr. Zur *theologia crucis* und *theologia resurrectionis* bei Paulus', *ZThK* 94 (1997), 25-38.

Seeley, D., *The Noble Death. Graeco-Roman Martyrology and Paul's Concept of Salvation* (Sheffield: Sheffield Academic Press, 1990).

Straub, E., 'Der Irdische als der Auferstandene: Kritische Theologie bei Johannes ohne ein Wort vom Kreuz', in A. Dettwiler and J. Zumstein (eds), *Kreuzestheologie im Neuen Testament* (Tübingen: Mohr Siebeck, 2002), pp. 239-64.

Stuhlmacher, P., *Biblische Theologie des Neuen Testaments* (2 vols; Göttingen: Vandenhoeck & Ruprecht, 1992/1999).

Versnel, H.S., 'Quid Athenis et Hierosolymis? Anmerkungen über die Herkunft von Aspekten des "Effective Death"', in J.W. van Henten (ed.), *Die Entstehung der jüdischen Martyrologie* (Leiden, Brill, 1989), pp. 162-96.

Chapter 17

The Trinity and the New Testament

Frances Young, Birmingham

When Thou, O Lord, was baptized in the Jordan,
The worship of the Trinity was made manifest.
For the voice of the Father bore witness unto Thee,
Calling Thee the beloved Son,
And the Spirit, in the form of a dove,
Confirmed his word as sure and steadfast.
O Christ our God, who has appeared and enlightened the world,
Glory to Thee.

So runs the troparion for Epiphany in the Eastern Orthodox tradition. But in scholarly circles no one has imagined for a very long time that such a revelation might have been in the minds of any of the Gospel writers as they told the story of the baptism. The modern consciousness of historical difference has excluded such dogmatic readings. How to speak of 'New Testament theology' responsibly in these changed circumstances has been Bob Morgan's persistent enquiry, and it is a privilege to join in honouring him by making this contribution to the discussion.

Speaking of those texts in the New Testament where Christ is associated with pre-existent wisdom, Morgan (2003) has said: 'these passages are part of the scriptural foundations of Christian belief, but they contribute to theology *in*directly, by quickening the Christian imagination that reads Scripture to strengthen its faith, and is then better equipped to build its theology on what the myth and other New Testament materials are getting at . . .' He suggests that these passages probably originated in liturgical contexts, that they should not be treated as expressing a fully worked out incarnational theology, and that to speak of a 'Wisdom-Christology' is 'potentially misleading, a product of a one-sidedly doctrinal emphasis in

New Testament theology'. He goes on: 'When this "makes doctrine out of what is not doctrine" [a quotation from Wrede] and turns myth into metaphysics instead of interpreting these texts in accordance with their intention to *celebrate* Jesus as the saving revelation of God, rather than define his nature, it is open to the charge of misreading the New Testament. Finding the later *doctrine* of pre-existence or incarnation in these hymnic passages is anachronistic and involves a category mistake.'

This critique is offered to contemporary New Testament scholarship, implying that despite 200 years of historico-critical endeavour it is still affected by anachronistic readings. Interestingly Morgan's position here is reinforced by my own recent researches into wisdom in the Apostolic Fathers – Wisdom-Christology is notable for its absence from these texts, and the first unambiguous indication of anything like a Wisdom-Christology is to be found in the works of Justin Martyr who conflates passages like Proverbs 8:22–31 with the Johannine Prologue and Stoic philosophy (Young 2005). Be that as it may, if Morgan takes such a radical view of 'doctrinal reading' with respect to Christology, how much more would he say this of later Trinitarian doctrine!

The troparion with which we began comes from a liturgical context; it is the voice of the church 'celebrating Jesus', and 'talking of God by interpreting these texts'. This constitutes Christian theological interpretation of scripture, according to Morgan. He points out the weaknesses both of doctrinal proof-texting and of 'pure history' for Christian theological interpretation, calling instead for a literary type of theological interpretation, and for 'living the life, which includes singing the songs . . . and reading the scriptures' in liturgy. On the other hand, he remains committed to historical enquiry and the search for authorial intention as 'the best control against arbitrary interpretations which do violence to a text by imposing the interpreter's beliefs on it.' So is historical radicalism to outlaw the troparion's celebratory and liturgical reading of the baptism as an epiphany of the Trinity?

The topic I was asked to tackle was 'New Testament theology from the perspective of emerging Trinitarian theology'. This seems to presuppose a developmental model: from the perspective of this later developed doctrine the embryonic character of New Testament theology becomes apparent. This way of conceiving the relationship between doctrine and scripture is widespread, but it is an assumption I want to challenge. What I hope to do is to explore another approach to the relationship, which may be seen as taking forward some of Morgan's own proposals, though not uncritically. For it is still worth asking whether Trinitarian theology does or does not actually reflect the implications of the New Testament.

The 'Emergence' of Trinitarian Theology

Trinitarian theology is the product of exegesis of the biblical texts, refined by debate and argument, and rhetorically celebrated in liturgy. It is 'discourse', a way of talking about God, and discourse does not develop like an oak tree growing from an acorn – it did not evolve from a 'primitive' to a more 'mature' form, and there was nothing inevitable about it. These evolutionary models are as all pervasive in our intellectual climate as Platonism was in the days of Origen, and their cultural locus needs to be exposed. They may appear convenient for those who want to make Christian doctrine historically relative, or those who by hindsight want to see the process teleologically – even as providentially guided; but they obscure the way in which the doctrine 'emerged'. The doctrine of the Trinity is the outcome of reading the scriptural texts with particular questions in mind, questions which do not seem to have occurred to the earliest Christians at all, questions generated by the socio-political context in which the Church Fathers found themselves. To that extent it is a conceptual superstructure built on the foundations of the New Testament. Rather than using organic metaphors, we need to take seriously the dialectical process of shaping the building blocks, and the factors which contributed to that shaping.

To undertake that task is to be disturbed. There are two reasons for this. The first is that Christian doctrine begins to look as if it might simply be the product of particular cultural pressures – the Neoplatonic trinity, for example, parallels the Christian Trinity and is a response to many of the same intellectual questions. The second is that the reading of scripture on which the eventual doctrinal edifice depends is profoundly different from anything modern scholars would regard as valid. Systematic theology, by simply accepting the traditions of Christian doctrine and trying to make them intellectually plausible in our (post-) modern world, conveniently overlooks the shaky foundations on which the doctrinal tradition rests, at least from the point of view of the different intellectual world in which we operate. This is not an easy challenge to which to respond.[1] Yet in the end the Fathers may well contribute some crucial pointers towards the theological reading of scripture which Morgan wants to discover.

We will take a look at two moments in early Christian history which were vital for the formation of Christianity's distinct discourse about God. In the process we will observe how the Fathers created a discourse in need of ever more refined specificity; and how they found balance by oscillation between one pole and another of what the biblical 'data' seemed to require.

The Monarchian controversies

Christian discourse focused on the *monarchia* of God throughout the second century. The one true God, the Creator and Sovereign of all, is the 'overseer' of all, even the thoughts in a person's heart, and to this God all will be accountable. Such is the theology already found in the Pastoral Epistles and the Apostolic Fathers. It is expressed liturgically in Melito's *Peri Pascha*. It figures large in apologetic – Justin, Tatian, Athenagoras and Theophilus, all alike contrast this one God with the polytheism of the religious world of the Roman Empire. It also informed resistance to Gnostic fragmentation of the divine (Hübner 1999).

Emphasis on God's oneness had a profoundly moral thrust, with the spectre of ultimate judgement to the fore; but it was also of fundamental cosmological significance, and questions about creation were primary in this period (May 1994, Ehrhardt 1968, Young 1991). It was in the second century that various challenges to biblical perspectives were presented. The predominant outlook tended to regard the material world as inferior to the spiritual world, and God as too transcendent to be too directly involved in creation. Gnosticism took this to further extremes, treating the material world as the product of a fallen Demiurge, and salvation as escape from matter. In Platonic philosophy there was a debate about whether the creation is eternal, the myth of the *Timaeus* articulating the constant relationship of agent, material and design (= form or idea), or whether cosmological origins were to be attributed to a Demiurge creating what now exists through the shaping of pre-existent matter. These ideas impinged on the Christian claims about God's *monarchia*, and before the century was out the radical doctrine of creation 'out of nothing' had been asserted. If Justin could align the Genesis account with the *Timaeus*, and imply that God ordering chaos was the Demiurge creating out of pre-existent matter, Theophilus would assert that God's creative activity did not require any pre-existent medium – indeed, it was precisely this that distinguished God's power from that of a human craftsman. Tertullian[2] summed it all up: God could not create out of the divine self, or everything would be divine; God could not create out of eternal matter, or there would be a second divine entity (note that *monarchia* can refer either to a single sovereignty or to a single source or first principle); so God must have created 'out of nothing'.

The consequence of this universal insistence on the uniqueness of God the Creator was a liturgical rhetoric which sounds 'modalist', if we may use an anachronistic term. There was a delight in the paradoxes implied by the notion of incarnation: the invisible is seen, the impassible suffers, and the immortal dies. It has been argued that second-century

theology was fundamentally monarchian (Hübner 1999), despite the
many accounts which suggest that the development of Logos theology
produced a binitarian theology.[3] This is probably an overstatement; at
least one function of the Logos doctrine was to give an account of God's
creative and saving activity which did not compromise divine transcendence, and Justin had even used the phrase, 'a second god'. It might be
better to say that the logical challenges of Christian devotion to Christ
alongside their explicit monotheism had barely been articulated.[4] It was
opponents who perceived the problems, Jews who accused Christians
of blasphemy and critics like Celsus, who may have been reacting against
the position of Justin:

> If these people worshipped no other god but one, perhaps they would
> have a valid argument against the others. But in fact they worship to an
> extravagant degree this man who appeared recently, and yet think it is not
> inconsistent with monotheism if they also worship his servant.[5]

Towards the end of the century such issues surfaced within the
Christian community in the so-called Monarchian controversies. Both
sides claimed that the scriptures and Christian teachers of the past supported their own view, probably with some justification. The issues had
not been explicit before, but the charge of 'ditheism' seems to have provoked a reaction against Logos theology.

So when these questions became explicit, what manner of arguments
were deployed? And what were the drivers on each side? In the main
their arguments are of a kind that Morgan would doubtless characterize
as 'proof-texting', proof-texting moreover which draws across the whole
of the scriptures without distinguishing historical or authorial sources,
Old and New Testament. Yet interestingly the 'drivers' may put this
conclusion into a different perspective.

Modern historical scholarship has distinguished two forms of monarchianism, so-called 'dynamic' and 'modalist' types. The first argued that
Jesus was a human being 'empowered' by God; the second that Father,
Son and Spirit were different 'modes' of the one God. According to
Novatian,[6] both had noticed that it is written that there is only one God;
and it is perhaps significant that the teaching of someone like Paul of
Samosata may well have evidenced aspects of both. The argument with
the modalists is best documented,[7] and here a series of texts keep
recurring: Exodus 20:3 – 'You shall have no other gods but me'; Isaiah
44:6 – 'I am the first and the last, and besides me there is no other'.
Of particular importance was Baruch 3:35–7: 'This is our God. No other
will be compared to him. He found out the whole way of knowledge

and gave it to Jacob his son and to Israel who is his beloved. Afterwards
he was seen on earth and conversed with men'. From this Noetus
apparently deduced that the God who is the one alone was subsequently
seen and talked with human beings, and so felt himself bound to
'submit to suffering' the single God that exists.[8] The modalists also
appealed to various New Testament texts: John 14:11 – 'Do you not
believe that I am in the Father and the Father in me?'; John 10:30 – 'I and
the Father are one'; and Romans 9:5, which seemed to describe Christ as
God over all.

Those responding to this appeal to texts appeal to other texts, of
course. But what lies behind the proof-texting? Clearly the Monarchians
were driven by the second-century arguments for monotheism, both
apologetic and anti-Gnostic. If God is the sole Creator, providentially
engaged with the world he has created, what is so difficult about extending that engagement to the incarnation? The doctrine of creation is
already counter-cultural in the sense that the involvement of the transcendent God with matter was widely regarded as impossible. So why
not Patripassianism? Isn't this what the liturgical paradoxes express? It
is interesting that modern theology has often challenged the Fathers on
precisely this point. What the Monarchians wanted to preserve was the
sense that it really is the one true God who is at work in the whole story.
Callistus is presented[9] as teaching that the Logos himself is Son and
himself Father, being one indivisible Spirit; the Father is not one person
and the Son another, but they are one and the same, all things, transcendent and immanent, being full of the divine Spirit. The Spirit which
became incarnate in the Virgin's womb was not different from the Father.
Exactly such argumentation, together with the same proof-texts, has been
advanced in the twentieth century by Oneness Pentecostals in their reaction against a Trinitarianism that appeared tritheistic. The Monarchians
accused 'Hippolytus' and his followers of being Ditheists. Surely
the drivers have a profound validity in terms of presenting the thrust of
the overall biblical witness: what happened in the 'New Testament' is the
work of the one true God to which the 'Old Testament' bears witness.

If this is true of those who became treated as heretics, what of those
who proved to be history's winners? What drove them to oppose these
'Monarchianisms'? How did they build their conceptual superstructure
on scripture? Certainly they had competing proof-texts, but there were
more fundamental concerns. Tertullian betrays[10] some of his with that
classic remark, 'They crucify the Father and put the Paraclete to flight!'
The rhetoric shows that he thought the reaction to this would be shock
and horror! He could not conceive of the transcendent God submitting
to suffering. How could the immortal die, let alone be born? Such

questions would go on haunting Christian teachers and splitting the church for centuries to come, especially as the divinity of the Logos incarnate in Jesus was unequivocally affirmed in the post-Nicene context. But meanwhile Tertullian's solution is to claim that the incarnate Logos makes it possible for the invisible to be seen. The Logos is God, but the 'dispensation' of God allows for a kind of buffer. Equally important for Tertullian is recognition of the activity of the Spirit in the church – he is by now a Montanist (though that could well mean he still belongs to the 'mainstream' church in Carthage, just as charismatics continue to belong to 'mainstream' denominations these days). The great driver for Tertullian is to find concepts that allow God's transcendence to be secure while divine immanence and activity in the world is still affirmed. Distinctions are important, but so is continuity. Tertullian would deny any intention to preach two or three gods rather than one.

Tertullian has in common with Hippolytus this appeal to the 'dispensa-tion' or 'economy' of God. They mean God's providential arrangements (*oikonomia* = 'household management') in relation to the created order. This, they suggest, disposes unity into trinity, creating a plurality without division. Tertullian draws attention to the one empire, and the fact that, without the sovereignty being divided, the emperor may still share the one sovereignty with his son as agent – even noting that provincial governors do not detract from the single monarchy, so that the analogy is extended to the angels and not just the Son and the Spirit! If, as Brent (1999) has suggested, the imperial cult provides the background to Callistus' favourable views of Monarchianism, this might be a good *ad hominem* argument. Be that as it may, it certainly reveals the cultural embedding of the arguments. Of course, *monarchia* may well imply 'single *arche*', not only as 'rule', but as 'first principle', 'source', 'origin' or 'beginning'. And this is where the opponents of Monarchianism show their consistency. Creation is no more the direct involvement of the transcendent God with matter than is incarnation. The Logos and Spirit, as Irenaeus had suggested, are the 'two hands' of God, so to speak, the instruments through which God handles creation at arms' length, as it were. There is ultimately one *arche* of everything, as the apologists argued, namely the one Creator God. But divine 'dispensation' disposes the unity into trinity. It is no wonder that this is often called 'economic Trinitarianism'.

But all this sounds as if the principal drivers were philosophical rather than exegetical considerations. I suspect that is too simple a view. The second-century legacy was a discourse honed by the need to defend the scriptures as well as the oneness of God. The Gnostics and Marcion had in their several ways challenged the assumption that the Jewish scriptures spoke of the same God as Jesus Christ. The argument came down to the question what overarching story was to be told, which texts were to be used, and how were the diverse texts of scripture to be related to the whole. Irenaeus had already insisted that the Rule of Faith or Canon of Truth provided the interpretative key, and this Rule of Faith, though a malleable summary appearing in different forms in the works of Irenaeus, Tertullian and Origen, has a consistent three-fold shape, just as baptismal questions and creeds would have: God the Creator; Christ Jesus, the Son of God who became incarnate for our salvation; and the Holy Spirit, who foretold in the prophets all that God would do in Christ. Scripture is to be read according to this pattern (Young 1990, 1997) – hence the Christological reading of the 'Old Testament', which is crucial to the doctrine of the Trinity, and the point at which modern exegetes part company decisively with patristic hermeneutics.

The arguments about scripture in the Monarchian controversies did not proceed simply by proof-texting. The question was how you expounded the texts you quoted, and one of the most important techniques was the adducing of texts from elsewhere so that a collage of witness was built up. The legacy of Justin Martyr was important: he had justified[11] with a catena of texts the claim that before all creatures God begat a Beginning, which is now named in scripture as the Glory of the Lord, now the Son, now Wisdom, now Angel, then God, then Lord and Logos. Appeal is then made to Genesis: 'Let us make man in *our* own image'; 'Behold Adam has become as *one of us*'. Clearly two were involved in creation, and the one addressed is the one Solomon calls Wisdom, begotten as a Beginning before all creatures. This kind of approach is taken up by Tertullian[12] and amplified, for example with reference to 1 Cor 15:27-8, which speaks of the Son reigning until God has put all his enemies under his feet, and then being subjected himself so that God may be all in all – clearly there are two sharing the 'monarchy' as well as the act of creation. John's Gospel is also exploited to demonstrate the dispensation whereby there are two, yet 'I and the Father are one' (John 10:30).

Hippolytus[13] insists that texts must be put in context – a good exegetical principle, yet applied in ways that few would commend today. Tackling the Monarchian proof-texts – including such passages as that mentioned from Baruch – he suggests that other indications in the passages point to Jesus Christ, confirming this by cross-references. His peroration is telling, celebrating the Word who is at the Father's side and whom the Father sent for the salvation of humanity. The Word is the one proclaimed through the Law and the Prophets, the one who became the 'new man' from the virgin and the Holy Spirit, not disowning what was human about himself – hungry, exhausted, weary, thirsty, troubled when he prays, sleeping on a pillow, sweating in agony and wanting release from suffering, betrayed, flogged, mocked, bowing his head and breathing his last. He took upon himself our infirmities, as Isaiah had said. But he was raised from the dead, and is himself the Resurrection and the Life. He was carolled by angels and gazed on by shepherds, received God's witness, 'This is my beloved Son', changed water into wine, reproved the sea, raised Lazarus, forgave sins. 'This is God become man on our behalf – he to whom the Father subjected all things. To him be glory and power as well as to the Father and the Holy Spirit in the Holy Church, both now and always and from age to age. Amen.' The motivations were both exegetical and liturgical. The conceptual discourse was driven by the need to articulate the devotional discourse in the face of challenging questions. But was this 'ditheism', as the Monarchians claimed?

It was of course the concept of the Logos, borrowed and developed from philosophy but validated by the Prologue to the Gospel of John, that enabled the opponents of Monarchianism to give a reasoned account. As Tertullian puts it,[14] God was alone, yet not alone, because he had his Logos within, and this 'Reason' became 'Discourse' when God spoke and so created. Thus there was the Word, the Son, a Person, another beside God, yet never separated from God, and of the same 'substance', as the shoot is 'son of the root', the river 'son of the spring', the beam 'son of the sun'. The Son is not other than the Father by diversity but by distribution, not by division but by distinction, and there is a third, the Holy Spirit making up this relationship. This is the vital 'economy', which must be affirmed alongside the oneness of God. But holding that delicate balance would prove difficult as new questions were raised. The discourse would require further shaping and refining. We turn to the second important moment of challenge which exposed the difficulties inherent in the sort of settlement reached in response to Monarchianism.

The Arian controversy

Hierarchy was built into pre-Nicene discourse. The Logos and the Spirit mediated the transcendent God, providing the vital link between the Creator and created things – indeed constituted the divine spirit and wisdom inherent in the human creation, as well as the divine order and rationality built into the universe by the Creator. So in Christ the impossible was possible: the invisible was made visible, the untouchable was touched, the impassible became passible and the immortal died. In Origen's version of Logos theology the multiplicity of *epinoiai* that belong to the one Son of God implicitly make him the 'One-Many' which

Middle Platonism canvassed as the 'Indefinite Dyad' required for the One to generate the diversity of the Many. The Logos is thus one with the Father, and yet not so – if not a second god, at least a secondary being though derived from the Father. To some extent that secondariness was counteracted by the notion of eternal generation – Origen's argument that, for the unchangeable God to be Father, he must always have had a Son; but its force was somewhat undermined by the parallel argument that for the unchangeable God to be Creator creation must be eternal. If some degree of hierarchy is implicit in 'economic Trinitarianism', this is notably the case in Origen's version of it. Whatever else was going on in the Arian controversy, its effect was to expose and put in question this implicit hierarchy.

Arius (see further Young 1983, 2003) shared with other Christian teachers a belief in the pre-existent divine Logos through whom God created everything. He understood that Christ was the incarnation of this pre-existent Logos or Wisdom of God. Nobody questioned the long-established view that Prov 8:22–31 was about this pre-existent Wisdom or Logos. The argument about Arius' motivations or background is probably beside the point: like the Monarchians he wanted to be true to the biblical tradition that there is only one God, and easily attracted the accusation, as they did, of being over-reliant on logic and syllogisms, while in fact taking certain texts of scripture with the utmost seriousness. As read since Justin Martyr, Prov 8:22 stated that 'the Lord created me a Beginning of his ways' and went on to speak of Wisdom as the one who pre-existed everything else and was God's co-creator. Arius deduced that the Logos was the first and greatest of God's creatures, through whom God created everything else. There was only one being that had never come into being (or was 'ingenerate' – *agenetos*), namely the one and only God. The Son was the 'only-begotten' (*monogenes* and therefore 'generated'); the Proverbs passage used both 'begat' (*genna(i)*) and 'created' (*ektisen*), which Arius took to be synonyms. The combination of scriptural exegesis, monotheistic assumptions and logical deductions was typical of Christian discourse in this period, and the same combination would characterize the reply to Arius. From the standpoint of modern biblical criticism, neither side had satisfactory arguments for the superstructure they built.

Arius was probably reacting against a statement made by his bishop that appeared 'Sabellian' – by now the accepted label for all forms of 'modalist' doctrine. In order to counter this he emphasized the 'secondary' and mediating character of the Logos. Athanasius, on whose writings we principally depend for discerning the issues at stake, counters with his own exegetical and logical armoury. He recognizes that Arius' position cuts the Logos off from God – the Logos is God's creature, not the Logos of the divine self, and so Wisdom is not God's own Wisdom either. Arius has produced two Wisdoms and two Logoi, and the Logos incarnate in Jesus is created out of nothing like all other creatures, potentially changeable, not necessarily sinless, only Son of God by grace not nature. Maybe that was one thing Arius sought – a Saviour who had to struggle alongside the rest of us, genuinely tempted and tried in all points (Gregg and Groh 1981). But for many Christians this undermined the possibility of salvation being guaranteed, and for Athanasius the imparting of divine life to those adopted as sons through the true Son Jesus Christ was rendered impossible. One way or another the substantial relationship of Son and Father had to be reasserted. The Nicene Creed resorted to *homoousios* – a non-scriptural term, because Arius would accept anything couched only in biblical language. Athanasius is at pains to argue that only thus could the 'mind' or 'sense' of scripture be maintained.[15]

So once again appeal is made to some overarching view of what scripture is about. True this is backed up by examination of the scriptural sense of particular words, and by drawing up collages of texts to establish this. There is a good deal of what might be described as proof-texting, as well as some very dubious exegesis, not least with respect to Prov 8:22–31. Athanasius wants to assert that the verb 'created' is used of the incarnation, whereas 'begat' is used of the Son's generation from the Father, a proposal which does violence to the sequence of the Proverbs text – even if modern readers were prepared to allow the simple identification of Wisdom in this passage with the pre-existent Logos who became incarnate in Jesus depicted in John 1, which is not very likely! Arius had also appealed to Gospel texts to show the 'creaturely' character of the Logos – he was tired, ignorant, changeable and passible. Athanasius has to distinguish between texts which speak of the Logos qua human being and those which clearly point to his divine nature, with some rather disjunctive effects – on one occasion he (or almost certainly someone writing in his name) is even led to suggest that the Logos 'imitated' our condition – a docetic hostage to doctrinal fortune![16] It is easy to dismiss all this as imposing a predetermined doctrine on the biblical material. Yet this was the manner in which Trinitarian theology was arrived at. Discourse was honed and refined in the context of controversy, and matters of exegesis were at the heart of the debates.

It is important to recognize that the exegetical arguments can all be illuminated by comparison with the procedures accepted in the schools of the Greco-Roman world (see further Young 1997) – in other words they belong to a particular intellectual culture. All education in the Roman world was based on literature and its interpretation, whether the ultimate aim was rhetorical prowess or philosophical competence. Christians were using the same tools to produce teaching from their texts as everyone else was using to find, say, Neo-platonic philosophy in Homer. Homer was used to interpret Homer, in the sense of establishing Homeric vocabulary and its sense by cross-referencing. Rhetoricians learned to determine the subject matter or argument behind the wording; for necessarily there were many different ways in which something could be said, and the style should be appropriate to the topic. Trinitarian theology was genuinely an attempt to uncover the truth about God inadequately articulated in human language; for God had accommodated the divine self to our linguistic and conceptual limitations in scripture, just as the Logos had accommodated himself to our physical limitations in the incarnation. So the task of exegesis was to uncover the 'mind' of scripture or the 'intent' of the Spirit, and to create a discourse adequate to articulating that. If Hanson called it 'the search for the Christian doctrine of God' – a significant move on from the 'development' model – we may need to go further and describe it as a process of creative construction, or as Morgan suggests, of building on the foundation provided by the New Testament.

New Testament Theology and the Trinity

The questions that now arise are these: Does this particular construction permit a better view of what the New Testament is about; or does the New Testament rather provide a 'foundation' on which a variety of different edifices might be built? And is this particular building a Tower of Babel – an hybristic attempt to define God, or indeed an imposition of false categories on the New Testament? But first we might ask: is Morgan's category of 'myth' a better rhetorical category for New Testament discourse than doctrine, and does that mean that it is inappropriate to look at the theology of the New Testament from the perspective of emerging Trinitarian theology?

New Testament theology – 'myth', 'doctrine' or what?

All words carry baggage, which makes this question particularly ambiguous. What Morgan wishes to say is that there is no worked-out conception of a Wisdom-Christology in the New Testament, treating 'doctrine' as propositional and metaphysical, the kind of discourse whose articulation we have traced. But there is plenty of 'doctrine' in the New Testament if we give the word its original force; and replacing it with 'myth' may not do much to clarify the situation.

The Latin-derived word 'doctrine', like its parallel 'dogma' from the equivalent Greek, simply means 'teaching'. The context in which such words have their currency was and is the world of education – schools, primary, secondary, tertiary, now; then, grammatical, rhetorical and philosophical. Schools often engaged in teaching of a moral and religious kind, but teaching was not generally associated with religious activities as such in the Greco-Roman world. The earliest churches may have had some similarities to *collegia*, which had a religious aspect,[17] but generally speaking their activities were more like those of synagogues (Segal 2002). Synagogues, like schools, were the carriers of culture, Jewish in this case rather than Greco-Roman, and both did this through the interpretation of texts. So synagogue and church had many features akin to a school,[18] especially their focus on morality, and recommending a way of life on the basis of the texts studied. The church offered exegetical comment on the scriptures in the light of what had happened recently through Jesus Christ, and exhortation to a particular lifestyle based on this exegesis of scripture and its fulfilment in Christ. This constituted the teaching of this school-like community. Not for nothing are the followers of Jesus called 'disciples': Jesus is consistently presented as a teacher with his circle of pupils. The New Testament is full of this kind of 'doctrine'.

Explicit teaching in the New Testament concerns practical issues: what are the commandments that should be followed by believers? But behind this teaching lies a set of theological assumptions providing the warrants. The overriding perspective is that the God of the scriptures has decisively acted in Jesus Christ and imparted the Spirit to the community of the 'new' covenant', writing the law on their hearts. Much of this is illuminated by assuming that the eschatological outlook of apocalyptic writings has shaped the mind-set of the earliest believers, who see the scriptures fulfilled in recent events. Whether we call this 'myth' or not is a moot question – 'myth' has proved to be a word which introduces obfuscation rather than clarity.[19] Maybe 'rhetoric' would capture the distinction from 'philosophy' which Morgan seems to need. What we certainly see is an ever-increasing conglomeration of ideas, roles, symbols, prophecies, whether found in the Jewish scriptures or traceable in other literature from approximately the same era, all overlaying one another as they are exploited to draw out the significance of Jesus Christ (Young 1977, 1996). In other words we have the kind of discourse which needs, as Morgan suggests, a literary hermeneutic: it appeals to the imagination, it provides creative insight, it stimulates to action, it does not systematize,

it is doxological. If Christian discourse later refined and honed the
underlying sense of all this, shifting the discourse from the rhetoric of
apocalyptic prophecy and cultic celebration to philosophy, logic and
metaphysics, it is nevertheless interesting that Triadic formulae already
appear to have been used, especially in liturgical contexts. We undoubtedly have the curious phenomenon of a group of people who offer
cultic devotion to Jesus, while believing they remain within the monotheistic traditions of Judaism;[20] or, as Morgan puts it, 'this conviction that
in having to do with Jesus we are having to do with God is what all
New Testament Christology and subsequent orthodoxy are getting at'
(Morgan 2003, p. 36). So the other questions come into play. Is 'emerging
Trinitarian theology' a valid perspective from which to view New
Testament theology?

A clearer view?

The debates which generated the discourse of Trinitarian theology certainly show that different edifices could be built on the foundation of the
New Testament. Deductive processes actually produced (and as some of
my asides indicated, still produce) a variety of models: as different issues
were raised and different considerations came into play, we can trace
oscillation from one point to another on a kind of spectrum of thought.
But the 'orthodox' voices consistently appeal to a unitive narrative or
'mind' of scripture, recognizing that the overall thrust is more important
than discrete proof-texts, while also seeking to be true to the confession
of the church in its liturgical life, a life in which the texts were read and
interpreted for the needs of the time. It is therefore not implausible that
their reading more faithfully represents the thrust of New Testament
theology. I would argue that the New Testament consistently presents the
activity of Christ and the Spirit as the work of the one true God of the
Law and the Prophets, Psalms and Wisdom. Under pressure that relationship had to be articulated in ways that the New Testament writers themselves had not envisaged,[21] but it was always there, at least in narrative
form. The new formulation may appear to depend on proof-texting and
on the Christological reading of the 'Old Testament', but surely there are
other ways of conceiving that fundamental sense of the underlying unity
of God's purpose, and indeed of the scriptures, which may cut more ice
in our different cultural environment.[22]

Trinitarian theology is sometimes treated as if it intended to produce
a definition of God. One of the most liberating aspects of studying the
texts written to oppose the neo-Arian Eunomius[23] is the discovery that
this is fundamentally erroneous. It was Eunomius who insisted that God

is knowable – indeed, completely comprehensible because he is a simple unity. God is always and absolutely one, remaining uniformly and unchangeably God, never becoming sometimes one and sometimes another, nor changing from being what he is, never separated or divided into more. The defining characteristic of this God is *agenesia*, which means that the Supreme and Absolute One is isolated from the second and third, which came after and are therefore inferior. The hierarchical view is reasserted on the basis of *defining* God as the one and only being that has not come into being.

By contrast, for Gregory of Nyssa God is *infinite* – without boundaries and therefore indefinable, in principle beyond our comprehension. To say otherwise is to reduce God to the size of our own creaturely minds. This perception lay at the heart of his spirituality – no finite mind can ever grasp the infinite God, so there is a constant journey of apprehension. Knowledge of God requires intellectual humility, a *kenosis* modelled on that of Christ – only this produces the true theologian.[24] No 'names' are adequate to God. Yet the language used in scripture is not arbitrary. God accommodates the divine self to our limitations. So we have to stretch our language and conceptions beyond their earthly meanings, and even then only catch a glimpse of the outskirts of his ways. What we do see, however, through creation, through scripture, is the common will and activity of Father, Son and Spirit, all three subjects belonging to the same indivisible, incomposite and infinite Godhead. *Theologia* is literally mind-blowing – speculation about inner-Trinitarian relations is always to be restrained by awareness of our creaturely incapacity; while God's *oikonomia*, the divine outpouring of love and grace, is perceptible and converting. Scripture contributes both to the constraints on speculation and to the stimulation of endless creative possibilities.

The poetry of Ephrem makes very similar moves (Brock 1985, pp. 44, 49):

> In the case of the Godhead, what created being is able to
>   investigate Him?
> For there is a great chasm between him and the Creator . . .

But God clothed the divine self in the metaphors and types of scripture:

> He clothed himself in our language, so that He might clothe us
> In his mode of life . . .
> It is our metaphors that He put on . . .

The Divine Being that in all things is exalted above all things
In his love bent down from on high and acquired from us our own
habits . . .

Trinity and incarnation are expressions of wonder and response to the gracious saving *kenosis* to which scripture bears witness.

So the Cappadocians and Ephrem the Syrian, not to mention John Chrysostom whose homilies on God's incomprehensibility bring the discourse right into the context of preaching and worship, celebrate God's indefinability. I would argue that in the process of opposing Eunomius they produce a theology which does indeed allow better insight into what the New Testament is all about – certainly better than their opponents. They allow the categories of human conceptuality and limitations of language to be challenged, in the light of what the New Testament proclaims. They reflect the 'intent' of New Testament theology in seeing that 'doctrine' provides warrant for a way of life in response to the saving grace of God. They produced the outline of a model that has proved constantly fruitful and generative over the centuries of Christian devotion and reading of scripture. They permitted a thousand flowers to bloom, and it is a wise insight that sets beauty alongside goodness and truth.

Morgan insists on the historical meaning as a criterion by which ana- chronistic and inappropriate readings of New Testament theology are to be avoided. But quite apart from the practical difficulties of ever produc- ing definitive historical meaning, there is no presuppositionless interpre- tation; and if the New Testament is to be read Christianly, we need to take seriously the hermeneutical principle that the future meaning of the text is as significant as its past meaning. Ancient rhetorical theory sug- gested that *pistis* (which means 'persuasion' as well as 'faith') is produced by the interaction of the *ethos* of the speaker (the authority given by good character), the *logos* of the speech (that is, the validity of the argu- ment) and the *pathos* of the audience (the way the hearers are swayed and moved to action).[25] This three-way approach to the interaction of author, text and reader perhaps provides a hermeneutical model for the complex interactions involved in reading New Testament theology from later perspectives. It may be true that only hindsight uncovers the true significance of things, and that a better view emerges from climbing the ladder or ascending the mountain – along with the vertigo of standing on the cliff and attempting to 'see' God in the Cloud of the Presence. It was Gregory of Nyssa, who particularly developed the mountain imagery for the theological and spiritual journey, and I guess that he and others

who articulated the Trinitarian doctrine were in fact doing what Morgan recommends: discovering the truth through living the life, singing the songs and reading the scriptures.
What they perceived was a 'theodrama'[26] with three characters and one action. This was the revelation incarnated in stories like the baptism. So Christians sing,

> When Thou, O Lord, was baptized in the Jordan,
> The worship of the Trinity was made manifest.
> For the voice of the Father bore witness unto Thee,
> Calling Thee the beloved Son,
> And the Spirit, in the form of a dove,
> Confirmed his word as sure and steadfast.
> O Christ our God, who has appeared and enlightened the world,
> Glory to Thee.

Notes

1. As proved by the debate in response to my paper on 'The "Mind" of Scripture – theological readings of the Bible in the Fathers' at the Society for the Study of Theology conference, 2004.
2. *Adversus Hermogenem.*
3. The thrust of Logos theology prior to the questions raised by the monarchians is hard to assess: e.g. Theophilus' view is interpreted as 'monarchian' by Wallace-Hadrill (1982) and Hübner (1999); and as 'subordinationist' by Kelly (1960).
4. The basic argument of Hurtado (2003) I accept – the earliest Christians show cultic devotion to the resurrected Jesus without accepting that this challenged their essential monotheism.
5. Quoted by Origen, *Contra Celsum* VIII.12 (ET Henry Chadwick [Cambridge: Cambridge University Press 1980]).
6. Novatian, *De Trinitate,* 30.
7. Though there are grave critical difficulties in attributing some of the crucial texts. The debate in Rome is documented by *The Refutation of all Heresies,* attributed to Hippolytus, and the arguments are developed in the *Contra Noetum,* another text whose provenance is disputed. The most recent discussion attributes the *Contra Noetum* to Hippolytus the martyr, who died with Pontianus, dating it later than Tertullian's *Adversus Praxeam. The Refutation* is earlier, takes a different theological position from the *Contra Noetum* and is not by Hippolytus but a member of his 'school'. See Brent (1995).
8. Hippolytus, *Contra Noetum* 2.5.
9. *The Refutation of all Heresies,* Book IX.
10. *Adversus Praxeam* 1.

11. *Dialogue with Trypho* 61-2.
12. *Adversus Praxeam* 5-8
13. *Contra Noetum* 4.7.
14. *Adversus Praxeam* 5-8.
15. *De Decretis.*
16. *Contra Arianos* III. 57.
17. The social parallels to the early church have been discussed since Meeks (1983). For a recent overview, see Ascough (2002). *Collegia*, philosophical schools and synagogues were often gatherings in private houses, like the early church.
18. The school-like character of early Christianity is now widely accepted; see e.g. Lampe (2003), Brent (1995, especially pp. 402ff).
19. Cf. the response to Hick (1977).
20. Cf. Hurtado (2003) for justification of this statement, though its expression is in fact an anachronistic shorthand – 'monotheism' being a word devised in the eighteenth century!
21. 'The loyal and uncritical repetition of formulae is seen to be inadequate as a means of securing continuity at anything more than a formal level; Scripture and tradition require to be read in a way that brings out their strangeness, their non-obvious and non-contemporary qualities, in order that they may be read both freshly and truthfully from one generation to another.' So Rowan Williams in the 'Postscript (Theological)' to his book *Arius. Heresy and Tradition* (Williams 1987). That theology is necessary, because new questions demand new thinking and so new exegesis, would appear to be the thrust of his argument, as of this essay. From the perspective of the fresh questions, a clearer view of the theological implications of the New Testament may well be possible.
22. It is along these lines that an answer needs to be developed to the challenge I presented to systematic theologians at SST – cf. note 1 above. Christian reading of scripture presupposes the acceptance of a framework of 'doctrine', and the fruitful interaction between that sense of the thrust of the biblical witness with what is actually found in the text.
23. Gregory of Nyssa, *Contra Eunomium* is fundamental here; but cf. also John Chrysostom's homilies, *On God's Incomprehensibility.*
24. Cf. Gregory of Nazianzus, *First Theological Oration.*
25. For an interesting development of this see Kinneavy (1987).
26. To borrow a term from Hans Urs von Balthasar.

References

Ascough, R.S., 'Greco-Roman philosophic, religious and voluntary associations', in R.N. Longenecker (ed.), *Community Formation in the Early Church and in the Church Today* (Peabody, MA: Hendrickson, 2002), pp. 3–19.
Brent, A., *Hippolytus and the Roman Church in the Third Century* (Leiden: Brill, 1995).

Brent, A., *The Imperial Cult and the Development of Church Order. Concepts and Images of Authority in Paganism and Early Christianity before the Age of Cyprian* (Leiden: Brill, 1999).
Brock, S., *The Luminous Eye. The Spiritual World Vision of St Ephrem* (Rome: CIIS Publications, 1985).
Ehrhardt, A., *The Beginning: a Study in the Greek Philosophical Approach to the Concept of Creation from Anaximander to St. John* (Manchester: Manchester University Press, 1968).
Gregg, R.C. and Groh, D.E., *Early Arianism: A View of Salvation* (London: SCM Press, 1981).
Hick, J. (ed.), *The Myth of God Incarnate* (London: SCM Press, 1977).
Hübner, R.M., *Der paradox Eine. Antignostischer Monarchianismus im zweiten Jahrhundert* (Leiden: Brill, 1999).
Hurtado, L., *Lord Jesus Christ* (Grand Rapids, MI: Eerdmans, 2003).
Kelly, J.N.D., *Early Christian Doctrines* (London: A. and C. Black, 1960).
Kinneavy, J.L., *Greek Rhetorical Origins of Christian Faith* (New York and Oxford: Oxford University Press, 1987).
Lampe, P., *From Paul to Valentinus: Christians at Rome in the First Two Centuries* (ET London: T. & T. Clark [Continuum], 2003).
May, G., *Creatio ex nihilo. The Doctrine of 'Creation out of Nothing' in Early Christian Thought* (ET Edinburgh: T. & T. Clark, 1994).
Meeks, W.A., *The First Urban Christians: the Social World of the Apostle Paul* (New Haven: Yale University Press, 1983).
Morgan, Robert, 'Jesus Christ, the Wisdom of God (2)', in David F. Ford and Graham Stanton (eds), *Reading Texts, Seeking Wisdom* (London: SCM Press, 2003), pp. 22–37.
Segal, A.F., 'The Jewish experience: temple, synagogue, home and fraternal groups', in R.N. Longenecker (ed.), *Community Formation in the Early Church and in the Church Today* (Peabody, MA: Hendrickson, 2002), pp. 20–35.
Wallace-Hadrill, D.S., *Christian Antioch* (Cambridge: Cambridge University Press, 1982).
Williams, R., *Arius. Heresy and Tradition* (London: DLT, 1987).
Young, F., 'A cloud of witnesses' and 'Two roots or a tangled mass?', in J. Hick (ed.), *The Myth of God Incarnate* (London: SCM Press, 1977).
Young, F., *From Nicaea to Chalcedon* (London: SCM Press, 1983).
Young, F., *The Art of Performance: towards a Theology of Holy Scripture* (London: DLT, 1990).
Young, F., '"Creatio ex nihilo": a context for the emergence of the Christian doctrine of creation', *SJT* 44 (1991), 139–51.
Young, F., 'From analysis to overlay: a sacramental approach to Christology', in D. Brown and Ann Loades (eds), *Christ: The Sacramental Word* (London: SPCK, 1996).
Young, F., *Biblical Exegesis and the Formation of Christian Culture* (Cambridge: Cambridge University Press, 1997).

Young, F., 'Proverbs 8 in interpretation (2): Wisdom personified', in David F. Ford and Graham Stanton (eds), *Reading Texts, Seeking Wisdom* (London: SCM Press, 2003).

Young, F., 'Wisdom in the Apostolic Father and the New Testament', in Andrew F. Gregory and Christopher M. Tuckett (eds), *Trajectories through the New Testament and the Apostolic Fathers* (Oxford: Oxford University Press, 2005), pp. 85–104.

Index of Biblical References

Ezekiel	23	5:1, 17, 21–2	89
16:9	148	5:17	121
		5:33–7	216
Daniel	44, 196	5:39	212
6	23	7:12	212
7:13	84	7:13–14	121
12:2–3	171	7:24–7	89
		8:11–12	212
Hosea		8:17	5
6:6	220	8:19	83
11:1	5, 79	9:13	118, 220
		11:19, 25–30	91
Amos		11:25–7	83
7:1–4	22	12:7	220
		12:28	82
Apocrypha	79, 273, 299	13:41–9	174
Wisdom		15:24	82
7:22–6	91	16:13–18	117
9:1–2	91	16:16, 21	79
		16:63–5	79
Baruch		18:17	240–1
3:35–7	290, 293	22:14	174
		23	132, 241
2 Esdras		24:30–1	84
6:53–9	84	24:43	35
		25	175
2 Maccabees		25:1–13	174
7:10	171–2	25:31–46	174, 183n
12:39–45	171	25:40	241
14:46	172	26:13	204
		26:28	68
4 Maccabees	172	26:36–46	118
		26:39, 42	134n
New Testament		26:56	79
Matthew	66, 89,	27:45–50	82
	97–102, 103,	27:46	134n
	131	28	129
1–2	88		
1:1, 18	77	Mark	43, 45, 66,
2:15	5		97–102, 141–2,
3:8–9	212		144–5, 158, 266,
3:57	83		267
4:17	82	1:1	75, 77, 81, 88,
4:23	82		92n, 280
5	91	1:1–13	88